السنية

بشرح المقدمة الآجرومية

تأليف

محمد محيي الدين عبد الحميد

A Commentary on

al-Ājrūmiyyah

A bilingual rendition of Muḥammad Muḥī al-Dīn ibn ʿAbd al-Ḥamīd's (d. 1393h) renowned commentary on Ibn Ājurūm's (d. 723h) primer entitled *al-Tuḥfat al-Saniyyah bi Sharḥ al-Muqaddimah al-Ājrūmiyyah.*

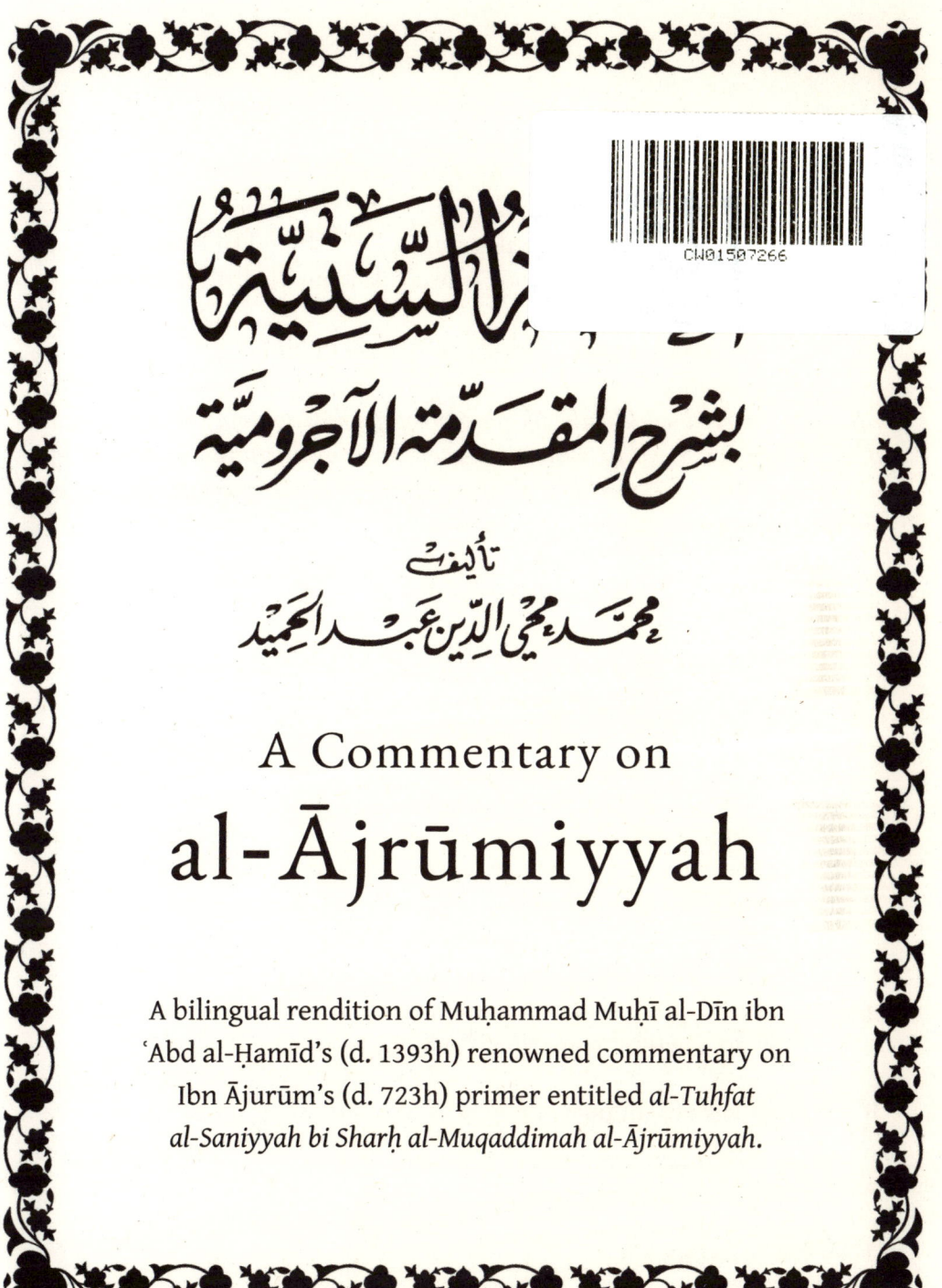

ISBN: 978 1 7392940 4 5

British Library Cataloguing in Publishing Data
A catalogue record for this book is available from the British Library

Revised fourth edition, 2022

Prepared and published by Dar al-Arqam Publishing
Birmingham, United Kingdom

www.daralarqam.bigcartel.com
Email: daralarqam@hotmail.co.uk

Translated by Adnan Karim
Head of translation at Dar al-Arqam. He has translated and edited a number of works for Dar al-Arqam.

Reviewed by Ash-Shafie Abdullah
BA in the Arabic Language from the Islamic University of Madinah, MA in teaching Arabic to non-native speakers from the Islamic University of Madinah.

بسم الله الرحمن الرحيم

"The house of al-Arqam is the house of Islām"

Al-Ḥākim (d.405 h.) in *al-Mustadrak 'ala al-Ṣaḥiḥayn* (6185)

A COMMENTARY ON

AL-ĀJRŪMIYYAH

Muḥammad Muḥī al-Dīn ibn ʿAbd al-Ḥamīd (d. 1393/1973)

DAR AL-ARQAM

الفهرس

Contents

تقديم الطبعة الثالثة

Note for the Third Edition

I would like to thank my dear brothers Alomgir, Ayman, ash-Shafie and Amr for their help in reviewing and providing corrections to this edition.

Adnan Karim
Birmingham, UK
19th October 2020

تقديم المترجم

Translator's Note

The main purpose of this translation is twofold:

Firstly, to aid teachers in delivering classes on *al-Tuḥfat al-Saniyyah*. Having access to a translation will allow the teacher to spend more time in explaining the book rather than preparing a translation. Furthermore it can help to bridge the gap between the stronger and weaker students in a class (in terms of their Arabic comprehension), which sometimes gives difficulty to the teacher in assessing the level of teaching which should be delivered.

Secondly, to serve as a bridge for students who may have learned the basics of Arabic but are not at a level yet to read an Arabic grammar book cover to cover purely in Arabic without difficulty. Depending on the level of the student they can read the Arabic and review their understanding with the English or use the English as an aid whilst reading the Arabic.

In order to fulfil this, the complete Arabic text has been provided and the translation has been kept as literal as possible, exceptions being in rare places where the translation would be strange if it was done in this manner.

Some grammatical terms have been transliterated to aid the flow of the translation and due to the importance of them being known to the student. This has most commonly been done for the following terms:

- *Al-rafʿ, al-naṣb, al-khafḍ/al-jarr* and *al-jazm*. These refer to the nominative, accusative, genitive and jussive states respectively. Words in these states are referred to as: *marfūʿ*, *manṣūb*, *makhfūḍ/majrūr* and *majzūm*.
- The parts of the *iḍāfah* (possessive) construction: *al-muḍāf* (the possessed) and the *muḍāf ilayh* (the possessor).

Supplementary notes have been extracted from the works of Shaykh ibn al-ʿUthaymin and from classical works quoted in *al-Ḥulal al-Dhahabiyyat ʿalā al-Tuḥfat al-Saniyyah.*

I ask Allah to accept this and cause it to aid the teaching of the language of His book, and that it become widespread in benefit like the illustrious works of our *shaykh*, Dr. V. Abdur Rahim (may Allah preserve him).

التقديم

Foreword

All Praises belong to Allah, the Lord of all of creation and may the best of Blessings and most complete of salutations be upon the leader of the Prophets and Messengers, our leader Muhammad, and upon his family and his companions.

To begin:

[Before you is] the book *al-Tuḥfat al-Saniyyah bi Sharḥ al-Muqadimmat al-Ājrūmiyyah* which was authored by the noble Shaykh Muḥammad Muḥī al-Dīn ʿAbd al-Ḥamīd al-Miṣri in explanation of *al-Muqadimmat al-Ājrūmiyyah*. The *Muqadimmah* is a book which students used to memorise by heart from an elementary level in their studies in Arabic grammar. The *Muqadimmah* features rules which are very concise and because of this, some of the students found it difficult to understand. As a result, many scholars after the book was authored stood to explain its contents, and perhaps from the very last of them was the *shaykh* who authored this explanation. Shaykh Muḥammad gave heavy importance to editing the books of Arabic grammar, and in other disciplines; especially concentrating on the books of al-Allāmah ibn Hishām including *al-Shudhūr*, *al-Qaṭr*, *al-Mughnī*, as well as others.

As for this book in particular, the *shaykh* includes all the rules mentioned in the book of *al-Ājrumiyyah* and also adds to it correct examples and wordings which add clarity, which are fantastic and very easy to digest.

With this initiative given to the books of Arabic grammar—in order to make such books easier for beginner learners to benefit from—it creates a momentum to complete bigger and more complex books of grammar in a similar fashion. So when the beginner learner completes his studies from books like this, it opens the path for him to read books which are more extensive than this. Benefiting from all of this, the student of knowledge then—with the praise of Allah—will have a strong grasp of the Arabic language.

So I ask Allah to reward those who worked on this book with the best of rewards for their efforts, that he has mercy upon the author, and that we all benefit from our righteous deeds.

In the end, all Praises are for Allah, the Lord of all creation.[1]

1 This has been summarised from a foreword written by Shaykh ʿAbd al-Ghanī al-Daqr.

هذا الكتاب

[About] This Book

This small but beneficial treatise competes itself in popularity amongst Arabic grammar books with the masterpiece of Ibn Mālik entitled *al-Alfiyyah*. It is a highly beneficial work with an objective of brevity. The author incorporated aspects of the book *al-Jumal* which was written by al-Allāmah Abu Qāsim 'Abd al-Rahmān ibn Isḥāq al-Zujājī. The book was authored in Makkah, may Allah preserve its honour, whilst the author was sitting in front of the Noble Ka'bah. As a result, Allah, the Most High, has accepted this work and increased its presence in lands from the east to the west. Beginner students of knowledge dedicated themselves to memorising this book by heart, thus it transpired that this book became the first building block for every student of knowledge who wanted to give Arabic grammar its utmost importance and in gaining a firm grounding of it.

Just as the students of knowledge dedicated themselves to this book, the scholars and annotators also dedicated themselves to it in seeking to clarify the rules in the book—it being full of benefit whilst maintaining brevity. The scholars have not left the opportunity to poeticise the book slip away, and they competed in this just as they competed with one another in publishing the book in order for it to have mass distribution.

This book was one of the preceding Arabic grammar books which were printed for the first time in Rome, around five centuries ago in 1592. For this reason, Allah, the Most High, decreed that this book reach Egypt and the great grammarian Shaykh Khālid al-Azharī explained the book and had it printed in Amsterdam in 1756.

This concise explanation that we have in front of us is from the contemporary explanations given to *al-Muqadimmah al-Ājrumiyyah*, which is beneficial in its own right. Shaykh Muḥammad Muhī al-Dīn 'Abd al-Ḥamīd (may Allah have Mercy on him) has excelled in its explanation, keeping it easy to understand and its simple layout leaves it very easy to follow and comprehend. More so, the book connects the topics and grammar rules in the book efficiently, featuring beneficial exercises for the student to practice. The students are quizzed in order for them to monitor their progress or to broaden their thought processes via constantly self-evaluating in the answers they give.

So I ask Allah, the Most High, that He gives us the ability to do whatever He loves and is pleased with, and that He accepts from us—through His favour and generosity—into our record of good deeds and the good deeds of our fathers and our scholars. Truly, He is able to do this and all praises are for Allah, the One by Whose favour that good deeds are completed by.[2]

2 This has been summarised from an introduction written by ʿAbd al-Jalīl al-ʿAṭā al-Bakrī.

ترجمة المؤلف

Biography of the Author

Abu ʿAbdullāh Muḥammad ibn Muḥammad ibn Dāwud al-Ṣinhājī al-Ājurrūmī comes from a tribal family which stems from a suburb town called Ṣafrawā in the Rīf area in Morocco. He himself was born in a city called Fās in 672/1273.

He spent his early years studying in Fās during which he studied a range of Islamic disciplines. Thereafter he travelled east to Makkah for Ḥajj and passed through Cairo and studied Arabic grammar there under the scholarly figure of Abū Ḥayyān Muḥammad ibn Yūsuf al-Gharnāṭī al-Andalusī. Here, he gained a certificate to teach (إجازة).

Shaykh Muḥammad ibn Ājurrūm (may Allah have Mercy upon him) was a profound and unique *faqīh*, a well accomplished grammarian and a masterful mathematician. He was an ocean of knowledge in the different recitations of the Qur'ān and in the sciences of *tajwīd*. He was a writer and was known to have a lot of blessing and goodness in his works.

It is not possible for us to display the true breadth of his works due to many of them being lost. However his works that have been found truly display his possession of deep knowledge. From them are:

- *Al-Muqaddimah al-Ājrūmiyyah fī Mabādī ʿIlm al-ʿArabīyyah.*
- *Farā'id al-Maʿānī fī Sharḥ Ḥirz al-Amānī.* This is a commentary on the poem of al-Shāṭibī regarding the seven *qirā'āt* (methods of recitation). This invaluable book displays the author's prowess, and a manuscript of it is present in his handwriting.
- *Majmūʿat Arājīz fī al-Qirā'āt wa al-Tajwīd wa al-Adab wa Ghayrihā.*

He used to teach the people of his city Fās and later died in his hometown in 723/1323. He was buried in the Andalūs area. May Allah have mercy upon him and reward him immensely for his efforts.

ترجمة الشارح

Biography of the Commentator

Abū Rajā Muḥammad Muḥī al-Dīn ibn ʿAbd al-Ḥamīd ibn Ibrāhīm al-Miṣrī was born in 1318/1900, in a village in the eastern province of Egypt.

He began his studies in the city of Damietta and then later was accepted into the famous university of al-Azhar in Cairo. He graduated in 1925 and held teaching jobs in Egypt and neighbouring Sudan. He continued to build his reputation until he was chosen to be the dean of the Faculty of Arabic Studies at al-Azhar and a member of the Panel of Arabic Linguistics in Cairo in 1924. He led the linguistic verdict (*fatwa*) panel at al-Azhar and he eventually retired from his post after leaving behind a firm legacy at the university.

The *shaykh* became famous for authoring and editing books until the number of books published by the *shaykh* numbered in their tens in a range of different disciplines. His major focus was in Arabic linguistics in which he wrote extensively in explanation, commentary, etymology and so forth. His works included revising and adding to the explanation of the *Alfiyyah* of Ibn Mālik by Ibn ʿAqīl and an explanation of *al-Sirājiyyah* in Ḥanafi Fiqh. He gave special attention to the books of Ibn Hishām, presenting his annotated editions of many of his works such as *Sharḥ al-Qaṭr* and *Mughnī al-Labīb*. He also wrote in the fields of history and biography.

This is how Shaykh Muḥammad Muḥī al-Dīn became a renowned scholar of this Ummah and a well-established researcher, to the extent that some even coined the nicknamed of "*Suyūṭī al-ʿAṣr*" (the Suyūṭī of this era) for him. This is also tantamount to the efforts he exerted as such a level of respect can only come about through hard work and extreme precision.

He passed away in Cairo during the year 1393/1973, May Allah have mercy upon the *shaykh* with an abundance of His mercy.

مقدمة الشارح

Introduction of the Commentator

بسم الله الرحمن الرحيم

الحمد لله وكَفَى، وسلامه على عباده الذين اصْطَفَى.

In the name of Allah, the Most Merciful, the Most Beneficent. All praises are for Allah alone and His Peace be upon His Slaves that He has Chosen.

هذا شَرْح واضح العبارة، ظاهر الإشارَة ، يَانِعُ الثَّمَرَة، دَانِي القِطَاف، كثير الأسئلة والتمرينات، قصدت به الزُّلْفَى إلى الله تعالى بتيسير فهم (المقَدِّمَة الآجُرُّومِيَّةِ) على صغار الطلبة ؛ لأنها الباب إلى تَفَهُّم العربية التي هي لُغَةُ سيدنا ومولانا رسول الله صلى الله عليه و على آله وصَحْبه وسلم، ولُغَةُ الكتاب العزيز.

This explanation is clear in its meanings, apparent in its directions, full of fruits, easy to pick from, plentiful in its questions and exercises. I seek by this book to gain proximity to Allah, the Most High, via making easy the understanding of al-Muqadimmat al-Ājrumiyyah for novice students of knowledge. Studying the likes of this book opens the doors for a person to learn Arabic—which is the language spoken by our leader and master, the Messenger of Allah (peace and blessings of Allah be upon him, his family and companions), and it is the language of the Kitāb al-Azīz (the Qur'ān).

وأرجو أن أستحق به رضا الله عز وجل ؛ فهو خير ما أسْعَى إليه.

I hope with this effort that I am eligible to gain the pleasure of Allah, the Glorified and the Exalted, as this is from the best ways I can travel towards Him.

رَبَّنَا عليك توكلنا ، وإليك أنَبْنَا ، وإليك المصير ، رَبَّنَا اغفر لي وَلِوَالِدَيَّ وللمؤمنين

والمؤمنات يومَ يَقُومُ الحساب

Our Lord, upon you we have relied upon and to You we turn and to You is our final end. Our Lord, forgive me and my parents and the believers on the Day of Accountability.

كتبه المعتز بالله تعالى وحده

Written by the one who seeks to be honoured by Allah alone,

محمد محيي الدين عبد الحميد

Muḥammad Muḥī al-Dīn ʿAbd al-Ḥamīd

المقدمات

An Introduction [to Grammar]

تعريف النحو ، موضوعه، ثمرته ، نسبته ، واضعه ، حكم الشارع فيه.

[In this section we will cover:] the definition of grammar, its subject matter, its benefits, where it belongs to, its formulator, and the Islamic ruling related to it.

التعريف : كلمة (نحو) تطلق في اللغة العربية على عدَّة معان؛ منها الْجِهَةُ ، تقول (ذَهَبْتُ نَحْوَ فلاَنٍ)، أي :جِهَتَهُ . ومنها الشّبْهُ والمِثْلُ ، تقول (مُحَمَّدٌ نَحْوُ عَلِيّ)، أي شِبْهُهُ وَمِثْلُهُ .

The definition of the word *naḥw* in the Arabic language has many different meanings. From them it includes "the direction" such as a person saying, "I left to go in the direction of such and such person". It also includes a resemblance and an imitation of, such as a person saying Muḥammad is like 'Alī.

وتطلق كلمة (نحو) في اصطلاح العلماء على: (العلم بالقواعد التي يُعْرَف بها أحكامُ أوَاخِرِ الكلمات العربية في حال تركيبها ؛ من الإعراب ، والبناء، وما يتبع ذلك) .

The word *naḥw* in its technical definition is defined as, "The knowledge of maxims which are used to define the rulings connected to word endings in the Arabic language within their structural contexts. This includes [words that take] inflection, and [words that have] fixed word-endings, and that which follows it."

الموضوع : وموضوعُ علمِ النحوِ : الكلمات العربيةُ ، من جهة البحث عن أحوالها المذكورة.

The subject matter of Arabic grammar is the Arabic vocabulary, i.e. studying their [grammatical] cases, as mentioned above.

الثمرة : وثمرة تَعَلُّم علم النحو : صِيَانَةُ اللسان عن الخطأ في الكلام العَرَبِّي ، وَفَهْمُ القرآنِ الكريم والحديثِ النبويّ فَهْماً صحيحاً ، اللذَيْنِ هما أصْلُ الشَّرِيعَةِ الإسلامية وعليهما مَدَارُها .

The benefit of studying Arabic grammar is that it trains the tongue against making mistakes in Arabic speech. It enables the learner to understand the Noble Qur'ān and the Prophetic narrations with the correct understanding; both of which are the primary sources of the Islamic Sharī'ah which the whole religion revolves around.

نسبته : هو من العلوم العربية .

Arabic grammar belongs to the broader discipline of Arabic sciences.

واضعه : والمشهور أن أوَّل واضع لعلم النحو هو أبو الأسْوَدِ الدُّؤلِيُّ ، بأمر أمير المؤمنين عليّ بن أبي طالب رضى الله عنه .

It is widely circulated that the initial formulator of Arabic grammar was Abū 'l-Aswad al-Du'alī after being commanded by the Commander of the Faithful, 'Alī ibn Abī Ṭālib ﷺ.

حكم الشارع فيه : وتعلمُه فَرْضٌ من فروض الكفاية ، وربما تَعَيَّنَ تَعَلُّمُهُ على واحد فَصَار فَرْضَ عَيْنٍ عليه .

The ruling on studying Arabic grammar is that it is a communal obligation, however someone may be specified to study it thus it becomes an individual obligation upon him.

[الكلام وأنواعه]
[Speech and Its Types]

قال المصَنِّف : وهو أبو عبد الله محمد بن داود الصَّنْهَاجِيُّ المعروف بابن آجُرُّوم ، والمولود في سنة ٦٧٢ اثنين وسبعين وستمائة ، والمتوفى في سنة ٧٢٣ ثلاث وعشرين وسبعمائة من الهجرة النبوية ـ رحمه الله تعالى .

The author said: And he is Abū ʿAbdullāh Muḥammad ibn Muḥammad ibn Dāwud al-Ṣinhājī—famously referred to as Ibn Ājurrūm. He was born in the year 672 and passed away in 723, and [both dates] are according to the Hijrah of the Prophet, may Allāh the Most High have mercy upon his soul.

الكَلاَمُ هُوَ اللَّفْظُ الْمُرَكَّبُ الْمُفِيدُ بِالْوَضْعِ .

He said: Speech is the compound utterance which brings forth benefit and is established [upon the Arabic language].

وأقول : لِلَفْظِ (الكلام) معنيَان : أحدهما لغوي ، والثاني نحويّ.

I say: Speech has two meanings, the first of them in the linguistic sense and the second in the grammatical sense.

أما الكلام الغوي فهو عبارة عَمَّا تَحْصُلُ بسببه فَائِدَةٌ ، سواءٌ أَكان لفظاً ، أم لم يكن كالخط والكتابة والإشارة.

As for speech in the linguistic sense, it can be defined as: An expression through which a benefit is obtained, irrespective of whether the expression is verbalised or not, such as scripting, writing or gesticulation.

وأما الكلامُ النحويُّ ، فلا بُدَّ من أن يجتمع فيه أربعة أمور : الأول أن يكون لفظاً ، والثاني

أن يكون مركَّباً ، والثالث أن يكون مفيداً ، والرابع أن يكون موضوعاً بالوضع العربي .

As for speech in the grammatical sense, it must possess four traits: (i) it must be an oral utterance, (ii) it must be compounded, (iii) it must be something which is comprehensible, and (iv) it must be established in the medium of the Arabic language.

ومعنى كونه لفظاً : أن يكون صَوْتاً مشتملاً على بعض الحروف الهجائية التي تبتدئ بالألف وتنتهي بالياء، ومثاله (أحمد) و(يكتب) و(سعيد) ؛ فإن كل واحدٍ من هذه الكلمات الثلاث عند النطق بها تكون صَوْتاً مشتملاً عَلَى أربعة أَحْرُفٍ هجائية ؛ فالإشارة ــ مثلاً ــ لا تسمَّى كلاماً عند النحويين ؛ لعدم كونها صوتاً مشتملاً على بعض الحروف ، وإن كانت تسمى عند اللغويين كلاماً ؛ لحصول الفائدة بها .

"Utterance": The meaning of this is that it must be an oral sound, formulated from some of the alphabet—that begins with *alif* and ends with *yā*. Examples being "Aḥmad", "*Yaktabu*" and "Saʿīd". Each of these three words—when verbally expressed—form a sound consisting of four letters of the alphabet. However gesticulation, for example, is not considered to be speech according to the grammarians. This is due the absence of sound consisting of the Arabic letters. The linguists do consider gesticulation to be speech, as it serves as a medium of communication.

ومعنى كونه مركباً : أن يكون مؤلفاً من كلمتين أو أكْثَرَ ، نحو : (مُحَمَّدٌ مُسَافِرٌ) و(الْعِلْمُ نَافِعٌ) و(يَبْلُغُ الْمُجْتَهِدُ الْمَجْدَ) و(لِكُلِّ مُجْتَهِدٍ نَصِيبٌ) و(الْعِلْمُ خَيْرُ مَا تَسْعَى إِلَيْهْ) فكل عبارة من هذه العبارات تسمى كلاماً ، وكل عبارة منها مؤلفةٌ من كلمتين أو أكْثَرَ.

"Compound": The meaning of this is that it must be composed of two words or more. Examples being "Muḥammad is a traveller", "Knowledge is beneficial", "The hard worker attains glory", "For every hard worker is a dividend" and "Knowledge is the best of what you pursue". Each of the aforementioned expressions is termed as speech, and each of them is composed of two words or more.

فالكلمة الواحدة لا تسمَّى كلاماً عند النحاة إلا إذا انْضَمَّ غيرها إليها : سواءٌ أَكان انضمام غيرها إليها حقيقةً كالأمثلة السابقة ، أم تقديراً ، كما إذا قال لك قائل : مَنْ أَخُوكَ؟ فتقول : مُحَمَّدٌ ، فهذه الكلمة تُعتَبَرُ كلاماً ، لأن التَّقدِير : مُحَمَّدٌ أَخِي : فهي في التقدير عبارة مؤلَّفة من ثلاث كلمات .

Thus a singular word is not termed as speech according to the grammarians until it is connected to another [word,] whether it is connected with other words like in the compound sentences that have preceded, or in the case of the meaning being implicitly inferred, as in the case where someone says to you, "*Man akhūka* (who is your brother)?" and you reply, "*Muḥammadun*". This statement (i.e. "*Muḥammadun*") is considered to be speech due to the inferred meaning i.e. "*Muḥammadun akhī* (Muḥammad is my brother)". So the inferred meaning here comprises of three words (the *yā* at the end of "*akhī*" is a first person pronoun).

ومعنى كونه مفيداً : أن يَحْسُنَ سكوتُ المتَكلم عليه ، بحيث لا يبقى السَّامِعُ منتظراً لشيءٍ آخر ، فلو قلت (إِذَا حَضَرَ الأُستَاذ) لا يسمى ذلك كلاماً ، ولو أَنَّه لفظ مركب من ثلاث كلمات ؛ لأن المخاطب ينتظر ما تقوله بعد هذا مِمَّا يَتَرَتَّبُ على حضور الأستاذ . فإذا قلت : (إِذَا حَضَرَ الأُسْتَاذُ أَنْصَتَ التَّلَامِيذُ) صار كلاماً لحصول الفائدة .

"Something which is comprehensible": This means that the listener is sufficed with what he hears and does not require any further explanation from the speaker. For instance, if it is said, "When the teacher is present," this is not classified as speech—though it is an utterance composed of three words. This is because the listener would be waiting for further clarification as to what will happen in relation to the teacher's presence. If it is said, "When the teacher is present the students listen," this is considered to be speech, due to the comprehensible benefit it exerts.

ومعنى كونه موضوعاً بالوضع العربيِّ : أن تكون الألفاظ المستعملة في الكلام من الألفاظ

التي وَضَعَتْهَا العربُ للدَّلالة على معنى من المعاني : مثلاً (حَضَرَ) كلمة وضعها العربُ لمعنًى ، وهو حصول الحضور في الزمان الماضي ، وكلمة (محمد) قد وضعها العربُ لمعنًى ، وهو ذات الشخص المسمى بهذا الاسم ، فإذا قُلْتَ (حَضَرَ مُحَمَّدٌ) تكون قد استعملت كلمتين كُل منهما مما وَضعه العرب ، بخلاف ما إذا تكلمْتَ بكلام مما وضعه العَجَمُ : كالفرس ، والترك ، والبربر ، والفرنج ، فإنه لا يسمى في عُرف علماءِ العربية كلاماً ، وإن سمَّاهُ أهل اللغة الأخرى كلاماً.

"It must be established in the medium of the Arabic language": Meaning that the lexis used must be the same lexis which Arabs use to communicate in order to convey a message. Examples are: "*Ḥadara*", which is a word utilised by the Arabs to bring forth the meaning of someone being present in the past tense. "Muḥammad", which is a word utilised by the Arabs to bring forth the meaning of the existence of an individual known by this name. Now if it were said, "*Ḥadara Muḥammadun*", this is formed from two words, both of them composed from the Arabic language. This is converse to words composed from the languages of the non-Arabs, such as: Persian, Turkish, Berber or a European language, [of which the utilisation] is not considered to be speech according to the scholars of Arabic, even though they are considered to be so by the speakers of the other languages.[3]

أمثلة للكلام المستوفي الشروط :

Examples of speech that fulfil these conditions are:

الْجَوُّ صَحْوٌ . الْبُسْتَانُ مُثْمِرٌ . الْهِلاَلُ سَاطِعٌ . السَّمَاءُ صَافِيَةٌ . يُضِيءُ الْقَمَرُ لَيْلاً . يَنْجَحُ الْمُجْتَهِدُ . لاَ يُفْلِحُ الكَسُولُ . لاَ إِلَهَ إِلاَّ الله . مُحَمَّدٌ صَفْوَةُ الْمُرْسَلِينَ . الله رَبُّنَا . محمد نَبِيُّنَا .

3 Shaykh ibn al-'Uthaymīn—in *Sharḥ al-Ājrūmiyyah* (p. 13)—added another aspect to the explanation of it being "established". The other aspect he mentioned is, "That it be established intentionally. This removes from its definition the speech of the intoxicated, the insane, the sleeping and the delirious. Their words are not termed as speech."

The weather is clear. The orchard is fruitful. The crescent is shining. The sky is clear. The moon illuminates the night. The hard-worker is successful. The lazy will not succeed. There is no deity worthy of being worshipped besides Allah. Muḥammad ﷺ is the elite of those who were sent. Allah is our Lord. Muḥammad ﷺ is our prophet.

أمثلة للفظ المفرد :

Examples of singular words:

محمد . علي . إبراهيم . قامَ . مِنْ .

Muḥammad, 'Alī, Ibrāhīm, he stood and from.

أمثلة للمركب الغير مفيد :

Examples of compound statements that are not comprehensible:

مدينة الإسكندرية . عَبْدُ الله . حَضْرَمَوْتُ . لو أَنْصَفَ الناس . إذا جاءَ الشتاءُ . مَهْمَا أَخْفَى المُرَائِي . أن طَلَعَتِ الشَّمسُ .

The city of Alexandria. The slave of Allah. Ḥadramawt. If the people were fair. When the winter comes. No matter the two faced conceals. If the sun rises.

أسئلة على ما تقدم

Questions Regarding What Has Preceded[4]

ما هو الكلام ؟

What is speech?

ما معنى كونه لفظاً ؟

What is the meaning of "it is an utterance"?

4 [T] The reader should attempt to answer all questions and exercises in Arabic.

ما معنى كونه مفيداً ؟

What is the meaning of "something that is comprehensible"?

ما معنى كونه مُركَّباً ؟

What is the meaning of "it is compound"?

ما معنى كونه موضوعاً بالوضع العربي ؟

What is the meaning of "it is established in the medium of the Arabic language"?

مَثِّلْ بخمسة أمثِلة لما يسمى عند النحاة كلاماً .

Bring five examples which would be considered as speech by the grammarians.

أنواع الكلام

Types of Speech

قال : وأَقْسَامُهُ ثَلاثَةٌ : اسْمٌ ، وَفِعْلٌ ، وَحَرْفٌ جَاءَ لِمَعْنًي .

He said: And it is divided into three groups[5]: *Ism* (noun), *fi'l* (verb) and the *ḥarf* (particle) which conveys meaning.

وَأقول : الألفاظُ التي كان الْعَرَبُ يَسْتَعْمِلُونَهَا في كلامِهِمْ ونُقِلَتْ إلينا عنهم ، فنحن نتكلم بها في مُحاوراتنا ودروسنا ، ونقرؤها في كُتُبِنا ، ونكتب بها إلى أهلينا وأصدقائنا ، لا يخلو واحد منها عن أن يكون واحدًا من ثلاثة أشياء : الاسم ، والفعل ، والحرف .

I say: The words that are used by the Arabs in their speech and that have been transmitted to us from them, that we speak with in our discussions and classes, that we read in our books, that we write in our letters to family and friends, none of the above is free from having one of the following three: the noun, the verb and the particle.

أما الاسمُ فهو في اللغة : ما دلَّ على مُسَمًّى .

The noun, in the linguistic sense, is defined as that which indicates towards something named.

وفي اصطلاح النحويين : كلمةٌ دَلَّتْ عَلى معنىً في نفسها ، ولم تقترن بزمان ، نحو : محمد ، عليّ ، ورَجُل ، وَجَمل ،ونَهْر ، وتُفَّاحَة ، ولَيْمُونَةٌ ، وَعَصًا ، فكل واحد من هذه الألفاظ يدل على معنى ، وليس الزمان داخلاً في معناه ، فيكون اسماً .

---

5 In *al-Kawākib al-Durriyyah* (1/29-30) it says, "This categorisation is in terms of the words (*al-kalimah*) and not speech (*al-kalām*), so one should take note."

In the grammatical sense, it is defined as a word that indicates a meaning in of itself and which cannot be linked to a tense (past, present or future).[6] Examples are: "Muḥammad", "'Alī", "a man", "a camel", "a river", "an apple", "a lemon" and "a stick". Each one of these words indicates a meaning in and of themselves, and none of them change according to their tense in time, this is what defines a noun.

وأما الفعل فهو في اللغة : الْحَدَثُ .

The verb, in the linguistic sense, is defined as an occurrence.

وفي اصطلاح النحويين : كلمة دلَّتْ على معنى في نفسها ، واقترنت بأحد الأزمنة الثلاثة ـ التي هي الماضي ، والحال ، والمستقبل .

In the grammatical sense, it is defined as a word that indicates a meaning in of itself and that is linked to one of three tenses: *al-māḍī* (past tense), *al-ḥāl* (present tense), *al-mustaqbal* (future tense).

نحو (كَتَبَ) فإنه كلمةٌ دالةٌ على معنى وهو الكتابة ، وهذا المعنى مقترن بالزمان الماضي .

An example being "*kataba*", which is a word that indicates a meaning i.e. writing. This meaning is linked to the *māḍī* tense.

ونحو (يَكْتُبُ) فإنه دال على معنى ـ وهو الكتابة أيضاً ـ وهذا المعنى مقترن بالزمان الحاضر .

Another example is "*yaktubu*", which also indicates the meaning of writing. However its meaning is linked to the *ḥādir* (present) tense.

ونحو (اكْتُبْ) فإنه كلمة دالة على معنى ـ وهو الكتابة أيضاً ـ وهذا المعنى مقترن بالزمان

6 Al-Khuḍarī said in his *Ḥāshiyat 'alā ibn 'Aqīl* (1/17), "His statement 'which cannot be linked to a tense'. This excludes verbs, not adverbs of time such as 'yesterday' and 'now'. This is because the time is their meaning, and they are not linked to it."

المستقبل الذي بعد زمان التكلم .

Another example is "*uktub*", which also indicates the command of writing. Its meaning is linked to the *mustaqbal* tense that takes place after the moment it is spoken.

ومثل هذه الألفاظ:

Examples of these words:

نَصَرَ وَيَنْصُرُ وَانْصُرْ ،وَفَهِمَ وَيَفْهَمُ وَافْهَمْ ، وَعَلِمَ وَيَعْلَمُ وَاعْلَمْ ، وَجَلَسَ وَيَجْلِسُ وَاجْلِسْ ، وَضَرَبَ وَيَضْرِبُ وَاضْرِبْ .

[Written above are a list of Arabic verbs in the *māḍī*, *ḥādir* and *mustaqbal* tenses:] He helped—he helps—help. He understood—he understands—understand. He knew—he knows—know. He sat—he sits—sit. He hit—he hits—hit.

والفعل على ثلاثة أنواع : ماضٍ و مُضَارِعٌ وأَمْرٌ :

The verb is of three types: the *māḍi*, *muḍāri'* and the *'amr*.

فالماضي ما دَلّ على حَدَثٍ وَقَعَ في الزَّمَانِ الذي قبل زمان التكلُّم ، نحو: كَتَبَ ، وَفَهِمَ ، وَخَرَجَ ، وَسَمِعَ ، وَأَبْصَرَ ، وَتَكَلَّمَ ، وَاسْتَغْفَرَ ، وَاشْتَرَكَ .

The *māḍī*: It indicates that the action took place before the speaker spoke. Examples being: He wrote, he understood, he left, he heard, he saw, he spoke, he sought forgiveness and he associated.

والمضارع : مَا دَلَّ عَلَى حدثٍ يقع في زمان التكلُّم أو بعده ، نحو: يَكْتُبُ ، وَيَفْهَمُ ، وَيَخْرُجُ ، وَيَسْمَعُ ، وَيَنْصُرُ ، وَيَتكلمُ ، وَيَستَغْفِرُ ، وَيَشْتَرِكُ .

The *mudāri'*: It indicates that the action is taking place whilst the speaker is speaking or in the time after he has spoke.[7] Examples being: He writes, he understands, he leaves, he hears, he helps, he speaks, he seeks forgiveness and he associates.

وَالأمرُ : ما دَلَّ على حَدَثٍ يُطْلَبُ حُصوله بعد زمان التكلُّم ، نحو: اكْتُبْ ، وَافْهَمْ ، واخْرُجْ ، واسْمَعْ ، وَانْصُرْ ، وَتَكَلَّمْ ، وَاسْتَغْفِرْ ، وَاشْتَرِكْ .

The *'amr*: It indicates that an action has been commanded after the time the word is spoken.[8] Examples being: Write, understand, leave, listen, help, speak, seek forgiveness and associate.

وأما الحرف : فهو في اللغة الطرَفُ .

The particle, in the linguistic sense, is defined as "the side".

وفي اصطلاح النُّحَاة : كلمة دَلَّتْ على مَعْنًى في غيرها ، نحو (مِنْ) ، فإنَّ هذا اللفظ كلمة دلَّتْ على معنى - وهو الابتداءُ - وهذا المعنى لا يتمُّ حتَّى تَضمَّ إلى هذه الكلمة غيرَهَا ، فتقول : (ذَهَبْتُ مِنَ الْبَيْت) مثلاً .

According to the nomenclature of the grammarians, it is defined as a word

7 Al-Ahdal said in *al-Kawākib al-Durriyyah* (1/41), "Neither of the two tenses of the *muḍāri'* are specified except by the appearance of an indicator. When they appear free of an indicator, either of the two tenses can be assumed. The future tense is specified if the verb is preceded by the letter *sīn* or *sawfa*. The present tense is specified if the verb is connected to a word such as 'now' (*al-ān*)."

8 This definition has some shortness. The definition given by al-Ahdal in *al-Kawākib* (1/42) is, "It is a verb that is linked to the future tense always. This is because the request given is for the attainment of what has not been attained e.g. **{Arise and warn.}** Or it can be for the continuation of what has been requested e.g. **{O Prophet, fear Allah.}**" The definition given by the author (i.e. Shaykh Muḥī al-Dīn) would not encompass the second *āyah* as Allah stated this whilst he was fearful of Him. If the reason for this order is questioned, then this was answered by Shaykh al-Shanqīṭī in *Mudhakirah fī Uṣūl al-Fiqh* (p. 35), "He (Allah) wanted from this continuation upon the state, or He ordered his Ummah through this command, as he is an example for them." See also the book of Shaykh 'Abd al-Raḥmān ibn Nāṣir al-Sa'dī entitled *al-Qawā'id al-Ḥisān li Tafsīr al-Qur'ān* (pp. 119-120), principle number forty six.

which is dependent upon another to have a meaning. An example being the word "*min*" (from). This is a word that has a meaning—which is *al-ibtidā* (lit. beginning i.e. "I left from the house".)—however this meaning is not completed until it is adjoined to other than it, e.g. "I went from the house".

أمثلة للاسم :

Examples of the noun are:

كتابٌ ، قَلَمٌ ، دَوَاةٌ ، كرَّاسَةٌ ، جَرِيدَةٌ ، خليل ، صالح، عمران ، وَرَقَةٌ ، سَبُعٌ ، حمَارٌ ، ذِئْبٌ ، فَهْدٌ ، نَمِرٌ ، لَيْمُونَة ، بُرْتقَالَةٌ ، كُمَّثْرَاةٌ ، نَرْجِسَةٌ ، وَرْدَةٌ ، هَؤلاءِ ، أنتم .

أمثلة للفعل :

Examples of the verb are:

سافَرَ يُسَافِرُ سَافِرْ ، قالَ يَقُولُ قُلْ ، أَمِنَ يَأْمَنُ إِيمَنْ ، رَضِيَ يَرْضَى ارْضَ ، صَدَقَ يَصْدُقُ اصْدُقْ ، اجْتَهَدَ يَجْتَهِدُ اجْتَهِدْ ، اسْتَغْفَرَ يَسْتَغْفِرُ اسْتَغْفِرْ .

أمثلة للحرف :

Examples of the particle are:

مِنْ ، إلى ، عَنْ ، عَلَى ، إلا ، لكِنْ ، إنَّ ، أَنْ ، بَلى ، بَلْ ، قَدْ ، سَوْفَ ، حَتَّى ، لَمْ ، لا ، لَنْ ، لَوْ ، لَمَّا ، لعَلَّ ، مَا ، لاَتَ ، لَيْت ، إنْ ، ثُمَّ ، أَوْ .

أسئلة

Questions

ما الاسم ؟ مَثِّل للاسْم بعشَرة أمثلة .

What is a noun? Provide ten examples of a noun.

ما الفعل ؟ إلى كم ينقسم الفعل ؟

What is a verb? How many categories is it split into?

ما المضارع ؟ ما هو الأمر ؟ ما الماضي ؟ مَثِّل للفعل بعشرة أمثلة .

What is the *muḍāriʿ*? What is the *ʾamr*? What is the *māḍī*? Bring ten examples of the verb.

ما هو الحرف ؟ مَثِّل للحرف بعشرة أمثلة .

What is the particle? Provide ten examples of the particle.

علامات الاسم

The Signs of the Noun

قال : فالاسمُ يُعْرَفُ : بِالْخَفْضِ ، وَالتَّنْوِينِ ، وَدخولِ الأَلِفِ وَاللَّامِ ، وَحُرُوفِ الْخَفْضِ ، وَهِيَ : مِنْ ، وَإِلَى ، وَعَنْ ، وَعَلَى ، وَفِي ، وَرُبَّ ، وَالْبَاءُ ، والْكَافُ ، وَاللَّامُ ، وَحُرُوفُ الْقَسَمِ ، وَهِيَ : الْوَاوُ ، وَالْبَاءُ ، وَالتَّاءُ .

He said: The noun is known by *al-khafḍ* (the acceptance of *jarr*), *al-tanwīn* (a mark which indicates indefiniteness), the acceptance of *alif* and *lām* (the definite article "al-"), the particles of *al-khafḍ*—which are: *min, ilā, 'an, 'alā, fī, rubba, al-bā, al-kāf, al-lām*, and the particles of *al-qasam* (particles of avowal)—which are: *al-wāw, al-bā* and *al-tā*.

أقول : للاسم علامات يتميَّز عن أَخَوَيْه الفِعْلِ والْحَرْفِ بوجودِ واحدةٍ منها أو قَبُولِها ، وقد ذكر المؤلف ـ رحمه الله ـ من هذه العلامات أَرْبَعَ علاماتٍ ، وهي الْخَفْضُ ، والتَّنْوِينُ ودخولُ الأَلِف واللَّام ، ودُخولُ حرفٍ من حروف الخفض .

I say: The noun has indicators that differentiate it from its two siblings (the verb and the particle) through the presence or the acceptance of one of them. The author mentioned here—may Allah have mercy upon him—four from these signs. They are: (i) *al-khafḍ*, (ii) *al-tanwīn*, (iii) the acceptance of *alif* and *lām*, (iv) the use of a particle from the particles of *al-khafḍ*.

أما الخفض فهو في اللغة : ضد الارتفاع .

As for *al-khafḍ*, linguistically it is the opposite of rising.

وفي اصطلاح النحاة : عبارة عن الكسرة التي يُحْدِثُهَا الْعامل أوْ ما ناب عنها ، وذلك مثل كسرة الراءِ من (بكرٍ) و(عمرو) في نحو قولك : (مَرَرْتُ بِبَكْرٍ) وقولك (هذا

كِتابُ عَمْرٍو) فبكْر وعمرو: اسمان لوجود الكسرة في آخر كل واحِدٍ منهما .

And in terms of the nomenclature of the grammarians it means: The state expressed by the diacritical mark *al-kasrah* that is brought about by an *'āmil* (governor), or what takes the place of the *kasrah*. Examples of this are the *kasrahs* on the letter *rā* in "Bakrin" and "'Amrin", when utilised in a statement such as, "I passed by Bakr," and, "This is the book of 'Amr." In both cases the two nouns Bakr and 'Umar have a *kasrah* present at their end.

وأما التنوين ، فهو في اللغة التَّصْويت ، تقول (نَوَّنَ الطَّائِرُ) أي : صَوَّتَ .

As for *al-tanwīn*,[9] linguistically it means phonation i.e. if it is said "The bird voiced a sound."

وفي اصطلاح النُّحَاة هو : نُونٌ ساكنةٌ تَتْبَعُ آخِرَ الاسم لفظاً ، وتفارقهُ خَطا للاستغناء عنها بتكرار الشَّكلة عند الضبْطِ بالقلم ، نحو : محمدٍ ، وكتابٍ ، وإيهٍ ، وصَهٍ ، ومُسْلِمَاتٍ ، وفَاطِمَاتٍ ، وحِينَئِذٍ ، وَسَاعَتَئِذٍ ، فهذه الكلمات كلها أسماء، بدليل وجود التنوين في آخِرِ كلِّ كلمة منها .

And in terms of the nomenclature of the grammarians it means: It is the nunation (i.e. the adding of the sound "*un*" to a word) that vocally follows the end of a word, it is a verbalised *nūn* although it is not written, as writing the *tanwīn's* diacritic serves against repetition in punctuating the *nūn's* written form. Examples of this are: Muḥammad, a book, shush, be quiet, Muslim women, Fāṭimahs, at that time and at that hour. All of these words are nouns, and the evidence for this is the presence of the *tanwīn* at the end of each of them.

العلامة الثالثة من علامات الاسم : دخول (أَلْ) في أول الكلمة ، نحو : الرجل ، والغلام ، والفرس ، والكتاب ، والبيت ، والمدرسة . فهذه الكلمات ، كلها أسماء لدخول الألف واللام في أوَّلها .

---

9 The *tanwīn* is of ten types, see *al-Kawākib* (1/31-34) and *Ḥāshiyat al-Fākihī 'alā al-Qaṭr* (1/22).

The third from the signs of the noun: The use of "*al-*" at the start of the word. Examples of this are: *al-rajul*, *al-ghulām*, *al-fars*, *al-kitāb*, *al-bayt*, *al-madrasah*. All of these words are nouns, and the evidence for this is the use of the letters *alif* and *lām* at their start.

العلامة الرابعة : دخول حرفٍ من حروف الخفض ، نحو (ذهبتُ من البيت إلى المدرسَةِ) فكل من (البيت) و(المدرسة) اسم ، لدخول حرف الخفض عليهما ، ولوجود (أَلْ) في أَوَّلهما .

The fourth sign: The use of a particle from the particles of *al-khafḍ* e.g. "I went from the house to the *madrassah*." Both *al-bayt* (the house) and *al-madrassah* here are nouns due to the use of a particle of *khafḍ* and the presence of "*al-*" at the start of both of them.

وحروف الخفض هي : (من) ولها معانٍ : منها الابتداءُ ، نحو (سَافَرْتُ مِنَ الْقَاهِرَةِ).

The particles of *al-khafḍ*[10] are: *Min*, and it has a number of meanings. From them is beginning e.g. "I travelled from Cairo."

و(إلى) من معانيها الانتهاء ، نحو (سَافَرْتُ إلى الإسْكَنْدَرِيَّةِ).

Ilā, from its meanings include the ending point e.g. "I travelled to Alexandria."

و(على) ومن معانيها الاستعلاءُ ، نحو (صَعِدْتُ عَلَى الْجَبَلْ).

ʿAlā, from its meanings is rising e.g. "I ascended upon the mountain."

و(عن) ومن معانيها مجاوزة، نحو: (رميت السهم عن القوس).

ʿAn, from its meanings is exceeding something e.g. "I shot the arrow from the bow."

10 For investigation into the meaning of the particles, one should study *Mughnī al-Labīb* by Ibn Hishām, in which he details and suffices, may Allah have mercy on him.

و(فِي) ومن معانيها الظرفية نحو (الْمَاءُ في الْكُوز).

Fī, and from its meanings is its use as an adverbial e.g. "The water is in the pitcher."

و(رُبَّ) ومن معانيها التقليل، ونحْو (رُبَّ رَجُلٍ كرِيمٍ قَابَلَنِي).

Rubba, and from its meanings is the minimising of possibility e.g. "Few a generous man have met me."

و(الْبَاءُ) ومن معانيها التعدية ، ونحو (مَرَرْتُ بالْوَادِي).

Al-bā, and from its meanings is its use as a transitive e.g. "I passed by the valley."

و(الكافُ) ومن معانيها التشبيه ، نحو (لَيْلى كالْبَدْرِ.).

Al-kāf, and from its meanings is its use for comparatives e.g. "Laylā is like the full moon."

و(اللام) ومن معانيها الْمِلْكِ نحْو (المالُ لمحمد)، والاختصاصُ ، نحو (البابُ للدَّار) ، و(الْحَصيرُ لِلْمَسْجِدِ) والاستحقاقُ نحو (الْحَمْدُ لله).

Al-lām, and from its meaning is (i) possessive e.g. "The money belongs to Muḥammad," (ii) specification e.g. "The door of the house," and, "The mat of the *masjid*," (iii) entitlement e.g. "All praise is due to Allāh."

ومن حروف الخفض : حُرُوف الْقَسَمِ ، وهي ثلاثة أحرف :

And from the particles of *al-khafḍ* are the particles of *al-qasam* (swearing of an oath), and these consist of three letters:

الأول : الواو ، وهي لا تَدْخُلُ إلا عَلَى الاسم الظاهِرِ ، ونحو (والله) ونحو ﴿وَالطُّورِ ۝ وَكتابٍ مَسْطُورٍ﴾ ونحو ﴿وَالتِّينِ وَالزيْتُون ۝ وَطُورِ سِينِين﴾

Firstly: *Al-wāw*. And this can only be used with a noun e.g. "By Allah", **{By the mount, and [by] a Book inscribed.}**[11] And also: **{By the fig and the olive, and by Mount Sinai.}**[12]

والثاني : الباءُ ، ولا تختص بلفظ دون لفظ ، بل تدخل على الاسم الظاهر ، نحو (بالله لأَجْتَهِدَنَّ) وعلى الضمير ، نحو (بكَ لأَضْرِبَنَّ الكَسُولَ).

Secondly: *Al-bā*. And this is not specific to a certain form of word, but can be used with a clear noun such as, "By Allah I will strive," or a pronoun such as, "[I swear] by you, I will hit the lazy person."

والثالث : التاءُ ، ولا تدخل إلا على لفظ الجلالة نحو ﴿وتاللهِ لأَكِيدَنَّ أَصْنَامَكُمْ﴾

Thirdly: *Al-tā*. And this is only used as an oath along with the Majestic Name of Allah, such as: **{And [I swear] by Allah, I will surely plan against your idols.}**[13]

أسئلة

Questions

ما علامات الاسم ؟

What are the signs of the noun?

ما معنى الخفض لغة واصطلاحاً ؟

Define *al-khafḍ* in the linguistic sense and in terms of nomenclature.

ما هو التنوين لغةً واصطلاحاً ؟

Define *al-tanwīn* in the linguistic sense and in terms of nomenclature.

---

11 Al-Ṭūr: 2-1

12 Al-Tīn: 1-2

13 Al-Anbiyāh: 57

على أي شيءٍ تدلُّ الحروف الآتية :(من) ، اللام ، الكاف ، (ربَّ) ، (عن) ، (فِي)؟

What do the following prepositions denote: *min*, *al-lām*, *al-kāf*, *rubba*, *'an* and *fī*?

ما الذي تختص واو القسم بالدخول عليه من أنواع الأسماء ؟

Which type of noun alone is used alongside the *wāw* of swearing an oath?

ما الذي تختصُّ تاءُ القسم بالدخول عليه ؟

Which type of noun alone is used alongside the *tā* of swearing an oath?

مَثِّل لباءِ القسم بمثالين مختلفين .

Bring two contrasting examples of the *bā* of swearing an oath

تمارين

Exercises

ميِّز الأسماءَ التي في الجمل الآتية مع ذكر العلامة التي عرفتَ به اسميتها : ﴿بسم الله الرحمن الرحيم﴾ . ﴿الحمد لله رب العالمين﴾. ﴿إن الصَّلاَةَ تَنْهَى عَنِ الْفَحْشَاءِ وَالْمُنْكَرِ﴾ . ﴿وَالْعَصْرِ۞إِنَّ الإِنْسَانَ لَفِي خُسْرٍ﴾ . ﴿وَإِلٰهُكُمْ إِلٰهٌ وَاحِدٌ﴾ . ﴿الرَّحْمٰنُ فَسْأَلْ بِهِ خَبِيرًا﴾. ﴿قل إِنَّ صَلاَتِي وَنُسُكِي وَمَحْيَايَ وَمَمَاتِي لله رَبِّ العَالَمِينَ۞لاَ شَرِيكَ لَهُ ، وَبِذَلِكَ أُمرتُ ، وَأَنَا أَوَّلُ المسْلِمِينَ﴾ .

Identify the nouns that are in the above *āyāt* and also mention the signs that show their status as nouns.

علامات الفعل

The Signs of the Verb

قال : والفِعْلَ يُعْرَفُ بِ(قَدْ) ، وَالسينِ و(سَوْفَ) وَتَاءِ التَأْنيثِ السَّاكِنة .

He said: The verb is known by *qad*, *al-sīn*, *sawfa*, and the non-vowelised *tā* of femininity.

وأقول : يَتَميز الفعْلُ عن أَخَوَيْهِ الاسمِ وَالْحرفِ بأَرْبعِ علاماتٍ ، متى وَجَدْت فيه واحدةً منها ، أو رأيتَ أنه يقبلها عَرَفْتَ أَنَّه فعلٌ :

I say: The verb is differentiated from its siblings the noun and the particle by four signs. If you come to find it with one of these signs or if you see that it accepts them, know that this is a verb.

الأولى : (قد) والثانية : (السين) والثالثة : (سوف) والرابعة: تاءُ التأْنيث الساكنة .

The first of them is "*qad*", the second is "*al-sīn*", the third is "*sawfa*" and the fourth is the non-vowelised *tā* of femininity.

أما (قد) : فتدخل على نوعين من الفعل ، وهما : الماضي ، والمضارع .

As for *qad*, it enters upon two types of the verb, and they are the *māḍī* and the *muḍāri'*.

فإذا دخلت على الفعل الماضي دلَّتْ على أحد مَعْنَيَيْن ـ وهما التحقيق والتقريب ـ فمثالُ دلالتها على التحقيق قولُه تعالى: ﴿قَدْ أَفْلَحَ الْمُؤْمِنُونَ﴾ وقولُه جل شأْنه: ﴿لَقَدْ رَضِيَ اللهُ عَنِ الْمُؤْمِنِينَ﴾ وقولنا : (قَدْ حَضَر مُحَمَّدٌ) وقولنا : (قد سافَرَ خَالِدٌ) ومثالُ دلالتها على التقريب قولُ مُقيم الصلاة : (قَدْ قَامَتِ الصَّلاَةُ) وقولك : (قَدْ غَرَبَت الشَّمْسِ) .

If it enters upon a *māḍi* verb it can indicate one of two meanings: (i) as an intensifier (used to reinforce or strengthen meaning) and (ii) the imminent beginning of an event/verb. Examples of where it indicates intensification is the statement of the Most High: **{Successful indeed are the believers.}**[14] And His statement: **{Certainly was Allah pleased with the believers.}**[15] Also our statements, "Certainly, Muḥammad was present," and, "Certainly, Khālid travelled." An example of where it indicates the imminent beginning of an event/verb is the statement at the establishment of the prayer, "Certainly the prayer is about to be established." Another example is the statement, "Certainly the sun is about to set."[16]

إذا دخلتْ على الفعل المضارع دلَّتْ على أحدِ مَعْنَيَيْن أيضاً ـ وهما التقليل ، والتكثير ـ فأما دلالتها على التقليل، فنحو قولك : (قَدْ يَصْدُقُ الكَذُوبُ) وقولك : (قَدْ يَجُودُ الْبَخِيلُ) وقولك : (قَدْ يَنْجَحُ الْبَلِيدُ) . وأما دلالتها على التكثير ؛ فنحو قولك : (قَدْ يَنَالُ الْمُجْتَهِدُ بُغْيَتَه) وقولك : (قَدْ يَفْعَلُ التَّقِيُّ الْخيرَ) وقول الشاعر :

If it enters upon a *muḍari*ʿ verb it can also indicate one of two meanings: a minimisation of the possibility or an augmentation of the possibility. Examples of where it indicates a minimisation of the possibility can be seen in the following statements: "Rarely is the liar truthful," "Rarely is the miser generous," and, "Rarely does the fool succeed." As for where it indicates an augmentation of the possibility, examples can be seen in the following statements: "Indeed the hard working will attain what he seeks," and, "Indeed the pious one performs good." Likewise the statement of the poet:

قَدْ يُدْرِكُ الْمُتَأَنِّي بَعْضَ حَاجَتِهِ   وَقَدْ يَكُونُ مَعَ الْمُسْتَعْجِلِ الزَّلَلُ

Indeed the one who deliberates will attain some of his need,

While indeed the one who rushes will be prone to error.

---

14 Al-Mu'minūn: 1

15 Al-Fath: 18

16 This is only the case if this is said before the sun sets. If it is said after it sets then it possesses the meaning of an intensifier.

وأما السين و(سوف) : فيدخلان على الفعل المضارع وَحْدَهُ ، وهما يدلان على التنفيس ، ومعناه الاستقبال ، إلاّ أنّ (السين) أقلُّ استقبالاً من (سوف) . فأما السين فنحو قوله تعالى : ﴿سَيَقُولُ السُّفَهَاءُ مِنَ النَّاسِ﴾ ، ﴿سَيَقُولُ لَكَ الْمُخَلَّفُونَ﴾ وأما (سوف) فنحو قوله تعالى : ﴿وَلَسَوْفَ يُعْطِيكَ رَبُّكَ فَتَرْضَى﴾ ، ﴿سَوْفَ نُصْلِيهِمْ نَارًا﴾ ، ﴿سَوْفَ يُؤْتِيهِمْ أُجُورَهُمْ﴾ .

As for *al-sīn* and *sawfa*, they specifically enter upon the *mudāriʿ* verb. Both of these indicate *al-tanfīs*, which means the future tense. However the scope of *al-sīn* in terms of the future tense is less intense than that of *sawfa*.[17] As for *al-sīn*, it can be seen in the statements of the Most High: {**The foolish among the people will say ...**}[18] and {**Those who remained behind [of the Bedouins] will say to you.**}[19] As for *sawfa*, it can be seen in the statements of the Most High: {**And your Lord is going to give you, and you will be satisfied**},[20] {**We will burn them in Fire**}[21] and {**To those He is going to give their rewards.**}[22]

وأما تاءُ التأْنيث الساكنة : فتدخل على الفعل الماضي دون غيره ؛ والغرض منها الدلالة على أنَّ الاسْمَ الذي أُسند هذا الفعلُ إليه مؤنَّثٌ ؛ سواءٌ أكان فاعلاً ، نحو (قَالَتْ عَائِشَةُ أُمُّ الْمُؤْمِنِينَ) أم كان نائبَ فاعل ، نحو (فُرِشَتْ دَارُنَا بِالْبُسُطِ) .

As for the non-vowelized *tā* of femininity, it enters upon the *māḍī* verb specifically. The purpose of it is to indicate that the noun that the verb is connected to is feminine. This is the case irrespective of whether there is (i) a *fāʿil* (the the subject of the verb) e.g. "ʿĀʾishah, the Mother of the Believers said ..." (ii) or if it is a *nāʾib fāʿil* (when the person/subject doing the action is unknown or

17 This is not a point of consensus. The grammarians of Kūfah viewed that *sīn* and *sawfa* are equal in this matter. This was the view of Ibn Mālik and he was followed by Ibn Hishām. See *al-Mughnī* (1/138-139) by Ibn Hishām, *Ḥāshiyat al-Dusūqī ʿalā al-Mughnī* (1/149), *Ḥāshiyat al-Ṣibbān ʿalā Sharḥ al-Ashmūnī* (1/74).

18 Baqarah: 142

19 Al-Fath: 11

20 Al-Duhā: 5

21 Al-Nisā: 56

22 Al-Nisā: 152

omitted) e.g. "Our abode was furnished with rugs."

والمراد أنها ساكنة في أصل وَضْعها ؛ فلا يضر تحريكها لعارض التخلص من التقاء الساكنين في نحو قوله تعالى : ﴿وَقَالَتِ اخْرُجْ عَلَيْهِنَّ﴾ ،﴿إِذْ قَالَتِ امْرَأَتُ عِمْرَانَ﴾ ، ﴿قَالَتَا أَتَيْنَا طَائِعِينَ﴾ .

The meaning of it being non-vowelized is in relation to the root of its construction. However it is not an issue if it is vowelized in order to prevent the meeting of two non-vowelized words, as in the statements of the Most High: **{She said, "Come out before them."}**,[23] **{When the wife of 'Imrān said}**,[24] and **{They said, "We have come willingly."}**[25]

ومما تقدم يتبين لك أن علامات الفعل التي ذكرها المؤلف على ثلاثة أقسام : قسم يختص بالدخول على الماضي ، وهو تاءُ التأنيث الساكنة ، وقسم يختص بالدخول على المضارع ، وهو السين وسوف ، وقسم يشترك بينهما، وهو قَدْ .

That which has been mentioned makes clear that the signs of the verb mentioned by the author are of three categories: (i) that which is specific to the *māḍī* verb i.e. the non-vowelized *tā* of femininity, (ii) that which is specific to the *muḍāri'* verb i.e. *al-sīn* and *sawfa*, (iii) that which is shared between both types of verb i.e. *qad*.

وقد تركَ علامة الفعل الأمر ، وهي دلالته على الطلبِ مع قبول ياءَ المخاطبة أو نون التوكيد ، نحو (قُمْ) و(اقْعُدْ) و(اكْتُبْ) و(انْظُرْ) فإن هذه الكلمات الأَرْبَعَ دَالَّةٌ على طلب حصول القيام والقعود والكتابة والنظر ، مع قبولها ياء المخاطبة في نحو : (قُومِي) ، و(اقْعُدِي) أو مع قبولها نون التوكيد في نحو (اكْتُبَنَّ)، و(انْظُرَنَّ إلى مَا يَنْفَعُكَ).

He did not mention the sign of the command verb,[26] which is: an indication

---

23 Yūsuf: 31

24 Āli 'Imrān: 9

25 Fussilat: 11

26 This is because he followed the way of the Kūfans i.e. that the verb is of two types:

of request or command, alongside the acceptance of the *yā* of the feminine second person singular or the *nūn* of emphasis. Examples are "stand", "sit", "write" and "look". These four words indicate a command requesting to stand, to sit, to write and to look. They also accept the *yā* of the feminine second person e.g. "stand" and "sit" or they may also accept the *nūn* of emphasis e.g. "write (emphasised)" and "look (emphasised) upon that which benefits you."

أسئلة

Questions

ما هي علامات الفعل ؟

What are the signs of the verb?

إلى كم قسم تنقسم علامات الفعل ؟

Into how many categories are these signs of the verb categorised?

ما هي العلامات التي تختص بالفعل الماضي ؟

Which of these signs is specific to the *māḍī* verb?

كم علامة تختص بالفعل المضارع ؟

How many of these signs are specific to the *muḍāri'* verb?

ما هي العلامة التي تشترك بين الماضي والمضارع ؟

Which of these signs is shared between the *māḍī* and *muḍāri'* verbs?

ما هي المعاني التي تدلُّ عليها (قد) ؟

---

the *māḍī* and the *muḍāri'*, and the *'amr* falls under the *muḍāri'*. This is because it is derived from the *muḍāri'*, the proof of which is the fact that it is built upon that which the *muḍāri'* becomes *majzūm* with. See *al-Mughnī* of Ibn Hishām (1/227) and *al-Kawākib* of al-Ahdal (1/37).

What are the meanings indicated to by *qad*?

على أي شيءٍ تدل تاءُ التأنيث الساكنة ؟

What does the non-vowelized *tā* of femininity indicate?

ما هو المعنى الذي تدلُّ عليه السين وسوف ؟ وما الفَرْقُ بينهما ؟

What is the meaning indicated to by *al-sīn* and *sawfa*? And what is the differentiation in this meaning between them?

هل تعرف علامة تميز فعل الأمر ؟

Do you know the sign that makes the imperative verb distinct?

مَثِّل لمثالين لـ(قد) الدالَّة على التحقيق .

Give two example sentences with *qad* where it indicates intensification.

مثِّل بمثالين تكون فيهما (قد) دالة على التقريب .

Give two example sentences with *qad* where it indicates the meaning of the imminent beginning of a verb.

مَثِّلْ بمثالين تكون (قد) في أحدهما دالة على التقريب وفِي الآخر دالة على التحقيق .

Give two example sentences with *qad*, in the first of them use it to indicate the meaning of the imminent beginning of a verb, and in the second of them use it to indicate intensification.

مثِّل بمثالين تكون (قد) في أحدهما دالة على التقليل وتكون في الآخر دالة على التكثير .

Give two example sentences with *qad*, in the first of them use it to indicate a minimisation of the possibility, and in the second of them use it to indicate an augmentation of the possibility.

مثِّل بمثالٍ واحدٍ تحتمل فيه (قد) أن تكون دالة على التقليل والتكثير .

Give one example of a sentence with *qad* where either a minimisation of the possibility or an augmentation of the possibility could be assumed.

مثِّل لـ(قد) بمثالٍ واحدٍ تحتمل فيه أن تكون دالة على التقريب أو التحقيق ، وبيِّن في هذا المثال متى تكون دالة على التحقيق ومتى تكون دالة على التقريب ؟

Give one example of a sentence with *qad* where either the meaning of imminent beginning or intensification could be assumed. Identify in this example when it indicates the meaning of the imminent beginning of a verb and when it indicates an intensification.

تمرين

Exercises

ميِّز الأسماء والأفعال التي في العبارات الآتية ، وميِّز كل نوع من أنواع الأفعال ، مع ذكر العلامة التي استدللت بها عَلَى اسمية الكلمة أو فعليتها ، وهي : ﴿إِنْ تُبْدُو خَيْرًا أَوْ تُخْفُوهُ أَوْ تَعْفُو عَنْ سُوءٍ ، فإِنَّ الله كَانَ عَفُوًّا قَديرًا﴾ ، ﴿إِنَّ الصَّفَا وَالْمَرْوَةَ مِنْ شَعَائِرِ الله فَمَنْ حَجَّ الْبَيْتَ أَوْ اعْتَمَرَ فَلاَ جُنَاحَ عَلَيْهِ أَنْ يَطوَّفَ بهمَا ، وَمَنْ تَطَوَّعَ خَيْرًا فإِنَّ الله شَاكِرٌ عَلِيمٌ﴾ .

Identify the nouns and verbs that are in the following sentences. Furthermore, identify each type from the types of verbs that arise. Also mention the signs which cause you to identify the words as nouns or verbs. The sentences are as follows: **{If [instead] you show [some] good or conceal it or pardon an offense—indeed, Allāh is ever Pardoning and Competent.}**[27] and **{Indeed, al-Safā and al-Marwah are among the symbols of Allah. So whoever makes Hajj to the House or performs 'Umrah—there is no blame upon him for walking between them. And whoever volunteers good—then indeed, Allah is appreciative and Knowing.}**[28]

27 Al-Nisā: 149
28 Al-Baqarah: 158

قال صلى الله عليه وسلم : ((سَتَكُونُ فِتَنٌ الْقَاعِدُ فِيهَا خَيْرٌ مِنَ القَائم ، وَالْقَائِمُ فِيهَا خَيْرٌ مِنَ المَاشِي ، وَالمَاشِي فِيهَا خَيْرٌ مِنَ السَّاعِي ، مَنْ تَشَرَّفَ لَهَا تَسْتَشْرِفْه ، وَمَنْ وَجَدَ فيهَا مَلْجَئًا أَوْ مَعَاذًا فَلْيَعُذْ بِهِ))

He ﷺ said, "There will be afflictions during which a sitting person will be better than a standing one, and the standing one will be better than a walking one, and the walking one will be better than a running one, and whoever will expose himself to these afflictions, they will destroy him. So whoever can find a place of protection or refuge from them, should take shelter in it."[29]

29 *Saḥīḥ al-Bukhārī* (7082)

الحرف

Al-Ḥarf (The Particle)

قال : والْحَرْفُ مَالاَ يَصْلُحُ مَعَهُ دَلِيلُ الاِسْمِ وَلاَ دَلِيلُ الْفِعْلِ .

He said: And the *ḥarf* (particle) is that which does not accept any of the signs of the noun or the signs of the verb.

وأقول : يتميّز الحرف عن أَخَوَيْهِ الاسمِ والفعلِ بأنه لا يصح دخول علامة من علامات الأسماءِ المتقدمة ولا غيرها عليه ، كما لا يصح دخولُ علامة من علامات الأفعال التي سبق بيانُها عليه ، ومثلُه (مِنْ) و(هَلْ) و(لمْ) فهذه الكلمات الثلاثة حروفٌ ، لأنها لا تقبل (أَلْ) ولا التنوين ، ولا يجوز دخول حرف الخفض عليها ، فلا يصح أن تقول : (المِنْ) ، لا أن تقول: (منٌ) ، ولا أن تقول : (إلى مِنْ) ، وكذلك بقية الحروف ، وأيضاً لا يصح أن تدخل عليها السينُ ، ولا (سوف) ولا تاءُ التأْنيثِ الساكِنةُ ، ولا (قَدْ) ولا غيرها مما هو علاماتٌ على أن الكلمة فِعلٌ .

I say: The particle stands out from the noun and verb by the fact that it is not valid for the signs of a noun to be used with it—those we have mentioned and any other signs. Likewise, it is improper for a particle to have the signs of a verb (that we have explained above) to enter upon it. Examples of the particle are *min* (from), *hal* (an interrogative particle) and *lam* (a particle of negation).[30] All three of these are particles as they do not accept "*al-*", the *tanwīn*, and the particles of *al-khafḍ* cannot be entered upon them. So it is not correct to say "*al-min* (the from)", nor "*minun*", nor "*ilā min* (to from)" and the same

30 The use of these three particles by the author is to indicate towards the particle consisting of three types: (i) that which is specific to the noun e.g. "*min*", (ii) that which is not specific to the noun or verb e.g. "*hal*", and (iii) that which is specific to the verb e.g. "*lam*". See *Ḥāshiyat al-Kafrāwī* (p. 13) and *al-Kawākib* (1/44).

is the case for the other *ḥurūf* (pl. of *ḥarf*). Likewise it is not correct for *al-sīn* to enter upon them, nor *sawfa*, nor the non-vowelized *tā* of femininity, nor *qad* and anything else from the signs of the verb.

تمرين

Exercises

١- ضع كل كلمة من الكلمات الآتية في كلام مفيد يحسن السكوت عليه :

One. Put each of the words below into a comprehensible compound sentence.

النَّخْلَةُ . الفيلُ . ينامُ . فَهِمَ . الحديقةُ . الأرضُ . الماءُ . يأكلُ . الثمرةُ . الفاكِهة . يَحْصُدُ . يُذاكِرُ .

❁❁❁

٢- ضع في المكان الخالي من كل مثال من الأمثلة الآتية كلمةً يتم بها المعنى ، بيِّن بعد ذلك عدد أجزاء كل مثال ، ونَوْعَ كل جزءٍ .

Two. Fill in the gaps to complete the sentences. Mention the number of separate parts of speech (noun, verb and particle) in each example, and label them.

(أ) يَحْفَظُ ... الدَّرْسَ	(ب) ... الثّور الأرْضَ
(ج) يَسْبَحُ ... في النَّهْر	(ح) الْوَلَدُ ... الْمؤَدَّبُ
(د) تَسِير ... في الْبِحَارِ	(ز) الْوَالِدُ ... عَلَي ابْنِهِ
(ه) يَرْتَفِعُ ... في الْجَوِّ	(ي) ... عَلِيٌّ الزَّهْرَ
(و) يَكْثُرُ ... بِبلادِ مِصر	(ط) ... السَّمَك في الماءِ

❁❁❁

٣- بيِّن الأفعال الماضية ، والأفعال المضارعة ، وأفعال الأمر ، والأسماء والحروف ، من العبارات الآتية :

Three. Identify the *māḍī* verbs, *muḍāri*ʿ verbs, the command verbs, the nouns and particles in the following sentences:

﴿مَا جَعَلَ اللهُ لِرَجُلٍ مِنْ قَلْبَيْنِ فِي جَوْفِهِ﴾ ... يَحْرِصُ الْعَاقِلُ عَلَى رِضَا رَبِّهِ ... احْرُث لِدُنْيَاكَ كَأَنَّكَ تَعِيشُ أَبَدًا ... يَسْعَى الْفَتَى لِأُمُورٍ لَيْسَ يُدْرِكُها ، لَنْ تُدْرِكَ الْمَجْدَ حَتَّى تَلْعَقَ الصَّبْرَ ... إِنْ تَصْدُقْ تَسُدْ ... ﴿قَدْ أَفْلَحَ مَنْ زَكَّاهَا ۝ وَقَدْ خَابَ مَنْ دَسَّاهَا﴾.

بابُ الإعْرَابِ

Chapter of Inflection

قال: الإعْرَابُ هُوَ : تَغْيِيرُ أَوَاخِرِ الْكلِمِ لِاخْتِلَافِ الْعَوَامِلِ الْداخِلَة عَلَيهَا لَفْظاً أَوْ تَقْدِيراً .

He said: Inflection is the changing of the end of words according to a variance in grammatical governors,[31] whether it is explicit or implicitly inferred.

وأقول الإعراب له مَعْنَيَانِ : أحدهما لُغويٌّ ، والآخر اصطلاحيٌّ .

I say: Inflection has two meanings: The first of them is the linguistic meaning and the other is in terms of the nomenclature of the grammarians.

أما معناه في اللغة فهو : الإظهار والإبانة ، تقول : أَعْرَبْتُ عَمَّا فِي نَفْسِي ، إذا أَبَنْتَهُ وأَظْهَرْتَهُ .

Its linguistic meaning is showing and expressing. An example is if it is said, "I expressed (*aʿrabtu*) what was within myself," with the meaning of announcing and making apparent what was within the self.

وأما معناه في الاصطلاح فهو ما ذكره المؤلف بقوله : (تَغْيِيرُ أَوَاخِرِ الكَلِم... إلخ).

As for the meaning in terms of the nomenclature [of the grammarians], it is what the author stated, "Inflection is the changing of vowel markings at the end of words … [until the end]."

والمقصود من (تَغْيِير أَوَاخِرِ الْكَلِم) تَغْيِيرُ أَحْوَالِ أَوَاخِر الكلم ، ولا يُعْقَل أن يُرَادَ تغييرُ

31 Al-Ahdal said in *al-Kawākib* (1/44), "The word *ʿawāmil* (governors) is the plural of *ʿāmil*. It refers to that which mandates the end of a word to have a specific state from *rafʿ*, *naṣb*, *jarr* or *jazm*."

نفس الأَوَاخِرِ، فإنَّ آخِر الكلمة نَفْسَهُ لا يتغير ، وتغيير أحوال أواخِر الكلمة عبارة عن تحوُّلها من الرفع إلى النصب أو الجر : حقيقة ، أو حُكماً ، ويكون هذا التَّحَوُّل بسبب تغيير العوامل : من عامل يقتضي الرفع على الفاعلية أو نحوها ، إلى آخَرَ يقتضي النصبَ على المفعولية أو نحوها ، وهلم جرا .

The intention behind, "The changing of the end of words," is the alteration of the state of the end of the word, and it should not be understood that this is intended to mean that the ending in of itself is altered. Rather, the ending of the word in of itself does not change, and the [mention of] change occurring in the state of the word is an expression of it shifting from the state of *al-rafʿ* to *al-naṣb* or *al-jarr*—in the actual sense or by ruling. The reason behind this alteration is the impact of a governor—and from the governors is that which causes the state of *al-rafʿ* due to the word being a subject of the verb or similar, while another governor will cause the state of *al-naṣb* due to the word being the object or similar, and so on.

مثلاً إذا قلت: (حَضَرَ مُحَمَّدٌ) فمحمد : مرفوع ؛ لأنه معمول لعامل يقتضي الرفع على الفاعلية ، وهذا العامل هو (حضر).

For example, if it is said, "Muḥammad was present." Muḥammad is *marfūʿ* due it being the operative of a governor that requires the state of *al-rafʿ* to be enforced upon its subject. The governor in this case is "[he] was present."

فإن قلت : (رأيت محمداً) تغير حال آخر (محمد) إلى النصب ؛ لتغير العامل بعامل آخر يقتضي النصبَ وهو (رأيت).

Whereas if it is said, "I saw Muḥammad," the state of the end of Muḥammad is altered to *al-naṣb*. This is due to the different governor here dictating [the end of the word] to alter to *al-naṣb*. The governor here is "I saw."

فإذا قلت (حظيتُ بمحمدٍ) تغير حالُ آخره إلى الجر ؛ لتغير العامل بعامل آخر يقتضي الجر وهو الباء .

Whereas if it is said, "I received Muḥammad," the state of the end of Muḥammad is altered to *al-jarr*, and this is due to the different governor here dictating [the end of the word] to alter to *al-jarr*. The governor here is the *bā*.

وإذا تأَمَّلْتَ في هذه الأمثلة ظهر لك أن آخِرَ الكلمة ـ وهو الدال من (محمد)ـ لم يتغير ، وأن الذي تغير هو أحوالُ آخرها : فإنك تراه مرفوعاً في المثال الأوَّل ، ومنصوباً في المثال الثاني ، ومجروراً في المثال الثالث .

If you were to contemplate over these examples, it would be clear to you that the end of the word—and that is the *dāl* of Muḥammad—does not change. Rather, what changes is the state of the ending. You should be able to see that it is *marfūʿ* in the first example, *manṣūb* in the second example and *majrūr* in the third example.

وهذا التغير من حالة الرفع إلى حالة النصب إلى حالة الجرِّ هو الإعراب عند المؤلف ومن ذهب مذهبه ، وهذه الحركات الثلاث ـ التي هي الرفع ، والنصب ، الجر ـ هي علامة وأَمَارَةُ على الإعراب .

This alteration from the state of *al-rafʿ* to the state of *al-naṣb* to the state of *al-jarr* is what constitutes inflection according to the author and those who followed the same school of thought. So these three cases—which are *al-rafʿ*, *al-naṣb* and *al-jarr*—are the signs and marks of inflection.

ومثلُ الاسم في ذلك الفعلُ المضارعُ .

The *muḍāriʿ* verb is similar to the noun in this sense.

فلو قلت : (يُسَافِرُ إبراهيمُ) فـ(يسافر) : فعل مضارع مرفوع ؛ لتجرده من عامل يقتضي نصبه أو عامل يقتضي جزمه .

If it is said, "Ibrāhīm travels," "travels" is a *marfūʿ muḍāriʿ* verb. This is due to it being free from any governor which would dictate it to be in *naṣb*, or a governor which would dictate it to be in the state of *jazm*.

فإذا قلت : (لَنْ يُسَافِرَ إبراهيمُ) تغير حال (يسافر) من الرفع إلى النصب ، لتغير العامل بعامل آخر يقتضي نصبه ، وهو (لَنْ) .

If one said, "Ibrāhīm will not travel," the state of the verb *yusāfir* ([he] travels) has altered from *al-rafʿ* to *al-naṣb*. This is due to the different governor here dictating it to become in the state of *naṣb*, and this is "*lan*" (will not).

فإذا قلت : (لَمْ يُسَافِرْ إبراهيمُ) تَغَيَّرَ حالُ (يسافر) من الرفع أو النصب إلى الجزم ، لتغير العامل بعامل آخر يقتضي جزمه ، وهو (لم).

If it is said, "Ibrāhīm did not travel," the state of the verb *yusāfir* has altered from *al-rafʿ* or *al-naṣb* to *al-jazm*. This is due to the different governor here dictating it to become *majzūm*, and this is "*lam*" (did not).

واعلم أن هذا التغير ينقسِمُ إلى قسمين : لَفْظِيٌّ ، وتقديري .

Know, that this process of alteration is categorised into two: explicit and implicit.

فأما اللفظي فهو : مالا يمنع من النطق به مانع كما رأيت في حركات الدال من (محمد) وحركات الراء من (يسافر).

As for the category of the explicit inflection, it is that which is not prevented by something from being articulated, as can be seen in the diacritical points of the letter *dāl* in "Muḥammad" and the diacritical points of the letter *rā* in "*yusāfir*".

وأما التقديري : فهو ما يمنع من التلفظ به مانع من تَعَذُّر ، أو استِثقال ، أو مناسَبَة ؛ تقول : (يَدْعُو الفتَى والْقَاضِي وغلامِي) فـ(يدعو) : مرفوع لتجرده من الناصب والجازم ، و(الفتى) : مرفوع لكونه فاعلاً ، و(القاضي) و(غلامي): مرفوعان لأنهما معطوفان على الفاعل المرفوع ، ولكن الضمة لا تظهر في أواخر هذه الكلمات ، لتعذرها في (الفتى) وثقلها في (يَدْعُو) وفي (الْقَاضِي) ولأجل مناسبة ياء المتكلم في (غُلاَمِي)

؛ فتكون الضمة مقدّرة على آخر الكلمة منع من ظهورها التعذر ، أو الثقل ، أو اشتغال المحل بحركة المناسبة .

As for the category of the implicit inflection, it is that which is prevented from being articulated by something. This can be due to impracticability, heaviness (i.e. where it is difficult to do so), or appropriateness.[32] If it is said, "The boy, the judge and my servant called." "Called" here is *marfūʿ* due to it being free of any governor that would dictate it to be in the state of *naṣb* or *jazm*. "The boy" is *marfūʿ* due to it being the subject. "The judge" and "my servant" are both *marfūʿ* due to them being linked to the *marfūʿ* subject. However the *dammah* cannot be seen at the end of these words. This is due to the impracticability of doing so with "the boy", and the heaviness of doing so for "called" and "the judge". In "my servant", it is due to the connection (i.e. appropriation) of the *yā* of the first person. Thus the *dammah* is implicit at the end of these words due to being prevented by impracticability, heaviness or the occupation of the place with the appropriate diacritical mark.

وتقول : (لَنْ يَرْضَى الْفَتَى وَالْقَاضِي وَغُلاَمِي) وتقول : (إِنَّ الْفَتَى وَ غُلاَمِي لَفَائِزَانِ) وتقول : (مَرَرْتُ بِالْفَتَى وغُلاَمِي والْقَاضِي) .

And it is said, "The boy, the judge and my boy servant will not be pleased," "Verily the boy and my servant boy are both winners," and, "I passed by the boy, my servant boy and the judge."

فما كان آخره ألفاً لازمة تُقَدَّر عليه جميعُ الحركات للتعذر ، ويسمى الاسمُ المنتهي بالألف مقصوراً ، مثل (الفتى) ،و(العَصا) ، و(الحِجَى) ، و(الرَّحَى) ، و(الرِّضَا).

32 Impracticability refers to, "The impracticability brought about by the diacritic appearing upon a defective letter and so this becomes impractical for the tongue to emit its sound." Heaviness refers to, "The difficulty brought about by the diacritic appearing upon a defective letter and so this becomes heavy for the tongue to emit its sound. The diacritic can be expressed however with heaviness and discomfort." Appropriateness refers to, "The presence of a diacritic at the end of a noun which is required due to its connection to another noun. An example is the letter *yā*, it is not appropriate for it to be preceded by any diacritic besides the *kasrah*. So the diacritic present before the letter *yā* is termed as the appropriate diacritic." See *al-Naḥwu al-Muṣaffī* (pp. 84-85 and 92).

That which ends with the letter *alif* demands the implication of all diacritical points due to impracticability. The noun that ends with an *alif* is called *maqṣūr* (broken)[33] e.g. the boy, the stick, the Hajj pilgrim, the hand-mill and the content.

وما كان آخره ياء لازمَة تُقَدَّر عليه الضمة والكسرة للثقل ، ويسمى الاسمُ المنتهي بالياءِ منقوصاً ، وتظهر عليه الفتحة لخفتها ، نحو : (القَاضِي) ، و(الدَّاعِي) ، و(الْغَازِي) ، و(السَّاعِي)، و(الآتي) ، و(الرّاَمِي).

That which ends with the letter *yā* demands the implication of the *ḍammah* and *kasrah* diacritical points due to heaviness. The noun that ends with *al-yā* is called *manqūṣ* (incomplete)[34], and the *fatḥah* (in explicit form) is visible upon it due to the phonetic ease of doing so. Examples being: the judge, the caller, the soldier, the courier, the coming and the thrower.

ما كان مضافاً إلى ياء المتكلم تُقَدَّر عليه الحركاتُ كلُّها للمناسبةِ ، نحو : (غلامِي) ، و(كِتابي) ، و(صَديِقِي) ، و(ابني) ، و(أُستاذي) .

What is appended to the *yā* of the first person demands the implication of every diacritical point upon it due to appropriation. Examples being: my servant, my book, my friend, my son, my teacher.

ويقابل الإعرابَ البناء ، ويتضح كل واحدٍ منهما تمامَ الاتّضَاحِ بسبب بيان الآخرَ . وقد ترك المؤلفُ بيان البناء ، ونحن نبينه لك على الطريقة التي بيَّنا بها الإعراب ، فنقول :

33 Al-Ahdal said in *al-Kawākib* (1/85), "[It is called this] because it is the opposite of the *mamdūd* (elongated) or because it is shortened, i.e. it is prevented from showing its diacritics." The definition of the *maqṣūr* noun, as given by Ibn ʿAqīl (1/81) is, "It is the inflectable noun which ends with the requisite (*lāzim*) letter *alif*."

34 Al-Ahdal said in *al-Kawākib* (1/86), "[It is called this] because there is a decrease in its diacritics and because its *lām kalimah* (which is the letter *yā*) is removed if there is a *tanwīn*—e.g. the word قاضٍ (the letter *yā* has been removed here)—in order to prevent the meeting of two *sukūns*." The definition of the *manqūṣ* noun, as given by Ibn ʿAqīl (1/81) is, "It is the inflectable noun which ends with the letter *yā* which dictates being preceded by a *kasrah*."

Al-binā (fixed endings i.e. words that do not accept inflection) is the opposite of *al-ʿirāb*, and both can be made completely clear by analysing the other. The author decided not to explain the words that do not accept inflection, however we will detail them to you in the same manner that we did so for the words that do accept inflection. So we say:

للبناء معنيان : أحدهما لغويّ ، والآخر اصطلاحيّ :

Al-binā has two definitions, the first being in the linguistic sense and the other is in terms of the nomenclature of the grammarians:

فأما معناه في اللغة فهو عبارة عن وَضْع شيءٍ على شيءٍ على جهَة يُرَادُ بها الثبوتُ واللزومُ .

As for its definition in the linguistic sense, it is an expression indicating the placing of something upon another in order to provide firmness and permanence.

وأما معناه في الاصطلاح فهو لُزُومُ آخر الكلمة حالةً واحدةً لغير عامل ولا اعتلال ، وذلك كلزوم (كَمْ) و(مَنْ) السكون ، وكلزوم (هؤلاءِ) و(حَذَامِ) و(أَمْسِ) الكَسْرَ ، وكلزوم (مُنْذُ) و(حَيْثُ) الضمَّ ، وكلزوم (أيْنَ) و(كَيْفَ) الفتحَ .

As for its definition in terms of nomenclature, it is that its end remains consistent in one state, in spite of the entry of different governors and not due to defectiveness in its construction. Examples of this consistency are the words "how many/much" and "who" upon the ending of *al-sukūn*, "these", "*ḥadhāmi*" and "yesterday" upon the ending of *al-kasrah*, "since" and "wherein" upon the ending of *al-ḍammah*, "where" and "how" upon the ending of *al-fatḥah*.

ومن هذا الإيضاح تعلم أن ألقابِ البناءِ أربعة : السكون ، والكسر ، والضم ، والفتح .

From this it is clearly seen that the forms of *al-binā* are four: *al-sukūn*, *al-kasrah*, *al-ḍammah*, and *al-fatḥah*.

وبعد بيان كل هذه الأشياء لا تَعْسُرُ عليك معرفة المعرب والمبني ، فإن المعرب : ما تَغَيَّرَ حالُ آخِرِهِ لفظاً أو تقديراً بسبب تغيُّرَ العوامل ، والمبني : ما لزم آخرُهُ حالَةً واحدةً لغير عامل واعتلال .

After comprehension of the aforementioned there will be no difficulty upon the reader in understanding the inflectable and the non-inflectable. The inflectable is that in which the state of the ending changes in wording or through implication due to the impact of a governor. The non-inflectable is that which its ending remains consistent in one state in spite of different governors and not due to defectiveness in its construction.

تمرين

Exercises

بيّن المعرب بأنواعه ، والمبني ، من الكلمات الواقعة في العبارات الآتية :

Identify the inflectable according to its types, and the non-inflectable that arise in the below sentences:

قال أعرابيٌّ : الله يُخْلِفُ مَا أَتْلَفَ الناسُ ، والدَّهْرُ يُتْلِفُ ما جَمَعُوا ، وكم مِنْ مَيْتَةٍ عِلَّتها طَلَبُ الحياةِ ، وحياةٍ سَببُهَا التَّعَرُّضُ لِلْمَوْتِ .

سأَل عُمَرُ بن الخطّابِ عَمْرو بنَ مَعْدِ يَكَرِبَ عَنِ الْحَرْبِ ، فقال لهُ : هي مُرَّةُ المَذَاقِ ، إذا قَلَصَتْ عن سَاقٍ ، مَنْ صَبَرَ فِيها عُرِفَ ، ومَنْ ضَعُفَ عنها تَلِفَ...

﴿والضُّحى ۝ والليْلِ إِذَا سجى ۝ ما وَدَّعك ربُّكَ وما قَلى ۝ للآخِرَةُ خَيْرٌ لَكَ مِنَ الأُولي﴾

{By the morning brightness, and [by] the night when it covers with darkness, your Lord has not taken leave of you, [O Muḥammad], nor has He detested [you]. And the Hereafter is better for you than the first [life].}[35]

35 Al-Ḍuḥā: 1-4

إنا الْعُلاَ حَدَّثَنِي وَهْيَ صادقةٌ   فيما تُحَدِّثُ أَنَّ العِزَّ في النُّقَل

إذا نامَ غِرٌّ في دُجى الليل فاسْهَرِ   وقم لِلْمَعَالِي والعَوَالي وشَمِّرِ

إذا أنت لم تُقْصِرْ عن الْجَهْلِ والخَنا   أَصَبْتَ حَليماً أو أصابك جاهلُ

الصَّبْر على حُقوق المُروءَةِ أشدُّ مِنَ الصَّبْر على ألم الحاجةِ، وذِلَّةُ الفَقْرِ مانِعةٌ من عزّ الصبر ، كما أن عزّ الغني مانِعٌ مِنْ كرم الإنصافِ .

أسئلة

Questions

ما هو الإعراب ؟ ما هو البناء ؟ ما هو المعرب ؟ ما هو المبني ؟

What is inflection? What is non-inflection? What is the inflectable? What is the non-inflectable?

ما معنى تغير أواخر الكلم؟ إلى كم قسم ينقسم التغير ؟ ما هو التغير اللفظي ؟ ما هو التغير التقديري ؟ ما أسباب التغير التقديري ؟

What is the meaning of "an alteration at the ending of a word"? How many types is this alteration categorised into? What is an explicit alteration and what is an implicit alteration? What are the reasons for the occurrence of an implicit alteration?

اذكر سببين مما يمنع النطق بالحركة .

Mention two reasons that prevent the pronunciation of a diacritic.

ايتِ بثلاثة أمثلة لكلام مفيد ، بحيث يكون في كل مثالٍ اسمٌ معرب بحركة مقدرة منع من ظهورها التعذر.

Bring three examples of comprehensible speech of which each contains a noun that inflects with an implicit diacritic that is prevented from being displayed due to impracticality.

ايت بمثالين لكلام مفيد في كل واحد منهما اسم معرب بحركة مقدرة منع من ظهورها الثقل .

Bring two examples of comprehensible speech of which each contains a noun that inflects with an implicit diacritic that is prevented from being displayed due to heaviness.

ايت بثلاثة أمثلة لكلام مفيد في كل مثال منها اسم مَبْنِيٌّ.

Bring three examples of comprehensible speech of which each contains a non-inflectable noun.

ايت بثلاثة أمثلة لكلام مفيد يكون في كل مثال منها اسم معرب بحركة مقدرة منع من ظهورها المناسبة .

Bring three examples of comprehensible speech of which each contains a noun that inflects with an implicit diacritic that is prevented from being displayed due to appropriation.

أنواع الإعراب

The Types of Declension

قال : وأقسامه أربعة : رَفْعٌ ، وَنَصْبٌ ، وَخَفْضٌ، وَجَزْمٌ ، فللأسمَاءِ مِنْ ذَلِكَ الرَّفْعُ ، والنَّصْبُ ، والخَفْضُ ، ولا جَزمَ فيها ، وللأفعال مِنْ ذَلِكَ الرَّفْعُ ، والنَّصبُ ، والجَزْمُ ، ولاَ خَفْضَ فيها .

He said: Its types are four: (i) *rafᶜ*, (ii) *naṣb*, (iii) *khafḍ* and (iv) *jazm*. Those applicable to the noun from these are: (i) *al-rafᶜ*, (ii) *al-naṣb*, (iii) *al-khafḍ* and it does not accept the *jazm* state. Those applicable to the verb are: (i) *al-rafᶜ*, (ii) *al-naṣb*, (iii) *al-jazm* and it does not accept the state of *khafḍ*.

وأقول : أنواع الإعراب التي تقع في الاسم والفعل جميعاً أربعة : الأوَّل : الرفع ، والثاني : النصب ، والثالث : الخفض ، والرابع : الجزم ، ولكل واحد من هذه الأنواع الأربعة معنى في اللغة، ومعنى في اصطلاح النحاة.

I say: The types of declension that take place upon the noun and verb are four in total: (i) *al-rafᶜ*, (ii) *al-naṣb*, (iii) *al-khafḍ* and (iv) *al-jazm*. Each of these four types has a linguistic definition and a definition according to the nomenclature of the grammarians:

أما الرفع فهو في اللغة : العُلُوُّ والارتفاعُ ، وهو في الاصطلاح : تغير مخصوصٌ علامَتُهُ الضمة وما ناب عنها ، وستعرف قريباً ما ينوب عن الضمة في الفصل الآتي إن شاء الله ، ويقع الرفع في كل من الاسم والفعل ، نحو : (يَقُومُ عَليٌّ) و(يَصْدَحُ البُلْبُلُ).

The linguistic meaning of *al-rafᶜ* is highness and ascension. Its meaning in terms of nomenclature is a specific alteration that occurs with the sign of *al-ḍammah* or its substitute. We will explain these substitutes for the *ḍammah* in the coming section, Allah willing. The state of *al-rafʿ* affects both the noun and verb. E.g. "'Alī stood" and, "The nightingale sings".

وأما النصبُ فهو اللغة : الاسْتِواءُ والاسْتِقَامَة ، وهو في الاصطلاح : تغير مخصوص علامته الفَتْحَة وما ناب عنها ، ويقع النَّصْبُ في كل من الاسم والفعل أيضاً ، نحو : (لَنْ أُحِبَّ الكَسَلَ) .

The linguistic meaning of *al-naṣb* is straightness and uprightness. Its meaning in terms of nomenclature is a specific alteration that occurs with the sign of *al-fatḥah* or its substitute. The state of *al-naṣb* also affects both the noun and verb. An example is, "I will not love laziness."

وأما الخفض فهو في اللغة : التَسَفُّلُ ، وهو في الاصطلاح : تغيُّر مخصوصٌ علامتُهُ الكَسْرَة وما نابَ عنها ، ولا يكون الخفض إلا في الاسم ، نحو : (تَألَّمْتُ مِنَ الكَسُولِ).

The linguistic meaning of *al-khafḍ* is lowering. Its meaning in terms of nomenclature is a specific alteration that occurs with the sign of *al-kasrah* or its substitute. The state of *al-khafḍ* only affects the noun, e.g. "I suffered from laziness."

وأما الجزم فهو في اللغة : القَطْعُ ، وفي الاصطلاح يغيرٌ مخصُوصٌ علامتُهُ اَلسُّكونُ وما نابَ عنه ، ولا يكون الجَزْمُ إلا في الفعل المضارع ، نحو (لَمْ يَفُزْ مُتَكَاسِلٌ) .

The linguistic meaning of *al-jazm* is a cut. Its meaning in terms of nomenclature is a specific alteration that occurs with the sign of *al-sukūn* or its substitute. The state of *al-jazm* only affects the *muḍāriʿ* verb, e.g. "The lazy one did not triumph."

فقد تبين لك أن أنواع الإعراب على ثلاثة أقسام : قسم مشترك بين الأسماء والأفعال ، وهو الرفع والنصب ، وقسم مختصٌّ بالأسماء ، وهو الخفض ، وقسم مختص بالأفعال

، وهو الجزْم .

It has been displayed to you above that the types of declension are of three categories: (i) those that are shared by the noun and the verb i.e. *al-rafʿ* and *al-naṣb*, (ii) that which is specific to the noun i.e. *al-khafḍ* and (iii) that which is specific to the verb i.e. *al-jazm*.

أسئلة

Questions

ما أنواع الأعراب ؟

What are the types of declension?

ما هو الرفع لغة واصطلاحاً ؟

What is the meaning of *al-rafʿ* in the linguistic sense and in terms of nomenclature?

ما هو النصب لغة واصطلاحاً ؟

What is the meaning of *al-naṣb* in the linguistic sense and in terms of nomenclature?

ما هو الخفض لغة واصطلاحاً ؟

What is the meaning of *al-khafḍ* in the linguistic sense and in terms of nomenclature?

ما هو الجزم لغة واصطلاحاً ؟

What is the meaning of *al-jazm* in the linguistic sense and in terms of nomenclature?

ما أنواع الإعراب التي يشترك فيها الاسم والفعل ؟

Which of the types of declension are shared by the noun and the verb?

ما الذي يختص به الاسم من علامات الإعراب ؟

Which of the types of declension are specific to the noun?

ما الذي يختص به الفعل من علامات الإعراب ؟

Which of the types of declension are specific to the verb?

مَثِّلْ بأربعة أمثلة لكُلٍّ من الإسم المرفوع ، والفعل المنصوب ، والاسم المخفوض ، والفعل المجزوم .

Provide four examples of the *marfūʿ* noun, *manṣūb* verb, *makhfūḍ* noun and *majzūm* verb.

باب معرفة علامات الإعراب

Chapter: Understanding the Signs of Declension

قال: للرفعِ أَرْبَعُ عَلاَمَاتٍ :الضَّمَّةُ ، والوَاوُ ، وَالأَلِفُ ، وَالنُّونُ .

He said: There are four signs of *al-rafʿ*: *al-ḍammah*, *al-wāw*, *al-alif* and *al-nūn*.

وأقول : تستطيع أن تَعْرِفَ أن الكلمة مرفوعة بوجود علامة في آخرها من أربع علامات : واحدة منها أصلية ، وهي الضمة ، وَثَلاَثٌ فُرُوعٌ عنها ، وهي : الواو ، والألف ، والنون .

I say: It is possible to ascertain that a word is *marfūʿ* by the presence of four signs upon its ending: the first—and it is its original sign—is *al-ḍammah*. The other three signs are subsidiaries of it, they are: *al-wāw*, *al-alif* and *al-nūn*.

مواضع الضمة

Positions of the Ḍammah

قال : فَأَمَّا الضَّمَّةُ فَتَكُون عَلاَمَةً للرَّفْعِ في أَرْبَعَةِ مَوَاضِيعَ : الإِسمِ المُفْرَدِ ، وجَمْعِ التَّكْسِيرِ ، وَجَمْعِ الْمُؤَنثِ السَّالِمِ ، والْفِعْل الْمُضَارِعِ الذي لَمْ يَتَّصلْ بآخره شَيْءٌ .

He said: As for *al-ḍammah*, it is an indicator of *al-rafʿ* in four instances: (i) the singular noun (ii) the broken plural (iii) the sound feminine plural (iv) the *muḍāriʿ* verb which has nothing attached to the end of it.

وأقول: تكون الضمة علامَةً على رَفْعِ الكلمة في أربع مواضع :

I say: The *ḍammah* is an indication of a word being *raf*ʿ in four instances:

الموضع الأول : الاسم المفرد ، والموضع الثاني : جمع التكسير ، والموضع الثالث : جمع المؤنث السالم ، والموضع الرابع : الفعل المضارع الذي لم يَتَّصِلْ به ألف اثنين ، ولا واو جماعة ، ولا ياء مخاطبة ، ولا نون توكيد خفيفةٌ أو ثقيلةٌ ، ولا نُونِ نِسْوَة .

The first instance: the singular noun. The second instance: the broken plural. The third instance: the sound feminine plural. The fourth instance: the *muḍari*ʿ verb of which its ending is not connected to the *alif* of duality, the *waw* of plurality, the *yā* of the feminine second person, neither the light *nūn* of emphasis, nor the heavy one, and neither the *nun* of feminine plurality.

أما الإِسم المفرد فالمراد به ههنا : ما ليس مُثَنَّى ولا مجموعاً ولا ملحقاً بهما ولا من الأسماء الخمسة .

As for the singular noun, the meaning of it here is: what is not dual, not plural, not attached to either of them and not from the five nouns.

سواءٌ أكان المراد به مذكراً مثل : محمد ، وعلي ، وحمزة ، أم كان المراد به مؤنثاً مثل : فاطمة ، وعائشة ، وزينب .

It includes that which is masculine e.g. Muḥammad, ʿAlī and Ḥamzah, or that which is feminine e.g. Fāṭimah, ʿĀishah and Zaynab.

وسواءٌ أكانت الضمة ظاهرة كما في نحو (حَضَرَ مُحَمَّدٌ) و(سّافَرَتْ فَاطِمَةُ)، أم كانت مُقَدَّرَةً نحو (حَضَرَ الْفَتَى والْقَاضِي وَأَخِي) ونحو (تَزَوَّجَتْ لَيْلَى ونُعْمى) فإن (محمد) وكذا (فاطمة) مرفوعان ، وعلامة رفعهما الضمة الظاهرة ، و(الفتى) ومثله (ليلى) و(نعمى) مرفوعات ، وعلامَةُ رَفعِهِنَّ ضمة مُقَدَّرَةٌ على الألف منع من ظهورها التعذر.

It includes that which has an explicit *ḍammah*, as in: "Muḥammad was present", "Fāṭimah travelled". It includes that which has an implicit *ḍammah*, such as "The boy, the judge and my brother were present" and "Laylā and Nuʿmā got married". Muḥammad and Fāṭimah are both *marfū'* and the sign of their state is the explicit *ḍammah*. The boy, Laylā and Nu'mah are all *marfu'*, and the sign of their state is the implicit *ḍammah* upon the *alif*, prevented from being displayed due to impracticality.

و(الْقَاضِي) مرفوع ، وعلامة رفعه ضمة مقدرة على الياء منع من ظهورها الثقل ، و(أَخِي) مرفوع ، وعلامة رفعه ضمة مقدرة على ما قبل ياءِ المتكلم منع من ظهورها حركةُ المناسَبَةِ .

And *al-qāḍī* is *marfū'*, and the sign of its state is an implicit *ḍammah* upon the *yā*, prevented from being displayed due to heaviness. And "*akhī*" is also *marfū'*, and the sign of its state is an implicit *ḍammah* upon that which comes before the *yā* of the first person, prevented from being displayed due to appropriation.

أما جمع التكسير فالمراد به : ما دَلَّ على أكثر من اثنين أو اثنتين مع تَغَيُّر في صيغة مفردهِ .

As for the broken plural, what it refers to here is that which indicates to more than two in the masculine or feminine gender, with an alteration of the singular form of the word.

وأنواع التغير الموجودة في جموع التكثير ستة :

The types of alteration correlating with the broken plural are six:

١- تَغَيُّرٌ بالشكل لَيْسَ غَيْرُ ، نحو : (أَسَدٌ وأُسْدٌ) ، وَ(نَمِرٌ ونُمُرٌ)؛ فإن حروف المفرد والجمع في هذين المثالين مُتَّحِدَة ، والاِخْتلاَف بين المفرد والجمع إنما هو في شكلها.

One. Alteration in the diacritics only e.g. "lion-lions" and "tiger-tigers". In these two examples the letters of the singular and the plural are the same. The difference between the two is in the diacritics.

٢- تَغَيُّرٌ بالنقص لَيْسَ غَيْرُ ، نحو : (تُهَمَة وتُهَمٌ) ، و(تُخَمَةٌ وتُخَمٌ) ، فأنت تجد الجمع قد نقص حرفاً في هذه الكلمات - وهو التاء - وباقي الحروف على حالها في المفرد.

Two. Alteration through a decrease only e.g. "charge-charges" and "indigestion-indigestions". You will notice that in the plural here the decrease is in a letter of the words—and that letter is *al-tā*—and the rest of the letters are the same as in the singular.

٣- تغير بالزيادة ليس غير ، نحو : (صِنْوٌ و صِنْوَان) ، في مثل قوله تعالى : ﴿صِنْوَانٌ وَغَيْرُ صِنْوَانٍ﴾

Three. Alteration through an increase only (ان) e.g. "twin-twins". This can be seen in the statement of the Most High: {[**And date palms,**] **some having twin trunks and some having a single one.**}[36]

٤- تغير في الشكل مع النقص ، نحو : (سَرِير وسُرُر) ، و(كِتَاب وكُتُب) ،و(أَحْمَر وحُمْر) ، و(أَبْيَض وبيض) .

Four. Alteration in the diacritics and through a decrease (i.e. taking away a ي or ا) e.g. "bed-beds", "book-books", "red (s)-red (p)" and "white (s)-white (p)".

٥- تغير في الشكل مع الزيادة ، نحو : (سَبَب وَأَسْبَاب) ، وَ(بَطل وأبطال) ، وَ(هِنْد وَهُنُود)، وَ(سَبُع وَسِبَاع) ، وَ(ذِئْب وَذِئَاب) ، و(شُجَاع وشُجْعَان).

Five. Alteration in the diacritics and through an increase (adding an ا or و) e.g. "cause-causes", "hero-heroes", "Hind-Hinds", "predatory animal-predatory animals", "wolf-wolves" and "brave (s)-brave (p)".

٦- تغير في الشكل مع الزيادة والنقص جميعاً ، نحو : (كَرِيم وكُرَمَاء) ، وَ(رَغِيف وَرُغْفَان)، و(كَاتِب وَكُتَّاب) ، وَ(أَمِير وأُمَرَاء).

36 Al-Ra'd: 4

Six. Alteration in the diacritics and through an increase and decrease together e.g. "generous (s)-generous (p)", "a loaf [of bread]-loafs", "writer-writers" and "leader-leaders".

وهذه الأنواع كلها تكون مرفوعة بالضمة ، سواءٌ أكان المراد من لفظ الجمع مذكراً ، نحو : (رِجَال) ، و(كُتاب)، أم كان المراد منه مؤنثاً ، (هُنُود) ، وَ(زَيَانِب)، وسواءٌ أكانت الضمة ظاهرة كما في هذه الأمثلة ، أم كانت مقدرة كما في نحو : (سكَارَى)، وَ(جَرْحَى) ، ونحو : (عَذَارَى)، وَ(حَبَالَى) تقول : (قامَ الرِّجالُ والزَّيَانِبُ) فتجدهما مرفوعين بالضمة الظاهرة ، وتقول : (حَضَرَ الْجَرْحَى والعَذَارَى) فيكون كل من (الْجَرْحَى) و(العَذَارَى) مرفوعاً بضمة مقدرة على الألف منع من ظهورها التعذر .

All of these types become *marfūʿ* with a *ḍammah*, regardless whether the wording refers to the plural male e.g. "men" and "writers" or if it refers to the plural female e.g. "Hinds" and "Zaynabs". This is also the case regardless whether the *ḍammah* is visible—as in these examples—or if it is implicit e.g. "drunkards", "wounded", "chaste" and " pregnant women". If you say, "The men and Zaynabs stood," you will find that they are both *marfūʿ* with an explicit *ḍammah*. And if you say, "The wounded and the chaste were present," you will find that they are both *marfūʿ* with an implicit *ḍammah* upon the *alif*, prevented from being displayed due to impracticality.

أما جمع المؤنث السالم فهو : ما دلَّ عَلَى أكثر من اثنتين بزيادة ألفٍ وَتاءٍ في آخره ، نحو : (زَيْنَبَات) ، و(فاطمات)، و(حَمَّامات) تقول (جَاءَ الزَّيْنَبَاتُ)، و(سافر الفاطمات) فـ(الزينبات) و(الفاطمات) مرفوعان ، وعلامة رفعهما الضمة الظاهرة ، ولا تكون الضمة مقدرة في جمع المؤنث السالم ، إلا عند إضافته لياء المتكلم نحو : (هَذِهِ شَجَرَاتِي وَبَقَرَاتِي).

As for the sound feminine plural it is that which indicates towards more than two with the addition of the letters *alif* and *tā* at the end of the word.[37] Exam-

37 One could say that this definition does not fully encompass the matter fully. The reason for this is that the author said, "That which indicates towards more than two (and the

ples are, "Zaynabs", Fāṭimahs" and "doves". If it is said, "The Zaynabs came" and "The Fāṭimahs travelled", the words "the Zaynabs" and "the Fātimahs" are *marfū'*. The sign of them being *marfū'* is the presence of the explicit *ḍammah*. The implicit *ḍammah* does not arise in relation to the sound feminine plural except when it connects to the *yā* of the first person e.g. "These are my trees and my cows."

فإن كانت الألف غيرَ زائدةٍ : بأن كانت موجودة في المفرد نحو (القاضي والقُضَاة) ، و(الداعي والدُّعَاةُ) لم يكن جمع مؤنث سالماً ، بل هو حينئذٍ جمعُ تكسيرٍ .

If the *alif* is not an addition i.e. it was present in the singular e.g. "judge-judges" and "caller-callers", it is not considered to be a sound feminine plural and it is instead considered to be a broken plural.

وكذلك لو كانت التاء ليست زائدة : بأن كانت موجودة في المفرد نحو (ميت وأمْوَات) ، و(بَيْت وأبيات) ، و(صوت وأصْوَات) كان من جمع التكسير ، ولم يكن من جمع المؤنث السالم .

Likewise if the *tā* is not an addition i.e. it was present in the singular e.g. "dead (s)-dead (p)", "house-houses" and "sound-sounds", it is considered to be a

---

word he used for "two" was "*ithnatayn*" which is specific to the feminine gender). However he then mentioned the example of "doves", of which the singular form is masculine. So according to this definition "doves" would not be considered to be a sound feminine plural. An alternative definition is that which was given by Ibn Hishām in *al-Shudhūr* (p. 39) and *al-Qaṭr* (p. 68), "That which becomes plural with the addition of the letter *alif* and *tā*." Ibn Mālik preceded him on this in his *Alfiyyah* with the couplet,

وما بتا وألف قد جمعا ... يكسر في الجر وفي النصب معا

That which becomes plural with alif and tā combined, it has a kasrah both in al-jarr and in naṣb.

Regarding the question that may arise to the student regarding why it is called the sound feminine plural though these words are not always feminine in their singular forms, al-Ahdal said in *al-Kawākib* (1/54), "This word (i.e. the sound feminine plural) became part of the nomenclature of the grammarians in reference to that which becomes plural with the addition of the *alif* and *tā* though they differ in their singular forms. This is a case of naming something after the part which forms its majority."

broken plural and not a sound feminine plural.

وأما الفعل المضارع فنحو (يَضْرِبُ) و(يَكْتُبُ) فكل من هذين الفعلين مرفوع ، وعلامة رفعه الضمة الظاهرة ، وكذلك (يدعو) ، و(يَرْجُو) فكل منهما مرفوع وعلامة رفعه ضمة مقدرة عَلَى الواو منع من ظهورها الثقل ، وكذلك (يَقْضِي) ، و(يُرْضِي) فكل منهما مرفوع ، وعلامة رفعه ضمة مقدرة على الياء منع من ظهورها الثقل ، وكذلك (يَرْضَى) ، و(يَقْوَى) فكل منهما مرفوع ، وعلامة رفعه ضمة مقدرة عَلَى الألف منع من ظهورها التعذر .

As for the *muḍāriʿ* verb e.g. "he hits" and "he writes", both of these verbs are *marfūʿ*, and the sign of them being in the state of *rafʿ* is the explicit *ḍammah*. Likewise "he calls" and "he hopes" are both *marfūʿ*, and the sign of them being so is the implicit *ḍammah* upon the letter *wāw*, prevented from being displayed due to heaviness. Likewise "he judges" and "he satisfies" are both *marfūʿ*, and the sign of them being so is the implicit *ḍammah* upon the letter *yā*, prevented from being displayed due to heaviness. Likewise "he is satisfied" and "he becomes strong" are both *marfūʿ*, and the sign of them being so is the implicit *ḍammah* upon the letter *alif*, prevented from being displayed due to impracticality.

وقولنا (الذي لم يتصل به ألفُ اثنين أو واو جماعة أو ياءُ مخاطبة) يُخْرِجُ ما اتصل به واحد من هذه الأشياء الثلاثة ؛ فما اتصل به ألف الاثنين نحو (يَكْتُبَانِ)، و(يَنْصُرَان) وما اتصل به واو الجماعة نحو : (يَكْتُبونَ)، و(يَنْصُرونَ) وما اتصل به ياءُ المخاطبة نحو : (تَكْتُبِينَ)، و(تَنْصُرِينَ) ، ولا يرفع حينئذ بالضمة ، بل يرفع بثبوت النون ، والألفُ أو الواو أو الياء فاعل ، وسيأتي إيضاح ذلك .

Our statement, "The *muḍariʿ* verb of which its ending is not connected to the *alif* of duality, the *waw* of plurality, the *yā* of the feminine second person" excludes that which is connected to any of these three things. Whatever is connected to the *alif* of duality—such as "Them two write" and "Them two help", to the *wāw* of plurality—such as "They write" and "They help", and to the *yā* of the feminine second person—such as "You write" and "You help" are not made *marfū'* here by a *ḍammah*. Rather they are *marfū'* by the presence of the *nūn*, the *alif*, the *wāw* or the *yā* of the *fā'il* (i.e. the subject of the verb). We will explain this matter shortly.

وقولنا (ولا نون توكيد خفيفة أو ثقيلة) يُخْرِجُ الفِعْلَ المضارعَ الذي اتصلت به إحدى النونين ، نحو قوله تعالى : ﴿لَيُسْجَنَنَّ وَلَيَكُونًا مِن الصَّاغِرِينَ﴾ والفعل حينئذٍ مبني على الفتح .

Our statement, "Neither the light *nūn* of emphasis, nor the heavy one" excludes the *muḍāri'* verb that is connected to either of these *nūns*. An example is in the statement of the Most High: **{He will surely be imprisoned and will be of those debased.}**[38] The verb here is non-inflectable upon a *fatḥa*.

وقولنا (ولا نون نسوة) يُخْرِجُ الفعلَ المضارعَ الذي اتصلت به نون النسوة ، نحو قوله تعالى ﴿وَالْوَالِدَتُ يُرْضِعْنَ﴾ والفعلُ حينئذ مبنيٌّ على السكون .

Our statement, "And neither the *nūn* of feminine plurality" excludes a *muḍāri'* verb that is connected to the *nūn* of feminine plurality. An example is in the statement of the Most High: **{The mothers may breastfeed.}**[39] The verb here (*yurḍi'na*) is non-inflectable upon a *sukūn*.

تمرين

Exercises

١- بيّن المرفوعات بالضمة وأنواعها ، مع بيان ما تكون الضمة فيه ظاهرة وما تكون الضمة فيه مقدرة ، وسبب تقديرها ، من بين الكلمات الواردة في الجمل الآتية :

Detail that which is *marfū'* with a *ḍammah* and the types of them, and while doing so, make clear that which has an explicit *ḍammah* and that which has an implicit *ḍammah*—with the reason for its inferred meaning—in the fol-

38 Yūsuf: 32
39 Al-Baqarah: 233

lowing sentences:

قالَتْ أَعْرَابِيّةٌ لِرَجُلٍ : مَالَكَ تُعْطِي وَلاَ تَعِدُ ؟ قالَ : مَالَكَ وَالْوَعْدَ ؟ قَالَت : يَنْفَسِحُ بِهِ الْبَصَرُ ، وينْتَشِرُ فِيهِ الأَمَلُ ، وَتَطِيبُ بِذِكْرِهِ النُّفُوسُ ، وَيُرْخَى بِه الْعَيْشُ ، وَتُكْتَسَبُ بِهِ الْمَوَدَّاتُ ، ويُرْبَحُ بِهِ الْمَدْحُ والْوَفاءُ ... الْخَلْقُ عِيَالُ الله ، فَأَحَبُّهُمْ الله أَنْفَعَهُم لِعِيَالِهِ .. أَوْلى النَّاس بالعفو أَقدَرُهُمْ عَلَى العُقُوبَةِ .. النِّساءُ حَبائِلُ الشَّيْطان.. عِنْدَ الشدَائِد تُعْرَفُ الإِخْوانُ .. تهُونُ البَلاَيَا بالصَّبْر .. الْخَطَايا تُظْلِمُ الْقَلْبَ .. القِرى إِكْرَامُ الضَّيْفِ .. الدَّاعِي إلى الْخَيرِ كَفَاعِلِه .. الظُّلْمُ ظلُماتٌ يَوْمَ الْقِيَامَة .

أسئلة

Questions

في كم موضع تكون الضمة علامة للرفع ؟

In how many situations is the *ḍammah* a sign of *al-rafʿ*?

ما المراد بالاسم المفرد هنا ؟ مَثِّل للاسم المفرد بأربعة أمثلة بحيث يكون الأول مذكراً والضمة ظاهرة على آخره ، والثاني مذكراً والضمة مقدرة ، والثالث مؤنثاً والضمة ظاهرة ، والرابع مؤنثاً والضمة مقدرة .

What is meant here by a singular noun? Provide four examples of the singular noun wherein the first of them is in the masculine gender and the *ḍammah* is explicit at its end, the second of them is in the masculine gender and the *ḍammah* is implicit, the third of them is in the feminine gender and the *ḍammah* is explicit, the fourth of them is in the feminine gender and the *ḍammah* is implicit.

ما هو جمع التكسير ؟ عَلَى كم نوع يكون التغير في جمع التكسير مع التمثيل لكل نوع بمثالين ؟ مثل لجمع التكسير الدال عَلَى مذكرِينَ والضمة المقدرة ، ولجمع التكسير

الدال على مؤنثات والضمة الظاهرة .

What is the broken plural? How many forms of alteration in the broken plural are there? Provide two examples for each type. Provide an example of a broken plural that is in the masculine gender and the *ḍammah* is implicit, and also a broken plural that is in the feminine gender and the *ḍammah* is explicit.

ما هو جمع المؤنث السالم ؟ هل تكون الضمة مقدرة في جمع المؤنث السالم ؟ إذا كانت الألف غير زائدة في الجمع الذي آخره ألف وتاء فمن أي نوع يكون مع التمثيل ؟ وكيف يكون إعرابه ؟

What is the sound feminine plural? Does the implicit *ḍammah* arise in relation to the sound feminine plural? If the *alif* is not an addition in the plural word that ends with the letters *alif* and *tā*, which type of plural is this considered to be (with an example)? How does it inflect?

متى يرفع الفعل المضارع بالضمة ؟ مثّل بثلاثة أمثلة مختلفة للفعل المضارع المرفوع بضمة مقدرة.

When is the *muḍāriʿ* verb made *marfūʿ* by a *ḍammah*? Provide three varying examples of the *muḍāriʿ* verb that is made *marfūʿ* with an implicit *ḍammah*.

نيابة الواو عن الضمة

The Letter *Wāw* as a Representative of the *Ḍammah*

قال : وأمَّا الْوَاوُ فتَكونُ عَلامَةً لِلرَّفْعِ في مَوْضعَيْن : في جَمْع المذكَّر السَّالم ، وفي الأَسْمَاءِ الْخَمْسَةِ ، وَهِيَ : أَبُوكَ ، وأَخوكَ ، وحَمُوكَ ، وفُوكَ ، وذو مَال .

He said: As for the letter *wāw*, it is an indicator of *rafʿ* in two cases: (i) the sound masculine plural and (ii) the five [exceptional] nouns which are: your father, your brother, your father in law, your mouth, and possessor of wealth.

أقول: تكون الواو علامة على رَفْعِ الكلمة في موضعين ، الأول : جَمْعُ المذكر السالم ، والموضع الثاني : الأسماء الخمسة .

I say: The letter *wāw* is a sign of the *marfūʿ* state of a word in two instances: In the sound masculine plural and the five nouns.[40]

أما جمع المذكر السالم ، فهو : اسمٌ دَلَّ عَلَى أكثر من اثنين ، بزيادة في آخره ، صالح للتَّجْرِيد من الزيادة ، وعَطَفِ مثله عليه ، نحو :﴿فَرِحَ المخَلَّفون﴾ ، ﴿لَّـٰكِنِ الرَّاسِخُونَ فِي الْعِلْمِ مِنْهُمْ وَالْمُؤْمِنُونَ﴾ ، ﴿وَلَوْ كَرِهَ الْمُجْرِمُونَ﴾ ، ﴿إِن يَكُن مِّنكُمْ عِشْرُونَ صَابِرُونَ﴾ ، ﴿وَآخَرُونَ اعْتَرَفُوا بِذُنُوبِهِمْ﴾ . فكل من ﴿المخلفون﴾ و﴿الراسخون﴾ و﴿المؤمنون﴾ و﴿المجرمون﴾ و﴿صابرون﴾ و﴿آخرون﴾ جمعُ مذكر سالمٌ ، دالٌ عَلَى أكثر من اثنين ، وفيه زيادة في آخره - وهي الواو والنون - وهو صالح للتجريد من هذه الزيادة .

As for the sound masculine plural, it is a noun that indicates to a number exceeding two with an addition to its end, and when this addition is removed the root word remains sound i.e. in its original form and its like (i.e. singular

40 Some add a sixth, هنوك (*hanūk*—your thing).

words) are to be conjoined[41] to it (i.e. to the masculine plural form). Examples being: **{Those who remained behind rejoiced}**,[42] **{But those firm in knowledge among them and the faithful believers}**,[43] **{Even if the criminals disliked it}**,[44] **{If there are among you twenty [who are] steadfast}**,[45] and **{And [there are] others who have acknowledged their sins}**.[46] All of the words, "those who remained behind", "those firm in knowledge", "the faithful believers", "the criminals", "the steadfast" and "the others" are sound masculine plurals. They indicate towards a number exceeding two and there is an addition at the end i.e. a *wāw* and a *nūn*, and when this addition is stripped the word remains sound.

ألا ترى أنك تقول : (مُخَلَّفٌ) ، و(رَاسِخٌ)، و(مُؤْمِنٌ)، و(مُجْرِمٌ)، و(صَابِرٌ)، و(آخَرٌ)، وكل لفظ من ألفاظ الجموع الواقعة في هذه الآيات مرفوعٌ ، وعلامة رفعه الواو نيابة عن الضمة ، وهذه النون التي بعد الواو عِوَضٌ عن التنوين في قولك : (مُخَلَّفٌ) وأخواته ، وهو الاسم المفرد.

The reader should be able to see [that the singular forms of these words are]: "The one who remained behind", "firm", "faithful believer", "criminal", "steadfast" and "other". All of the words that are present in the *āyāt* above are *marfū'*, and the sign of their state is the *wāw* serving in place of the *ḍammah*. The letter *nūn* that we see after the letter *wāw* is a compensatory mechanism for the exclusion of the *tanwīn* found in "*mukhalla<u>fun</u>*" and its sisters, and this (i.e. *mukhallafun*) is the singular form of the noun.

وأما الأسماء الخمسة فهي هذه الألفاظ المحصورة التي عَدَّها المؤلف - وهي : أبُوكَ ، وأخوكَ ، وحَمُوكَ ، وفُوكَ ، وذو مَالٍ ، وهي تُرْفَعُ بالواو نيابة عن الضمة ، تقول: (حَضَرَ

41 The meaning of this is that the original statement would be, "Zayd, Zayd and Zayd arrived" and then they are combined, so it is said, "The Zayds (Zaydūn) arrived." See *Ḥashiyat al-Ḥāmidī* (p. 36).

42 Al-Tawbah: 81

43 Al-Nisā: 162

44 Al-Anfāl: 8

45 Al-Anfāl: 65

46 Al-Tawbah: 102

أبُوكَ ، وأخُوكَ ، وَحَمُوكَ ، وفُوكَ ، وذُو مَالٍ) ، وكذا تقول : (هذا أبُوكَ) وتقول (أبُوكَ رَجُلٌ صَالِحٌ) وقال الله تعالى ﴿وَأَبُونَا شَيْخٌ كَبِيرٌ﴾، ﴿مِنْ حَيْثُ أَمَرَهُمْ أَبُوهُمْ﴾ ، ﴿وإنهُ لَذُو عِلْمٍ﴾ ، ﴿إني أنا أخُوكَ﴾ فكلُّ اسمٍ منها في هذه الأمثلة مرفوعٌ ، وعلامة رفعه الواوُ نيابةً عن الضمة ، وما بعدها من الضمير أو لفظ (مال) أو لفظ (علم) مضافٌ إليه.

As for the five nouns, they are the small number of words mentioned by the author i.e. your father, your brother, your father in law, your mouth and possessor of wealth. They become *marfūʿ* with the letter *wāw*, which is the delegate for the *ḍammah*. It is said, "Present was your father, your brother, your father in law, your mouth, and a possessor of wealth." Likewise it is said, "This is your father" and "Your father is a righteous man." It was also said by Allah ﷻ: **{And our father is an old man}**,[47] **{From where their father had ordered them}**,[48] **{And indeed, he was a possessor of knowledge}**[49] and **{Indeed, I am your brother.}**[50] All of the nouns in these examples are *marfūʿ*, and the sign of them being so is the *wāw* serving as a substitute for the *ḍammah*. That which comes after them such as pronouns, the word "[possessor of] wealth" or "[possessor of] knowledge" are *muḍāf ilayhi*.

واعلم أن هذه الأسماء الخمسة لا تُعْرَبُ هَذا الإعراب إلا بشروط ، وهذه الشروط منها ما يشترط في كلها ، ومنها ما يشترط في بعضها :

Understand that the five nouns do not inflect in this specific manner unless they meet certain conditions, some of which are related to all of the nouns and some of which are specific to certain ones.

أما الشروط التي تشترط في جميعها فأربعة شروط :

As for the conditions that correspond to all of the nouns, they are four in number:

---

47 Al-Qaṣaṣ: 23
48 Yūsuf: 68
49 Yūsuf: 68
50 Yūsuf: 69

الأول : أن تكون مُفْرَدَةً ، والثاني : أن تكون مُكبَرةً ، والثالث أن تكون مضافة ، والرابع : أن تكون إضافتها لغير ياء المتكلم .

Firstly, that it is singular. Secondly, that it is in the augmentative form. Thirdly, that it is the *muḍāf* (possessed). Fourthly, that it is possessed by anything in the possessive compound besides the letter *yā* of the first person singular.

فخرج بـ(اشتراط الأفراد) ما لو كانت مُثَنَّاةً أو مجموعة جمع مذكر أو جمع تكسير؛ فإنها لو كانت مجموعة جمع تكسير أُعربت بالحركات الظاهرة ، تقول : (الآباءُ يُرَبُّونَ أَبْنَاءَهُمْ) وتقول : (إخْوانُكَ يَدُكَ التي تبْطِشُ بِهَا) ، وقال الله تعالى :﴿آباؤكم وأبْنَاؤُكم﴾، ﴿إنما الْمُؤمِنُونَ إِخْوَةٌ﴾ ، ﴿فأصْبَحْتُمْ بِنِعْمَتِهِ إخْوَاناً﴾ .

The condition of singularity excludes these words when they are in the dual form, the plural male form, or the broken plural. If they are in the broken plural form, they inflect with a visible diacritic. Examples are: "Fathers cultivate their sons", "Your brothers are your hands with which you attack", and the statements of Allah: **{[If] your fathers, and your sons}**,[51] **{Verily the faithful believers are brothers}**[52] and **{And you became—through his favour—brothers.}**[53]

ولو كانت مُثَنَّاةَ أُعربت إعرابَ المثنى؛ بالألف رفعاً وبالياء نصباً وجرًّا ، وسيأتي بيانه قريباً ، تقول : (أَبَوَاكَ رَبَّيَاكَ) وتقول : (تَأَدَّبْ في حَضْرَةِ أَبَوَيكَ) وقال الله تعالى : ﴿وَرَفَعَ أَبَوَيْهِ عَلَى العَرْشِ﴾ ، ﴿فَأَصْلِحُوا بَيْنَ أَخَوَيْكُمْ﴾ .

If they are in the dual form, they inflect in the manner of the dual—*marfū'* with the letter *alif*, *manṣūb* and *majrūr* with the letter *yā*. We will cover this shortly. Examples are: "Your parents cultivated you", "Show good manners in the presence of your parents", and the statements of Allah: **{And he raised his**

51 Al-Tawbah: 24
52 Al-Ḥujurāt: 10
53 Ālī 'Imrān: 103

parents upon the throne}[54] and **{So make peace between your two brothers.}**[55]

ولو كانت مجموعة جمع مذكر سالماً رُفعت بالواو على ما تقدم ، ونصبت وجرت بالياءِ ، وتقول : (هؤلاَء أبُونَ وأخُونَ) ، وتقول : (رَأيتُ أَبِينَ وَأَخِينَ) ولم يجمع بالواو والنون غيرُ لفظ الأب والأخ ، وكان القياسُ يقتضي ألا يُجمع شيءٌ منها هذا الجمعَ .

If they are in the sound masculine plural form, they become *marfūʿ* with the letter *wāw*—as we have mentioned—, and they become *manṣūb* and *majrūr* with the letter *yā*. Examples are: "These are fathers and brothers" and "I saw fathers and brothers." None from them (i.e. from the five exceptional nouns) becomes plural with the letters *wāw* and *nūn* except for the words "father" and "brother," and deduction from this dictates that none of the others become plural through this pattern.

وخرج بـ(اشتراط : أن تكون مكبرة) ما لو كانت مُصَغَّرَةً ، فإنها حينئذ تعرب بالحركات الظاهرة ، تقول : (هذا أُبَيٌّ وأُخَيٌّ) ؛ وتقول : (رأيت أبيا وأخيا)، وتقول : (مَرَرْتُ بِأُبَيٍّ وأُخَيٍّ) .

The condition that it must be in the augmentative form excludes these words when they are in the diminutive form. In the instance of them being in the diminutive form they inflect with visible diacritics. Examples are: "This is a small father and a small brother, "I saw a small father and a small brother" and "I passed by a small father and a small brother."

وخرج بـ(اشتراط أن تكون مُضَافة) ما لو كانت منقطعة عن الإضافة ؛ فإنها حينئذٍ تُعرب بالحركات الظاهرة أيضاً ، تقول : (هذا أبٌ) وتقول : (رأيْتُ أباً) وتقول : (مَرَرْتُ بأب) وكذلك الباقي ، وقال الله تعالى : ﴿وَلَهُۥٓ أَخٌ أَوْ أُخْتٌ﴾ ، ﴿إِن يَسْرِقْ فَقَدْ سَرَقَ أَخٌ لَّهُۥ مِن قَبْلُ﴾ ، ﴿قَالَ ٱئْتُونِى بِأَخٍ لَّكُم مِّنْ أَبِيكُمْ﴾ ، ﴿إِنَّ لَهُۥٓ أَبًا شَيْخًا كَبِيرًا﴾ .

The condition that it must be a *muḍāf* (possessed) excludes these words that

54 Yūsuf: 100
55 Al-Ḥujurāt: 10

are separate from the possessive compound. In this case they would inflect with visible diacritics as well. Examples are: "This is a father", "I saw a father", "I passed by a father" and likewise is the case for the others [from the five]. Further to these examples, Allah ﷻ states: **{And has a brother and a sister}**,[56] **{If he steals—a brother of his has stolen before}**,[57] **{He said, "Bring me a brother of yours from your father}**,[58] and **{Indeed he has a father who is an old man.}**[59]

وخرج بـ(اشتراط أن تكون إضافتها لغير ياءِ المتكلم) ما لو أضيفت إلى هذه الياء ؛ فإنها حينئذٍ تعرب بحركات مقدرة على ما قبل ياء المتكلم منع من ظهورها اشتغالُ المحلِّ بحركة المناسبة؛ تقول : (حَضَرَ أبِي وأخِي) ، وتقول : (احْتَرَمْتُ أبِي و أخِي الأكْبَرَ) وتقول : (أنَا لا أتكلَّمُ في حَضْرَةِ أبِي وأخِي الأكْبَرِ) وقال الله تعالى : ﴿إِنَّ هٰذَا أَخِي﴾ ، ﴿أَنَا يُوسُفُ وَهَٰذَا أَخِي﴾ ، ﴿فَأَلْقُوهُ عَلَىٰ وَجْهِ أَبِي﴾ .

The condition that it is possessed by anything in the possessive compound besides the letter *yā* of the first person singular excludes that which is so. In this case they inflect with an implicit diacritic upon the letter that comes before the *yā* of the first person singular, prevented from being displayed due to the position being occupied with the appropriate diacritic. Examples of this are: "My father and my brother were present", "I honoured my father and my elder brother", and "I do not speak in the presence of my father and elder brother." Examples from the statements of Allah ﷻ are: **{Verily, this brother of mine}**,[60] **{I am Yūsuf and this is my brother}**,[61] and **{And cast it over the face of my father.}**[62]

وأمّا الشروط التي تختص ببعضها دون بعض؛ فمنها أن كلمة (فُوكَ) لا تُعْرَبُ هذا

56 Al-Nisā: 12

57 Yūsuf: 77

58 Yūsuf: 59

59 Yūsuf: 78

60 Ṣād: 23

61 Yūsuf: 90

62 Yūsuf: 93

الإعرابَ إلاّ بشرط أن تخلو من الميم ، فلو اتصلت الميم أُعربت بالحركات الظاهرة ، تقول : (هذَا فَمٌ حَسَنٌ) ، وتقول : (رأَيْتُ فَماً حَسَناً) ، وتقول : (نَظَرْتُ إلَى فَمٍ حَسَنٍ) وهذا شرط زائد في هذه الكلمة بخصوصها على الشروط الأربعة التي سبق ذكرها .

As for the conditions that are specific to certain words from the five nouns, from them is in regard to the word "mouth". It does not take the declension [of the five nouns] except if it is free from the letter *mīm* (in Arabic the word mouth is normally "*fam*"). If the *mīm* is found in the word then it takes the declension with visible diacritics. Examples are: "This is a sound mouth", "I saw a sound mouth" and "I looked at a sound mouth". This is an additional condition to the four we have mentioned previously and it is specific to this word.

ومنها أن كلمة (ذو) لا تعربُ هذا الإعرَابَ إلا بِشرطين : الأول : أن تكون بمعنى صاحب ، والثاني : أن يكون الذي تضاف إليه اسمَ جنس ظاهراً غَيْرَ وَصْفٍ ؛ فإن لم تكن بمعنى (صاحب) بأن كانت موصولة فهي مَبْنيَّةٌ .

Also from them is that the word "possessor of" does not take the declension of the five nouns unless it meets two conditions: (i) that it has the meaning of "possessor" and (ii) that the word connected to it in the possessive compound is a clear noun[63] and not an adjective. If it does not have the meaning of "possessor", such as if it serves as a demonstrative pronoun, then it is un-inflectable.

ومثالُها غيرَ مَوْصُولة قولُ أبي الطيب المتنبي :

63 Regarding the term "clear noun" (اسمَ جنس ظاهراً), al-Ḥamādī said in *Ḥāshiyat al-Kafāwī* (p. 36), "It is that which is correct to be given the attribute of less and more such as wealth." Yasin said in his *Ḥāshiyat 'alā al-Fākihī* (p. 36), "The meaning of their statement [that it is compounded to an *ism jins*] is that which is opposite to an adjective, as stated in *Sharḥ al-Tashīl*. [After defining it, its author said,] 'It has been falsely assumed by some lacking intelligence that the meaning of the *ism jins* here refers to the indefinite. This contradicts certain examples from the Qur'ān and ḥadīth."

An example of it not coming as a demonstrative pronoun is the couplet of Abī al-Ṭayyib al-Mutanabbī:

ذُو الْعَقْلِ يَشْقَى فِي النَّعِيمِ بِعَقْلِهِ   وَأَخُو الْجَهَالَةِ فِي الشَّقَاوَةِ يَنْعَمُ

The intelligent is wretched in bliss due to his intellect (i.e. due to foreseeing the consequences),

But the brother of ignorance finds bliss in wretchedness (i.e. due to not foreseeing the consequences).

وهذان الشرطان زائدانِ في هذه الكلمة بخصوصها على الشروط الأربعة التي سبق ذكرها .

These are two additional conditions to the four we have mentioned previously and they are specific to this word (i.e. "*dhu*").

تمرين

Exercises

١- بيّن المرفوعِ بالضمة الظاهرة ، أو المُقدّرة ، والمرفوعَ بالواو ، مع بيان نوع كل واحد منها ، من بين الكلمات الواردة في الجمل الآتية :

One. Make clear in the following sentences that which is *marfuʿ* with an explicit *ḍammah*, an implicit *ḍammah*, and with the letter *wāw*—whilst also defining the type of each one.

قال الله تعالى : ﴿قَدْ أَفْلَحَ الْمُؤْمِنُونَ ، الَّذِينَ هُمْ فِي صَلاَتِهِمْ خَاشِعُونَ ، وَالَّذِينَ هُمْ عَنِ اللَّغْوِ مُعْرِضُونَ ، وَالَّذِينَ هُمْ لِلزَّكَاةِ فَاعِلُونَ ، وَالَّذِينَ هُمْ لِفُرُجِهِمْ حَافِظُونَ﴾ وقال الله تعالى : ﴿وَرَأَى الْمُجْرِمُونَ النَّارَ فَظَنُّوا أَنَّهُمْ مُوَاقِعُوهَا وَلَمْ يَجِدُوا عَنْهَا مَصْرِفاً﴾ .

الْفِتْنَةُ تُلْقِحُهَا النَّجْوَى وتُنتِجُهَا الشَّكْوَى .. إِخْوَانُكَ هُمْ أَعْوَانُكَ إِذَا اشْتَدَّ بِكَ الْكَرْبُ ، وَأُسَاتُكَ إِذَا عَضَّكَ الزَّمَانُ .. النَّائِبَاتُ مِحَكُّ الأَصْدِقَاءِ .. أَبُوكَ يَتَمَنَّى لَكَ الْخَيْرَ وَيَرْجُو

لَكَ الْفَلاَحَ .. أَخُوكَ الَّذِي إذا تَشْكُو إِلَيْهِ يُشْكِيكَ.. وَإِذَا تَدْعُوهُ عِنْدَ الكَرْبِ يُجِيبُكَ .

٢ـ ضع في الأماكن الخالية من العبارات الآتية اسماً من الأسماء الخمسة مرفوعاً بالواو :

Two. In the below sentences, enter a noun from the five nouns that is *marfū'* with the letter *wāw*.

(أ) إِذَا دَعَاكَ ... فَأَجِبْهُ .　　(ج) ... كَانَ صديقا لي .

(ب) لَقَدْ كانَ مَعِي ... بالأَمْسِ .　　(د) هذا الكتابُ أَرْسَلَهُ لَكَ ...

٣ـ ضع في المكان الخالي من الجمل الآتية جمع تكسيرٍ مرفوعاً بضمة ظاهرة في بعضها ، ومرفوعاً بضمة مقدرة في بعضها الآخر :

Three. In the below sentences, enter a broken plural that is *marfū'* with an explicit *ḍammah* in some of them, and *marfū'* with an implicit *ḍammah* in the others.

(أ) ... أَعْوَانُكَ عِنْدَ الشدَّةِ .　　(ج) كانَ معنا أمْسِ... كِرَامٌ.

(ب) حضرَ... فَأَكْرَمْتُهُمْ .　　(د) ... تفْضَحُ الكَذُوبَ .

أسئلة

Questions

في كم موضع تكون الواو علامة للرفع ؟

In how many situations is the *wāw* an indication of a word being *marfū'*?

ما هو جَمع المذكر السالم ؟

What is a sound masculine plural?

مثل لجمع المذكر السالم في حال الرفع بثلاثة أمثلة .

Provide three examples of the sound masculine plural in the *marfūʿ* state.

اذكر الأسماءُ الخمسة .

What are the five nouns?

ما الذي يشترط في رفع الأسماء الخمسة بالواو نيابة عن الضمة ؟

What are the conditions required for the five nouns to become *marfūʿ* with the letter *wāw* as a representative for the *ḍammah*?

لو كانت الأسماءُ الخمسة مجموعة جمع تكسير فبماذا تعربها ؟

If the five nouns are in the broken plural, what do they inflect with?

لو كانت الأسماء الخمسة مثناة فبماذا تعربها ؟

If the five nouns are in the dual form, what do they inflect with?

مثّل بمثالين لاسمين من الأسماء الخمسة مثنيين ، وبمثالين آخرين لاسمين منها مجموعين .

Provide two examples of words from the five nouns in the dual form, and two examples from them in the plural form.

لو كانت الأسماءُ الخمسة مصغرة فبماذا تعربها ؟

If the five nouns are in the diminutive form, what do they inflect with?

لو كانت مضافة إلى ياء المتكلم فبماذا تعربها ؟

If they are connected in a possessive compound to the letter *yā* of the singular first person, with what do they inflect with?

ما الذي يشترط في (ذو) خاصة ؟

What are the conditions specific to the word "possessor of"?

ما الذي يشترط في (فوك) خاصة ؟

What is the condition specific to the word "your mouth"?

نيابة الألف عن الضمة

The Letter *Alif* as a Representative of the *Ḍammah*

قال : وأمَّا الألفُ فتكُونُ عَلامَةً لِلرَّفْعِ فِي تَثْنِيَةِ الأسْمَاءِ خَاصَّةً .

He said: As for the *alif*, it is an indicator of *rafʿ* specifically in the dual form.

وأقول : تكون الألف علامة على رفع الكلمة في موضع واحد ، وهو الاسم المثنى ، نحو (حَضَرَ الصّدِيقَانِ) فالصديقان : مثنى ، وهو مرفوع لأنه فاعل ، وعلامة رفعه الألف نيابة عن الضمة ، والنون عوضٌ عن التنوين في قولك : (صَدِيقٌ) ، وهو الاسم المفرد .

I say: The letter *alif* is a sign of a word being *marfūʿ* in only one situation; which is when the noun is in the dual form. An example is, "The two friends were present." The word "two friends" here is in the dual form, it is *marfūʿ* due to it being the subject, and the sign of it being *marfūʿ* is the letter *alif* serving in place of the *ḍammah*. The letter *nūn* that we see [after the letter *alif*] is a compensatory mechanism for the exclusion of the *tanwīn* found in "*ṣadīqun*", the singular noun.

والمثنى هو : كل اسم دَلَّ على اثنين أو اثنتين ، بزيادة في آخره ، أغْنَتْ هذه الزيادة عن العاطف والمعطوف ، نحو (أَقْبَلَ العُمَرانِ ، والهِنْدَانِ) فالعُمران : لفظ دلَّ على اثْنَيْنِ اسْمُ كلِّ واحدٍ منهما (عُمَرُ) ، بسبب وجود زيادة في آخره ، وهذه الزيادة هي الألف والنون ، وهي تُغْنِي عن الإتيان بواو العطف وتكرير الاسم بحيث تقول : (حَضَرَ عُمَرُ وَعُمَرُ) وكذلك (الهندان)؛ فهو لفظ دَالٌّ على اثنتين كلٌّ واحدة منهما اسمها (هِنْدٌ) ، وسَبَبُ دلالته عَلى ذلك زيادة الألف والنون في المثال ، ووجود الألف والنون يغنيك عن الإتيان بواو العطف وتكرير الاسم بحيث تقول : (حَضَرَتْ هِنْدٌ وَهِنْدٌ).

The dual form is that which indicates to two masculine things, or two feminine things, with an addition to the end of the word. This addition removes the need of mentioning a conjoined and linked word, an example being "The two ʿUmars and two Hinds came." Here the word "*ʿUmarān*" is a word that indicates towards two males, each of them named ʿUmar, and the tool with which this is indicated is the addition of the letters *alif* and *nūn* to its end. This is a compensatory mechanism for the letter *wāw* of conjunction that would have appeared and the repetition of the names i.e. "ʿUmar and ʿUmar were present." Likewise, the word "Hindān" is a word that indicates towards two females, each of them named Hind, and the tool with which this is indicated is the addition of the letters *alif* and *nūn* to its end. This is a compensatory mechanism for the letter *wāw* of conjunction that would have appeared and the repetition of the two names i.e. "Hind and Hind were present."

تمرينات

Exercises

١ـ رُدَّ كلَّ جمع من الجموع الآتية إلى مفرَدِهِ ، ثم ثَنِّ المفردات ، ثم ضع كل مثنى في كلام مفيد بحيث يكون مرفوعاً ، وها هي ذي الجموعُ :

One. Return all of the following plurals into the singular form. Then convert the singular words into the dual form and utilise them in beneficial sentences where they are *marfūʿ*. These are the plural words:

جِمالٌ ، أفْيَالٌ ، سُيُوفٌ ، صَهَارِيجُ ، دُوِيٌّ ، نُجُومٌ ، حَدَائِقُ ، بَسَاتِينُ ، قَرَاطِيسُ ، مَحَابِرُ ، أحْذِيَةٌ ، قُمُصٌ ، أطِبَّاءُ ، طُرُقٌ ، شُرَفَاءُ ، مَقَاعِدُ، عُلَمَاءُ ، جُدْرَانٌ ، شَبَابِيك ، أبْوَابٌ ، نَوَافِذُ ، آنِسَاتٌ ، رُكَّعٌ ، أُمُورٌ ، بِلادٌ ، أقْطَارٌ ، تفاحَات .

٢ـ ضع كل واحد من المثنيات الآتية في كلام مفيد :

Two. Put each of the below dual forms into beneficial speech:

الْعَالِمَانِ ، الوَالِيَانِ ، الأَخوَانِ ، المجتَهدانِ ، الهَادِيَانِ ، الصَّدِيقَانِ ، الحَديقَتَانِ ، الفَتَاتَّانِ ، الكِتَابَانِ ، الشريفَانِ ، القُطْرَانِ ، الجِدَارَانِ ، الطِبيبَانِ ، الأمْرَانِ ، الفَارِسَانِ ، المَقْعَدَانِ ، الْعَذْرَاوَانِ ، السَّيْفَانِ ، المَاجِدَانِ ، الخِطَابَانِ ، الأبَوَانِ ، البَلَدَانِ ، البُسْتَانَانِ ، الطَّرِيقَانِ ، راكِعَانِ ، دَوَاتَانِ ، بَابَانِ ، تُفَّاحَتَانِ ، نَجْمَانِ .

٣- ضع في الأماكن الخالية من العبارات الآتية ألفاظاً مثناة :

Three. Place dual form words within the empty spaces found in the statements below:

(أ) سافر... إلى مصر ليشاهدا آثارها .

(ب) حَضَرَ أخي ومعه.. فأكرمتهم .

(ج) وُلِدَ لخالد ... فسمى أحدهما (محمداً) وسمى الآخر (عليًّا).

أسئلة

Questions

في كم موضع تكون الألف علامة على رفع الكلمة ؟

In how many situations is the letter *alif* a sign of a word being *marfū*?

ما هو المثنى ؟

Define the dual form.

مثّل للمثنى بمثالين : أحدهما مذكر ، والآخر مؤنث .

Provide two examples of the dual form, the first of them in the male gender and the second in the feminine.

نيابة النون عن الضمة

The Letter *Nūn* as a Representative of the *Ḍammah*

قال : وأمَّا النُونُ فَتكُونُ عَلاَمَةَ للرَّفع في الفِعْلِ المُضَارع ، إذا اتصَلَ بِهِ ضمِير تَثْنِيةٍ ، أوْ ضَمِيرُ جَمْعٍ ، أوْ ضَمِيرُ المُؤنَّثةِ الْمُخَاطَبَةِ .

He said: As for the letter *nūn*, it is an indicator of *rafʿ* in the *muḍāriʿ* verb if it is connected to an attached pronoun of duality, an attached pronoun of plurality, or an attached pronoun used to address the female gender.

وأقول : تكون النون علامة على أن الكلمة التي هي فيها مرفوعة في موضع واحد ، وهو الفعل المضارع المسند إلى ألف الاثنين أو الاثنتين ، أو المسند إلى واو جماعة الذكور ، أو المسند إلى ياء المؤنثة المخاطبة.

I say: The letter *nūn* is a sign of a word being *marfūʿ* when it falls [at the end of] it in one instance, and that is the *muḍāriʿ* verb connected to the letter *alif* of male or female duality, or connected to the letter *wāw* of male plurality, or connected to the letter *yā* of the feminine second person.

أما المسند إلى ألِفِ الاثنين فنحو (الصَّدِيقَانِ يُسَافِرَانِ غداً) ، ونحو (أَنْتُمَا تُسَافِرَانِ غَداً) فقولنا : (يسافران) وكذا (تسافران) فعل مضارع مرفوع لتجرده من الناصب والجازم ، وعلامة رفعه ثُبُوتُ النون ، وألف الاثنين فاعل ، مبني على السكون في محل رفع .

As for when it is connected to the letter *alif* of duality, examples are, "The two friends travel tomorrow" and "You two travel tomorrow". The words "two [friends] travel" and "you two travel" are both *marfūʿ muḍāriʿ* verbs due to the absence of a governor of the *naṣb* and *jazm* states. The sign of them being *marfūʿ* is the presence of the letter *nūn*, and the letter *alif* is the dual form subject, non-inflectable upon a *sukūn* in the state of *rafʿ*.

وقد رأيت أن الفعل المضارع المسنَدَ إلى ألف الاثنين قد يكون مبدوءًا بالياء للدلالة على الْغَيْبَةَ كما في المثال الأوَّل ، وقد يكون مبدوءًا بالتاء للدلالة على الخطاب كما في المثال الثاني .

We have seen that the *muḍārīʿ* verb connected to the letter *alif* of duality will sometimes begin with the letter *yā* indicating the third person—as in the first example—and sometimes begin with the letter *tā* indicating the second person—as in the second example.

وأما المسند إلى ألف الاثْنَتَين فنحو (الهِندَانِ تُسَافِرانِ غَداً) ، ونحو : (أَنْتُمَا يا هِنْدَانِ تُسَافِرَانِ غَداً) فـ(تسافران) في المثالين : فعل مضارع مرفوع بثبوت النون ، والألف فاعل ، مبني على السكون في محل رفع .

As for when it is connected to the letter *alif* of feminine duality, examples are, "The two Hinds travel tomorrow" and "You two—O Hinds—travel tomorrow." The word "travel" in the two examples is a *muḍārīʿ* verb which is *marfūʿ* due to the presence of the letter *nūn*, and the letter *alif* is the dual subject, non-inflectable upon a *sukūn* in the *marfūʿ* state.

ومنه تعلم أن الفعل المضارع المسند إلى ألف الاثنتين لا يكون مبدوءًا إلا بالتاء للدلالة على تأنيث الفاعل ، سواءٌ أكان غائباً كالمثال الأوَّل ، أم كان حاضراً مُخَاطَباً كالمثال الثاني .

From this it can be seen that the *muḍārīʿ* verb connected to the *alif* of feminine duality will not begin with anything besides the letter *tā* so as to indicate towards the feminine subject. This is the case regardless if it is in the third person—as in the first example—or in the second person—as in the second example.

وأما المسند إلى واو الجماعة فنحو (الرِّجَالُ الْمُخْلِصُونَ هُمْ الَّذِينَ يَقُومُونَ بواجبهم) ، ونحو (أَنْتُمْ يَا قَوْمُ تَقُومُونَ بِواجبكم) فـ(يقومون) ـ ومثله (تقومون) ـ فعل مضارع مرفوع

، وعلامة رفعه ثبوت النون ، وواو الجماعة فاعل ، مبني على السكون في محل رَفْعٍ .

As for when it is connected to the letter *wāw* of plurality, examples are, "The sincere men are those whom stand by their duties", and "You, O people, stand by your duties." The word "[whom] stand by" and also "you stand" are *muḍārī*ʿ verbs in the state of *raf*ʿ. The sign of them being *marfū*ʿ is the presence of the letter *nūn* and the letter *wāw* is the plural subject, non-inflectable upon a *sukūn* in the *marfū*ʿ state.

ومنه تعلم أن الفعل المضارع المسنَدَ إلى هذه الواو قد يكون مَبْدُوءًا بالياء للدلالة على الغيبة ، كما في المثال الأوّل ، وقد يكون مَبْدُوءًا بالتاء للدلالة على الخطاب ، كما في المثال الثاني .

From this it can be seen that the *muḍārī*ʿ verb connected to this letter *wāw* will sometimes commence with the letter *yā* to indicate the third person—as in the first example—and sometimes commence with the letter *tā* to indicate the second person—as in the second example.

وأما المسند إلى ياء المؤنثة المخاطبة فنحو (أنْتِ يا هِنْدُ تَعْرِفِينَ وَاجِبَكِ) فـ(تعرفين) : فعل مضارع مرفوع ، وعلامة رفعه ثبوت النون ، وياءُ المؤنثة المخاطبة فاعل ، مبني على السكون في محل رفع .

As for when it is connected to the letter *yā* of the feminine second person, an example is, "You, O Hind are aware of that which is incumbent upon you." The word "are aware" is a *muḍārī*ʿ verb in the state of *raf*ʿ. The sign of it being *marfū*ʿ is the presence of the letter *nūn* and the letter *yā* is the feminine second person subject, non-inflectable upon a *sukūn* in the state of *raf*ʿ.

ولا يكون الفعلُ المسند إلى هذه الياء إلاَّ مبدوءًا بالتاء ، وهي دَالة على تأنيثِ الفاعل .

A verb is not connected to this letter *yā* except that it begins with the letter *tā*, and it indicates to a feminine subject.

فتَلَخَّصَ لك أن المسند إلى الألف يكون مبدوءًا بالتاء أو بالياء ، والمسند إلى واو كذلك

يكون مبدوءًا بالتاء أو الياء ، والمسند إلى الياء لا يكون مبدوءًا إلا بالتاء .

This can be summarised for the reader by stating that [the *muḍārīʿ* verb] connected to the letter *alif* can commence with either the letter *tā* or *yā*. [The *muḍārīʿ* verb] connected to the letter *wāw* likewise can commence with either the letter *tā* or *yā*. [The *muḍārīʿ* verb] connected to the letter *yā* does not commence except with the letter *tā*.

ومثالها : يَقُومَانِ ، وَتَقُومَان ، وَيَقُومُون ، وَتَقُومون ، وتقومِينَ ، وتُسَمَّى هذه الأمثلة (الأَفْعَالِ الْخَمْسَةَ) .

Examples of it are: "They both stand", "they (fem.) both stand", "they stand", "you stand" and "you (fem.) stand." These are called the five verbs.

تمرينات

Exercises

١- ضع في كلّ مكان من الأمكنة الخالية فعلاً من الأفعال الخمسة مناسباً ، ثم بيّن على أي شيءٍ يدل حرف المضارعة الذي بدأته به :

One: Place in the empty spaces below the appropriate verb from the five verbs. Then clarify what the beginning letter of the *muḍārīʿ* indicates.

(أ) الأولاد ... في النَّهْرِ .

(ب) الآباءُ ... على أبناءهم .

(ج) أنتما أيها الغُلاَمَان ... ببطء .

(د) هؤلاَءِ الرجال ... في الحقل .

(ه) أَنْتِ يا زَيْنَبُ ... وَاجِبَكِ.

(و) الفَتَاتَان ... الْجُنْدِيّ .

(ز) أَنْتُمْ أيها الرجال ... أوطانكم .

(ح) أنْتِ يا سُعَادُ ... بالكُرَةِ .

٢- استعمل كل فعل من الأفعال الآتية في جملة مفيدة :

Two: Use each of the following verbs in a beneficial sentence:

تَلْعَبَانِ ، تَؤدِّينَ ، تَزْرَعُونَ ، تَحْصُدَانِ ، تُحَدِّثانِ ، تَسِيرُونَ ، يَسْبَحُون ، تَخْدُمُونَ ، تُنْشِئَانِ ، تَرْضَيْنَ .

❁❁❁

٣- ضع مع كل كلمة من الكلمات الآتية فعلاً من الأفعال الخمسةُ مناسباً ، واجعل مع الجميع كلاما مفيدا :

Three. Place with each of the below words an appropriate verb from the five verbs, and utilise them to provide beneficial sentences:

الطَّالِبانِ ، الغِلْمَانُ ، المُسْلِمون ، الرِّجَال الذين يؤدُّون واجبَهم ، أنتِ أيتها الفتاة ، انتم يا قوم ، هؤلاءِ التلاميذ ، إذا خالفتِ أوامر الله .

❁❁❁

٤- بيِّن المرفوع بالضمة، والمرفوع بالألف ، والمرفوع بالواو ، والمرفوع بثبوت النون ، مع بيان نوع كل واحد منها ، من بين الكلمات الواردة في العبارات الآتية :

Four. Identify from the below words that which is made *marfūʿ* by the *ḍammah*, *marfūʿ* by the letter *alif*, *marfūʿ* by the letter *wāw* and *marfūʿ* by the presence of the letter *nūn*. Also detail the type that each of the words in the paragraph below fall into:

كُتَّابُ الْمُلُوكِ عَيْبَتُهمْ المَصُونَةُ عِنْدَهُمْ ، وَآذَانُهمُ الْوَاعِيَةُ ، وَأَلْسِنَتُهمُ الشَّاهِدَةُ ، الشَّجَاعَةُ غَرِيزَةٌ يَضَعُهَا الله ، لِمَنْ يَشَاءُ مِنْ عِبَادِهِ ، الشُّكْرُ شُكْرَانِ : بِإِظْهَارِ النِّعْمَةِ ، وَبِالتَّحَدُّثِ بِاللِّسَانِ ، وَأَوَّلُهُمَا أَبْلَغُ مِنْ ثَانيِهما ، المُتَّقُونَ هُمُ الَّذينَ يُؤْمِنُونَ بِالله وَالْيَومِ الآخِرِ .

أسئلة

Questions

في كم موضع تكون النون علامة على رفع الكلمة ؟

In how many situations is the letter *nūn* a sign of a word being *marfūʿ*?

بماذا يبدأُ الفعل المضارِع المسند إلى ألف الاثنين ؟ وعلى أي شيءٍ تدل الحروف المبدوء بها ؟

With what does the *muḍāriʿ* verb connected to the letter *alif* of duality begin with? And what do the letters that appear at the beginning of it indicate?

بماذا يُبْدَأُ الفعل المضارع المسند للواو أو الياء ؟

With what does the *muḍāriʿ* verb connected to the letter *wāw* or *yā* begin with?

مَثِّل بمثالين لكل من الفعل المضارع المسند إلى الألف وإلى الواو وإلى الياء .

Provide two examples of the *muḍāriʿ* verb connected to the letter *alif*, the letter *wāw* and the letter *yā*.

ما هي الأفعال الخمسة ؟

What are the five verbs?

علامات النصب

The Signs of *al-Naṣb*

قال : ولِلنَّصبِ خَمْسُ عَلاَمَاتٍ الْفَتْحَةُ ، وَالأَلِفُ ، وَالكَسْرَةُ ، وَاليَاءُ ، وَحَذْفُ النُّونِ .

He said: And for the state of *al-naṣb* there are five signs: the *fatḥah*, the letter *alif*, the *kasrah*, the letter *yā* and the removal of the letter *nūn*.

وأقول : يمكنك أن تحكم على الكلمة بأنها منصوبةٌ إذا وجدَتَ في آخرها علامة من خمس علاماتٍ : واحدة منها أصلية ، وهي الفتحة ، وأربع فروع عنها ، وهي : الألف ، والكسرة ، والياء ، وحَذْفُ النون .

I say: It will be possible for you to rule a word to be *manṣūb* if you find at its end one of five signs: the *fatḥah*—which is the root sign—and four which are subsidiary signs: the letter *alif*, the *kasrah*, the letter *yā*, and the removal of the letter *nūn*.

الفتحة ومواضعها

The *Fatḥah* and Its Utilisation

قال : فَأَمَّا الفَتْحَةُ فَتَكُونُ عَلامَةً لِلنَّصْبِ في ثَلاثَةِ مَوَاضِعَ : فِي الِاسْمِ الْمُفْرَدِ ، وَجَمْعِ التَّكْسِيرِ ، وَالْفِعْلِ الْمُضَارِعِ إِذَا دَخَلَ عَلَيْهِ نَاصِبٌ ، وَلَمْ يَتَّصِلُ بِآخِرِهِ شَيْءٌ .

He said: As for the *fatḥah*, then it is an indicator of the state of *naṣb* in three instances: (i) In the singular noun, (ii) in the broken plural, (iii) in the *muḍāriʿ* verb if a *nāsib* (i.e. a governor that dictates a word to be *manṣūb*) precedes it and there is nothing attached to its end.

وأقول تكون الفتحة علامة على أن الكلمة منصوبة في ثلاثة مواضع ، الموضع الأوَّل : الاسم المفرد ، والموضع الثاني : جمع التكسير ، والموضع الثالث : الفعل المضارع الذي سَبَقَهُ ناصب ، ولم يتصل بآخره ألفُ اثنين ، ولا واو جماعة ، ولا ياء مخاطبة ، ولا نون توكيد ، ولا نون نسوة .

I say: The *fatḥah* is a sign of a word being *manṣūb* in three situations: (i) the singular noun, (ii) the broken plural, (iii) the *muḍāriʿ* verb that is preceded by a *nāṣib* and is not connected at the end to the letter *alif* of duality, the letter *wāw* of plurality, the letter *yā* of the feminine second person, the letter *nūn* of emphasis and the letter *nūn* of feminine plurality.

أما الاسم المفرد فقد سبق تعريفه .

As for the singular noun, we have preceded in defining it.

والفتحة تكون ظاهرة على آخره في نحو (لقيتُ عَلِيّاً) ونحو (قَابَلْتُ هِنْداً) فَ(عَلِيّاً)

، و(هنداً) : اسمان مفردان ، وهما منصوبان لأنهما مفعولان ، وعلامة نصبهما الفتحة الظاهرة ، والأول مذكر والثاني مؤنث .

The *fatḥah* is explicit at the end of the words such as: "I met 'Alī" and "I met Hind". In these two examples, 'Ali and Hind are both singular nouns, and they are both *manṣūb* as they are objects. The sign of them being *manṣūb* is the explicit *fatḥah*, the first of them is masculine and the second is feminine.

وقد تكونُ الفتحةُ مُقَدَّرَةً نحو :(لَقِيتُ الْفَتى) ونحو (حَدَّثْتُ لَيْلَى) فـ(الفتى) وَ(لَيْلَى) : اسمان مفردان منصوبان ؛ لكون كلّ منهما وقع مفعولاً به ، وعلامة نصبهما فتحة مقدره على الألف منع ظهورها التعذر ، والأول مذكر والثاني مؤنث .

And sometimes the *fatḥah* is implicit, such as "I met the boy" and "I told Laylā." In these two examples "the boy" and "Laylā" are both *manṣūb* singular nouns, due to them being objects. The sign of them being *manṣūb* is the implicit *fatḥah* on the *alif*, prevented from being displayed due to impracticality. The first of them is masculine and the second is feminine.

وأما جمع التكسير فقد سبق تعريفه أيضاً .

As for the broken plural, we have also preceded in defining it.

والفتحة قد تكون ظاهرة على آخره ، نحو (صَاحَبْتُ الرِّجَالَ) ونحو (رَعَيْتُ الْهُنُودَ) : فـ(الرجال) و(الهنود) جَمْعَا تكسير منصوبان ، لكونهما مفعولين ، وعلامة نصبهما الفتحة الظاهرة ، والأول مذكر ، والثاني مُؤَنث .

The *fatḥah* is sometimes visible upon its end such as "I accompanied the men" and "I shepherded the *Hinds* ('camels' in this sentence)." The two words here "men" and "*Hinds*" are broken plurals in the state of *naṣb* due to them being objects. The sign of them being *manṣūb* is the explicit *fatḥah*, the first of them is masculine and the second is feminine.

وقد تكون الفتحة مقدرة ، نحو قوله تعالى :﴿وَتَرَى النَّاسَ سُكَارَى﴾ ونحو قوله تعالى

﴿وَأَنْكِحُوا الأَيَامَى﴾ فـ﴿سُكَارَى﴾ و﴿الأَيَامَى﴾ : جَمْعَا تكسير منصوبان؛ لكونهما مفعولين، وعلامة نصبهما فتحة مقدرة على الألف منع من ظهورها التعذر .

And sometimes the *fatḥah* is implicit, such as in the statement of the Most High: **{And you will see the people [appearing] intoxicated}**[64] and **{And marry the single}**[65]. In these two examples the words "intoxicated" and "the single" are broken plurals in the *manṣūb* state, due to them being objects. The sign of them being *manṣūb* is an implicit *fatḥah* upon the letter *alif*, prevented from being displayed due to impracticality.

وأما الفعل المضارع المذكور فنحو قوله تعالى ﴿لَنْ نَبْرَحَ عَلَيْهِ عَاكِفِينَ﴾ فـ﴿نبرح﴾ فعل مضارع منصوب بـ(لَنْ) ، وعلامة نصبه الفتحة الظاهرة .

As for the aforementioned *muḍāri'* verb, an example is the statement of the Most High: **{We will never cease being devoted to it.}**[66] The word "cease" is a *muḍāri'* verb made *manṣūb* by the particle "never", and the sign of it being *manṣūb* is the explicit *fatḥah*.

وقد تكون الفتحة مقدرة ، نحو (يَسُرُّنِي أن تَسْعَى إلى المَجْدِ) فـ(تسعى) : فعل مضارع منصوب بـ(أنْ) ، وعلامة نصبه فتحة مقدرة على الألف منع من ظهورها التعذر .

The *fatḥah* is also implicit some times, e.g. in the statement, "It pleases me that you strive towards glory." The word "you strive" is a *muḍāri'* verb made *manṣūb* by the particle "that" and the sign of it being *manṣūb* is the implicit *fatḥah* upon the letter *alif*, prevented from being displayed due to impracticality.

فإن اتصل بآخر الفعل المضارع ألف اثنين ، نحو (لَنْ يَضْرِبَا) أو واو جماعة نحو (لَنْ تَضْرِبُوا) أو ياء مُخَاطَبَة ، نحو (لَنْ تَضْرِبِي) لم يكن نصبه بالفتحة ، فكُلٌّ من (تَضْرِبَا) و(تَضْرِبُوا) و(تَضْرِبِي) منصوب بـ(لَنْ) ، وعلامة نصبه حذف النون ، والألف أو

64 Al-Ḥajj: 2
65 Al-Nūr: 32
66 Ṭaha: 91

الواو أو الياء فاعل مبني على السكُون في محل رفع ، وستعرف ذلك فيما يأتي .

If the end of the *muḍāriʿ* verb is connected to the letter *alif* of duality e.g. "These two will not hit", the letter *wāw* of plurality e.g. "You will not hit", the letter *yā* of the feminine second person e.g. "You will not hit", it will not become *manṣūb* with a *fatḥah*. Each of the words "these two are hitting", "they are hitting", and "you are hitting" are *manṣūb* due to the particle "*lan*", however the sign of them being *manṣūb* is the removal of the letter *nūn*. The letters *alif*, *wāw* and *yā* are the subjects, non-inflectable upon a *sukūn* in the state of *rafʿ*. The reader will understand this at a later point.

وإن اتصل بآخره نون توكيد ثقيلة ، نحو (والله لَن تَذْهَبَنّ) أو خفيفة نحو (والله لَنْ تَذْهَبَنْ) فهو مبني على الفتح في محل نصب .

If the end [of the *muḍāriʿ* verb] is connected to the heavy letter *nūn* of emphasis e.g. "By Allah, indeed you will certainly not hit", or the light letter *nūn* of emphasis e.g. "By Allah, you will certainly not hit", it is non-inflectable upon a *fatḥah* in the state of *naṣb*.

وإن اتصل بآخره نون النسوة ، نحو (لَنْ تُدرِكْنَ المَجْدَ إلاَّ بالْعَفَافِ) فهو حينئذ مبني على السكون في محل نصب .

If the end [of the *muḍāriʿ* verb] is connected to the letter *nūn* of feminine plurality e.g. "You will not attain glory except with chastity", here it is non-inflectable upon a *sukūn* in the state of *naṣb*.

تمرينات

Exercises

١ـ استعمل الكَلِمَات الآتية في جمل مفيدة بحيث تكون منصوبة :

One. Utilise the following words in beneficial sentences where the words are *manṣūb*.

الحقل ، الزهرة ، الطلاب ، الأكرة ، الحديقة ، النهر ، الكتاب ، البستان ، القلم ، الفرس ، الغلمان ، العَذَارَى ، العصا ، الهُدَى ، يشرب ، يَرضى ، يَرتَجي ، تسافر .

❁❁❁

٢- ضع في مكان من الأمكنة الخالية في العبارات الآتية اسماً مُناسباً منصوباً بالفتحة الظاهرة ، واضبطه بالشكل :

Two. Place in the empty spaces within the below sentences an appropriate *manṣub* noun that is made *manṣūb* by an explicit *fatḥah*. Express the diacritics upon them.

(أ) إنَّ ... يَعْطِفون على أبنائهم .

(ب) أَطع ... لأنه يهذبك ويثقفك .

(ج) احْتَرِمْ ... لأنها رَبَّتْكَ .

(د) ذَاكِر ... قَبْلَ أَنْ تَحْضُرَهَا .

(ه) أَدِّ ... فَإِنَّكَ بهذا تَخْدُمُ وَطَنَكَ .

(و) كُنْ... فإنّ الْجُبنَ لاَ يُؤَخِّر الأَجل.

(ز) الْزمْ ...فإن الهذرَ عَيْبٌ .

(ح) احْفَظْ ... عن التكلم في الناس .

(ط) إن الرَّجُلَ ... هو الذي يؤدي واجبه.

(ى) مَنْ أَطَاعَ ... أَوْرَدَهُ المهالك .

(ك) اعْمَلْ ... وَلَو في غَيْرِ أَهْلِهِ .

(ل) أَحْسِنْ ... يَرْضَ عَنْكَ الله .

❁❁❁

أسئلة

Questions

في كم موضع تكون الفتحة علامة على النصب ؟

In how many instances is the *fatḥah* a sign of a word being *manṣūb*?

مثّل للاسم المفرد المنصوب بأربعة أمثلة : أحدها للاسم المفرد المذكر المنصوب

بالفتحة الظاهرة ، وثانيها للاسم المفرد المنصوب بفتحة مقدرة ، وثالثها للاسم المفرد المؤنث المنصوب بالفتحة الظاهرة ، ورابعها للاسم المفرد المؤنث المنصوب بالفتحة المقدرة.

Provide four examples of the singular noun that is *manṣūb*: The first of them should be a masculine singular noun in the state of *naṣb* with an explicit *fatḥah*. The second of them should be a singular noun in the state of *naṣb* with an implicit *fatḥah*. The third of them should be a feminine singular noun in the state of *naṣb* with an explicit *fatḥah*. The fourth of them should be a feminine singular noun in the state of *naṣb* with an implicit *fatḥah*.

مَثِّل لجمع التكسير المنصوب بأربعة أمثلة مختلفة.

Provide four different examples of the *manṣūb* broken plural.

متى يُنْصَبُ الفعل المضارع بالفتحة ؟ مثّل للفعل المضارع المنصوب بمثالين مختلفين .

When is the *muḍāri'* verb made *manṣūb* by a *fatḥah*? Provide two different examples of the *manṣūb muḍāri'* verb.

بماذا يُنْصبُ الفعل المضارع الذي اتصل به ألف اثنين ؟

With what is the *muḍāri'* verb connected to the letter *alif* of duality made *manṣūb* with?

إذا اتصل بآخر الفعل المضارع المسبوق بناصب نُونُ توكيد فما حكمه ؟

If a *muḍāri'* verb preceded by a *nāṣib* has the letter *nūn* of emphasis connected to its end, what is the ruling regarding it?

مثّل للفعل المضارع الذي اتصل بآخره نون النسوة وسَبَقَه ناصِبٌ مع بيان حكمه .

Provide an example of a *muḍāri'* verb that has a *nūn* of feminine plurality connected to its end and that is preceded by a *nāṣib*. Also clarify its ruling.

نيابة الألف عن الفتحة

The Letter *Alif* as a Representative of the *Fatḥah*

قال : وَأَمَّا الْأَلِفُ فَتَكُونُ عَلَامَةً لِلنَّصْبِ في الْأَسْمَاءِ الْخَمْسَةِ ، نَحْوَ (رَأَيْتُ أَبَاكَ
وَأَخَاكَ) وَمَا أَشْبَهَ ذلِكَ .

He said: As for the letter *alif*, then it is an indicator of the state of *naṣb* in the five nouns. Like the following example, "I saw your father and brother", and whatever resembles this.

وأقول : قد عرفْتَ فيما سبق الأسماءَ الخمسةَ ، وشَرطَ إعرابِها بالواو رفعاً والألف نصباً
والياء جَرًّا ، والآن نخبرك بأن العلامة الدالة على أن إحدى هذه الكلمات منصوبةٌ وجودُ
الألف في آخرها ، نحو (احْتَرِمْ أَبَاكَ) و(انْصُرْ أَخَاكَ) و(زُوري حَمَاكِ) و(نَظِّفْ
فَاكَ) و(لاَ تَحْتَرِمْ ذَا الْمَالِ لِمَالِه) فَكُل من (أباكَ) ، و(أخاكَ) ، و(حماكِ) ،
و(فاكَ) ، و(ذا الْمَالِ) في هذه الأمثلة ونحوها منصوبٌ ؛ لأنَّه وقع فيها مفعولاً به ،
وعلامة نصبِه الألف نيابة عن الفتحة ، وكل منها مضاف ، وما بعدُه من الكاف ، و(
الْمَال) مضاف إليه .

I say: You should have come to understand the five nouns from what has preceded. Their inflection is conditional upon the letter *wāw* in the state of *rafʿ*, the letter *alif* in the state of *naṣb* and the letter *yā* in the state of *jarr*. At the current juncture, I will clarify to you that the sign indicating one of these words to be *manṣūb* is the presence of the letter *alif* at its end. Examples are, "Honour your father", "Support your brother", "Visit (fem. singular) your father in law", "Clean your mouth" and, "Do not honour a possessor of wealth for his wealth". Each of the words "your father", "your brother", "your father in law", "your mouth" and "the possessor of wealth" in these examples and similar cases are *manṣūb* due to them being objects. The sign of them being *manṣūb* is the letter *alif* serving in place of the *fatḥah*. Each of them is the possessed object and that which comes after it e.g. the letter *kāf* and wealth is the possessor.

وليس للألفِ موضع تنوب فيه عن الفتحة سوى هذا الموضع .

The *alif* does not assume the position of serving as the representative of *fatḥah* except in this instance.

أسئلة

Questions

في كم موضع تنوب الألف عن الفتحة ؟

In how many instances does the letter *alif* serve as a representative for the *fatḥah*?

مَثِّل للأسماء الخمسة في حال النصب بأربعة أمثلة .

Provide four examples of the five nouns in the state of *naṣb*.

نيابة الكسرة عن الفتحة

The *Kasrah* as a Representative of the *Fatḥah*

قال : وَأَمَّا الْكَسْرَةُ فَتَكُونُ عَلاَمَةً لِلنَصْبِ في جَمْعِ المُؤَنَثِ السَّالِمِ .

He said: As for the *kasrah*, then it is an indicator of the state of *naṣb* for the sound feminine plural.

وأقول : قد عرفت فيما سبق جَمْعَ الْمُؤَنَّثِ السالم ، والآن نخبرك أنه يمكنك أن تستدلَّ على نصب هذا الجمع بوجود الكَسْرَة في آخره ، وذلك نحو قولك (إِنَّ الْفَتَيَاتِ الْمُهَذَّبَاتِ يُدْرِكْنَ الْمَجْدَ) فكُلٌّ من (الفتيات) و(المهذبات) جمعُ مؤنثٍ سالمٌ ، وهما منصوبان ؛ لكون الأول اسما لـ(إنّ) ، ولكون الثاني نعتاً للمنصوب ، وعلامة نصبهما الكَسْرَة نيابة عن الفتحة.

I say: I have previously defined the sound feminine plural form. At the current juncture, we will clarify to the reader that one can decipher one of these plural words to be *manṣūb* by the presence of a *kasrah* at its end. An example of this can be seen in the statement, "Verily the courteous girls will attain glory." The words "girls" and "courteous" are both sound feminine plurals and both are *manṣūb*. The first of them is *manṣūb* due to it being the noun of *inna* and the second one due to it being an adjective of a *manṣūb* word. The sign of them being *manṣūb* is the *kasrah* serving in place of the *fatḥah*.

وليس للكَسرة موضع تنوب فيه عن الفتحة سوى هذا الموضع .

The *kasrah* does not assume the position of serving as the representative of *fatḥah* except in this instance.

تمرينات

Exercises

١- اجمع المفردات الآتيَةَ جمعَ مؤنثٍ سالماً وهي :

One. Convert the following singular words into the sound feminine plural:

العاقلة ، فاطمة ، سُعْدَى ، المُدرِّسَة ، اللهاة ، الْحمَّام ، ذكرى .

٢- ضع كل واحد من جموع التأنيث الآتية في جملة مفيدة ، بشرط أن يكون في موضع نصبٍ ، واضبطه بالشكل ، وهي :

Two. Put each of the following feminine plurals into beneficial sentences, a stipulation upon you is to use them in sentences where they are *manṣūb*. Express the diacritics upon them. They are:

العاقلات ، الفاطمات ، سُعْدَيات ، المُدَرِّسَاتُ ، اللهَوات ، الْحَمَّامَات ، ذِكْرَيَات .

٣- الكَلِمَات الآتية مُثَنَّيَات ، فَرُدَّ كلَّ واحد منها إلى مفرده ، ثم اجمع هذا المفرد جمع مؤنث سالماً ، واستعمل كل واحد منها في جملة مفيدة ، وهي:

Three. The words that follow are feminine and in the dual form. Convert them into the singular form, then convert the singular form into the sound feminine plural and then utilise each of them in beneficial sentences. They are:

الزينبان ، الْحبْلَيَان ، الكاتبتان ، الرسالتان ، الحمراوان .

نيابة الياء عن الفتحة

The Letter *Yā* as a Representative of the *Fatḥah*

قال : وَأَمَّا الْيَاءُ فَتَكُونُ عَلامَةً لِلنَصْبِ في التَّثْنِيَةِ وَالْجَمْعِ .

He said: As for the letter *yā*, then it is an indicator of the state of *naṣb* in both the dual and plural forms.

وأقول قد عرفْتَ المثنى فيما مضى ، وكذلك قد عرفتَ جمع المذكر السالم والآن نخبرك أنه يمكنك أن تعرف نصْبَ الواحد منهما بوجود الياء في آخره ، والفرق بينهما أن الياء في المثنى يكُونُ ما قبلها مفتوحاً وما بعدها مَكْسُوراً ، والياء في جمع المذكر يكون ما قبلها مكْسُوراً وما بعدها مفتوحاً .

I say: You should know the dual form based upon what has preceded, and likewise the sound masculine plural. At this juncture we will explain to the reader that it is possible to ascertain one of them being *manṣūb* through the presence of the letter *yā* at its end. However there is a difference between the two, in the dual form that which is before the *yā* takes a *fatḥah* and that which follows it takes a *kasrah*, in the plural form that which is before the *yā* takes a *kasrah* and that which follows it takes a *fatḥah*.[67]

فمثال المثنى (نَظَرْتُ عُصْفُورَيْنِ فوق الشجرة) ونحو (اشترى أبي كِتَابَيْنِ لي ولأخي)، فكلٌ من (عصفورين) و(كتابين) منصوب لكونه مفعولاً به ، وعلامة نصبه الياء المفتوح ما قبلها المكسور ما بعدها ، لأنه مثنى ، والنون عوض عن التنوين في الاسم

67 Al-Ahdal said in *al-Kawākib* (1/73), "In its dual form, its *yā* is preceded by a *fatḥah*, and in its plural form it is preceded by a *kasrah*. This is because the dual form is more commonly used in speech than the plural and thus this configuration was specified for it to bring about ease." Also see *al-Taṣrīḥ* (1/69) and *Ḥāshiyat al-Ḥāmidī* (p. 42).

المفرد .

Examples of the dual form are, "I saw two sparrows above the tree" and, "My father purchased two books, one for me and one for my brother." Each of the words "two sparrows" and "two books" are *manṣūb* due to them being objects. The sign of them being *manṣūb* is the letter *yā* preceded by a letter with a *fatḥah* and followed by a letter with a *kasrah*. This is because they are in the dual form, the letter *nūn* that we see after the letter *yā* is a compensatory mechanism for the exclusion of the *tanwīn* present in the singular form.

ومثال جمع المذكر السالم (إن الْمُتَّقِينَ لَيَكْسِبُونَ رِضَا رَبِّهِمْ) ، ونحو : (نَصَحْتُ المجتهدِينَ بالانْكِبَابِ عَلَى المُذَاكرةِ) فكُلٌّ من (المتّقين) و(المجتهدين) منصوب ؛ لكونه مفعولاً به، وعلامة نصبه الياءُ المكسور ما قبلها المفتوح ما بعدها ؛ لأنه جمع مذكر سالم ، والنون عوض عن التنوين في الاسْمِ المفرد .

Examples of the sound masculine plural are, "Indeed the pious will earn the pleasure of their Lord" and "I advised the diligent workers to devote themselves to studying." Each of the words "the pious" and "diligent workers" are *manṣūb* due to them being objects.[68] The sign of them being *manṣūb* is the letter *yā* preceded by a letter with a *kasrah* and followed by a letter with a *fatḥah*. This is because they are in the sound masculine plural form, the letter *nūn* that we see after the letter *yā* is a compensatory mechanism for the exclusion of the *tanwīn* present in the singular form.

تمرينات

Exercises

١ـ الكلمات الآتية مفردة فثنها كلها ، واجمع منها ما يصح جمعه جمعَ مذكر سالماً ، وهي :

One. The following words are singular, place them in the dual form. Furthermore, convert into the sound masculine plural that which accepts it.

68 The word "the pious" is actually the noun of *inna*.

محمد ، فاطمة ، بكر، السبع ، الكاتب ، النَّمِر ، القاضي ، المُصْطَفى .

٢ـ استعمل كل مثنى من المثنيَات الآتية في جملة مفيدة بحيث يكون منصوباً ، واضبطه بالشكل الكامل ، وهي :

Two. Utilise each of the following dual form words in a beneficial sentence where they are in the *naṣb* state and place the full diacritics upon them. They are:

المحمدان ، الفاطمتان ، البَكرَانِ ، السَّبُعَان ، الكاتِبَان ، النَّمِرَانِ ، القاضِيَانِ ، المُصْطَفَيَانِ .

٣ـ استعمل كل واحد من الجموع الآتية في جملة مفيدة بحيث يكون منصوباً واضبطه بالشكل الكامل ، وهي :

Three. Utilise each of the following plurals in a beneficial sentence where they are in the *naṣb* state and place the full diacritics upon them. They are:

الراشدون ، الْمفْتُونَ ، العاقلون ، الكاتبون ، المُصْطفَون .

نيابة حذف النون عن الفتحة

The Removal of the Letter *Nūn* as a Representative of the *Fatḥah*

قال : وَأَمَّا حَذْفُ النُّونِ فَيَكُون عَلَامَةً لِلنَّصْبِ في الأَفْعَالِ الْخَمْسَةِ التي رَفْعُهَا بِثَبَاتِ النُّونِ .

He said: As for the removal of the letter *nūn*, then it is an indicator of the state of *naṣb* in the five verbs when the indicator of the state of *raf'* is the fixedness of the letter *nūn*.

وأقول : قد عرفت مما سبق ما هي الأفعال الخمسة ، والآن نخبرك أنه يمكنك أن تعرف نَصْبَ كل واحد منها إذا وجدت النون التي تكون علامة الرَّفْع مَحْذُوفَة ، ومثالها في حالة النصب قولُكَ : (يسرني أن تَحْفَظُوا درُوسَكُمْ) . ونحو : (يُؤلِمُني مِنَ الْكَسَالَى أن يُهْمِلُوا في وَاجِبَاتِهِمْ) ، فكلٌّ من (تحفظوا) و(يهملوا) فعلٌ مضارعٌ منصوبٌ بـ(أنْ) ، وعلامة نصبه حذف النون ، وواو الجماعة فاعل مبني على السكون في محل رفع .

I say: You should know the five verbs based upon what has preceded. At this juncture we will explain to the reader that it is possible to ascertain one of them being *manṣūb* through the removal of the letter *nūn*—which is used to indicate a word being *marfū'*—at its end. Examples of them being *manṣūb* are, "It pleases me that you all memorise your lessons" and "It hurts me from the lazy that they neglect their obligations". Each of the words "you preserve" and "they neglect" are *muḍāri'* verbs in the *naṣb* state due to "that". The sign of them being *manṣūb* is the absence of the letter *nūn*, the letter *wāw* of plurality is the subject, non-inflectable upon a *sukūn* in the state of *raf'*.

وكذلك المتصل بألف الاثنين ، نحو (يَسُرُّني أنْ تَنالاَ رَغبَاتِكُمَا) والمتصل بياء المخاطبة ، نحو : (يُؤْلِمُني أَنْ تُفرِّطِي في وَاجِبِكِ) ، وقد عَرَفْتَ كيف تُعْرِبُهُما .

Likewise is the case when they are connected to the letter *alif* of duality e.g. "It pleases me that you two have attained both of your desires", and when they are connected to the letter *yā* of the feminine second person e.g. "It hurts me that you (fem.) are lax in your (fem.) obligations." It should be known to you how these inflect.

تمرينات

Exercises

١ـ استعمل الكلمات الآتية مرفوعة مرة ، ومنصوبة مرة أخري ، في جمل مفيدة ، واضبطها بالشكل :

One. Utilise the following words—as *marfū'* once, and *manṣūb* once—in a beneficial sentence, and express their diacritics:

الكتاب ، القرطاس ، القلَم ، الدَّوَاة ، النَّمِر ، النهر ، الفيل ، الحديقة ، الجمل ، االبساتين ، المغانم ، الآداب ، يظهر ، الصادقات ، العفيفات ، الوالدات ، الإخوان ، الأساتذة ، المعلمون ، الآباءُ ، أخوك ، العَلم ، المروءة ، الصديقان ، أبوك ، الأصدقاء ، المؤمنون ، الزُّرَّاع ، المُتَّقُون ، تقومان ، يلعبان .

أسئلة

Questions

متى تكون الكسرة علامة للنصب ؟

When is the *kasrah* a sign of the state of *naṣb*?

متى تكون الياءُ علامة للنصب ؟

When is the letter *yā* a sign of the state of *naṣb*?

في كم موضع يكون حذف النون علامةً للنصب ؟

In how many instances is the removal of the letter *nūn* a sign of the state of *naṣb*?

مثّل لجمع المؤنث المنصوب بمثالين وأعرب واحداً منهما .

Provide two examples of the feminine plural in the state of *naṣb* and place the inflections for one of them.

مثّل للأفعال الخمسة المنصوبة بثلاثة أمثلة وأعرب واحداً منها .

Provide three examples of the five verbs in the state of *naṣb* and place the inflections for one of them.

مثّل لجمع المذكر السالم المنصوب بمثالين .

Provide two examples of the sound masculine plural in the state of *naṣb*.

مثّل لجمع المذكر السالم المرفوع بمثالين .

Provide two examples of the sound masculine plural in the state of *rafʿ*.

مثّل للمثنى المنصوب بمثالين .

Provide two examples of the dual form in the state of *naṣb*.

مثّل للمثنى المرفوع بمثالين .

Provide two examples of the dual form in the state of *rafʿ*.

مثّل للأفعال الخمسة المرفوعة بمثالين .

Provide two examples of the five verbs in the state of *rafʿ*.

علامات الخفض

The Signs of *al-Khafḍ*

قال : وَلِلْخَفْضِ ثَلاَثُ عَلاَمَاتٍ : الْكَسْرَةُ ، وَالْيَاءُ ، وَالْفَتْحَة .

He said: And for the state of *khafḍ*, there are three signs: the *kasrah*, the letter *yā*, and the *fatḥah*.

وأقول يمكنك أن تعرف الكلمة مخفوضةً إذا وجدت فيها واحداً من ثلاثة أشياء : الأول الكسرة ، وهي الأصل في الخفض ، والثاني الياء ، والثالث . الفتحة ، وهما فَرْعَانِ عن الكسرة ؛ ولكل واحد من هذه الأشياء الثلاثة مَوَاضع يكون فيها ، سنذكر ذلك تفصيلاً فيما يلي .

I say: It will be possible for you to know that a word is *makhfūḍ* if you notice one of three things: the first is the *kasrah*—which is the root sign of *al-khafḍ*—, the second is the letter *yā* and the third is the *fatḥah*—both of these are subsidiaries of the *kasrah*. For each of these three signs there are a number of instances where they are utilised, and we will provide details regarding them below.

الكسرة ومواضعها

The *Kasrah* and Its Utilisation

قال : فأَمَّا الْكَسْرَةُ فَتكُونُ عَلامَةً لِلْخَفْضِ في ثَلاثَةِ مَوَاضِعَ : في الاسْمِ الْمُفْرَدِ الْمُنْصَرِفِ ، وَجَمْعِ التَّكْسِيرِ المُنْصَرِفِ ، وَجَمْعِ المُؤَنْثِ السَّالِم .

He said: As for the *kasrah*, then it is an indicator of the state of *khafḍ* in three instances: (i) the singular noun which is a triptote,[69] (ii) the broken plural form which is a triptote, and (iii) the sound feminine plural.

وأقول: للكسرة ثلاثة مواضع تكون في كل واحِدٍ منها علامةً على أن الاسم مخفوض .

I say: There are three instances where the *kasrah* is utilised as a sign that a noun is *makhfūḍ*:

الموضع الأول : الاسم المفرد المنصرف ، وقد عرفت معنى كونه مفرداً ، ومعنى كونه منصرفاً : أن الصرف يلحق آخِرَه ، والصَّرْفُ : هو التَّنوين ، نحو (سَعَيْتُ إلى مُحَمَّدٍ) ونحو (رَضِيتُ عَنْ عَلِيٍّ) ونحو (اسْتَفَدْتُ مِنْ مُعَاشَرَةِ خَالِدٍ) ونحو (أَعْجَبَنِي خُلُقُ بَكْرٍ) فكل من (محمد) و(علي) مخفوض لدخول حرف الخفض عليه ، وعلامة خفضه الكسرة الظاهرة ، وكل من (خالد) ، و(بكر) مخفوض لإضافة ما قبله إليه ، وعلامة خفضه الكسرة الظاهرة أيضاً ، و(محمد) و(علي) و(خالد) و(بكر) : أسماء مفردة، وهي منصرفة ، لِلُحُوقِ التنوين لها .

The first instance: In the singular triptote noun. I have previously defined the meaning of singular. The meaning of it being a triptote is that its end can ac-

69 The triptote was stipulated here—in both cases—because that which is contrary to the triptote becomes *majrūr* with a *fatḥah* e.g. (مررتُ بأحمدَ) and (مررتُ بمساجدَ). This was not stipulated for the sound feminine plural due to it only coming as triptote.

cept *ṣarf*, and *ṣarf* is the *tanwīn*. Examples are "I paced to Muḥammad", "I was pleased with 'Alī", "I benefited from accompanying Khālid" and "I was amazed by Bakr's character." The words "Muḥammad" and "'Alī" are *makhfūḍ* due to being preceded by a particle of *al-khafḍ*, and the sign of them being *makhfūḍ* is the explicit *kasrah*. The words "Khālid" and "Bakr" are *makhfūḍ* due to what precedes them in the possessive compound, and the sign of them being *makhfūḍ* is the explicit *kasrah*. "Muḥammad", "'Alī", "Khālid", and "Bakr" are singular nouns, and they are triptote due to them accepting the *tanwīn*.

والموضع الثاني : جمع التكسير المنصرف ، وقد عرفت مما سَبَقَ معنى جمع التكسير ، وعرفت في الموضع الأول هنا معنى كونه منصرفاً ، وذلك أن الصرف يلحق آخره ، نحو (مَرَرْتُ بِرِجَالٍ كِرَامٍ) ونحو (رَضِيتُ عَنْ أَصْحَابٍ لَنَا شُجْعَانٍ) فكل من (رجال) و(أصحاب) مخفوض لدخول حرف الخفض عليه ، وعلامة خفضه الكسرة الظاهرة ، وكل من (كرام)، و(شُجعَان) مخفوض لأنه نعت للمخفوض ، وعلامة خفضه الكسرة الظاهرة أيضاً ، و(رجال) و(أصحاب) و(كرام) و(شُجْعَان) : جموعُ تكسير ، وهي منصرفة ؛ للحوق التنوين لها .

The second instance: In the broken plural form which is a triptote. I have previously defined the meaning of the broken plural. Likewise I have explained the meaning of triptote in the previous paragraph, i.e. that its end accepts *ṣarf*. Examples are, "I passed by the noble men" and "I was pleased with our courageous companions". Each of the words "men" and "companions" are *makhfūḍ* due to the entrance of a particle of *khafḍ* upon them, and the sign of them being *makhfūḍ* is the explicit *kasrah*. The words "noble" and "courageous" are *makhfūḍ* due to being adjectives of *makhfūḍ* words. Each of the words "men", "companions", "noble" and "courageous" are broken plurals, and they are triptotes due to them accepting the *tanwīn*.

والموضع الثالث : جمع المؤنث السالم ، وقد عرفت فيما سبق معنى جمع المؤنث السالم ، وذلك نحو (نَظَرْتُ إلى فَتَيَاتٍ مُؤَدَّبَاتٍ) ، ونحو (رَضِيتُ عن مُسْلِمَاتٍ قَانِتَاتٍ) فكل من (فَتَياتٍ) ، وَ(مسلمات) مخفوض ؛ لدخول حرف الخفض عليه

، وعلامة خفضه الكسرة الظاهرة . وكل من (مؤدَّبات) ، و(قانتات) مخفوض ؛ لأنه تابع للمخفوض ، وعلامة خفضه الكسرة الظاهرة أيضاً ، وكل من : (فتيات) ، و(مسلمات) ، و(مؤدبات) ، و(قانتات) : جمع مؤنث سالم .

The third instance: In the sound feminine plural. I have previously defined the meaning of the sound feminine plural. Examples are, "I looked at the well-mannered girls" and, "I was pleased with the devout Muslim women." In these examples, the words "young girls" and "Muslim women" are *makhfūḍ* due to them being preceded by a particle of *al-khafḍ*, and the sign of them being *makhfūḍ* is the explicit *kasrah*. Each of the words "well-mannered" and "devout" are *makhfūḍ* due to them being followers of a *makhfūḍ* word, and the sign of them being *makhfūḍ* is the explicit *kasrah*. Each of the four aforementioned words are sound feminine plurals.

أسئلة

Questions

ما هي المواضع التي تدل الكسرة فيها على خفض الاسم ؟

In which instances does the *kasrah* indicate that a noun is *makhfūḍ*?

ما معنى كون الاسم مفرداً منصرفاً ؟

What is the meaning of a word being a singular triptote noun?

ما معنى كونه جمع تكسير منصرفا ؟

What is the meaning of a word being a triptote broken plural?

مثّل للاسم المفرد المنصرف المجرور بأربعة أمثلة ، وكذلك لجمع التكسير المنصرف المجرور .

Provide four examples of the triptote singular noun which is *majrūr* (synonym of *makhfūd*). Likewise provide the same for the triptote broken plural which is *majrūr*.

مثّل لجمع المؤنث السالم المجرور بمثالين .

Provide two examples of the sound feminine plural which is *majrūr*.

نيابة الياء عن الكسرة

The Letter *Yā* as a Representative of the *Kasrah*

قال: وَأَمَّا الْيَاءُ فَتَكُونُ عَلامَةً لِلْخَفْضِ في ثَلاثَةِ مَوَاضِعَ : في الأَسْمَاءِ الْخَمْسَةِ ، وَفي التَّثْنِيَةِ ، وَالْجَمْعِ .

He said: As for the letter *yā*, then it is an indicator of the state of *khafḍ* in three instances: (i) the five nouns, (ii) the dual form and (iii) the plural form.

وأقول: للياء ثلاثةُ مواضعَ تكون في كل واحدٍ منها دالة على خفض الاسم .

I say: There are three instances where the letter *yā* indicates that a noun is *makhfūḍ*.

الموضع الأول : الأسماء الخمسة ، وقد عرفتها ، وعرفت شروطَ إعرابها مما سبق ، وذلك نحو (سَلِّمْ عَلَى أَبِيكَ صَبَاحَ كلِّ يَوْمٍ) ونحو (لا تَرْفَعْ صَوْتَكَ عَلَى صَوْتِ أَخِيكَ الأَكْبَرِ) ونحو (لاَ تَكُن مُحِبًّا لذي المال إلاَّ أن يكون مُؤَدَّباً) فكل من (أبيك) ، و(أخيك) و(ذي المال) مخفوض ؛ لدخول حرف الخفض عليه ، وعلامة خفضه الياءُ ، والكاف في الأوَّلَيْنِ ضميرُ المخاطَب ، وهي مضافٌ إليه مبني على الفتح في محل خفض ، وكلمة (المال) في المثال الثالث مضافٌ إليه أيضاً ، مجرور بالكسرة الظاهرة .

The first instance: The five nouns, and these have been defined. Likewise I have explained the conditions of their declension from what has preceded. Examples are, “Give the greetings to your father during the morning of every day”, “Do not raise your voice above the voice of your older brother” and, “Do not love the possessor of wealth except if he has good manners.” Each of the words “your father”, “your brother” and “possessor of wealth” are *makhfūḍ* due to being preceded by a particle of *al-khafḍ*, and the sign of them being *makhfūḍ* is the letter *yā*. The letter *kāf* (your) in the first two examples is the second person pronoun and the *muḍāf ilayhi*, non-inflectable upon a *fatḥah* in the state of *khafḍ*. The word "wealth" in the third example is also the *muḍāf ilayhi*, *majrūr* with an explicit *kasrah*.

الموضع الثاني : المثنى ، وذلك نحو (انْظُرْ إلى الْجُنْدِيَّيْنِ) ، ونحو (سَلِّمْ عَلَى الصَّدِيقَيْنِ) فكل من (الجنديين) ، و(الصديقين) مخفوض ؛ لدخول حرف الخفض عليه ، وعلامة خفضه الياءُ المفتوح ما قبلها المكسور ما بعدها ، وكل من (الجنديين) ، و(الصديقين) مُثنًّى ؛ لأنه دال على اثنين .

The second instance: The dual form. Examples are, "Look at the two soldiers" and, "Give greetings to the two friends". Each of the words "two soldiers" and "two friends" are *makhfūḍ* due to their acceptance of a particle of *al-khafḍ*, the sign of them being *makhfūḍ* is the letter *yā* preceded by a letter with a *fatḥah* and followed by a letter with a *kasrah*. Each of the words "two soldiers" and "two friends" are dual forms, as they indicate towards two.

الموضع الثالث : جمع المذكر السالم ، نحو (رَضِيتُ عَنِ الْبَكْرِينَ) ، ونحو (نَظَرْتُ إلى المُسْلِمِينَ الْخَاشِعِينَ) فكل من (البكرين)، و(المسلمين) مخفوض ؛ لدخول حرف الخفض عليه ، وعلامة خفضه الياءُ المكسور ما قبلها المفتوح ما بعدها ، وكل منهما جمع مذكر سالم .

The third instance: The sound masculine plural. Examples are, "I was pleased with the two Bakrs" and, "I looked at the submissive Muslims". Each of the words, "the two Bakrs" and "the two Muslims" are *makhfūḍ* due to their acceptance of a particle of *khafḍ* and the sign of them being *makhfūḍ* is the letter *yā* preceded by a letter with a *kasrah* and followed by a letter with a *fatḥah*. Each of them is a sound masculine plural.

تمرين

Exercises

١- ضَعْ كُلَّ فعل من الأفعال الآتية في جملتين بحيث يكون مرفوعاً في إحداهما ، ومنصوباً في الأخري :

One. Place all of the following verbs in two sentences, in the first of them the verb should be *marfū'* and in the second of them the verb should be *manṣūb*:

يجري ، يبني ، ينظف ، يركب ، يَمْخر ، يشرب ، تضيء .

❁❁❁

٢- ضع كلَّ اسمٍ من الأسماء الآتية في ثلاث جمل ، بحيث يكون مرفوعاً في إحداها ومنصوباً في الثانية ومخفوضا في الثالثة ، واضبط كل ذلك بالشكل :

Two. Place all of the following nouns into three sentences, in the first of them the noun should be *marfū'*, in the second of them it should be *manṣūb*, and in the third of them it should *makhfūḍ*. Express the appropriate diacritics upon them.

والدك ، إخوتك ، أسنانك ، الكتاب ، القطار ، الفاكهة ، الأم ، الأصدقاء ، التلميذان ، الرجُلاَنِ ، الجنديُّ ، الفتاة ، أخوك ، صديقك ، الجنديَّان ، الفَتيَانِ ، التاجر ، الوَرْد ، النيل ، الاستحمام ، النشاط ، المهمِلُ ، المهذبات.

❁❁❁

أسئلة

Questions

ما هي المواضع التي تكون الياءُ فيها علامة على خفض الاسم ؟

What are the instances in which the letter *yā* is a sign that a noun is *makhfūḍ*?

ما الفَرْقُ بين المثنى وجمع المذكر في حال الخفض ؟

What is the difference between the manner the dual form and plural form take the state of *al-khafḍ*?

مثّل للمثنى المخفوض بثلاثة أمثلة .

Provide three examples of the dual form in the state of *al-khafḍ*.

مثّل لجمع المذكر المخفوض بثلاثة أمثلة أيضاً .

Provide three examples of the sound masculine plural in the state of *al-khafḍ*.

مثّل للأسماء الخمسة بثلاثة أمثلة يكون الاسم في كل واحد منها مخفوضاً .

Provide three examples of the five nouns, in each example the noun should be *makhfūḍ*.

نيابة الفتحة عن الكسرة

The *Fatḥah* as a Representative of the *Kasrah*

قال : وَأَمَّا الْفَتْحَةُ فَتَكُونُ عَلامَةَ لِلْخفضِ في الاسمِ الذِي لا يَنْصَرِفُ .

He said: As for the *fatḥah*, then it is an indicator of the state of *khafḍ* for the nouns which are diptotes.

وأقول : للفتحة موضع واحد تكون فيه علامة على خفض الاسم ، وهو الاسم الذي لا ينصرف .

I say: There is one instance where the *fatḥah* provides the sign of a noun being *makhfūḍ*, and this is in the diptote noun.

ومعنى كونه لا ينصرف : أنه لا يَقْبَلُ الصَّرْفَ ، وهو التنوين ، والاسم الذي لا ينصرف هو : الذي أشْبَهَ الفعل في وجود علتين فرعيتين : (إحداهما ترجع إلى اللفظ ، والأخرى ترجع إلى المعنى) ، أو وُجدَ فيه علَّة واحدة تقوم مَقام العِلَّتَين .

The meaning of it being diptote is that it does not accept *ṣarf* i.e. the *tanwīn*. The noun that is diptote is: That which resembles a verb[70] through the pres-

70 To explain this further: A verb does not inflect with a *tanwin* nor as a *makhfūḍ*. As for the common noun, it does inflect with these. However, if the noun has two secondary reasons, it is no longer a common noun but rather it is deemed as the resemblance of a verb. Both of these, meaning verbs and (non-common) nouns which diptote, become subsidiaries. So the non-common noun that doesn't inflect is a subsidiary of a common noun which does inflect, due to the two reasons within them. Whereas the verb is a subsidiary of a triptote noun because it is derived from it ([t] i.e. from the infinitive), according to the correct opinion, as well as it being dependent upon it ([t] i.e. to a *fā'il* (doer) of the verb). So if you understand the likeness between such nouns that diptote and verbs then we can draw a principle, 'If something resembles another then it carries the same ruling as it', meaning it usually takes the same ruling. See: *Ḥāshiyat al-Khudriyyah 'ala*

ence of two subsidiary reasons[71]: The first of them returns to its pronunciation, the other returns to its meaning. Or it can be due to the presence of one reason in the place of two.

والعلل التي توجد في الاسم وتَدُلُّ على الفرعية وهي راجعة إلى المعنى اثنتان لَيْسَ غَيْرُ : الأولى العَلَمِيَّةُ ، والثانية الوَصْفية ، ولابد من وجود واحدة من هاتين العلتين في الاسم الممنوع من الصرف بسبب وجود علتين فيه .

The reason that is found in the noun and which indicates that it is subsidiary (i.e. subsidiary of verbs due to resembling them) and it returns to the meaning consists of two and not more, (i) the proper noun and (ii) the descriptive noun. It is essential for one to find one of these reasons in the diptote noun that is diptote due to the two reasons.

والعلل التي توجد في الاسم وتدل على الفرعية وتكون راجعة إلى اللفظ ستُّ عِلَلٍ ، وهي : التأنيث بغير ألف ، والْعُجْمَة ، والتركيب ، وزيادة الألف والنون ، وَوَزنُ الْفِعْلِ ، والعَدْلُ ، ولابد من وجود واحدة من هذه العلل مع العلمية فيه ، وأما مع الوصفية فلا يوجد منها إلا واحدةٌ من ثلاث ، وهي : زيادة الألف والنون ، أو وزن الفعل أو العدل .

The reason that is found in the noun and which indicates a subsidiary and it returns to the word itself consists of six. They are: (i) a feminine name without an *alif*, (ii) a non-Arab name, (iii) compounding, (iv) the addition of the letters *alif* and *nūn*, (v) [a noun upon] the word structure of the verb and (vi) a word altered from its original form. It is essential to find one of these six when the word is a proper noun. However when it is a descriptive noun, only one of three from these are found: (i) the addition of the letters *alif* and *nūn*, (ii) the word structure of the verb, and (iii) a word altered from its original form.

Ibn ʿAqīl (2/97) and *Ḥāshiyat al-Sujāʿī ʿala al-Qaṭr* (p. 26).

71 Al-Ḥamidī said in *Ḥāshiyat ʿalā al-Kafrāwī* (p. 44): "The meaning of *illah* (reason) linguistically is the unnatural occurrence that entails an unnatural situation. Terminologically it is that which entails a ruling; and the ruling here refers to the ruling of being diptote, either (i) entailing two reasons or (ii) one in place of the two."

فمثال الْعَلَمِية مع التأنيث بغير ألف : فاطمة ، وزينب ، وحمزة .

Examples of the proper noun that is feminine without an *alif* are: Fāṭimah, Zaynab and Ḥamzah.

ومثالُ العلمية مع العجمة : إدريس ، ويعقوب ، وإبراهيم .

Examples of the proper noun that is non-Arab are: Idrīs, Ya'qūb and Ibrāhīm[72].

ومثالُ العلمية مع التركيب : مَعْدِيكَرِبُ ، وبَعْلَبَكُّ ، وقَاضِيخَانُ ، وبُزُرْجَمِهْرُ ، ورَامَهُرْمُز .

Examples of the proper noun that is a compound (i.e. when two names are made into one) are: Ma'dīkarib, Ba'labakk, Qāḍīkhān, Buzurjamihr and Rāmahurmuz.

ومثال العلمية مع زيادة الألف والنون : مَرْوَانُ ، وعُثْمَانُ ، وغَطَفَانُ ، وعَفَّانُ ، وسَحْبَانُ ، وسُفْيَانُ ، وعِمْرَانُ ، وَقَحْطَانُ ، وَعَدْنَانُ .

Examples of the proper noun that has an addition of the letter *alif* and *nūn* are: Marwān, 'Uthmān, Ghaṭāfān, 'Affān, Saḥbān, Sufyān, 'Imrān, Qaḥṭān and 'Adnān.

ومثال العلمية مع وزن الفعل : أَحْمَد ، وَيَشْكُرُ ، وَيَزِيدُ ، وتَغْلِبُ ، وَتَدْمُرُ .

Examples of the proper noun on the pattern of the verb are: Aḥmad, Yashkuru, Yazīd, Taghlib and Tadmur.

ومثالُ العلمية مع العدل : عُمَرُ ، وَزَفَرُ ، وَقُثَمُ ، وَهُبَلُ ، وَزُحَلُ ، وجُمَحُ ، وَقزَحُ ، وَمُضَرُ ، ودلف ، وبلع ، وهذل ، وثعل ، وجشم ، وعصم ، وجحا .

---

72 Non-Arab names refer to names which are foreign to the Arabic language, but became proper nouns in the Arabic language. However, if they are not proper nouns in their foreign language, then the correct view is that these proper nouns must be longer than three letters long. If these three conditions are not present then it becomes a noun which does inflect. See: *Sharḥ Ibn 'Aqīl* (3/332), *Shuthūr al-Dhahab* (P. 454) and *al-Kawākib* (1/98-100).

Examples of the proper noun with an alteration from its original form[73] are: ʿUmar, Zufar, Qutham, Hubal, Zuḥal, Jumaḥ, Quzaḥ, Muḍar, Dulaf, Bulaʿ, Hudhal, Thuʿal, Jusham, ʿUṣam and Juḥā.

ومثالُ الوصفية مع زيادة الألف والنون : رَيَّانُ ، وشَبْعَانُ ، ويَقْظَانُ .

Examples of the descriptive noun with an addition of the letter *alif* and *nūn*: Rayyān, Shabʿān and Yaqẓān.

ومثالُ الوصفية مع وزن الفعل : أَكْرَمُ ، وَأَفْضَلُ ، وَأَجْمَلُ .

Examples of the descriptive noun upon the word structure of the verb are: Akram, Afḍal, and Ajmal.

ومثالُ الوصفية مع العدل : مَثْنَى ، وَثُلاَثُ ، وَرُبَاعُ ، وَأُخَرُ .

Examples of the descriptive noun with alteration from its original form are: Mathnā, Thulāth, Rubāʿu and Ukharu.

وأما العلتان اللتان تقوم كل واحدة منهما مقام العلتين فهما : صيغة منتهى الجموع ، ألف التأنيث المقصورة أو الممدودة .

As for the two reasons that each serve in the place of two reasons, they are: (i) those that are pluralised upon the pattern of *muntahā al-jumūʿ* (the utmost

73 Ibn Hishām said in *al-Qaṭr* (p. 447), "*Al-ʿadl* is the transformation of a noun from its form to another whilst retaining its original meaning. [...] It is found in two morphological patterns in the definite nouns. The first of them is "*fuʿal*" (فُعَل), and this is specific to the masculine gender. It is transformed from the pattern "*fāʿil*" (فاعل) e.g. ʿUmar (which is transformed from ʿĀmir). The second of them is "*faʿāl*" (فَعَال) , and this is specific to the feminine gender. It is transformed from the pattern "*fāʿilah*" (فاعلة) e.g. *ḥadhām*, and this is a rule specific to the linguistic rules of the people of Tamīm." Al-Ḥaṭāb said in *al-Mutammimah*, as it is also stated in *al-Kawākib* (1/49), "[Examples] are the proper nouns upon the morphological pattern of '*fuʿal*' e.g. ʿUmar, Zufar, Zuḥal. It is stated that they are diptotes, and there is no apparent reason causing this besides the fact that these names indicate transformation i.e. ʿUmar is from ʿĀmir, Zufar is from Zāfir and Zuḥal is from Zāḥil."

plural)[74], (ii) words made feminine by an *alif maqṣūrah* or *mamdūdah*.

أما صيغة منتهى الجموع فضابِطُهَا : أن يكون الإسْمُ جمعَ تكسير ، وقد وقع بعد ألف تكسيره حرفان نحو : مَسَاجِدَ ، وَمَنَابِرَ ، وَأَفاضِلَ ، وَأَمَاجِدَ ، وَأماثِلَ ، وَحَوَائِض ، وَطَوامِثَ ، أو ثلاثةُ أحْرُف وَسَطُهَا ساكنٌ ، نحو : مَفَاتِيح ، وَعَصَافير ، وقَناديل .

As for those that are pluralised upon the pattern of *muntahā al-jumū'*, its condition is that the noun is in the broken plural state that has two letters after the *alif* of brokenness. Examples are, *masjids*, *minbars*, virtuous, majestic, examples, menstruating females and girls on their first period (this word has a number of different meanings that refer to menstruating women and in the verbal form it also refers to intimate touching e.g. "none had touched them"). Or it may have three letters, the middle of them having a *sukūn* e.g. keys, sparrows and lamps.

وأما ألف التأنيث المقصورة فنحو : حبْلَى ، وَقُصْوَى ، وَدُنْيَا ، وَدَعْوى .

As for the noun with a feminine *alif al-maqṣūrah*, examples are: pregnant, farthermost, world and allegation/lawsuit.

وأما ألف التأنيث الممدودة فنحو : حَمْرَاء ، وَدَعْجَاء ، وَحسنَاء ، وَبَيْضَاء ، كحْلاَء ، نافِقَاء ، وأصدقاء ، وعُلَمَاء .

As for the noun with a feminine *alif al-mamdūdah*,[75] examples are: red, wide-

74 Regarding the meaning of the *muntahā al-jumū'*, al-Ahdal said in *al-Kawākib* (1/89), "It refers to the highest point of plural found in the language of the Arabs." Shaykh Ibn al-'Uthaymīn said in his *Sharḥ* (p. 101), "This refers to the plural that comes on the pattern of 'مفاعل' or 'مفاعيل'."

75 Al-Hamalāwī said in *Shadhā al-'Arf* (p. 87), "The letter *alif* here is of two types: (i) the singular i.e. the *maqṣūrah* e.g. *ḥublā* (pregnant) and *bushrā* (glad tidings), (ii) that besides the singular [i.e. the *mamdūdah*] which is preceded by an *alif* and is transformed into the letter *hamzah* e.g. red and maiden." In the book *al-Naḥwu al-Musaffā* (p. 41) it says, "Take note: The *alif al-mamdūdah* causes the word to become a diptote when it possesses two characteristics: (i) it appears after three or more letters, whereas if it comes after two letters it is a triptote e.g. رُغاءٌ, رِعاءٌ, بِناءٌ, نِداءٌ, رِداءٌ, (ii) it is an addition in the word wherein it is found, whereas if it is in the original form of the word or the form trans-

eyed with heavy contrast between the black and white [of the eyes], beautiful, white, kohl-eyed, burrows, friends and scholars.

فكلُّ ما ذكرناه من هذه الأسماء ، وكذا ما أشبهها ، لا يجوز تنوينُهُ ، ويُخفَضُ ، بالفتحة نيابة عن الكسرة ، نحو : (صَلّى الله عَلَى إبْرَاهِيمَ خلِيلِه) ونحو : (رَضِيَ الله عَنْ عُمَرَ أمير المؤمنين) : فكل من (إبراهيم) و(عمر) : مخفوض ؛ لدخول حرف الخفض عليه ، وعلامة خفضهما الفتحة نيابة عن الكسرة ؛ لأن كل واحد منهما اسم لا ينصرف ، والمانع من صرف (إبراهيم) العلمية والعُجْمَةُ ، والمانع من صرف (عُمَرَ) : العلمية والعَدْلُ .

For each of these nouns which we have mentioned—and those like them—it is not permissible to give them *tanwīn*. They are made *makhfūḍ* by the *fatḥah* in place of the *kasrah*. Examples of this are, "Allah blessed upon Ibrāhīm, his *khalīl*" and, "Allah was pleased with ʿUmar, the leader of the faithful." Each of the words Ibrāhīm and ʿUmar are *makhfūḍ* due to the entry of a particle of *al-khafḍ* upon them, and the sign of them being *makhfūḍ* is a *fatḥah* serving in place of the *kasrah*. This is because each of them is a diptote, Ibrāhīm is prevented from being a triptote due to it being a non-Arab proper noun.[76]

---

formed from the original form then the word is triptote e.g. أعداءٌ, أسماءٌ, أبناءٌ, نداءٌ, رداءٌ."

76 Al-Ḥamidī said in *Hāshiyat ʿalā al-Kafrāwī* (p. 45), "The names of the Prophets are non-Arab proper nouns except for Muḥammad, Ṣāliḥ, Shuʿayb and Hūd. All of their names are diptotes except for these four due to them not being non-Arab names. The names Nūḥ, Lūṭ and Shīth are also triptote. This is due to them being non-Arab proper nouns but not meeting the condition of the diptote non-Arab noun that it consist of more than three letters. All of the names of the Angels are also diptotes due to being non-Arab proper nouns except for four: Munkar, Nakīr, Mālik and Riḍwān (the *tanwīn* is prevented from being displayed in Riḍwān due to it being a proper noun with the addition of the letter *alif* and *nūn*). The names of the months are triptote except for Jumādā al-Ūlā and Jumādā al-Thāniyah which are diptote due to the *alif al-maqṣūrah* of femininity, Shaʿbān and Ramaḍān due to them being proper nouns with the addition of the letters *alif* and *nūn*, and the words Ṣafar and Rajab when used to refer to someone specifically, then they are diptote due to them being proper nouns, and altered from their original forms i.e. al-Ṣafar and al-Rajab (in any other case they are triptote)." See *al-Kawākib* (1/98-99).

Note: It is not established in the Qur'ān and Sunnah that Shīth is a prophet. Our Shaykh

Whereas ʿUmar is prevented from being a triptote due to it being a proper noun that is altered from its original form.

وقِسْ على ذلك الباقي .

Apply this rule to all other proper nouns which are similar to them.

ويشترط لخفض الإسم الذي لا ينصرف بالفتحة : أن يكون خالياً من (أل) وألا يُضافَ إلى اسْم بعده ، فإن اقترن بـ(أل) أو أُضيف ، خُفِضَ بالكسرة ، نحو قوله تعالى ﴿وَأَنْتُمْ عَاكِفُونَ فِي الْمَسَاجِدِ﴾ ونحو : (مَرَرْتُ بحسْنَاءِ قُرَيشٍ) .

There are conditions for one of these words to become *makhfūḍ* with a *fatḥah*. They are: (i) It remains free from "*al-*" (the) and (ii) it is not compounded to a noun after it through possession. If it is connected to "*al-*" or in a possessive compound with a noun after it, then it is made *makhfūḍ* with a *kasrah*. An example is the statement of the Most High: **{As long as you are staying for worship in the *masjids*}**[77] and the statement, "I passed by the beautiful women of Quraysh."

تمرين

Exercises

١- بيّن الأسباب التي تُوجِبُ مَنْعَ الصرف في كل كلمة من الكلمات الآتية :

Abu ʿAbd al-Rahmān [Muqbil] al-Wādiʿī stated this, Allah increase his benefits.

As for the names of the two angels Munkar and Nakīr, then this has been reported by al-Tirmidhī in his *Jāmiʿ* (3/383, 1071) in which he classified it as being *hasan gharīb*, Ibn Abī ʿĀsim in al-Sunnah (No. 864), al-Ājurri in *al-Sharīʿah* (p. 365), Ibn Ḥibbān in his *al-Ihsān* (7/No. 3117), on the authority of Abu Hurayrah that the Messenger of Allah said, 'When the deceased is placed in the grave, two angels come to him, black in complexion and with blue eyes. One of them is called al-Munkar and the other al-Nakīr...'"

Benefit: In origin, names of locations are diptotes except for certain names that were narrated from the Arabs as triptotes.

77 Al-Baqarah: 187

One. Detail the reasons that prevent the following words from being triptotes:

زَيْنَبُ ، مُضَرُ ، يُوسُفُ ، إبراهيمُ ، أَكْرَمُ مِنْ أَحْمَدَ ، بَعْلَبَك ، رَيَّان ، مَغَاليق ، حَسَّان ، عَاشُوراء ، دُنْيَا .

۞۞۞

٢ـ ضع كل كلمة من الكلمات الآتية في جملتين ، بحيث تكون في إحداهما مجرورة بالفتحة نيابة عن الكسرة ، وفي الثانية مجرورة بالكسرة الظاهرة .

Two. Place all of the following words into two sentences, in the first of which it should be *majrūr* with a *fatḥah* in place of the *kasrah*, and in the second of which it should be *majrūr* with an explicit *kasrah*.

دَعْجاء ، أَمَاثِل ، أَجْمَلُ ، يقظان .

۞۞۞

٣ـ ضع في المكان الخالي من الجمل الآتية اسماً ممنوعاً من الصرف واضبطه بالشكل ، ثم بين السبب في منعه :

Three. In the empty spaces found in the sentences below, enter an appropriate diptote noun and express the diacritics upon them, then explain the reason for it being prevented from being a triptote.

۞۞۞

(أ) سَافِرْ مَعَ ... أَخِيكَ .

(ب) ... خَيْرٌ مِنْ ...

(ج) كانَتْ عِنْدَ ... زَائِرَةٌ مِنْ ...

(ه) هذه الْفَتَاةُ ...

(و) ... يَظْهَرُ بَعْدَ المطرِ .

(ز) مَرَرْتُ بِمِسْكِينٍ ... فَتَصَدَّقْتُ عليه.

(د) مَسْجِد عَمْرٍو أَقْدَمُ مَا بِمِصْرَ مِنْ ... (ح) الإِحْسَانُ إلى المسيء ...إلى النّجاة

(ه) هذه الفتاة ... (ط) ... تعطف عَلَى الْفُقَرَاء .

أسئلة

Questions

ما هي المواضع التي تكون الفتحة فيها علامةً على خفض الاسم ؟

What are the instances in which the *fatḥah* is utilised as a sign of a noun being *makhfūḍ*?

وما معنى كون الاسم لا ينصرف ؟

What is the meaning of a noun being a diptote?

ما هو الاسم الذي لا ينصرف ؟

What are the nouns that are diptotes?

ما هي العلل التي ترجع إلى المعنى ؟

What are the reasons that return to the meaning of the word?

ما هي العلل التي ترجع إلى اللفظ ؟

What are the reasons that return to the pronunciation of the word?

كم عِلَّة من العلل اللفظية توجد مع الوصفية ؟

How many of the pronunciation related reasons are found with descriptive nouns?

كم علة من العلل اللفظية توجد مع العلمية ؟

How many of the meaning related reasons are found with proper nouns?

ما هما العلّتانِ اللتانِ تقوم الواحدة منهما مقام علتين ؟

What are the two reasons that each take the place of two reasons?

مَثِّلْ لاسم لا ينصرف لوجود العلمية والعدل ، والوصفية والعدل ، والعلمية ، وزيادة الألف والنون ، والوصفية وزيادة الألف والنون ، والعلمية والتأنيث ، والوصفية ووزن الفعل ، والعلمية والعجمة .

Provide an example of the diptote noun due to it being: (i) a proper noun that is altered from its original form, (ii) a descriptive noun that is altered from its original form, (iii) a proper noun with the addition of the letters *alif* and *nūn*, (iv) a descriptive noun with the addition of the letters *alif* and *nūn*, (v) a proper noun that is feminine, (vi) a descriptive noun with the word structure of the verb, and (vii) a proper noun that is non-Arab.

علامتا الجزم

The Two Signs of the *Jazm*

قال : وَلِلْجَزْمِ عَلامَتَانِ : السُّكُونُ ، وَالْحَذْفُ .

He said: And for the state of *jazm*, there are two signs: (i) the *sukūn* and (ii) removal.

وأقول : يمكنك أن تحكم على الكلمة بأنها مجزومة إذا وَجَدْتَ فيها واحداً من أمرين ؛ الأول : السكون ، وهو العلامة الأصلية للجزم ، والثاني : الحذف ، وهو العلامة الفرعية ، ولكل واحد من هاتين العلامتين مواضع سنذكرها:

I say: It is possible for you to rule a word to be *majzūm* if you find in it one of two things. The first is the *sukūn*, and it is the root sign for the state of *jazm*. The second is removal (*ḥadhf*), and it is the subsidiary sign. Each of these signs have their specific positions that we will now mention.

موضع السكون

Instances of the *Sukūn*

قال : فَأَمَّا السُّكُونُ فَيَكُونُ عَلَامَةً لِلْجَزْمِ في الْفِعْلِ الْمُضَارِعِ الصحيح الآخر .

He said: As for the *sukūn*, then it is an indicator of the state of *jazm* in the *muḍāri'* verb which ends with a sound letter.

وأقول : للسكون موضع واحد يكون فيه علامةً على أن الكلمة مجزومةٌ ، وهذا الموضع هو الفعل المضارع الصحيح الآخر ، ومعنى كونه صحيح الآخر أن آخره ليس حرفا من حروف العلة الثلاثة التي هي الألف والواو والياءُ .

I say: There is one instance where the *sukūn* is a sign of a word being *majzūm*, and this instance is the *muḍāri'* verb which ends with a sound letter. The meaning of "which ends with a sound letter" is that it does not end with one of the three defective letters, i.e. (i) *al-alif*, (ii) *al-wāw* and (iii) *al-yā*.

ومثال الفعل المضارع الصحيح الآخر (يلْعبُ)، و(يَنْجَحُ)، و(يُسَافِرُ)، و(يَعِدُ) ، و(يَسْأَلُ) فإذا قلت (لَمْ يَلْعَبْ عَلِيٌّ) و(لَمْ يَنْجَحْ بَلِيدٌ) و(لَمْ يُسَافِرْ أَخُوكَ) و(لَمْ يَعِدْ إبراهيمُ خَالِداً) و(لَمْ يَسْأَلْ بكْرٌ الأُسْتاذ) .. فكلٌّ من هذِه الأفعال مجزومٌ ، لسبق حرف الجزم الذي هو (لم) عليه ، وعلامة جزمه السكون ، وكل واحدٍ من هذهِ الأفعال فعلٌ مضارع صحيح الآخر .

Examples of the *muḍāri'* verb ending with a sound letter are: "He plays", "he succeeds", "he travels", "he promises" and "he is asking". If it is said, "'Alī did not play", "A stupid person has not succeeded", "Your brother did not travel", "Ibrāhīm did not prepare Khālid" and, "Bakr did not question his teacher", each of the verbs in these statements is *majzūm*. The reason for them being *majzūm* is due to being preceded by a particle of *al-jazm* i.e. "did not", and the sign of them being *majzūm* is the *sukūn*. Each of these verbs is a *muḍāri'* verb which ends with a sound letter.

مواضع الحذف

Instances of Removal

قال : وأمَّا الْحذفُ فيَكُونُ عَلامَةً للجَزمِ في الْفِعْل الْمُضَارِع الْمُعْتل الآخِر ، وَفي الأفْعَالِ الْخَمْسةِ التي رفْعُهَا بثبَاتِ النُّونِ .

He said: As for removal, then it is an indicator of the state of *jazm* when the last letter in a *muḍāriʿ* verb is defective and it is also an indicator of the state of *jazm* in the five verbs when the sign of the state of *rafʿ* is the fixedness of the letter *nūn*.

وأقول : للحذف موضعان يكون في كل واحدٍ منهما دليلاً وعلامة على جَزْمِ الكلمة .

I say: There are two instances where removal is an indication of a word being *majzūm*.

الموضع الأول : الفعل المضارع المعتلُّ الآخِرِ ، ومعنى كونه مُعْتَلَّ الآخر أنَّ آخره حرف من حروف العلة الثلاثة التي هي الألف والواو والياء ؛ فمثال الفعل المضارع الذي آخره ألف : (يَسْعَى) ، وَ(يَرْضَى) ، وَ(يهْوَى) ، وَ(يَنْأَى) ، و(يشقى) ، و(يبْقى) .

The first instance: The *muḍāriʿ* verb that ends with a defective letter. The meaning of this is that the word ends with a letter from the three defective letters. These are: (i) *al-alif*, (ii) *al-wāw* and (iii) *al-yā*. Examples of *muḍāriʿ* verbs that end with the letter *alif* are: "he pursues", "he is pleased", "he likes", "he is at a distance", "he suffers" and "he remains".

ومثال الفعل المضارع الذي آخره واو: (يَدْعُو) ، وَ(يرْجُو) ، وَ(يبْلُو) ، وَ(يَسْمُو) ، وَ(يَقْسُو) ، وَ(ينبُو) .

Examples of *muḍāriʿ* verbs that end with the letter *wāw* are: "he calls", "he hopes", "he tests", "he names", "he stiffens" and "he appoints."

ومثالُ الفعل المضارع الذي آخره ياءٌ: (يُعْطِي) ، و(يَقْضِي) ، وَ(يَسْتَغْشِي) ، و(يُحْيي) ، وَ(يَلْوِي) ، وَ(يَهْدِي) .

Examples of *muḍāriʿ* verbs that end with the letter *yā* are: "he gives", "he judges", "to cover", "he gives life", "he contorts", and "he guides".

فإذا قلت : (لم يسْع عليٌّ إلى المجد) فإن (يسع) مجزوم ؛ لسبق حرف الجزم عليه ، وعلامة جزمه حذفُ الألف ، والفتحةُ قبلها دليل عليها ، وهو فعل مضارع معتل الآخر ، وإذا قلت : (لَمْ يدْعُ مُحمَّدٌ إلا إلى الحق) فإن (يَدْع) فعل مضارع مجزومٌ ؛ لسبق حرف الجزم عليه ، وعلامة جزمه حذف الواو ، والضمة قبلها دليل عليها ، وإذا قلت : (لَمْ يُعْطِ مُحمَّدٌ إلا خالداً) فإن (يُعْطِ) فعلٌ مضارع مجزوم لسبق حرف الجزم عليه ، وعلامة جزمه حذف الياء والكسرة قبلها دليل عليها ، وقِسْ على ذلك أخواتها .

If it is said, "ʿAlī did not pursue towards glory", the word "pursue" is *majzūm* due to it being preceded by a particle of *al-jazm*. The sign of it being *majzūm* is the removal of the letter *alif* and the *fatḥah* before it is an evidence to it. It is a *muḍāriʿ* verb with a defective ending. If it is said, "Muḥammad did not call except to the truth", the word "call" is a *majzūm muḍāriʿ* verb due it being preceded by a particle of *al-jazm*. The sign of it being *majzūm* is the removal of the letter *wāw*, and the *ḍammah* before it is an evidence to it. If it is said, "Muḥammad did not give except to Khālid," the word "give" is a *majzūm muḍāriʿ* verb due to it being preceded by a particle of *al-jazm*. The sign of it being *majzūm* is the removal of the letter *yā*, and the *kasrah* before it is an evidence of this. [This is the rule,] based on them apply the rule to everything which is similar to them.

الموضع الثاني : الأفعال الخمسة التي ترفع بثبوت النون ، وقد سبق بيانُها ، ومثالها (يضربان)، و(تضربان) ، و(يضربون) ، و(تضربون) ، و(تضربين) تقول (لَمْ يَضْرِبَا

) ، وَ(لمْ تَضْرِبَا) ، وَ(لَمْ يَضْرِبُوا) ، وَ(لَمْ تَضْرِبُوا) ، و(لمْ تَضْرِبِي) فكل واحد من هذه الأفعال فعل مضارعٌ مجزوم ؛ لسبق حرف الجزم الذي هو (لم) عليه ، وعلامة جزمه حذف النون ، والألف أو الواو أو الياء فاعل ، مبني على السكون في محل رفع .

The second instance: The five verbs that enter the state of *rafʿ* through the fixedness of the letter *nūn*, and we have explained this earlier. Examples are: "them two hit", "them/you two hit", "they hit", "you hit" and "you (fem.) hit." If it is said, "them two did not hit", "them/you two did not hit", "they did not hit", "you did not hit", "you (fem.) did not hit," each of these verbs is a *majzūm muḍāriʿ* verb due to them being preceded by a particle of *al-jazm* i.e. "did not". The sign of them being *majzūm* is the removal of the letter *nūn*, and the letter *alif*, *wāw* and *yā* are the subjects (*fāʿil*), non-inflectable upon a *sukūn* in the state of *rafʿ*.

تمرينات

Exercises

١- استعمل كل فعل من الأفعال الآتية في ثلاث جمل مفيدة ، بحيث يكون في واحدة منها مرفوعاً ، وفي الثانية منصوباً ، وفي الثالثة مجزوماً ، واضْبِطْهُ بالشكل التام في كل جملة :

One. Utilise each of the following verbs in three beneficial sentences. In the first of them they should be *marfūʿ*, in the second *manṣūb* and in the third *majzūm*. Express the complete diacritics upon them.

يَضْرِبُ ، تَنْصُرَانِ ، تُسَافِرِينَ ، يَدْنُو ، تَرْبَحُون ، يَشْتَرِي ، يَبْقَى ، يَسْبِقَانِ.

٢- ضع في المكان الخالي من الجمل الآتية فعلاً مضارعاً مناسباً ، ثم بيّن علامَة إعرابه :

Two. Place in the empty spaces below the appropriate *muḍāriʿ* verb and then identify the sign of their declension.

(أ) الكسول ... إلى نفسه ووطنه .

(ب) لَنْ ... المَجْد إلا بالعمل والمثابرة.

(ج) الصديق المخلص ... لفرح صديقه.

(د) الفتاتان المجتهدتان ... أباهُما .

(ه) الطلاب المجدُّون ... وطنهم .

(و) أنتم يا أصدقائي ... بزيارتكم.

(ز) من عَمِلَ الخِيْرَ فإنُّهُ ...

(ح) إذا أساءك بعض إخوانك فلا ...

(ط) يَسُرُّني أن ... إخْوَتَكَ.

(ي) إن أديت وَاجبَكَ ...

(ك) لم ... أبي أمس .

(ل) أنْتِ يا زينب ... واجبك .

(م) إذا زُرْتُمُوني ...

(ن) مَهْمَا أَخْفَيْتُمْ ...

أسئلة

Questions

ما هي علامات الجزم ؟

What are the signs of the state of *jazm*?

في كم موضع يكون السكون علامة للجزم ؟

In how many instances is the *sukūn* a sign of the state of *jazm*?

في كم موضع يكون الحذفُ علامة على الجزم ؟

In how many instances is the removal a sign of the state of *jazm*?

ما هو الفعل الصحيح الآخر؟

What is a verb with a sound ending?

مَثِّل للفعل الصحيح الآخرة بعشرة أمثلة ،

Provide ten examples of the verb with a sound ending.

ما هو الفعل المعتل الآخر ؟

What is a verb with a defective ending?

مَثِّل للفعل المعتل الذي آخره ألف بخمسة أمثلة، وكذلك الفعل الذي آخره واو .

Provide five examples of the verb with a defective ending with the letter *alif*, and likewise for the one ending with the letter *wāw*.

مثِّل للفعل الذي آخره ياءُ بمثالَيْنِ .

Provide two examples of the verb with a defective ending with the letter *yā*.

ما هي الأفعال الخمسة ؟

What are the five verbs?

بماذا تجزم الأفعال الخمسة ؟

How do the five verbs enter the state of *jazm*?

مثِّل للأفعال الخمسة المجزومة بخمسة أمثلة .

Provide five examples of the five verbs in the state of *jazm*.

المعربات

Inflectable [Words]

قال: (فصل) المعربات قِسمان: قسم يعرب بالحركات ، وقسم يعرب بالحروف .

He said: Section: The inflectable words are divided into two groups. One group inflects through diacritics while the other group inflects through letters.

وأقول: أراد المؤلف ـ رحمه الله تعالى ـ بهذا الفصل أن يبين على وجه الإجمال حكم ما سبق تفصيله في مواضع الإعراب.

I say: The intention of the author (may Allāh have mercy upon him) with this section is to explain in summary what we have previously explained in detail regarding the positions of inflection.

والمواضع التي سبق ذكر أحكامها في الإعراب تفصيلاً ثمانية، وهي: الاسم المفرد، وجمع التكسير، وجمع المؤنث السالم، والفعل المضارع الذي لم يتصل بآخره شيء، والمثنى، وجمع المذكر السالم، والأسماء الخمسة، والفعال الخمسة.

The positions that we have preceded in detailed explanation upon their rulings in inflection are eight, they are: (i) the singular noun, (ii) the broken plural, (iii) the sound feminine plural, (iv) the *muḍāriʿ* verb that has nothing connected to its end, (v) the dual form, (vi) the sound masculine plural, (vii) the five nouns and (viii) the five verbs.

وهذه الأنواع التي هي مواضع الإعراب ـ تنقسم إلى قسمين: القسم الأول يعرب بالحركات، والقسم الثاني يعرب بالحروف، وسيأتي بيان كل نوع منها تفصيلاً .

These types—i.e. these positions of inflection—are categorised into two: The first of them inflects through diacritics, and the second of them inflects through letters. We will now provide explanation of both of them in detail.

المعرب بالحركات

Inflectable Through Diacritics

قال: فالذي يعرب بالحركات أربعة أشياء: الاسم المفرد، وجمع التكسير، وجمع المؤنث السالم، والفعل المضارع الذي لم يتصل بآخره شيء .

He said: So the group which is identified by way of diacritics contains four types of nouns: (i) The singular noun, (ii) the broken plural, (iii) the sound feminine plural, and (iv) the *muḍāriʿ* verb which has nothing connected to its end.

وأقول: الحركات ثلاثة، وهي: الضمة والفتحة والكسرة، ويلحق بها السكون، وقد علمت أن المعربات على قسمين: قسم يعرب بالحركات، وقسم يعرب بالحروف .

I say: The diacritics are three: (i) *al-ḍammah*, (ii) *al-fatḥah*, (iii) *al-kasrah* and grouped with them is (iv) *al-sukūn*. You should know that the inflectable are of two types, (i) the type that inflects with diacritics and (ii) the type that inflects with letters.

وهذا شروع في بيان القسم الأول الذي يعرب بالحركات، وهو أربعة أشياء:

We commence at this juncture with detailing the first type i.e. the words that inflect with diacritics, and they are four things:

١ ـ الاسم المفرد، ومثاله (محمد) و(الدرس) من قولك: (ذاكرَ محمدٌ الدرسَ) فـ(ذاكر): فعل ماض مبني على الفتح لا محل له من الإعراب، و(محمد): فاعل مرفوع، وعلامة رفعه الضمة الظاهرة، و(الدرس): مفعول به منصوب، وعلامة نصبه الفتحة الظاهرة، وكلُ من (محمد) و(الدرس) اسم مفرد .

First: The singular noun, examples are "Muḥammad" and "the lesson" in the sentence, "Muḥammad revised the lesson." The word "revised" is a *māḍī* verb that is non-inflectable upon a *fatḥah* without a grammatical state. "Muḥammad" is the subject and is *marfuʿ*, and the sign of it being *marfuʿ* is the explicit *ḍammah*. "The lesson" is the object and it is *manṣūb*, and the sign of it being *manṣūb* is the explicit *fatḥah*. Both "Muḥammad" and "the lesson" are singular nouns.

٢ ـ جمع التكسير، ومثاله (التلاميذ) و(الدروس) من قولك: (حفظ التلاميذ الدروس) فـ(حفظ): فعل ماض مبني على الفتح لا محل له من الإعراب، و(التلاميذ) : فاعل مرفوع وعلامة رفعه الضمة الظاهرة، و(الدروس) : مفعول به منصوب، وعلامة نصبه الفتحة الظاهرة، وكل من (التلاميذ) ، و(الدروس) جمع تكسير.

Second: The broken plural, examples are the words "the students" and "the lessons" in the sentence, "The students memorised the lessons". The word "memorised" is a *māḍī* verb which is non-inflectable upon a *fatḥah* without a grammatical state. The word "the student" is the subject and it is *marfūʿ*, the sign of it being *marfūʿ* is the explicit *ḍammah*. The word "the lessons" is the object and it is *manṣūb*, the sign of it being *manṣūb* is the explicit *fatḥah*. Both of the words "the students" and "the lessons" are broken plurals.

٣ ـ جمعُ المؤنثِ السالمُ، ومثاله (المؤمنات)، و(الصلوات) من قولك: (خشعت المؤمنات في الصلوات) فـ(خشع) : فعل ماض مبني على الفتح لا محل له من الإعراب ، و(المؤمنات): فاعل مرفوع وعلامة رفعه الضمة الظاهرة ، و(في) حرف جر، و(الصلوات): مجرور بـ(في)، وعلامة جره الكسرة الظاهرة ، وكل من (المؤمنات)، و(الصلوات) جمع مؤنث سالم .

Third: The sound feminine plural, examples are the words "the female faithful believers" and "the prayers" in the sentence, "The female faithful believers humbled themselves in prayers." The word "humbled" is a *māḍi* verb which is non-inflectable upon a *fatḥah* without a grammatical state. The word "the female faithful believers" is the subject and it is *marfuʿ*, the sign of it being *marfu'* is the explicit *ḍammah*. The word "in" is a particle of *al-khafḍ*. The word "prayers" is *majrūr* due to the word "in" (*fī*), and the sign of it being *marfu'* is the explicit *kasrah*. Both of the words "the female faithful believers" and "prayers" are sound feminine plurals.

٤ ـ الفعل المضارع الذي لم يتصل بآخره شيء، ومثاله (يذهب) من قولك: (يذهب محمد) فـ(يذهب) : فعل مضارع مرفوع لتجرده من الناصب والجازم، وعلامة رفعه الضمة الظاهرة، و(محمد) فاعل مرفوع وعلامة رفعه الضمة الظاهرة .

Fourth: The *muḍāri'* verb that has nothing connected to its end, an example is the word "he goes" in the sentence, "Muḥammad goes." The word "he goes" is a *muḍāri'* verb and it is *marfū'* due to the absence of a *nāṣīb* (a governor that causes a word to become *manṣūb*) and a *jāzim* (a governor that causes a word to become *majzūm*), the sign of it being *marfū'* is the explicit *ḍammah*. The word "Muḥammad" is the subject, and the sign of it being *marfū'* is the explicit *ḍammah*.

الأصل في إعراب ما يعرب بالحركات، وما خرج عنه

The Root Signs of Inflection for That Which Inflects with Diacritics, and Its Exceptions

قال: وكلها ترفع بالضمة، وتنصب بالفتحة، وتخفض بالكسرة وتجزم بالسكون، وخرج عن ذلك ثلاثة أشياء: جمع المؤنثِ السالم ينصب بالكسرة، والاسم الذي لا ينصرف يخفض بالفتحة، والفعل المضارع المعتل الآخر يجزم بحذف آخره .

He said: In all of the previously mentioned nouns the state of *rafʿ* is indicated by the *ḍammah*, the state of *naṣb* is indicated by the *fatḥah*, the state of *khafḍ* is indicated by the *kasrah*, and the state of *jazm* is indicated by the *sukūn*. The only exceptions to this are three: (i) The sound feminine plural in which the state of *naṣb* is indicated by the *kasrah*, (ii) the state of *khafḍ* in diptote nouns is indicated by the *fatḥah*, (iii) the *muḍāriʿ* verb which ends with a defective letter enters the state of *jazm* with the removal of its last letter.

وأقول: الأصل في الأشياء الأربعة التي تعرب بالحركات: أن ترفع بالضمة وتنصب بالفتحة، وتخفض بالكسرة، وتجزم بالسكون .

I say: The root principle in the four things that take inflection with diacritics is: *marfūʿ* with the *ḍammah*, *manṣūb* with the *fatḥah*, *makhfūḍ* with the *kasrah* and *majzūm* with the *sukūn*.

١ ـ أما الرفع بالضمة فإنها كلها قد جاءت على ما هو الأصل فيها، فرفعُ جميعها بالضمة، ومثالها: (يسافر محمد والأصدقاء والمؤمنات). فـ(يسافر): فعل مضارع مرفوع لتجرده من الناصب والجازم، وعلامة رفعه الضمة الظاهرة، و(محمد): فاعل

مرفوع، وعلامة رفعه الضمة الظاهرة، وهو اسم مفرد، و(الأصدقاء): مرفوع لأنه معطوف على المرفوع، وعلامة رفعه الضمة الظاهرة، وهو جمع تكسير، و(المؤمنات): مرفوع، لأنه أيضا معطوف على المرفوع، وعلامة رفعه الضمة الظاهرة، وهو جمع مؤنث سالم .

First: As for the state of *rafʿ* with the *ḍammah*, it applies to everything that takes to the root principle, so they all become *marfūʿ* with the *ḍammah*. An example is in the sentence, "Muḥammad, the friends and the faithful female believers travel." The word "travel" is a *muḍāriʿ* verb and it is *marfūʿ* due to the absence of a *nāṣib* and a *jāzim*, the sign of it being *marfūʿ* is the explicit *ḍammah*. The word "Muḥammad" is the subject and *marfūʿ*, the sign of it being *marfūʿ* is the explicit *ḍammah* and it is a singular noun. The word "the friends" is *marfūʿ* due to it being conjoined to a *marfūʿ* word, the sign of it being *marfūʿ* is the explicit *ḍammah* and it is a broken plural. The word "faithful female believers" is *marfūʿ* due to it also being conjoined to a *marfūʿ* word, the sign of it being *marfūʿ* is the explicit *ḍammah*, and it is a sound feminine plural.

٢ ـ وأما النصب بالفتحة فإنها كلها جاءت على ما هو الأصل فيها، ما عدا جمع المؤنث السالم، فإنه ينصب بالكسرة نيابة عن الفتحة، ومثالها (لن أخالف محمداً والأصدقاء والمؤمنات). فـ(أخالف) : فعل مضارع منصوب بـ(لن) ، وعلامة نصبه الفتحة الظاهرة، و(محمداً) مفعول به منصوب وعلامة نصبه الفتحة الظاهرة أيضاً، وهو اسم مفرد كما علمت، و(الأصدقاء): منصوب لأنه معطوف على المنصوب وعلامة نصبه الفتحة الظاهرة أيضاً، وهو جمع تكسير كما علمت، و(المؤمنات) منصوب، لأنه معطوف على المنصوب أيضاً، وعلامة نصبه الكسرة نيابة عن الفتحة، لأنه جمع مؤنث سالم .

Second: As for the state of *al-naṣb* with the *fatḥah*, it applies to everything that takes to the root principle. An exception to this is the sound feminine plural, as it becomes *manṣūb* with the *kasrah* as a representative for the *fatḥah*. An example of this is in the sentence, "I will not differ with Muḥammad, the friends and the faithful female believers." The word "I differ" is a *muḍāriʿ*

verb made *manṣūb* due to being preceded by "never", and the sign of it being *mansūb* is the explicit *fatḥah*. The word "Muḥammad" is the object and it is *manṣūb*, the sign of it being *manṣūb* is likewise the explicit *fatḥah* and it is a singular noun as we have stated previously. The word "the friends" is *mansūb* due to it being conjoined to a *manṣūb* word and the sign of it being *manṣūb* is also the explicit *fatḥah*, it is a broken plural as we have mentioned previously. The word "the faithful female believers" is *manṣūb* due to also being conjoined to a *manṣūb* word, the sign of it being *manṣūb* is the *kasrah* serving in place of the *fatḥah* due to it being a sound feminine plural.

٣ ـ وأما الخفض بالكسرة فإنها كلها قد جاءت على ما هو الأصل فيها، ما عدا الفعل المضارع، فإنه لا يخفض أصلاً، وما عدا الاسم الذي لا ينصرف، فإنه يخفض بالفتحة نيابة عن الكسرة، ومثالها: (مررت بمحمد، الرجال، المؤمنات، واحمد)، فـ(مررت): فعل وفاعل، والباء حرف خفض، و(محمد): مخفوض بالباء، وعلامة خفضه الكسرة الظاهرة، وهو اسم مفرد منصرف كما عرفت، و(الرجال): مخفوض، لأنه معطوف على المخفوض، وعلامة خفضه الكسرة الظاهرة، وهو جمع تكسير منصرف كما عرفت أيضاً، و(المؤمنات): مخفوض، لأنه معطوف على المخفوض أيضاً، وعلامة خفضه الكسرة الظاهرة وهو جمع مؤنث سالم كما عرفت أيضاً، و(أحمد): مخفوض لأنه معطوف على المخفوض أيضاً، وعلامة خفضه الفتحة نيابة عن الكسرة، لأنه اسم لا ينصرف، والمانع له من الصرف العلمية ووزن الفعل.

Third: As for the state of *al-khafḍ* with the *kasrah*, it applies to everything that takes to the root principle. An exception to this is the *muḍāriʿ* verb as it does not become *makhfūḍ* at all (due to being a verb). Another exception is the diptote noun as it becomes *makhfūḍ* with the *fatḥah* which serves as a representative of the *kasrah*. An example of this is in the sentence, "I passed by Muḥammad, the men, the female faithful believers and Aḥmad." "I passed by" is a verb and includes the subject. The letter *bā* is a particle of *khafḍ*. The word "Muḥammad" is made *makhfūḍ* by the letter *bā* and the sign of it being *makhfūḍ* is the explicit *kasrah*, it is a triptote singular noun as we have mentioned previously. The word "the men" is *makhfūḍ* due to it being conjoined to a *makhfūd* word and the sign of it being so is the explicit *kasrah*, it is a triptote broken plural as we have mentioned previously. The word "the female faithful believers" is *makhfūḍ* due to it also being conjoined to a *makhfūḍ* word and the sign of it being *makhfūḍ* is the explicit *kasrah*, it is a sound feminine plural as we have mentioned previously. The word "Aḥmad" is *makhfūḍ* due to it also being conjoined to a *makhfūḍ* word and the sign of it being *makhfūḍ* is the *fatḥah* serving as a representative for the *kasrah* due to it being a diptote noun—prevented from taking inflection due to being a proper noun and on the word structure of the verb.

٤ ـ وأما الجزم بالسكون فأنت تعلم أن الجزم مختص بالفعل المضارع، فإن كان صحيح الآخر فإن جزمه بالسكون كما هو الأصل في الجزم، ومثاله: (لم يسافر خالد) فـ(لم) : حرف نفي وجزم وقلب، و(يسافر) : فعل مضارع مجزوم بـ(لم) ، وعلامة جزمه السكون، و(خالد) : فاعل مرفوع، وعلامة رفعه الضمة الظاهرة.

Fourth: As for the state of *al-jazm* with the *sukūn*, the reader should know that the state of *jazm* is specific to the *muḍāriʿ* verb. If its ending is with a sound letter, in this case it would be made *majzūm* by the *sukūn*, which is the root indicator of the state of *jazm*. An example of this is in the sentence, "Khālid did not travel". The word "did not" is a particle of negation and brings about the state of *jazm* and alteration (i.e. alteration in the tense, from the present tense to the past tense). The word "he travels" is a *muḍāriʿ* verb which is *majzūm* due to "did not", and the sign of it being *majzūm* is the *sukūn*. Khālid is *marfūʿ* and the subject, the sign of it being *marfūʿ* is the explicit *ḍammah*.

وإن كان الفعل المضارع معتل الآخر كان جزمه بحذف حرف العلة، ومثاله: (لم يسعَ بكر ، ولم يدعُ ، ولم يقض) فكل من (يسع) و(يدع)، و(يقض) فعل مضارع مجزوم بـ(لم)، وعلامة جزمه حذف الألف من (يسع)، والفتحة قبلها دليل عليها، وحذف الواو من (يدع)، والضمة قبلها، وحذف الياء من (يقض)، والكسرة قبلها دليل علها.

As for the *muḍāriʿ* verb that ends with a defective letter, it becomes *majzūm* through the removal of the defective letter. Examples are, "Bakr did not strive, he did not call nor did he carry out". Each of the words "strive", "call" and "carry out" are *muḍāriʿ* verbs made *majzūm* by "did not". The sign of them being *majzūm* is the removal of the letter *alif* from "he strives"—the *fatḥah* before it is a proof of this, the removal of the letter *wāw* from "he calls"—the *ḍammah* before it is a proof of this, and the removal of the letter *yā* from "he carries out"—the *kasrah* before it is a proof of this.

المعربات بالحروف

Inflectable Through Letters

قال: والذي يعرب بالحروف أربعة أنواع: التثنية، وجمع المذكر السالم، والأسماء الخمسة، والأفعال الخمسة، وهي: (يفعلان) ، و(تفعلان) ، و(يفعلون) ، و(تفعلون) ، و(تفعلين).

He said: And the group of words which inflect with letters are of four types: (i) the dual form, (ii) the sound masculine plural, (iii) the five nouns and (iv) the five verbs, they are: they both do, they (fem) both do, they (pl.) do, you do and you (fem) do.

وأقول: القسم الثاني من المعربات: الأشياء التي تعرب بالحروف، والحروف التي تكون علامة الإعراب أربعة، وهي: الألف والواو والياء، والنون، والذي يعرب بهذه الحروف أربعة أشياء:

I say: The second type of inflected word is that which inflects through letters. The letters that are utilised as indicators of inflection are four: (i) *al-alif*, (ii) *al-wāw*, (iii) *al-yā* and (iv) *al-nūn*. Four things inflect with these letters:

١ - التثنية، والمراد بها المثنى، ومثاله : (المصران) ، و(المحمدان) ، و(البكران) ، و(الرجلان) .

One. *Al-tathniyah*, and this means the dual form. Examples are, "the two regions", "the two Muḥammads", "the two Bakrs" and "the two men".

٢ - جمع المذكر السالم، ومثاله : (المسلمون) ، و(البكرون) ، و(المحمدون) .

Two. The sound masculine plural. Examples are, "the Muslims", "the Bakrs" and "the Muḥammads".

٣ ـ الأسماء الخمسة وهي : أبوك، وأخوك، وحموك، وفوك، وذو مال .

Three. The five nouns i.e. "your father", "your brother", "your father in law", "your mouth" and "possessor of wealth".

٤ ـ الأفعال الخمسة ومثالها : (يضربان) ، و(تكتبان) ، و(يفهمون) ، و(تحفظون) ، و(تسهرين).

Four. The five verbs i.e. the third person dual masculine form, the second person dual form, the third person plural masculine form, the second person plural masculine form and the second person singular feminine form.

وسيأتي بيان إعراب كل واحد من هذه الأشياء الأربعة تفصيلاً

We will discuss the inflection of these four matters in detail below.

إعراب المثنى

The Inflection of the Dual Form

قال: فأما التثنية فترفع بالألف، وتنصب وتخفض بالياء .

He said: As for the dual form, then the state of *rafʿ* is indicated by the letter *alif*, the states of *naṣb* and *khafḍ* are indicated by the letter *yā*.

وأقول: الأول من الأشياء التي تعرب بالحروف (التثنية) ، وهي: المثنى كما علمت، وقد عرفت فيما سبق تعريف المثنى.

I say: The first of the four things that inflect with the letters is *al-tathniyah* i.e. the dual form, as we mentioned above. You should already know the definition of the dual form from what has preceded.

وحكمه: أن يرفع بالألف نيابة عن الضمة، وينصب ويخفض بالياء المفتوح ما قبلها المكسور ما بعدها نيابة عن الفتحة أو الكسرة، ويوصل به بعد الألف أو الياء نون تكون عوضاً عن التنوين الذي يكون في الاسم المفرد، ولا تحذف هذه النون إلا عند الإضافة.

The rulings related to it: It becomes *marfūʿ* with the letter *alif* serving in place of the *ḍammah*. It becomes *manṣūb* and *makhfūḍ* with the letter *yā*, the letter before it has a *fatḥah* and that which comes after it has a *kasrah*, and this serves in place of the *fatḥah* or the *kasrah*. A letter *nūn* is connected to the end of the letter *alif* or *yā* and this serves as a compensatory mechanism for the *tanwīn* that is found in the singular noun. This *nūn* is not removed except in the possessive compound.

فمثال المثنى المرفوع (حضر القاضيان) ، و(قال رجلان) فكل من (القاضيان) ، و(رجلان) مرفوع لأنه فاعل، وعلامة رفعه الألف نيابة عن الضمة، لأنه مثنى، النون

عوض عن التنوين في الاسم المفرد .

Examples of the *marfūʿ* dual form are, "the two judges were present" and "two men said". Both of the words "the two judges" and "two men" are *marfūʿ* due to them being subjects. The sign of them being *marfūʿ* is the *alif* serving as a representative for the *ḍammah* due to them being in the dual form. And the letter *nūn* serves as a compensatory mechanism for the *tanwīn* that is found in the singular noun.

ومثال المثنى المنصوب (أحب المؤدبين) و(أكره المتكاسلين) فكل من (المؤدبين) ، و(المتكاسلين) منصوب، لأنه مفعول به، وعلامة نصبه الياء المفتوح ما قبلها المكسور ما بعدها نيابة عن الفتحة، لأنه مثنى، والنون عوض عن التنوين في الاسم المفرد .

Examples of the *manṣūb* dual form are, "I love the two well mannered ones" and "I dislike the two lazy ones." Both of the words the "two well mannered ones" and "the two lazy ones" are *manṣūb* due to being objects. The sign of them being *manṣūb* is the letter *yā*, preceded by a letter with a *fatḥah* and followed by a letter with a *kasrah*, serving as a representative for the *fatḥah* due to them being dual forms. The letter *nūn* at the end is a compensatory mechanism for the *tanwīn* found in the singular noun.

ومثال المثنى المخفوض (نظرت إلى الفارسين على الفرسين) فكل من (الفارسين) و(الفرسين) مخفوض، لدخول حرف الخفض عليه، وعلامة خفضه الياء المفتوح ما قبلها المكسور ما بعدها نيابة عن الكسرة، لأنه مثنى، والنون عوض عن التنوين في الاسم المفرد .

An example of the *makhfūḍ* dual form is, "I looked at the two riders upon the two horses." Both of the words "the two riders" and "the two horses" are *makhfūḍ* due to being preceded by a particle of *al-khafḍ*. The sign of them being *makhfūḍ* is the letter *yā*, preceded by a letter with a *fatḥah* and followed by a letter with *kasrah*, serving as a representative for the *kasrah* due to them being dual forms. The letter *nūn* at the end is a compensatory mechanism for the *tanwīn* found in the singular noun.

إعراب جمع المذكر السالم

The Inflection of the Sound Masculine Plural

قال: وأما جمع المذكر السالم فيرفع بالواو، وينصب ويخفض بالياء .

He said: As for the sound masculine plural, then the state of *raf*ʿ is indicated by the letter *wāw*, and both the conditions of *naṣb* and *khafḍ* are indicated by the letter *yā*.

وأقول: الثاني من الأشياء التي تعرب بالحروف جمع المذكر السالم وقد عرفت فيما سبق تعريف جمع المذكر السالم .

I say: The second of the four things that inflect with letters is the sound masculine plural. I have previously defined the sound masculine plural.

وحكمه: أن يرفع بالواو نيابة عن الضمة وينصب ويخفض بالياء، المكسور ما قبلها المفتوح ما بعدها نيابة عن الفتحة أو الكسرة، ويوصل به بعد الواو أو الياء نون تكون عوضاً عن التنوين في الاسم المفرد، وتحذف هذه النون عند الإضافة كنون المثنى.

The rulings related to it: It becomes *marfū*ʿ with the letter *wāw* serving as a representative for the *ḍammah*. It becomes *manṣūb* and *makhfūḍ* with the letter *yā* which is preceded by a letter with a *kasrah* and followed by a letter with a *fatḥah*, serving as a representative for the *fatḥah* or the *kasrah*. A letter *nūn* is connected to the end of the letter *wāw* or *yā* and this serves as a compensatory mechanism for the *tanwīn* that is found in the singular noun. This *nūn* is removed in the possessive compound, as mentioned in the dual form.

فمثال جمع المذكر السالم المرفوع (حضر المسلمون) و(أفلح الآمرون بالمعروف) فكل من (المسلمون) و(الآمرون) مرفوع لأنه فاعل وعلامة رفعه الواو نيابة عن الضمة:

لأنه جمع مذكر سالم، والنون عوض عن التنوين في الاسم المفرد.

Examples of the *marfūʿ* sound masculine plural are, "The Muslims were present" and "The enjoiners of good were successful". Each of the words "the Muslims" and "the enjoiners" is *marfūʿ* due to being the subjects of their verbs. The sign of them being *marfūʿ* is the letter *wāw* serving as a representative for the *ḍammah*, due to them being sound masculine plurals. A letter *nūn* is connected to the end of the letter *wāw* and this serves as a compensatory mechanism for the *tanwīn* that is found in the singular noun.

ومثال جمع المذكر السالم المنصوب (رأيت المسلمين)، و(احترمت الآمرين بالمعروف)، فكل من (المسلمين) و(الآمرين) منصوب، لأنه مفعول به، وعلامة نصبه الياء، المكسور ما قبلها المفتوح ما بعدها، لأنه جمع مذكر سالم، والنون عوض عن التنوين في الاسم المفرد.

Examples of the *manṣūb* sound masculine plural are, "I saw the Muslims" and "I respected the enjoiners of good." Each of the words "the Muslims" and "the enjoiners" are *manṣūb* due to being the objects of their verbs. The sign of them being *manṣūb* is the letter *yā*—preceded by a letter with a *kasrah* and followed by a letter with a *fatḥah*, due to them being sound masculine plurals. A letter *nūn* is connected to the end of the letter *yā* and this serves as a compensatory mechanism for the *tanwīn* that is found in the singular noun.

ومثال جمع المذكر السالم المخفوض: (اتصلت بالآمرين بالمعروف) و(رضي الله عن المؤمنين) فكل من (الآمرين)، و(المؤمنين) مخفوض، لدخول حرف الخفض عليه، وعلامة خفضه الياء المكسور ما قبلها المفتوح ما بعدها، لأنه جمع مذكر سالم، والنون عوض عن التنوين في الاسم المفرد.

Examples of the *makhfūḍ* sound masculine plural are, "I attached myself to the enjoiners of good" and "And Allah is pleased with the faithful believers". Each of the words "the enjoiners" and "the faithful believers" are *makhfūḍ* due to being preceded by a particle of *al-khafḍ*. The sign of them being *makhfūḍ* is the letter *yā*—preceded by a letter with a *kasrah* and followed by a letter with a *fatḥah* due to them being sound masculine plurals. A letter *nūn* is connected to the end of the letter *yā* and this serves as a compensatory mechanism for the *tanwīn* that is found in the singular noun.

إعراب الأسماء الخمسة

The Inflection of the Five Nouns

قال: وأما الأسماء الخمسة فترفع بالواو، وتنصب بالألف، وتخفض بالياء .

He said: As for the five nouns, then the state of *rafʿ* with them is indicated with the letter *wāw* and the state of *naṣb* is indicated with the letter *alif*, and the state of *khafḍ* is indicated with the letter *yā*.

وأقول: الثالث من الأشياء التي تعرب بالحروف الأسماء الخمسة وقد سبق بيانها وبيان شروط إعرابها هذا الإعراب .

I say: The third of the four things that inflect with the letters is the five nouns which have been previously explained as well as the conditions for their inflections.

وحكمها: أن ترفع بالواو نيابة عن الضمة، وتنصب بالألف نيابة عن الفتحة وتخفض بالياء نيابة عن الكسرة.

The rulings related to them: They become *marfūʿ* with the letter *wāw* serving in place of the *ḍammah*. They become *manṣūb* with the letter *alif* serving in place of the *fatḥah*. They become *makhfūḍ* with the letter *yā* serving in place of the *kasrah*.

فمثال الأسماء الخمسة المرفوعة (إذا أمرك أبوكَ فأطعه) و(حضر أخوك من سفره)، فكل من (أبوك) و(أخوك) مرفوع، لأنه فاعل، وعلامة رفعه الواو نيابة عن الضمة، لأنه من الأسماء الخمسة، والكاف مضاف إليه، مبني على الفتح في محل خفض .

Examples of the five nouns being *marfūʿ* are, "If your father commands you [to do something] then obey him" and "Your brother arrived from his journey". Each of the words "your father" and "your brother" are *marfūʿ* due to being subjects. The sign of them being *marfūʿ* is the letter *wāw* serving as a representative for the *ḍammah*, and this is due to them being from the five nouns. The letter *kāf* (i.e. *abū<u>ka</u>*) is the *muḍāf ilayhi*, non-inflectable upon a *fatḥah* in the state of *khafḍ*.

ومثال الأسماء الخمسة المنصوبة (أطع أباك) ، و(أحبب أخاك) فكل من (أباك) و(أخاك) منصوب، لأنه مفعول به، وعلامة نصبه الألف نيابة عن الفتحة، لأنه من الأسماء الخمسة، والكاف مضاف إليه، مبني على الفتح في محل جر، كما سبق .

Examples of the five nouns being *manṣūb* are, "Obey your father" and "Love your brother". Each of the words "your father" and "your brother" are *manṣūb* due to being the objects. The sign of them being *manṣūb* is the letter *alif* serving as a representative for the *ḍammah*, and this is due to them being from the five nouns. The letter *kāf* (i.e. *abū<u>ka</u>*) is the *muḍāf ilayhi*, non-inflectable upon a *fatḥah* in the state of *jarr*, as we have explained previously.

ومثال الأسماء الخمسة المخفوضة (استمع إلى أبيك) ، و(أشفق على أخيك) فكل من (أبيك) و(أخيك) مخفوض، لدخول حرف الخفض عليه، وعلامة خفضه الياء نيابة عن الكسرة، لأنه من الأسماء الخمسة، والكاف مضاف إليه كما سبق .

Examples of the five nouns being *makhfūḍ* are, "Listen to your father" and "Have compassion for your brother". Each of the words "your father" and "your brother" are *makhfūḍ* due to being preceded by a particle of *al-khafḍ*. The sign of them being *makhfūḍ* is the letter *yā* serving as a representative for the *kasrah*, and this is due to them being from the five nouns. The letter *kāf* (i.e. *abū<u>ka</u>*) is the *muḍāf ilayhi*, non-inflectable upon a *fatḥah* in the state of *jarr*, as we have explained previously.

إعراب الأفعال الخمسة

The Inflection of the Five Verbs

قال: وأما الأفعال الخمسة فترفع بالنون، وتنصب وتجزم بحذفها .

He said: As for the five verbs, then the state of *rafʿ* with them is indicated by [the presence] of the letter *nūn*. Both the states of *naṣb* and *jazm* are indicated by the removal of the letter *nūn*.

وأقول: الرابع من الأشياء التي تعرب بالحروف الأفعال الخمسة وقد عرفت فيما سبق حقيقة الأفعال الخمسة.

I say: The final one of the four things that inflect with letters is the five verbs—I have previously defined the five verbs mentioned here.

وحكمها: أنها ترفع بثبوت النون نيابة عن الضمة، وتنصب وتجزم بحذف هذه النون نيابة عن الفتحة أو السكون.

The rulings related to them: They become *marfūʿ* with the presence of the letter *nūn* serving as a representative for the *ḍammah*. They become *manṣūb* and *majzūm* with the removal of the letter *nūn*, and this serves as a substitute for the *fatḥah* or the *sukūn*.

فمثال الأفعال الخمسة المرفوعة (تكتبان) و(تفهمان) فكل منهما فعل مضارع مرفوع، لتجرده من الناصب والجازم، وعلامة رفعه ثبوت النون، والألف ضمير الاثنين فاعل، مبني على السكون في محل رفع .

Examples of the five verbs being *marfūʿ* are, "You two write" and "You two understand". Both of them are *marfūʿ muḍāriʿ* verbs due to the absence of any *nāṣib* or *jāzim*, and the sign of them being so is the presence of the letter *nūn*.

The letter *alif* is a pronoun of duality and the subject, un-inflectable upon a *sukūn* in the state of *raf*ʿ.

ومثال الأفعال الخمسة المنصوبة (لن تحزنا) و(لن تفشلا) فكل منهما فعل مضارع منصوب بـ(لن)، وعلامة نصبه حذف النون، والألف ضمير الاثنين فاعل مبني على السكون في محل رفع .

Examples of the five verbs being *manṣūb* are, "You two will not grieve" and "You two will not fail". Both of them are *manṣūb muḍāri*ʿ verbs due to the word "*lan*", and the sign of them being so is the removal of the letter *nūn*. The letter *alif* is a pronoun of duality and the subject, un-inflectable upon a *sukūn* in the state of *raf*ʿ.

ومثال الأفعال الخمسة المجزومة (لم تذاكرا) و(لم تفهما) فكل منهما فعل مضارع مجزوم بـ(لم) ، وعلامة جزمه حذف النون، والألف ضمير الاثنين فاعل مبني على السكون في محل رفع .

Examples of the five verbs being *majzūm* are, "You two don't revise" and "You two don't understand". Both of them are *majzūm muḍāri*ʿ verbs due to the word "*lam*", and the sign of them being so is the removal of the letter *nūn*. The letter *alif* is a pronoun of duality and the subject, un-inflectable upon a *sukūn* in the state of *raf*ʿ.

تمرينات

Exercises

١ ـ ضع كل كلمة من الكلمات الآتية في جملة مفيدة، بحيث تكون منصوبة وبين علامة نصبها :

One. Place all of the following words into beneficial sentences where they are in the *manṣūb* state, and identify the sign of them being *manṣūb*.

الجو، الغبار، الطريق، الحبل، مشتعلة، القطن، المدرسة، الثوبان، المخلصون،

المسلمات، أبي، العلا، الراضي .

❁❁❁

٢ - ضع كل كلمة من الكلمات الآتية في جملة مفيدة، بحيث تكون مخفوضة، وبين علامة خفضها:

Two. Place all of the following words into beneficial sentences where they are in the state of *khafḍ*, and identify the sign of them being *makhfūḍ*:

أبوك، المهذبون، القائمات بواجبهن، المفترس، أحمد، مستديرة، الباب، النخلتان، الفأرتان، القاضي، الورى .

❁❁❁

٣ - ضع كل كلمة من الكلمات الآتية في جملة مفيدة، بحيث تكون مرفوعه، وبين علامة رفعها:

Three. Place all of the following words into beneficial sentences where they are in the state of *raf'*, and identify the sign of them being *marfū'*.

أبويه، المصلحين، المرشد، الغزاة، الآباء، الأمهات، الباني، ابني، أخيك .

❁❁❁

٤ - بين في العبارات الآتية المرفوع والمنصوب والمجزوم من الأفعال، والمرفوع والمنصوب والمخفوض من الأسماء، وبين مع كل واحد علامة إعرابه:

Four. In the following sentences, detail the *marfū'*, *manṣūb* and *majzūm* verbs, and detail the *marfū'*, *manṣūb* and *makhfūd* nouns. Also provide for each one the sign of its inflection:

استشار عمر بن عبد العزيز في قوم يستعملهم، فقال له أصحابه: عليك بأهل العذر، قال: ومن هم؟ قال: الذين إن عدلوا فهو ما رجوت، وإن قصروا قال الناس: قد اجتهد عمر.

أحضر الرشيد رجلاً ليوليه القضاء، فقال له: إني لا أحسن القضاء ولا أنا فقيه، فقال الرشيد: فيك ثلاث خلال: لك شرف والشرف يمنع صاحبه من الدناءة، ولك حلم يمنعك من العجلة، ومن لم يعجل قل خطؤه، وأنت رجل تشاور في أمرك، ومن شاور كثر صوابه، وأما الفقه فسينضم إليك من تتفقه به، فولي فما وجدوا فيه مطعناً.

٥ ـ ثن الكلمات الآتية، ثم استعمل كل مثنى في جملتين مفيدتين بحيث يكون في واحدة من الجملتين مرفوعاً، وفي الثانية مخفوضاً .

Five. Convert the below words into the dual form, then utilise these dual form words into two beneficial sentences where in the first of them the dual form word is *marfūʿ* and in the second of them it is *makhfūḍ*.

الدواة، الوالد، الحديقة، القلم، الكتاب، البلد، المعهد .

٦ ـ اجمع الكلمات الآتية جمع مذكر سالماً، واستعمل كل جمع في جملتين مفيدتين بشرط أن يكون مرفوعاً في إحداهما ومنصوباً في الأخرى:

Six. Convert the below words into the sound masculine plural, then utilise these plural form words in two beneficial sentences where in the first of them the plural is *marfūʿ* and in the second of them it is *manṣūb*.

الصالح، المذاكر، الكسل، المتقي، الراضي، محمد .

٧ - ضع كل فعل من الأفعال المضارعة الآتية في ثلاث جمل مفيدة، بشرط أن يكون مرفوعاً في إحداها، ومنصوباً في الثانية، ومجزوماً في الثالثة:

Seven. Place all of the following *muḍāriʿ* verbs into three beneficial sentences. In the first sentence they should be *marfūʿ*, in the second sentence they should be *manṣūb* and in the third sentence they should be *majzūm*.

يلعب، يؤدي واجبه، يسأمون، تحضرين، يرجوا الثواب، يسافران .

أسئلة

Questions

إلى كم قسم تنقسم المعربات؟

Into how many categories is inflection categorised into?

ما هي المعربات التي تعرب بالحركات؟

What are the inflected words that inflect by diacritics?

ما هي المعربات التي تعرب بالحروف؟

What are the inflected words that inflect by letters?

مَثِّل للاسم المفرد المنصرف في حالة الرفع والنصب والخفض، ومثل لجمع التكسير كذلك.

Provide an example of the inflectable singular noun in the *rafʿ*, *naṣb* and *khafḍ* states. Provide the same for the broken plural.

بماذا ينصب جمع المؤنث السالم ؟

With what does the sound feminine plural become *manṣūb* with?

مثل لجمع المؤنث السالم في حالة النصب والرفع والخفض.

Provide an example of the sound feminine plural in the *naṣb*, *rafʿ* and *khafḍ* states.

بماذا يخفض الاسم الذي لا ينصرف؟

With what does the non-inflectable noun become *makhfūḍ* with?

مثل للاسم الذي لا ينصرف في حالة الخفض والرفع والنصب.

Provide an example of the non-inflectable noun in the *khafḍ*, *rafʿ* and *naṣb* states.

بماذا يجزم الفعل المضارع المعتل الآخر؟

With what does the *muḍāriʿ* verb with a defective ending become *majzūm*?

مثل للمضارع المعتل الآخر في حالة الجزم.

Provide an example of the *muḍāriʿ* verb with a defective ending in the state of *jazm*.

ما هي المعربات التي تعرب بالحروف؟

What are the inflected words that inflect with letters?

وبماذا يرفع المثنى؟

With what does the dual form become *marfūʿ* with?

وبماذا ينصب ويخفض؟

With what does it become *manṣūb* and *makhfūḍ*?

بماذا يرفع جمع المذكر السالم؟

With what does the sound masculine plural become *marfūʿ* with?

وبماذا ينصب ويخفض؟

And with what does it become *manṣūb* and *makhfūḍ* with?

مثل للمثنى في حالة الرفع والنصب والخفض.

Provide examples of the dual form in the state of *rafʿ*, *naṣb* and *khafḍ*.

ومثل لجمع المذكر السالم كذلك.

Provide examples of the sound masculine plural in a similar manner.

بماذا تعرف الأسماء الخمسة في حالة الرفع والنصب؟ وبماذا تخفض؟

How do you identify that the five nouns are in the state of *rafʿ* and *naṣb*? And how so for when they are in the state of *khafḍ*?

مثل للأسماء الخمسة في حالة الرفع والنصب، ومثل للأفعال الخمسة في أحوالها الثلاثة.

Provide an example of the five nouns in the state of *rafʿ* and *naṣb*. Provide an example of the five verbs in each of their three grammatical states.

باب الأفعال

Chapter of the Verbs

قال: الأفعال ثلاثة: ماض، ومضارع، وأمر، نحو: (ضرب) و(يضرب) و(اضرب).

He said: The verb is of three types: (i) *māḍi*, (ii) *muḍāri'* and (iii) *'amr*. Examples are "he hit", "he hits" and "hit".

❁❁❁

الأفعال وأنواعها

The Verbs and Their Types

وأقول: ينقسم الفعل إلى ثلاثة أقسام:

I say: The verb is separated into three types:

القسم الأول: الماضي، وهو ما يدل على حصول شيء قبل زمن التكلم، نحو: (ضرب) و(نصر)، و(فتح)، و(علم)، و(حسب)، و(كرم) .

The first type: The *māḍī*, and it is that which indicates the attainment of something before the time of speaking. Examples are: "he hit", "he supported", "he opened", "he knew", "he calculated" and "he honoured".

القسم الثاني: المضارع، وهو ما دل على حصول شيء في زمن التكلم، أو بعده، نحو (يضرب)، و(ينصر)، و(يفتح)، و(يعلم)، و(يحْسب)، و(يكرم).

The second type: The *muḍāri'*, and it is that which indicates the actioning of something at the time of speaking or after it. Examples are: "he hits", "he supports", "he opens", "he knows", "he calculates" and "he honours".

القسم الثالث: الأمر، وهو ما يطلب به حصول شيء بعد زمن التكلم، نحو: (اضرب) ، و(انصر) ، و(افتح) ، و(اعلم)، و(احسب)، و(اكرم) .

The third type: The *'amr* (command verb), and it is the seeking of the actioning of something after the time of speaking. Examples are: "hit", "support", "open", "know", "calculate" and "honour".

وقد ذكرنا لك في أول الكتاب هذا التقسيم، وذكرنا لك معه علامات كل قسم من هذه الأقسام الثلاثة .

We have explained this categorisation to you during the beginning of the book, and we mentioned to you alongside it the signs of each of these three categories.

أحكام الفعل

Rulings of the Verb

قال: فالماضي مفتوح الآخر أبداً، والأمر مجزوم أبداً، والمضارع ما كان في أوله إحدى الزوائد الأربع التي يجمعها قولك (أنيت)، وهو مرفوع أبداً، حتى يدخل عليه ناصب أو جازم .

He said: The *māḍī* verb always ends with a *fatḥah* and the *ʾamr* is always *majzūm*. The *muḍāriʿ* is preceded by one of four extra letters which are gathered together in the word "*anaytu*" and it is always in the state of *rafʿ* until a *nāṣib* or a *jāzim* enters upon it and alters its grammatical state.

وأقول: بعد أن بين المصنف أنواع الأفعال شرع في بيان أحكام كل نوع منها .

I say: After the author explained the types of the verbs, he commenced with detailing the rulings related to each type.

فحكم الفعل الماضي البناء على الفتح، وهذا الفتح إما ظاهر، وإما مقدر.

The ruling of the *māḍī* verb is that it is built upon a *fatḥah*, and this *fatḥah* is sometimes explicit and sometimes implicit.

أما الفتح الظاهر ففي الصحيح الآخر الذي لم يتصل به واو الجماعة، ولا ضمير رفع متحرك وكذلك في كل ما كان أخره واواً أو ياءً، نحو: (أكرم) ، و(قدم) ، و(سافر)، ونحو: (سافرت زينب) ، و(حضرت سعاد) ، ونحو: (رضي)، و(شقي) ، ونحو: (سَرُوَ)، وَ(بَذُوَ) .

As for the *fatḥah* that is explicit, it is in the *māḍī* verb that has a sound ending which is not connected to the letter *wāw* of plurality, nor the *marfūʿ* pronoun that is inflectable, likewise it is in that which ends with the letters *wāw* and *yā*. Examples are: "he honoured", "he advanced", "he travelled", "Zaynab travelled", "Suʿād was present", "he was pleased", "he was wretched", "he was pleased" and "he was rude".

وأما الفتح المقدر فهو على ثلاثة أنواع، لأنه :

As for the implicit *fatḥah*, it is of three types:

إما أن يكون مقدراً للتعذر، وهذا في كل ما كان آخره ألفاً، نحو: (دعا) ، و(سعى) . فكل منهما فعل ماض مبني على فتح مقدر على الألف منع من ظهوره التعذر .

Sometimes it is implicit due to impracticability, and this is the case for each *māḍi* verb that ends with the letter *alif*. Examples are, "he called" and "he strove". Each of these is a *māḍi* verb un-inflectable upon an implicit *fatḥah* on the letter *alif*, prevented from being displayed due to impracticability.

وإما أن يكون الفتح مقدراً للمناسبة، وذلك في كل فعل ماض اتصل به واو الجماعة، نحو: (كتبوا) ، و(سعدوا). فكل منهما فعل ماض مبني على فتح مقدر على آخره منع من ظهوره اشتغال المحل بحركة المناسبة، وواو الجماعة مع كل منهما فاعل مبني على السكون في محل رفع .

Sometimes it is implicit due to appropriation, and this is the case for each *māḍi* verb that is connected to the letter *wāw* of plurality. Examples are, "they wrote" and "they were happy". Each of these is an un-inflectable *māḍi* verb built upon an implicit *fatḥah* on its end, prevented from being displayed due to its place being assumed by the appropriate diacritic. The letter *wāw* of plurality in each of them is the subject, un-inflectable upon a *sukūn* in the state of *rafʿ*.

وإما أن يكون الفتح مقدراً لدفع كراهة توالي أربع متحركات، وذلك في كل فعل ماض اتصل به ضمير رفع متحرك، كتاء الفاعل ونون النسوة، نحو: (كتبت) ، و(كتبت)

، و(كتبت) ، و(كتبنا) ، و(كتبن). فكل واحد من هذه الأفعال فعل ماض مبني على فتح مقدر على آخره منع من ظهوره اشتغال المحل بالسكون العارض لدفع كراهة توالي أربع متحركات فيما هو كالكلمة الواحدة، والتاء، أو (نا) أو النون: فاعل، مبني على الضم أو الفتح، أو الكسر، أو السكون في محل رفع .

Sometimes it is implicit to prevent the disliked presence of four successive diacritics. This is the case for each *māḍī* verb that has a *mutaḥarik*[78] *marfūʿ* pronoun connected to it, e.g. the letter *tā* which is a subject and the letter *nūn* of feminine plurality. Examples are, "I wrote", "you wrote", "you (fem.) wrote", "we wrote", "they (fem.) wrote". Each of these words is a *māḍi* verb un-inflectable upon an implicit *fatḥah* at the end, prevented from being displayed due to its place being assumed by a *sukūn* which serves to prevent the disliked meeting of four diacritics in what appears as one word. The Arabic pronouns *tā*, *nā* and *nūn* are the subjects, un-inflectable upon a *ḍammah*, *fatḥah*, *kasrah* or *sukūn* in the state of *rafʿ*.

وحكم فعل الأمر: البناء على ما يجزم به مضارعه .

The ruling of the *ʾamr* verb is that it is built upon what its *muḍāriʿ* form becomes *majzūm* with.

فإن كان مضارعه صحيح الآخر، ويجزم بالسكون، كان الأمر مبنياً على السكون، وهذا السكون إما ظاهر، وإما مقدر، فالسكون الظاهر له موضعان، أحدهما: أن يكون صحيح الآخر ولم يتصل به شيء، نحو: (اضْربْ)، و(اكْتُبْ) . والثاني: أن تتصل به نون النسوة نحو: (اضْرِبْنَ) و(اكْتُبْنَ) مع الإسناد إلى نون النسوة.

As for the *muḍāriʿ* verb with a sound ending, it becomes *majzūm* with a *sukūn*, and so the *ʾamr* is built upon the *sukūn*. This *sukūn* can either be explicit or implicit. The explicit *sukūn* has two instances, the first of them is the *muḍāriʿ* verb with a sound ending that is not connected to anything e.g. "hit" and "write". The second of them is when its end is connected to the *nūn* of

78 I.e. with diacritics.

feminine plurality e.g. “you (pl.) hit” and “you (pl.) write”.

وأما السكون المقدر، فله موضع واحد ؛ وهو : أن تتصل به نون التوكيد خفيفة ، أو ثقيلة ؛ نحو (اضربَنْ) و(اكتبَنْ) . ونحو : (اضربَنَّ) و(اكتبَنَّ).

As for the implicit *sukūn*, it has one instance—that being when it is connected to the light or heavy letter *nūn* of emphasis e.g. “you should hit”, “you should write” and “you must hit”, “you must write”.

وإن كان مضارعه معتل الآخر فهو يجزم بحذف حرف العلة، فالأمر منه يُبنى على حذف حرف العلة، نحو (ادعُ) و(افضِ) و(اسعَ).

As for the *muḍāriʿ* verb with a defective ending, it becomes *majzūm* through the removal of the defective letter, and the *ʾamr* is built upon this removal of the defective letter e.g. “call”, “decree” and “strive”.

وإن كان مضارعه من الأفعال الخمسة فهو يجزم بحذف النون، فالأمر منه يُبنى على حذف النون، نحو (اكتبا) و(اكتبوا) و(اكتبي).

As for the *muḍāriʿ* from the five verbs, it becomes *majzūm* through the removal of the letter *nūn*, and the *ʾamr* is built upon this removal of the letter *nūn*. Examples being “you two write”, “you (pl.) write” and “write (fem.)”.

والفعل المضارع علامته أن يكون في أوله حرف زائد من أربعة أحرف يجمعها قولك: (أنيتُ) أو قولك (نأيتُ) أو قولك (أتين) أو قولك (نأتي).

The sign of the *muḍāriʿ* verb is that they commence with one of the four additional letters that are combined in the words “***anaytu***”, “***n'aytu***”, “***atayna***” or “***n'atī***”.

فالهمزة للمتكلم مذكراً كان أو مؤنثاً، نحو (أفهم) والنون للمتكلم الذي يعظم نفسه، أو للمتكلم الذي يكون معه غيره، نحو (نَفْهَمُ).

The letter *hamzah* denotes the singular first person for both genders e.g. "I understand". The *nūn* denotes the singular first person in the sense of glorifying oneself, or it denotes the speaker in addition to others alongside him e.g. "we understand."

والياء للغائب نحو (يقوم) والتاء للمخاطب ؛ أو الغائبة ؛ نحو : (أنت تفهم يا محمد واجبك)، ونحو: (تفهم زينب واجبها) .

The letter *yā* denotes the third person e.g. "he stands". The letter *tā* denotes the second person or the third person feminine gender e.g. "Do you understand your duty, O Muḥammad?", and "Zaynab understands her duty."

فإن لم تكن هذه الحروف زائدة، بل كانت من أصل الفعل، نحو: (أكل) ، و(نقل) ، و(تَفَلَ) ، و(يَنَعَ) ، أو كان الحرف زائداً، لكنه ليس للدلالة على المعنى الذي ذكرناه، نحو: (أكرم) ، و(تقدم) كان الفعل ماضياً لا مضارعاً .

If these letters are present but are not the aforementioned additions, rather they are part of the root word structure e.g. "to eat", "to move", "to spit", "to ripen", or they are additions but convey a meaning different to the ones above e.g. "he honoured" and "he served", they are *māḍī* verbs and not *muḍāriʿ*.

وحكم الفعل المضارع: أنه معرب ما لم تتصل به نون التوكيد ثقيلة كانت أو خفيفة أو نون النسوة، فإن اتصلت به نون التوكيد بني معها على الفتح، نحو قوله تعالى: ﴿لَيُسْجَنَنَّ وَلِيَكُوناً مِنَ الصَّاغِرِينَ﴾ وإن اتصلت به نون النسوة بني معها على السكون، نحو قوله تعالى ﴿وَالْوَالِدَاتُ يُرْضِعْنَ﴾ .

The ruling of the *muḍāriʿ* verb is that it is inflectable as long as it is not connected to the heavy or light letter *nūn* of emphasis or the *nūn* of feminine plurality. If the letter *nūn* of emphasis is connected to the *muḍāriʿ* verb then it becomes built upon a *fatḥah* alongside it, an example is the *āyah*: **{He will surely be imprisoned and will be of those debased.}**[79] If the letter *nūn* of feminine plurality is attached to the *muḍāriʿ* verb then it becomes built upon a

79 Yūsuf: 32

sukūn alongside it, an example is the *āyah*: **{Mothers may breastfeed their children.}**[80]

وإذا كان معرباً فهو مرفوع ما لم يدخل عليه ناصب أو جازم، نحو: (يفهم محمد)، فـ(يفهم) : فعل مضارع مرفوع لتجرده من الناصب والجازم، وعلامة رفع الضمة الظاهرة، و(محمد) : فاعل مرفوع بالضمة الظاهرة .

When it is inflectable, the *muḍāriʿ* verb is *marfūʿ* as long as a *nāṣib* or *jāzim* does not enter upon it. An example is, "Muḥammad understands." In this sentence "understands" is a *marfūʿ muḍāriʿ* verb due to the absence of any *nāṣib* or *jāzim* before it. The sign of it being *marfūʿ* is the explicit *ḍammah*. Muḥammad is the subject and it is *marfūʿ* with an explicit *ḍammah*.

فإن دخل عليه ناصب نصبه، نحو: (لن يَخيبَ مجتهد) فـ(لن) : حرف نفي ونصب واستقبال، و(يخيب) : فعل مضارع منصوب بـ(لن)، وعلامة نصبه الفتحة الظاهرة، و(مجتهد): فاعل مرفوع وعلامة رفعه الضمة الظاهرة.

If a *nāṣib* enters upon it then it becomes *manṣūb*. An example is, "Never will the hardworking be unsuccessful." "*Lan*" (never) is a particle of negation, *nāṣb* and future tense. The word "unsuccessful" is a *muḍāriʿ* verb made *manṣūb* by "*lan*" and the sign of it being *manṣūb* is the visible *fatḥah*. The word "hard-working" is the subject, it is *marfūʿ* and the sign of this is the explicit *ḍammah*.

وإن دخل عليه جازم جزمه، نحو: (لم يجزع إبراهيم) فـ(لم) : حرف نفي وجزم وقلب، و(يجزع) : فعل مضارع مجزوم بـ(لم) ، وعلامة جزمه السكون، و(إبراهيم) : فاعل مرفوع، وعلامة رفعه الضمة الظاهرة .

If a *jāzim* enters upon the *muḍāriʿ* verb then it becomes *majzūm*. An example is "Ibrāhīm did not become worried". "*Lam*" (did not) is a particle of negation, *jazm* and alteration (i.e. from the present/future tense to the past tense). "He worries" is a *muḍāriʿ* verb made *majzūm* by "*lam*", the sign of it being so is the *sukūn*. "Ibrāhīm" is the subject and it is *marfūʿ*, the sign of which being

80 Al-Baqarah: 233

the explicit *ḍammah*.

أسئلة

Questions

إلى كم قسم ينقسم الفعل؟

Into how many categories is the verb split into?

ما هو الفعل الماضي؟ ما هو الفعل المضارع؟ ما هو فعل الأمر؟

What is the *māḍī* verb? What is the *muḍāriʿ* verb? What is the *ʾamr* verb?

مثل لكل قسم من أقسام الفعل بخمسة أمثلة.

Provide five examples of each category of verbs.

متى يكون الفعل الماضي مبنياً على الفتح الظاهر؟

When is the *māḍī* verb un-inflectable upon an explicit *fatḥah*?

مثل لكل موضع يبنى فيه الفعل الماضي على الفتح الظاهر بمثالين.

Provide two examples of each instance where the *māḍī* verb is un-inflectable upon an explicit *fatḥah*.

متى يكون الفعل الماضي مبنياً على فتح مقدر؟

When is the *māḍī* verb *un-inflectable* upon an implicit *fatḥah*.

مثل لكل موضع يبنى فيه الفعل الماضي على فتح مقدر بمثالين، وبين سبب التقدير فيهما.

Provide two examples of each instance where the *māḍī* verb is un-inflectable upon an implicit *fatḥah*. Explain the reasons for the *fatḥah* being implicit.

متى يكون فعل الأمر مبنياً على السكون الظاهر؟

When is the *ʾamr* verb un-inflectable upon an explicit *sukūn*?

مثل لكل موضع يبنى فيه فعل الأمر على السكون الظاهر بمثالين.

Provide two examples of each instance where the *ʾamr* verb is un-inflectable upon an explicit *sukūn*.

متى يبنى الفعل الأمر على السكون المقدر؟

When is the *ʾamr* verb un-inflectable upon an implicit *sukūn*?

مثل لذلك بمثالين.

Provide two examples of this.

متى يبنى فعل الأمر على حذف حرف العلة ؟

When is the *ʾamr* verb un-inflectable upon the removal of the defective letter?

ومتى يبنى على حذف النون؟ مع التمثيل.

And when is it un-inflectable upon the removal of the letter *nūn*? Provide examples.

ما علامة الفعل المضارع؟ ما هي المعاني التي تأتي لها همزة المضارعة؟ وما هي المعاني التي تأتي لها نون المضارعة؟

What are the signs of the *muḍāriʿ* verb? What are the meanings indicated by the letter *hamzah* of the *muḍāriʿ*? And what are the meanings indicated by the letter *nūn* of the *muḍāriʿ*?

ما حكم الفعل المضارع؟ متى يبنى الفعل المضارع على الفتح؟ ومتى يبنى على السكون؟ ومتى يكون مرفوعاً ؟

What is the ruling of the *muḍāriʿ* verb? When is the *muḍāriʿ* verb un-inflectable upon a *fatḥah*? When is it un-inflectable upon a *sukūn*? When is it *marfūʿ*?

نواصب المضارع

Nawāṣib[81] of the *Muḍāri*ʿ Verb

قال: فالنواصب عشرة، وهي: (أن) ، و(لن) ، و(إذن) ، و(كي) ، و(لام (كي)) ، و(لام الجحود) ، و(حتى) ، والجواب بالفاء والواو، و(أو) .

He said: The *nawāṣib*[82] are ten[83] "*an*" (that), "*lan*" (will not), "*idhan*" (then), "*kay*" (so that), "*lām kay*" (in order to)[84], the letter *lām al-juḥūd*[85], *ḥattā* (until), the letters *fā* and *wāw* as the *jawāb* (answer) [of a *sharṭ* (condition)] and *aw* (or).

وأقول: الأدوات التي ينصب بعدها الفعل المضارع عشرة أحرف وهي على ثلاثة أقسام: قسم ينصب بنفسه، وقسم ينصب بـ(أن) مضمرة بعده جوازاً، وقسم ينصب بـ(أن) مضمرة بعده وجوباً .

I say: The apparatus that make the *muḍāri*ʿ verb after it *manṣūb* are ten particles, and they are categorised into three: (i) the type that produces the state of *naṣb* in of itself, (ii) the type that produces the state of *naṣb* with the allowance of an implicit "*an*" (that) after it and (iii) the type that produces the state of *naṣb* with an implicit "*an*" (that) after it that is mandatory to be so (i.e. im-

81 *Nawāṣib* is the plural of *nāṣib*, which refers to governors that cause the grammatical state of *naṣb*.
82 Al-Ḥāmidī (p. 59) said, "They have preceded the *jawāzim* due to their effect being discernible i.e. through a diacritic, in contrast to the *jawāzim* which [shows its effect] through absence. The former is more noble."
83 They are ten according to the Kūfī grammarians—and the author was a Kūfī. According to the Basran grammarians the *nawāsib* are four: "*an*", "*lan*", "*idhan*" and "*kay*", and this was the view preferred by Ibn Hishām in *Shudhūr* (p. 287).
84 The letter *lām* added to a *muḍāri*ʿ verb which adds the reason for the action.
85 This is to have a negation via *lam yakun* or *mā kāna* and the likes followed by a *lām* and a *muḍāri*ʿ verb. This expresses a complete negation using a *muḍāri*ʿ verb.

plicit).

أما القسم الأول: وهو الذي ينصب الفعل المضارع بنفسه - فأربعة أحرف وهي: (أن) ، و(لن) ، و(إذن) ، و(كي) .

As for the first category—and it is the type that produces the state of *naṣb* in of itself—it consists of four particles: "*an*", "*lan*", "*idhan*" and "*kay*".

أما (أن) : فحرف مصدر ونصب واستقبال، ومثالها قوله تعالى ﴿أَطْمَعُ أَنْ يَغْفِرَ لِي﴾ وقوله جل ذكره: ﴿وَأَخَافُ أَنْ يَأْكُلَهُ الذِّئْبُ﴾، وقوله تعالى: ﴿إِنِّي لَيَحْزُنُنِي أَنْ تَذْهَبُوا بِهِ﴾، وقوله تعالى: ﴿وَأَجْمَعُوا أَنْ يَجْعَلُوهُ﴾ .

As for "*an*", it is a particle of the infinitive, the *naṣb* state and the future tense. Examples of it can be found in the following *āyāt*: **{I aspire that He will forgive me}**,[86] **{And I fear that a wolf would eat him}**,[87] **{Indeed, it saddens me that you should take him}**,[88] and **{And they agreed to place him}**.[89]

أما (لن) فحرف نفي ونصب واستقبال، ومثاله قوله تعالى: ﴿لَنْ نُؤْمِنَ لَكَ﴾ وقوله تعالى: ﴿لَنْ نَبْرَحَ عَلَيْهِ﴾ ، وقوله تعالى: ﴿لَنْ تَنَالُوا الْبِرَّ﴾ .

As for "*lan*" (will not), it is a particle of negation, the *naṣb* state and the future tense. Examples of it can be found in the following *āyāt*: **{We will not believe in you}**,[90] **{We will not cease}**[91] and **{Never will you attain the good}**.[92]

وأما (إذن) فحرف جواب وجزاء ونصب، ويشترط لنصب المضارع بها ثلاثة شروط:

As for "*idhan*" (then), it is a particle of *jawāb*, apodosis (the main clause of

86 Al-Shu'rā: 82
87 Yūsuf: 13
88 Yūsuf: 13
89 Yūsuf: 15
90 Al-Baqarah: 55
91 Ṭaha: 91
92 Āli 'Imrān: 92

a conditional sentence), and the *naṣb* state.[93] There are three conditions that must be met for it to make the *muḍāriʿ* verb *manṣūb*:

الأول: أن تكون (إذن) في صدر جملة الجواب .

First: That the word "*idhan*" be situated at the start of a sentence of *al-jawāb*.

الثاني: أن يكون المضارع الواقع بعدها دالاً على الاستقبال.

Second: That the meaning of the *muḍāriʿ* verb present after it indicates towards the future tense.

الثالث: أن لا يفصل بينها وبين المضارع فاصل غيرُ القسم أو النداء أو ((لا) النافية) .

Third: There is not a division between it and the *muḍāriʿ* verb except an oath, the vocative or the *lā* of negation.[94]

ومثال المستوفية للشروط أن يقول لك أحد إخوانك: (سأجتهد في دروسي) فتقول له: (إذن تنجح) .

An example of it being with a *sharṭ* is if one of your brothers says to you, "I will work hard in my lessons", and you say, "Then you will be successful."

ومثال المفصولة بالقسم أن تقول (إذن والله تنجح)، ومثال المفصولة بالنداء أن تقول: (إذن يا محمد تنجح)، ومثال المفصولة بـ((لا) النافية) أن تقول: (إذن لا يخيب سعيك) أو تقول: (إذن والله لا يذهب عملك ضياعاً).

93 In regards to the meaning of "a particle of *jawāb*, apodosis, and the *naṣb* state" (حرف جواب وجزاء ونصب), al-Ahdal said in *al-Kawākib* (2/469), "*Idhan* is called a particle of *jawāb* (answer) due to it being used to answer something else. It can arise in the beginning, the middle or end of the sentence, however it does not cause the *naṣb* state unless it arises in the beginning. It is called a particle of apodosis due to its content being used to answer the content of something else." Also see *Hashiyat al-Ḥāmidī* (p. 64).

94 There is a difference of opinion regarding these three divisions as some increased upon them, see *al-Kawākib* (2/469), and some decreased on them, see *Sharḥ al-Qaṭr* (p. 82-83) and *Ḥāshiyat al-Kafrāwī* (p. 60).

An example of the division with an oath is if you say, "Then—by Allah—you will be successful." An example of the division with a vocative is if you say, "Then—O Muḥammad—you will be successful." An example of the division with the *lā* of negation is if you say, "Then your endeavour will not be unsuccessful," or if you say, "Then—by Allah—your work will not go in waste."

وأما (كي) فحرف مصدر ونصب، ويشترط في النصب بها أن تتقدمها لام التعليل لفظاً، نحو قوله تعالى: ﴿لِكَيْلَا تَأْسَوْا﴾، أو تتقدمها هذه اللام تقديراً، نحو قوله تعالى: ﴿كَىْ لَا يَكُونَ دُولَةً﴾، فإذا لم تتقدمها اللام لفظاً ولا تقديراً كان النصب بـ(أن) مضمرة، وكانت (كي) نفسها حرف تعليل.

As for "*kay*" (so that), it is a particle of the infinitive and the *naṣb* state. The condition for it producing the *naṣb* state is that it is preceded by the explicit letter *lām* of reasoning. An example of this is the *āyah*: **{In order that you not despair.}**[95] Or if it is preceded by an implied form of this *lām*, an example being the *āyah*: **{So that it will not be a perpetual distribution.}**[96] If it is not preceded by either the visible or implicit letter *lām* of reasoning, then [the *muḍāriʿ* verb] is made *manṣūb* by an implicit "*an*" (that) and the word "*kay*" in this instance is a particle of causation in of itself.

وأما القسم الثاني: وهو الذي ينصب الفعل المضارع بواسطة (أن) مضمرة بعده جوازاً - فحرف واحد وهو لام التعليل، وعبر عنها المؤلف بـ(لام (كي))، لاشتراكهما في الدلالة على التعليل، ومثالها قوله تعالى: ﴿لِيَغْفِرَ لَكَ اللهُ مَا تَقَدَّمَ مِن ذَنۢبِكَ وَمَا تَأَخَّرَ﴾، وقوله جل شأنه: ﴿لِيُعَذِّبَ اللهُ الْمُنَافِقِينَ والمنافِقاتِ﴾.

As for the second category—it is that which produces the state of *naṣb* upon the *muḍāriʿ* verb through the means of the particle "*an*" that is allowed to be implicit—and it is one particle, the letter *lām* of causation. It was expressed by the author through his words, "*lām kay*". This is due to them sharing the attribute of indicating *taʿlīl* (causation). Examples can be found in the two statements of Allah: **{That Allah may forgive for you what preceded of your**

95 Al-Ḥadīd: 23

96 Al-Ḥashr: 7

sin and what will follow}[97] and {[It was] so that Allah may punish the hyp-
ocrite.}[98]

وأما القسم الثالث: وهو الذي ينصب الفعل المضارع بواسطة (أن) مضمرة وجوباً ـ
فخمسة أحرف :

As for the third category—it is that which produces the state of *naṣb* upon the
muḍāri' verb through the means of the particle "*an*" that is mandatory to be
implicit—and it consists of five particles:

الأول: لام الجحود، وضابطها أن تسبق بـ(ما كان) أو (لم يكن) فمثال الأول
قوله تعالى : ﴿مَا كَانَ اللّٰهُ لِيَذَرَ الْمُؤْمِنِينَ عَلَى مَآ أَنْتُمْ عَلَيْهِ﴾، وقوله سبحانه : ﴿وَمَا كَانَ اللّٰهُ
لِيُعَذِّبَهُمْ﴾، ومثال الثاني قوله جل ذكره : ﴿لَمْ يَكُنِ اللّٰهُ لِيَغْفِرَ لَهُمْ وَلَا لِيَهْدِيَهُمْ سَبِيلًا﴾ .

The first of these is the letter *lām al-juḥūd*.[99] The governing principle for this
is that it is preceded by "*mā kāna*" or "*lam yakun*". Examples of the former
are the *āyahs*: {Allah would not leave the believers in that [state] you are in
[presently]}[100] and: {But Allah would not punish them.}[101] An example of the
latter is the *āyah*: {Allah will not forgive them, nor guide them on the (Right)
Way.}[102]

والحرف الثاني (حتى) وهو يفيد الغاية أوالتعليل، ومعنى الغاية أنَّ ما قبلها ينقضي
بحصول ما بعدها نحو قوله تعالى: ﴿حَتَّىٰ يَرْجِعَ إِلَيْنَا مُوسَىٰ﴾، ومعنى التعليل أن ما قبلها
علة لحصول ما بعدها، نحو قولك لبعض إخوانك (ذاكر حتى تنجح) .

---

97 Al-Fatḥ: 2
98 Al-Aḥzāb: 73
99 Al-Ahdal said (2/478), "It is termed as *lām al-juḥud* because it comes in the context
of negation by referring to the general whilst identifying something specific." Yasin said
in *Hashiyat 'ala al-Fākihī* (1/118), "It is called *juhd* because linguistically it reinforces a
previous negation whilst not being an absolute negation."
100 Āli 'Imrān: 179
101 Al-Anfāl: 33
102 Al-Nisā: 137

The second particle is *ḥattā* (until) and it can provide the meaning of *al-ghāyah* (the end point) or *al-taʿlīl* (causation). The meaning of *al-ghāyah* here is that the first part of the statement becomes null with the attainment of what comes after it, e.g. in the *āyah*: {**They said, "We will never cease being devoted to the calf until Mūsā returns to us."**}[103] And the meaning of *al-taʿlīl* here is that the first part of the statement is the reason for the attainment of what comes after it, e.g. if you say to one of your brothers, "Revise until you succeed."

والحرفان الثالث والرابع: فاء السببية، وواو المعية، بشرط أن يقع كل منها في جواب نفي أو طلب .

The third and fourth particles are the letter *fā* of causation[104] and the letter *wāw* of simultaneousness,[105] the condition upon them is that they are within a *jawāb* (lit. answer, technically it refers to the response to a condition (*sharṭ*)) of negation or request.

أما النفي فنحو قوله تعالى: ﴿لا يُقْضَى عَلَيْهِمْ فَيَمُوتُوا﴾

As for negation, an example is in the *āyah*: {**[Death] is not decreed for them so they may die.**}[106]

وأما الطلب فثمانية أشياء:

As for the demand, it consists of eight things:

الأمر، والدعاء، والنهي، والاستفهام، والعرض، والتحضيض، والتمني، والرجاء.

The command, the call, the prohibition, the question, the offer, incitement, the wish and the desire.

103 Ṭaha: 91

104 Al-Ahdal said in *al-Kawākib* (1/482), "This is when the intention behind its use is to indicate that which comes before it as the reason for that which follows it."

105 Al-Ahdal said in *al-Kawākib* (1/482), "It indicates the meaning of *maʿa* (with) and that the things before and after it occurred simultaneously."

106 Fāṭir: 36

أما الأمر فهو الطلب الصادر من العظيم لمن هو دونه، نحو قول الأستاذ لتلميذه: (ذاكر فتنجح) أو (وتنجح)

As for the command, it is a request emanating from the superior to the one lesser in rank than him. An example is the statement of the teacher to his student, "Revise then you will succeed."

وأما الدعاء فهو الطلب الموجه من الصغير إلى العظيم، نحو: (اللهم اهدني فأعمل الخير) أو (وأعمل الخير)

As for the *du'ā* then it is a request despatched from the inferior to the one higher in rank. An example is, "O Allah, guide me then I will do good."

وأما النهي فنحو: (لا تلعب فيضيعَ أملك) أو (ويضيعَ أملك) .

As for the prohibition, an example is, "Do not play so your aspirations will be ruined."

وأما الاستفهام فنحو: (هل حفظت دروسك فأسمعها لك)، أو (وأسمعها لك) .

As for the question, an example is, "Have you memorised your lessons so that I may test you?"

وأما العرض فهو الطلب برفق نحو: (ألا تزورنا فنكرمك)، أو(نكرمك) .

As for the offer, it is a gentle request. An example is, "Won't you visit us so that we can serve you?

وأما التحضيض فهو الطلب مع حث وإزعاج نحو: (هلا أديت واجبك فيشكرك أبوك) أو (ويشكرك أبوك)

As for *al-taḥḍīḍ*, it refers to the request that is accompanied by inducement and prodding. An example is, "Why don't you complete your duty so your father can thank you."

وأما التمني فهو طلب المستحيل، أو ما فيه عسر، نحو قول الشاعر:

As for the wish, it is the seeking of something unlikely to occur, or that which has an element of difficulty. An example is the statement of the poet:

ليت الكواكب تدنو لي فأنظمها   عقودَ مدحٍ فما أرضى لكم كَلِمِي

If only the stars descended to me so that I would arrange them,
Into a necklace of praises that you would not be pleased with my speech.[107]

ومثله قول الآخر:

Another example is the couplet:

ألا ليتَ الشبابَ يعودُ يوما   فأخبره بما فعل المشيبُ

If only the youth would return,
So I inform him of what the old age did.

ونحو: (ليت لي مالاً فأحج منه).

Also, "If only I had money then I would perform Ḥajj."

وأما الرجاء فهو طلب الأمر القريب الحصول نحو: (لعل الله يشفيني فأزورك).

As for the desire (*al-rajā*), it is the seeking for something that can be attained soon. An example is, "Perhaps if Allah cures me, I will visit you."

وقد جمع بعض العلماء هذه الأشياء التسعة التي تسبق الفاء والواو في بيت واحد هو:

Scholars have gathered these nine things that precede the letters *fā* and *wāw* into one couplet:

107 The one who recited this couplet was ʿAmārah ibn ʿAlī, as recorded in *Siyar Aʿlām al-Nubalā* (20/592-596) by al-Imām al-Dhahabī.

مُر، وادعُ، وانهُ، وسل، واعرض، لحضهم   تمنَّ، وارج؛ كذاك النفي، قد كمُلا

Command, call, prohibit, ask, offer so that they may be incited,
Wish, desire and likewise deny and this completes them (all nine forms of demanding and prohibiting).

وقد ذكر المؤلف أنها ثمانية، لأنه لم يعتبر الرجاء منها .

The author mentioned eight things, as he did not consider the desire to be from them.

الحرف الخامس (أو) ويشترط في هذه الكلمة أن تكون بمعنى (إلا) أو بمعنى (إلى)، وضابط الأولى: أن يكون ما بعدها ينقضي دفعة، نحو: (لأقتلن الكافر أو يسلم)

The fifth particle is "*aw*" (or) with the condition that this word has the meaning of "except/but" or "to". The governing principle of the first is that it is followed by something that recants [what came before it] completely e.g. "I will certainly fight the *kāfir*, except if he submits."

وضابط الثانية: أن يكون ما بعدها ينقضي شيئاً فشيئاً، نحو قول الشاعر:

The governing principle of the second is that it is followed by something that recants [what came before it] as it gradually proceeds, e.g. the statement of the poet:

لأستسهلن الصعبَ أو أدركَ المُنى   فما انقادت الآمال إلا لصابر

Indeed I shall endure difficulty until death comes to me,
As ambitions are achieved only by the patient.

تمرينات

Exercises

١ ـ أجب عن كل جملة من الجمل الآتية بجملتين في كل واحدة منهما فعل مضارع :

One. Answer each of the following sentences with two sentences, each of them containing a *muḍāri*ʿ verb.

(أ) ما الذي يؤخرك عن إخوانك؟

(ب) هل تسافر غداً؟

(ج) كيف تصنع إذا أردت المذاكرة؟

(د) أي الأطعمة تحب؟

(هـ) أين يسكن خليل؟

(و) في أي متنزه تقضي يوم العطلة؟

(ز) من الذي ينفق عليك؟

(ح) كم ساعة تقضيها في المذاكرة كل يوم؟

٢ - ضع في كل مكان من الأماكن الخالية فعلاً مضارعاً، ثم بين موضعه من الإعراب وعلامة إعرابه:

Two. Place a *muḍāri*ʿ verb in the empty spaces within the sentences below. Then explain their state of inflection and the sign that indicates such:

(أ) جئت أمس ... فلم أجدك.

(ب) يسرني أن ...

(ج) أحببت علياً لأنه ...

(د) لن ... عمل اليوم إلى غدٍ.

(ه) أنتما ... خالداً.

(و) زرتكما لكي ... معي إلى المتنزه.

(ز) هاأنتم هؤلاء ... الواجب.

(ط) من أراد ... نفسه فلا يقصر في واجبه.

(ي) يعز علي أن ...

(ك) أسرع السير كي .... أول العمل.

(ل) لن .... المسيء من العقاب.

(م) ثابري على عملك كي ...

(ن) أدوا واجباتكم كي ... على رضا الله.

(س) اتركوا اللعب ...

(ح) لا تكونون مخلصين حتى ... (ع) لولا أن ... عليكم لكلفتكم إدمان
أعمالكم. العمل.

أسئلة

Questions

ما هي الأدوات التي تنصب المضارع بنفسها؟

What are the apparatus that make a *muḍāri*ʿ verb *manṣūb* in of themselves?

ما معنى (أن) وما معنى (لن) وما معنى (إذن) وما معنى (كَي)؟

What is the meaning of "*an*", "*lan*", "*idhn*" and "*kay*"?

ما الذي يشترط لنصب المضارع بعد (إذن) وبعد (كي)؟

What are the conditions that must be met for a *muḍāri*ʿ verb to be made *manṣūb* by the particles "*idhn*" and "*kay*" that precede it?

ما هي الأشياء التي لا يضر الفصل بها بين (إذن) الناصبة والمضارعة؟

What are the things that do not impact "*idhn*" making the *muḍārī*ʿ verb *manṣūb* when they come between the word "*idhn*" and the verb?

متى تنصب (أن) مضمرة جوازاً؟ متى تنصب (أن) مضمرة وجوباً؟

When does the "*an*" that is allowed to be implicit produce the state of *naṣb*? When does the "*an*" that is mandatory to be implicit do so?

ما ضابط لام الجحود؟ ما معنى (حتى) الناصبة؟ ما هي الأشياء التي يجب أن يسبق واحداً منها فاء السببية أو واو المعية؟ مثّل لكل ما تذكره .

What is the governing principle of the letter *lām al-juḥūd*? What are the meanings of "*ḥattā*" when it is a *nāṣib*? What are the things that must be preceded by the letter *fā* of causation or the letter *wāw* of accompaniment? Provide an example for everything you have mentioned.

جوازم المضارع

Jawāzim of the *Muḍāriʿ* Verb[108]

قال: والجوازم ثمانية عشر، وهي: (لم) ، و(لمّا) ، و(ألم) ، و(ألما) ، و(لام الأمر، والدعاء) ، و((لا) في النهي والدعاء)، و(إن) و(ما) و(مهما) ، و(إذ ما)، و(أي) ، و(متى) ، و(أين) ، و(أيان) ، و(أنى) ، و(حيثما) ، و(كيفما) ، و(إذا) في الشعر خاصة.

He said: The *jawāzim* are eighteen: "*lam*", "*lammā*", "*alam*", "*alammā*", the letter *lām* of command and *du'ā*, "*lā*" in a prohibition or a *du'ā*, "*in*", "*mā*", "*mahmā*", "*idh mā*", "*ayyu*", "*matā*", "*ayna*", "*ayyān*", "*annā*", "*ḥaythumā*", "*kayfamā*" and "*idhā*" when it is used in poetry.

وأقول: الأدوات التي تجزم الفعل المضارع ثمانية عشر جازماً، وهذه الأدوات تنقسم إلى قسمين: القسم الأول: يجزم فعلاً واحداً، والقسم الثاني: يجزم فعلين.

I say: The apparatus that make the *muḍāriʿ* verb *majzūm* are eighteen. And these apparatus are categorised into two types: (i) that which makes one verb *majzūm* and (ii) that which makes two verbs *majzūm*.

أما القسم الأول، فستة أحرف، وهي: (لم) ، و(لما) ، و(ألم) ، و(ألما) ، و(لام الأمر، والدعاء) ، و(لا) في النهي والدعاء، وكلها حروف بإجماع النحاة.

As for the first type, it consists of six particles: "*lam*", "*lammā*", "*alam*", "*alammā*", the letter *lām* of command and *duʿā* and "*lā*" in a prohibition or a *duʿā*. All of these are considered to be *ḥurūf* (pl. of *ḥarf*) by the consensus of the grammarians.

---

108 *Jawāzim* is the plural of *jāzim*, which refers to agents that cause the grammatical state of *jazm*.

أما (لم) فحرف نفي وجزم وقلب، نحو قوله تعالى: ﴿لَمْ يَكُنِ الَّذِينَ كَفَرُوا﴾، وقوله سبحانه: ﴿قُل لَّمْ تُؤْمِنُوا﴾.

As for "*lam*", it is a particle of negation, *jazm* and alteration. Examples are the *āyahs*: **{Those who disbelieved were not}**[109] and: **{Say, "You have not [yet] believed ..."}**[110]

وأما (لما) فحرف مثل (لم) في النفي والجزم والقلب، نحو قوله تعالى: ﴿لَمَّا يَذُوقُوا عَذَابِ﴾.

As for "*lammā*" (not yet), it is a particle similar to "*lam*" in that it is a particle of negation, *jazm* and alteration. An example is the *āyah*: **{They have not yet tasted My punishment.}**[111]

وأما (ألم) فهو، (لم) زيدت عليه همزة التقرير، نحو قوله تعالى: ﴿أَلَمْ نَشْرَحْ لَكَ صَدْرَكَ﴾ .

As for "*alam*", it is the particle "*lam*" with the addition of a letter *hamzah* of affirmation. An example is in the *āyah*: **{Did We not expand for you, [O Muhammad], your breast?}**[112]

وأما (ألمّا) فهو (لما) زيدت عليه الهمزة نحو: (ألمّا أحسن إليك).

As for "*alammā*", it is "*lammā*" with the addition of the *hamzah*. An example can be seen in the statement, "Have I not yet been good to you?"

وأما اللام، فقد ذكر المؤلف أنها تكون للأمر والدعاء، وكل من الأمر والدعاء يقصد به طلب حصول الفعل طلباً جازماً، والفرق بينهما أن الأمر يكون من الأعلى للأدنى، كما في الحديث: ((فليقل خيراً أو ليصمت))، وأما الدعاء فيكون من الأدنى للأعلى، نحو

109 Al-Bayyinah: 1
110 Al-Hujarāt: 14
111 Ṣad: 8
112 Al-Sharḥ: 1

قوله تعالى: ﴿لِيَقْضِ عَلَيْنَا رَبُّكَ﴾.

As for the letter *lām*, the author has mentioned it here as coming for a command and a *du'ā*, and each of these has the element of seeking something assertively. However the difference between them is that the command is from the superior in rank to the inferior, as in the ḥadīth, "Then let him speak with good or remain silent."[113] The *du'ā*, on the other hand, is from the inferior in rank to the superior, as in the *āyah*: **{Let your Lord put an end to us.}**[114]

وأما (لا) فقد ذكر المؤلف أنها تأتي للنهي والدعاء، وكل منهما يقصد به طلب الكف عن الفعل وتركه، والفرق بينهما أن النهي يكون من الأعلى للأدنى، نحو: ﴿لا تَخَفْ﴾، ونحو: ﴿لا تَقُولُوا رَاعِنَا﴾، ﴿لا تَغْلُوا فِي دِينِكُمْ﴾

As for "*lā*", the author has mentioned that it comes for a prohibition and a *du'ā* and each of them express the seeking of the halt of an action and the leaving off of it. Regarding the difference between them: The prohibition is expressed from the superior in rank to the inferior, examples are in the *āyāt*: **{Fear not}**,[115] **{Say not [to the Messenger] *rā'inā*}**,[116] and, **{Do not commit excess in your religion}**.[117]

وأما الدعاء فيكون من الأدنى للأعلى نحو: ﴿رَبَّنَا لا تُؤَاخِذْنَا﴾، وقوله جل شأنه: ﴿وَلا تَحْمِلْ عَلَيْنَآ إِصْراً﴾.

The *du'ā* is expressed from the inferior in rank to the superior, as in the *āyahs*: **{Our Lord, punish us not}**[118] and, **{And lay not upon us}**.[119]

وأما القسم الثاني: وهو ما يجزم فعلين، ويسمى أولهما فعل الشرط، وثانيهما جواب

113 *Ṣaḥīḥ al-Bukhārī*: 6136
114 Al-Zukhruf: 77
115 Hūd: 70
116 Al-Baqarah: 104
117 Al-Nisā: 171
118 Al-Baqarah: 286
119 Al-Baqarah: 286

الشرط وجزاءه، وهو على أربعة أنواع:

As for the second type, it is that which makes two verbs *majzūm*. The first of them is the verb of the condition and the second is the answer and the apodosis of the condition. This consists of four categories:

النوع الأول: حرف باتفاق، والنوع الثاني: اسم باتفاق، والنوع الثالث: حرف؛ على الأصح، والنوع الرابع: اسم؛ على الأصح.

The first category is agreed upon to be a particle, the second is agreed upon to be a noun, the third is a particle—according to the strongest opinion, and the fourth is a noun—according to the strongest opinion.

أما النوع الأول: فهو (إن) وحده، نحو: (إن تذاكر تنجح)، فـ(إن) حرف شرط جازم باتفاق النحاة، يجزم فعلين: الأول فعل الشرط والثاني جوابه وجزاؤه، و(تذاكر) فعل مضارع فعل الشرط مجزوم بـ(إن) وعلامة جزمه السكون، وفاعله ضمير مستتر فيه وجوباً تقديره: أنت، و(تنجح): فعل مضارع جواب الشرط وجزاؤه، مجزوم بـ(إن) وعلامة جزمه السكون، وفاعله ضمير مستتر فيه وجوباً تقديره أنت.

The first category: It solely consists of "*in*". An example of it is in the sentence, "If you revise you will succeed." "*In*" is considered to be a conditional particle and a *jāzim* according to the consensus of the grammarians. It makes two verbs *majzūm*, the first of them is the verb of the condition and the second of them is the answer to it and the apodosis. [In this sentence] the word "you revise" is a *muḍāriʿ* verb and the verb of the condition, it is *majzūm* due to "*in*" and the sign of it being so is the *sukūn*. The subject is the hidden pronoun that is obligatory to be implied i.e. "*anta*" (you). The word "succeed" is a *muḍāriʿ* verb and the answer of the condition and its apodosis. It is made *majzūm* by "*in*" and the sign of it being so is the *sukūn*. The subject is the hidden pronoun that is obligatory to be implicit i.e. "*anta*" (you).

وأما النوع الثاني: وهو المتفق على أنه اسم - فتسعة أسماء وهي: (من)، و(ما)، و(

أي)، و(متى)، و(أيان)، و(أين)، و(أنى)، و(حيثما)، و(كيفما).

The second category: It is agreed upon as being a noun, and it consists of nine nouns. These are, "*man*", "*mā*", "*ay*", "*matā*", "*ayyān*" , "*ayna*", "*annā*", "*ḥaythumā*" and "*kayfamā*".

فمثال (من) قولك: (من يُكرم جارَه يُحمد)، و(من يذاكر ينجح) وقوله تعالى: ﴿فَمَن يَعمَل مِثقالَ ذَرَّةٍ خَيراً يَرَهُ﴾ .

Examples of "*man*" (who) can be seen in the statements, "He who honours his neighbour is praised" and, "He who revises succeeds." We can also see an example in the *āyah*: **{So whoever does an atom's weight of good will see it.}**[120]

ومثال (ما) قولك: (ما تصنع تجز به) و(ما تقرأ تستفيد منه) و﴿وَمَا تُنْفِقُوا مِنْ خَيْرٍ يُوَفَّ إِلَيْكُمْ﴾ .

Examples of "*mā*" (what) can be seen in the statements, "Whatever you make, you will be paid for", "Whatever you read, you will benefit from it", and in the *āyah*: **{And whatever you spend of good - it will be fully repaid to you.}**[121]

ومثال (أي) قولك: (أيَّ كتابٍ تقرأْ تستفيد منه) و﴿أَيّاً مَا تَدْعُوا فَلَهُ الْأَسْمَاءُ الْحُسْنَى﴾.

Examples of "*ayy*" (which) can be seen in the statement, "Whichever book you read, you will benefit from it", and the *āyah*: **{Whichever [name] you call—to Him belong the best names.}**[122]

ومثال (متى) قولك: (متى تلتفت إلى واجبك تنل رضا ربك) وقول الشاعر:

Examples of "*matā*" (when) can be seen in the statement, "When you pay heed to that which is mandated upon you, you will attain the pleasure of your Lord," and the statement of the poet:

120 Al-Zalzalah: 7
121 Al-Baqarah: 272
122 Al-Isrā: 110

أنا ابن جَلا وطلاع الثنايا   متى أضع العمامة تعرفوني

I am the son of distinction and traverser of mountain passes,
When I take off my turban you will know me.[123]

ومثال (أيان) قولك: (أيان تَلقَني أُكرِمكَ) وقول الشاعر:

Examples of "*ayyān*" (when) can be seen in the statement, "When you meet me I will honour you," and the statement of the poet:

فأيان ما تعدل به الريح تنزل

For wherever the wind blows, it will follow it .

مثال (أينما) قولك: (أينما تتوجه تلق صديقاً) وقوله تعالى: ﴿أَيْنَمَا يُوَجِّهْهُ لا يَأْتِ بِخَيْرٍ﴾ وقوله: ﴿أَيْنَمَا تَكُونُوا يُدْرِكْكُمُ الْمَوْتُ﴾

Examples of "*aynamā*" (wherever) can be seen in the statement, "Wherever you go, you will find friends," and the *āyahs*: **{Wherever he directs him, he brings no good}**[124] and, **{Wherever you may be, death will overtake you.}**[125]

ومثال (حيثما) قول الشاعر:

An example of "*haythumā*" (wherever) is the statement of the poet:

حيثما تستقيم يقدر لك اللـ   ـه نجاحاً في غابر الأزمان

Wherever you stand upright, Allāh will ordain for you
Success in every passing moment.

123 Al-'Aynī said in *Sharḥ Shawāhid al-Ashamūnī* (3/260), "This was stated by Suḥaym and it was said by al-Muthaqab al-'Abdī Abū Zubayd. Its attribution to al-Ḥajjāj is not correct, rather he copied it."
124 Al-Naḥl: 76
125 Al-Nisā: 78

ومثال (كيفما) قولك: (كيفما تكن الأمة يكن الولاة) و(كيفما تكن نيتك يكن ثواب الله لك).

Examples of "*kayfamā*" (however/howsoever)[126] can be seen in the statements, "However the state of a community, likewise will be its rulers," and, "Howsoever your intention is, like it will be the reward from Allah."

ويزاد على هذه الأسماء التسعة (إذا) في الشعر كما قال المؤلف، وذلك ضرورة نحو قول الشاعر:

In addition to these nine nouns, there is "*idhā*" when it is utilised in poetry—as mentioned by the author, and this is due to [poetic] necessity (i.e. due to the need of maintaining rhythm etc.).[127] An example is in the statement of the poet:

استغن ما أغناك ربك بالغنى   فإذا تصبك خصاصة فتجمل

Suffice yourself with what your Lord has made you rich by,
But if you are stricken with poverty then beautify yourself [with patience].

وأما النوع الثالث: وهو ما اختلف في أنه اسم أو حرف، والأصح أنه حرف - فذلك حرف واحد وهو (إذ ما) ومثله قول الشاعر:

The third category: There is a difference regarding whether this is a noun or a particle, and the stronger view is that it is a particle, and this category consists

126 It bringing the state of *jazm* is according to the Kūfī grammarians, whereas this is considered to be a grammatical mistake according to the Baṣrī grammarians. None from the Baṣrī grammarians agreed with this except for Qaṭrab, and Ibn Ājurūm followed the Kūfan opinion. See *al-Mughnī* by Ibn Hishām (1/205) and *al-Kawākib* (2/516).

127 In *al-Khaṣā'iṣ* (p. 150) Ibn Jinni stated, "Chapter: Is it permitted for us to change the diacritic for the purpose of rhythm in poetry, or not? I asked my teacher, Abu ʿAlī (may Allah have Mercy on him) about this and he said, 'Just as lyricists change the diacritics in their lyrics, likewise it is permissible for us poets to change the diacritics in our poetry, but this is only permissible out of necessity to make it rhyme, without this, just as they have been cautious then it is upon us to be cautious [lest we fall into *lahn*].'"

of a single particle: "*idh mā*" (whatever or whenever). An example is in the statement of the poet:

وإنك إذ ما تأت ما أنت آمر به تلف من إياه تأمر آتياً

Indeed, whenever you come with what you command others,
To do, you will find those you command doing so.

وأما النوع الرابع: وهو ما اختلف في أنه اسم أو حرف، والأصح أنه اسم - فذلك كلمة واحدة، وهي (مهما) ومثالها قوله تعالى: ﴿مَهْمَا تَأْتِنَا بِهِ مِنْ آيَةٍ لِتَسْحَرَنَا بِهَا فَمَا نَحْنُ لَكَ بِمُؤْمِنِينَ﴾، وقول الشاعر:

The fourth category: There is a difference regarding whether this is a noun or a particle, and the stronger view is that it is a noun, and this category consists of a single noun: "*mahmā*" (whatsoever). Examples can be seen in the *āyah*: **{Whatever signs you may bring to us, to work your sorcery on us, we shall never believe in you}**,[128] and the statement of the poet:

وإنك مهما تعط بطنك سؤله وفرجك نالا منتهى الذم أجمعا

Indeed, whatsoever you give to your stomach its request,
And your sexual organ, both shall attain the utmost blame together.[129]

تمرينات

Exercises

١ - عين الفعال المضارعة الواقعة في الجمل الآتية، ثم بين المرفوع منها والمنصوب والمجزوم، وبين علامة إعرابه:

One. Identify the *muḍāriʿ* verbs present in the following sentences. Then identify from them the *marfūʿ*, *manṣūb* and *majzūm*, and detail the signs in-

128 Al-Aʿrāf: 132

129 The one who recited this couplet was Ḥātim al-Ṭāʾī, as stated in Ibn Hishām's *al-Mughnī* (1/331).

dicating them to be so:

من يزرعِ الخير يحصد الخير . لا تتوان في واجبك . إياك أن تشرب وأنت تعب . كثرة الضحك تميت القلب . من يعرض عن الله يعرض الله عنه . إن تثابر على العمل تفز . من لم يعرف حق الناس عليه.. لم يعرف الناس حقه عليهم . أينما تسع تجد رزقاً . حيثما يذهب العالم يحترمه الناس . لا يجمل بذي المروءة أن يكثر المزاح . كيفما تكونوا يول عليكم . إن تدخر المال ينفعك . إن تكن مهملاً تسؤ حالك . مهما تبطن تظهره الأيام . لا تكن مهذاراً فتشقى .

❁❁❁

٢ ـ أدخل كل فعل من الأفعال المضارعة الآتية في ثلاث جمل، بشرط أن يكون مرفوعاً في واحدة منها، ومنصوباً في الثانية، ومجزوماً في الثالثة .

Two. Place each of the following *muḍāriʿ* verbs into three sentences, with the condition that they be *marfūʿ* in the first sentence, *manṣūb* in the second and *majzūm* in the third:

تزرعِ، تسافر، تلعب، تظهر، تحبون، تشربين، تذهبان، ترجو، يهذي، ترضى .

❁❁❁

٣ ـ ضع في كل مكان من الأماكن الخالية في الأمثلة الآتية أداة شرط مناسبة:

Three. Place in each of the empty spaces below the appropriate conditional instrument:

(أ) ... تحضر يحضر أبوك.

(ب) ... تصاحب أصحابه.

(د) ... تُخِف تظهره أفعالُكَ.

(ه) ... تذهب أذهب معك.

(ج) ... تلعب تندم. (و) تذاكر فيه ينفعك.

٤ ـ أكمل الجمل الآتية بوضع فعل مضارع مناسب، واضبط آخره:

Four. Complete the following sentences with an appropriate *muḍāriʿ* verb. Express the diacritic at the end of each of them.

(أ) إن تذنب ... (و) أينما تسر ...

(ب) إن يسقط الزجاج ... (ز) كيفما يكن المرء ...

(ج) مهما تفعلوا ... (ح) من يزرني ...

(د) أي إنسان تصاحبه ... (ط) أيان يكن العالم ...

(ه) إن تضع الملح في الماء ... (ي) أنى يذهب العلم ...

٥ ـ كوِّن من كل جملتين متناسبتين من الجمل الآتية جملة مبدوءة بأداة شرط تناسبهما:

Five. Formulate a single sentence from every two sentences (that allow a single conditional sentence to be formed) with the correct conditional instrument inserted as the commencement:

تنتبه إلى الدرس، تمسك سلك الكهرباء، تصل بسرعة، تستفد منه، تركب سيارة، تصعق، تغلق نوافذ حجرتك، تؤد واجبك، يسقط المطر، يفسد الهواء، يفز برضاء الناس، تفتح المظلة.

أسئلة

Questions

إلى كم قسم تنقسم الجوازم؟ ما هي الجوازم التي تجزم فعلاً واحداً؟ ما هي الجوازم التي تجزم فعلين؟

Into how many types have the *jawāzim* been categorised into? Which are the *jawāzim* that make one verb *majzūm*? Which are the *jawāzim* that make two verbs *majzūm*?

بين الأسماء المتفق على اسميتها والحروف المتفق على حرفيتها من الجوازم التي تجزم فعلين.

Detail from the [categories of] *jawāzim* that make two verbs *majzūm*, the nouns upon which there is consensus on them being nouns and the particles upon which there is consensus on them being particles.

مثل لكل جازم يجزم فعلاً واحداً بمثالين، ومثل لكل جازم يجزم فعلين بمثال واحد؛ مبيناً فيه فعل الشرط وجوابه.

Provide two examples of each *jawāzim* that makes one verb *majzūm*. Provide one example of each *jawāzim* that makes two verbs *majzūm*. Make clear in this sentence the conditional verb and the *jawāb*.

عدد المرفوعات وأمثلتها

The Types of the *Marfūʿ* Words and Examples of Them

قال: (باب مرفوعات الأسماء) المرفوعات سبعة، وهي: الفاعل، والمفعول الذي لم يسم فاعله، والمبتدأ، وخبره، واسم (كان) وأخواتها، وخبر (إن) وأخواتها، والتابع للمرفوع، وهو أربعة أشياء: النعت، والعطف، والتوكيد، والبدل.

He said: "Chapter of the *Marfūʿ* Nouns":[130] The types of the *marfūʿ* words are seven: (i) the subject,[131] (ii) the object where the subject is not named, (iii) the nominal subject and (iv) its predicate, (v) the noun of *kāna* and its sisters, (vi) the predicate of *inna* and its sisters, (vii) the follower of a *marfūʿ* word, and this consists of four: the adjective, the conjunction, the emphasis, and the substitute.

وأقول: قد علمت مما مضى أن الاسم المعرب يقع في ثلاثة مواقع: موقع الرفع، وموقع النصب، وموقع الخفض، ولكل واحد من هذه المواقع عوامل تقتضيه، وقد شرع المؤلف

---

130 Al-Ḥāmidī said (p. 74), "He commenced with these words due to them being the root, and he followed them with the *manṣūb* words due to their excellence. The *majrūr* words were mentioned last due to them being *manṣub* in their place." See *al-Kawākib* (1/154).

131 Al-Kafrāwī said (pp. 74-75), "He commenced with the subject due to it being the foundation of the *marfūʿ* words according to the majority of grammarians, and due to its governing agent being an explicit word. [...] And it is followed [by the *nāʾib* (representative) *fāʿil*] due to it being the representative of it. And it is followed by [the nominal subject and its predicate] due to them being both grammatical abrogators and followed, which precedes that which is only a grammatical abrogator or a grammatical follower. [Then he stated regarding *inna* and its sisters,] and he postponed it and what came before it, meaning the *ism kana* because the *ism kana* has the governing agent which abrogates, thus it was postponed as previously mentioned."

يبين لك ذلك على التفصيل، وبدأ بذكر المرفوعات، لأنها الأشرف، وقد ذكر أن الاسم يكون مرفوعاً في سبعة مواضع .

I say: You should have understood at this juncture, from what we have covered, that the inflectable noun falls into three positions: (i) the position of *raf*ʿ, (ii) the position of *naṣb* and (iii) the position of *khafḍ*. Each of these positions have governors causing them to be so. The author has now commenced with explaining these in detail, initiating with the *marfū*ʿ state as it is the most distinguished. So he mentions that the noun is *marfū*ʿ in seven places:

١ ـ إذا كان فاعلاً، ومثاله (علي) و(محمد) ؛ في نحو قولك (حضر علي)، (سافر محمد).

One. If it is the subject. Examples of this are the words "ʿAlī" and "Muḥammad" in the statements, "ʿAlī was present" and "Muḥammad travelled."

٢ـ أن يكون نائباً عن الفاعل، وهو الذي سماه المؤلف المفعول الذي لم يسم فاعله، نحو (الغصن) و(المتاع) من قولك: (قطع الغصن) و(سرق المتاع) .

Two. If it is deputising as the subject. The author has referred to it here as, "the object where the subject is not named." Examples are the words "the branch" and "the property" in, "The branch was cut" and "The property was stolen."

٣، ٤ ـ المبتدأ والخبر، نحو (محمد مسافر) و(علي مجتهد).

Three and Four. The nominal subject and its predicate. Examples are, "Muḥammad (nominal subject) is a traveller (predicate)", and "ʿAlī (nominal subject) is hard working (predicate)."

٥ ـ اسم (كان) أو إحدى أخواتها ؛ نحو (إبراهيم) و(البرد) من قولك: (كان إبراهيم مجتهداً) و(أصبح البرد شديداً) .

Five. The noun of *kāna* or of one of its sisters. Examples are the words "Ibrāhīm" and "cold" in the statements, "Ibrāhīm was hard working" and,

"The cold became severe."

٦ ـ خبر (إن) أو إحدى أخواتها، نحو (فاضل) و(قدير) من قولك: (إن محمداً فاضل) و(إن الله على كل شيء قدير).

Six. The predicate of *innā* or of one of its sisters. Examples are the words "virtuous" and "powerful" in the statements, "Indeed Muḥammad is virtuous" and "Indeed Allah is over all things powerful."

٧ ـ تابع المرفوع، والتابع أربعة أنواع:

Seven. The grammatical follower of a *marfū'* word, and this consists of four types:

الأول :النعت، وذلك نحو: (الفاضل) و(كريم) من قولك: (زارني محمد الفاضل) و(قابلني رجل كريم).

The first type: The adjective, and examples of this are the words "virtuous" and "noble" in the statements, "I was visited by the virtuous Muḥammad" and, "I was met by a noble man."

والثاني العطف، وهو على ضربين: عطف بيان، وعطف نسق، فمثال عطف البيان (عمر) من قولك: (سافر أبو حفص عمر)، ومثال عطف النسق (خالد) من قولك: (تشارك محمد وخالد).

The second type: The conjunct, and it is of two kinds: the conjunct for explanation and the conjunct for coordination. An example of the conjunct for explanation is the word "'Umar" in the statement, "Abū Ḥafṣ 'Umar travelled." An example of the conjunct for coordination is the word "Khālid" in the statement, "Muḥammad and Khālid are partnered."

والثالث: التوكيد، ومثاله: (نفسه) من قولك (زارني الأمير نفسه).

The third type: The emphasis, and an example of it is the word "himself" in the statement, "I was visited by the leader himself."

والرابع البدل، ومثاله (أخوك)، من قولك: (حضر علي أخوك) .

The fourth type: The substitute, and an example of it is "your brother" in the statement, "Your brother ʿAlī was present."

وإذا اجتمعت هذه التوابع كلها أو بعضها في كلام قدمت النعت، ثم عطف البيان، ثم التوكيد، ثم البدل، ثم عطف النسق، تقول: (جاء الرجل الكريم علي نفسه صديقك وأخوه).

If all or some of these are combined in a sentence, the order in which they are placed [in the sentence] are: the adjective, the explanatory conjunct, the emphasis, the substitute and then the conjunct for coordination. An example of this is the sentence, "The noble man himself, ʿAlī, your friend and his brother came."

تدريب على الإعراب

Exercises upon Grammatical Analysis

أعرب الأمثلة الآتية: (إبراهيم مُخلِص) ، ﴿وكان ربك قديراً﴾، (إن الله سميع الدعاء) .

Provide a grammatical analysis of the following examples: "Ibrāhīm is sincere", **{And your Lord is ever All-Powerful}**[132] and "Indeed Allah is hearing of supplications."

الجواب

Answers

١ - (إبراهيم) مبتدأ، مرفوع بالابتداء، وعلامة رفعه الضمة الظاهرة، (مخلص) خبر لمبتدأ، مرفوع بالمبتدأ، وعلامة رفعه الضمة الظاهرة .

132 Al-Furqān: 54

One. The word "Ibrāhīm" is the nominal subject, it is *marfūʿ* due to it being the commencement, and the sign of it being *marfūʿ* is the explicit *ḍammah*. The word "sincere" is the predicate of the nominal subject, it is *marfūʿ* due to the nominal subject and the sign of it being so is the explicit *ḍammah*.

٢ - (كان) فعل ماض ناقص، يرفع الاسم وينصب الخبر، (رب) اسم (كان) مرفوع بها، وعلامة رفعه الضمة الظاهرة، و(رب) مضاف، والكاف ضمير المخاطب مضاف إليه، مبني على الفتح في محل خفض، (قديراً) خبر (كان) منصوب بها، وعلامة نصبه الفتحة الظاهرة .

Two. The word "*kāna*" is a deficient *māḍī* verb that makes its noun *marfūʿ* and its predicate *manṣūb*. The word "Lord" is the noun of *kāna* and made *marfūʿ* by it, and the sign of it being so is the explicit *ḍammah*. The word "Lord" is also the *muḍāf* while the letter *kāf* (your) is the second person pronoun and the *muḍāf ilayh*. It is un-inflectable upon a *fatḥah* in the state of *khafḍ*. The word "All-Powerful" is the predicate of *kāna* and made *manṣūb* by it, and the sign of it being so is the explicit *fatḥah*.

٣ - (إن) حرف توكيد ونصب، (الله) لفظ الجلالة اسم (إن) منصوب به وعلامة نصبه الفتحة الظاهرة، (سميع) خبر (إن) مرفوع به، وعلامة رفعه الضمة الظاهرة، و(سميع) مضاف، و(الدعاء) مضاف إليه، مخفوض بالإضافة، وعلامة خفضه الكسرة الظاهرة.

Three. The word "*inna*" (indeed) is a particle of emphasis and *naṣb*. The word Allah is the name of the Majestic[133] and it is the noun of *inna*, made *manṣūb* by it and the sign of it being so is the explicit *fatḥah*. "Hearing" is the predicate of "*inna*" and made *marfūʿ* due to it, the sign of it being so is the explicit *ḍammah*. It is also the *muḍāf* while "supplications" is the *muḍāf ilayh*, made *makhfūḍ* due to being the possessor in a possessive compound and the sign of it being so is the explicit *kasrah*.

أسئلة

133 *Lafẓ al-jalālah* refers specifically to the word "Allah".

Questions

في كم موضع يكون الاسم مرفوعاً؟

In how many instances is the noun *marfū*?

ما أنواع التوابع؟ وإذا اجتمع التوكيد وعطف البيان والنعت فكيف ترتبها ؟ وإذا اجتمعت التوابع كلها فما الذي تقدمه منها؟

What are the types of the grammatical followers? When an emphasis, explanatory conjunct/conjoined word and an adjective are gathered in one sentence, in what order would they appear? When all of the followers are gathered, which one of them is given precedence over the others?

مثل للمبتدأ وخبره بمثالين، مثل لكل من اسم (كان) وخبر (إن) والفاعل ونائبه بمثالين .

Provide two examples of the nominal subject and the predicate. Provide two examples of the noun of *kāna*, predicate of *inna*, the subject and its deputy.

باب الفاعل

Chapter of the Subject

قال: (باب الفاعل) الفاعل هو: الاسم المرفوع المذكور قبله فعله.

He said: The subject is a *marfūʿ* noun which is preceded by the verb it applies to.

وأقول: الفاعل له معنيان: أحدهما لغوي والآخر اصطلاحي .

I say: The Arabic word *al-fāʿil* has two meanings, the first of them is linguistic and the other is technical.

أما معناه في اللغة فهو عبارة عمن أوجد الفعل.

As for the linguistic definition, it is an expression regarding the one who produces an action.

وأما معناه في الاصطلاح فهو: الاسم المرفوع المذكور قبله فعله، كما قال المؤلف.

As for its meaning according to the nomenclature of the grammarians, it is the *marfūʿ* noun which is preceded by the verb it applies to, as stated by the author.

وقولنا (الاسم) لا يشمل الفعل ولا الحرف، فلا يكون واحد منهما فاعلاً، وهو يشمل الاسم الصريح والاسم المؤول بالصريح.

Our statement "noun" negates the inclusion of the verb and particle, so evidently neither of them could be the subject. It consists of the explicit noun and the paraphrase of the explicit noun.

أما الصريح فنحو (نوح) و(إبراهيم) في قوله تعالى ﴿قَالَ نُوحٌ﴾، ﴿وَإِذْ يَرْفَعُ إِبْرَاهِيمُ﴾

As for the explicit noun, it consists of words similar to "Nūḥ" and "Ibrāhīm" in the statements of Allah: **{Nūḥ said}**[134] and **{And [mention] when Ibrāhīm was raising.}**[135]

وأما المؤول بالصريح فنحو قوله تعالى: ﴿أَوَلَمْ يَكْفِهِمْ أَنَّا أَنْزَلْنَا﴾، فـ(أن): حرف توكيد ونصب، و(نا) اسمه مبني على السكون في محل نصب، و(أنزلنا) فعل ماض وفاعله، والجملة في محل رفع خبر (أن)، و(أن) وما دخلت عليه في تأويل مصدر فاعل (يكفي) والتقدير: أولم يكفهم إنزالنا، ومثاله قولك: (يسرني أن تتمسك بالفضائل)، وقولك: (أعجبني ما صنعت)، التقدير فيهما: يسرني تمسكك، وأعجبني صنعك.

As for the paraphrase of the explicit noun, an example of it is in the statement of the Most High: **{And is it not sufficient for them that We revealed.}**[136] "*Anna*" (that) is a particle of emphasis and *naṣb*. The attached pronoun "*nā*" (we) is the *ism* of *anna*, un-inflectable upon a *sukūn* in the state of *naṣb*. "*Anzalnā*" (we revealed) consists of a *māḍī* verb and its subject, and as a sentence it is in the state of *rafʿ* due to it being the predicate of *anna*. *Anna* and what enters upon it are interpreted as an infinitive subject of "sufficient", and the implicit meaning is, "Does our revelation not suffice them?" More examples are, "I am pleased that you adhere to virtuousness", and, "I am marvelled by what you have manufactured." The implied meaning of both of these is, "I am pleased by your adherence" and "I am marvelled by your manufacturing."

وقولنا: (المرفوع) يخرج ما كان منصوباً أو مجروراً، فلا يكون واحد منهما فاعلاً.

Our statement "*marfūʿ*" negates the inclusion of the *manṣūb* and *majrūr*, so neither of them could be a subject.

وقولنا: (المذكور قبله فعله) يخرج المبتدأ واسم (إن) وأخواتها، فإنهما لم يتقدمهما

134 Nūḥ: 21
135 Al-Baqarah: 127
136 Al-ʿAnkabūt: 51

فعل البتة، ويخرج أيضاً اسم (كان) وأخواتها، واسم (كاد) وأخواتها، فإنهما وإن تقدمهما فعل فإن هذا الفعل ليس فعل واحدٍ منهما، والمراد بالفعل :ما يشمل شبه الفعل كاسم الفعل في نحو (هيهات العقيق) و(شتان زيد وعمرو) واسم الفاعل في نحوه (أقادم أبوك) فـ(العقيق) ، و(زيد) مع ما عطف عليه، و(أبوك) : كل منها فاعل.

Our statement, "which is preceded by the verb it applies to" negates the inclusion of the nominal subject and the noun of "*inna*" and its sisters, as both of these are never preceded by the verb. Likewise the noun of *kāna* and its sisters and the noun of *kāda* and its sisters are excluded from the definition of the subject, despite them being preceded by verbs—for neither of these action it. The intended meaning of the verb includes that which resembles the verb, such as the gerund e.g. "How far away is the canyon" and, "How unalike are Zayd and ʿAmr." The noun on the morphologic structure of the doer of the verb (*fāʿil*) e.g. "Is your father standing". The words "canyon", "Zayd" and the word conjoined to it (i.e. ʿAmr) and "your father" are all subjects.

أقسام الفاعل وأنواع الظاهر منه

Categories of the Subject and the Types of Apparent Ones from Them

قال: وهو على قسمين: ظاهر، ومضمر.

فالظاهر نحو قولك: (قام زيد، ويقوم زيد)، و(قام الزيدان، ويقوم الزيدان)، و(قام الزيدون، ويقوم الزيدون)، و(قام الرجال، ويقوم الرجال) ، و(قامت هند، وتقوم هند) ، و(قامت الهندان، وتقوم الهندان) ، و(قامت الهندات، وتقوم الهندات) ، و(قامت الهنود وتقوم الهنود)، و(قام أخوك ويقوم أخوك)، و(قام غلامي، ويقوم غلامي)، وما أشبه ذلك .

He said: It consists of two types: (i) the apparent, and (ii) the implicit. Examples of the apparent are the statements, "Zayd stood" and "Zayd stands", "the two Zayds stood" and "the two Zayds stand", "the Zayds stood" and "the Zayds stand", "the men stood" and "the men stand", "Hind stood" and "Hind stands", "the two Hinds stood" and "the two Hinds stand", "the Hinds stood" and "the Hinds stand", "your brother stood" and "your brother stands", "my boy stood" and "my boy stands", and other similar words.

وأقول: ينقسم الفاعل إلى قسمين: الأول الظاهر والثاني المضمر، فأما الظاهر فهو: ما يدل على معناه بدون حاجة إلى قرينة، وأما المضمر فهو: ما لا يدل على المراد منه إلا بقرينة تكلم أو خطاب غيبة.

I say: The subject is categorised into two: (i) the apparent and (ii) the inferred. As for the apparent, it is that which indicates towards a meaning without the need of an indicator. As for the inferred, it is that which does not display a meaning except through an indicator in the first person, second person or third person.

والظاهر على أنواع: لأنه إما أن يكون مفرداً أو مثنى أو مجموعاً جمعاً سالماً أو جمع تكسير، وكل من هذه الأنواع الأربعة إما أن يكون مذكراً وإما أن يكون مؤنثاً، فهذه ثمانية أنواع، وأيضاً فإما أن يكون إعرابه بضمة ظاهرة أو مقدرة، وإما أن يكون إعرابه بالحروف نيابة عن الضمة، وعلى كل هذه الأحوال إما أن يكون الفعل ماضياً، وإما أن يكون مضارعاً.

The apparent subject is of various types, and this is because sometimes it is: (i) singular, (ii) dual, (iii) plural: (iii-i) the sound plural or (iii-ii) the broken plural. And each of these four types is sometimes: (i) masculine, or (ii) feminine and thus this produces eight types. Further to this, sometimes it inflects with the explicit *ḍammah* or the implicit *ḍammah*, and sometimes it inflects with letters deputising for the *ḍammah*. And in all of these cases, it will either have a *māḍī* verb or a *muḍāriʿ* verb.

فمثال الفاعل المفرد المذكر: مع الفعل الماضي: (سافر محمد)؛ و(حضر خالد) ومع الفعل المضارع: (يسافر محمد)، و(يحضر خالد) .

Examples of the singular masculine subject with *māḍī* verbs are: "Muḥammad travelled" and "Khālid was present." Examples with *muḍāriʿ* verbs are, "Muḥammad travels" and "Khālid comes."

ومثال الفاعل المثنى المذكر: مع الفعل الماضي (حضر الصديقان) ، و(سافر الأخوان)، ومع الفعل المضارع (يحضر الصديقان) ، و(يسافر الأخوان) .

Examples of the dual masculine subject with a *māḍī* verb are: "the two friends were present" and "the two brothers travelled." Examples with a *muḍāriʿ* verb are: "the two friends come" and "the two brothers travel."

ومثال الفاعل المجموع جمع تصحيح لمذكر مع الفعل الماضي (حضر المحمَّدون) ، و(حجَّ المسلمون) ، ومع الفعل المضارع: (يحضر المحمَّدون) ، و(يحُج المسلمون).

Examples of the sound plural masculine subject with a *māḍī* verb are: "the Muḥammads were present" and "the Muslims performed Ḥajj". Examples with *muḍāri'* verbs are: "the Muḥammads are present" and "the Muslims are performing Ḥajj."

ومثال الفاعل المجموع جمع تكسير؛ وهو مذكر مع الماضي: (حضر الأصدقاء)، و(سافر الزعماء)، ومع المضارع: (يحضر الأصدقاء)، و(يسافر الزعماء) .

Examples of the broken plural masculine subject with a *māḍī* verb are: "the friends were present" and "the leaders travelled." Examples with a *muḍāri'* verb are: "the friends come" and "the leaders travel."

ومثال الفاعل المفرد المؤنث: مع الماضي (حضرت هند) ، و(سافرت سعاد) ، ومع المضارع: (تحضر هند) ، و(تسافر سعاد).

Examples of the singular feminine subject with a *māḍī* verb are: "Hind was present" and "Su'ād travelled". Examples with a *muḍāri'* verb are: "Hind comes" and "Su'ād travels".

ومثال الفاعل المثنى المؤنث: مع الماضي (حضرت الهندان) ، و(سافرت الزينبان) ، ومع المضارع (تحضر الهندان) ، و(تسافر الزينبان) .

Examples of the dual feminine subject with a *maḍī* verb are: "the two Hinds were present" and "the two Zaynabs travelled." Examples with a *muḍāri'* verb are: "the two Hinds come" and "the two Zaynabs travel."

ومثال الفاعل المجموع جمع تصحيح لمؤنث: مع الماضي (حضرت الهندات) ، و(سافرت الزينبات) ومع المضارع (تحضر الهندات) ، و(تسافر الزينبات) .

Examples of the sound plural feminine subject with a *māḍī* verb are: "the Hinds were present" and "the Zaynabs travelled". Examples with a *muḍāri'* verb are: "the Hinds are present" and "the Zaynabs travel".

ومثال الفاعل المجموع جمع تكسير، وهو لمؤنث: مع الماضي (حضرت الهنود) ، و(

سافرت الزيانب)، ومع المضارع: (تحضر الهنود) ، و(تسافر الزيانب) .

Examples of the broken plural feminine subject with a *māḍī* verb are: "the Hinds were present" and "the Zaynabs travelled." Examples with a *muḍāriʿ* verb are: "the Hinds come" and "the Zaynabs travel."

ومثال الفاعل الذي إعرابه بالضمة الظاهرة جميع ما تقدم من الأمثلة ما عدا المثنى المذكر والمؤنث وجمع التصحيح لمذكر.

All of these types that we have mentioned inflect with an explicit *ḍammah* except for the dual masculine form, the dual feminine form and the sound masculine plural.

ومثال الفاعل الذي إعرابه بالضمة المقدرة: مع الفعل الماضي (حضر الفتى) ، و(سافر القاضي) ، و(أقبل صديقي)، ومع المضارع (يحضر الفتى) ، و(يسافر القاضي)، و(يقبل صديقي) .

Examples of the subject that inflects with an implicit *ḍammah*, with a *māḍī* verb are: "The boy was present", "The judge travelled and "My friend approached." Examples with a *muḍāriʿ* verb are: "The boy is present", "The judge travels" and "My friend approaches."

ومثال الفاعل الذي إعرابه بالحروف النائبة عن الضمة ما تقدم من أمثلة الفاعل المثنى المذكر أو المؤنث، وأمثلة الفاعل المجموع جمع تصحيح لمذكر، ومن أمثلته أيضاً: مع الماضي (حضر أبوك) ، (سافر أخوك)، ومع المضارع (يحضر أبوك) ، و(يسافر أخوك) .

Examples were provided above of the subject that inflects with a letter serving as the representative for the *ḍammah*, this includes both the masculine and feminine dual forms, and also the sound masculine plural. From them is also [with *māḍī* verbs]: "your father was present" and "your brother travelled", and with *muḍāriʿ* verbs: "your father comes" and "your brother travels."

أنواع الفاعل المضمر

Types of the Implicit Subject

قال: والمضمر اثنا عشر، نحو قولك: (ضربت) ، و(ضربنا) ، و(ضربتَ) ، و(ضربتِ) ، و(ضربتُما) ، و(ضربتُم) ، و(ضربتن) ، و(ضربَ) ، و(ضربت) ، و(ضربا) ، و(ضربوا) ، و(ضربنَ).

He said: The implicit consists of twelve, examples are, "I hit", "we hit", "you hit", "you (fem.) hit", "you two hit", "you all hit", "you all (fem.) hit", "he hit", "she hit", "those two hit", "they hit" and "they (fem.) hit."

وأقول: قد عرفت فيما تقدم المضمر ما هو، والآن نعرفك أنه على اثني عشر نوعاً. وذلك لأنه:

I say: We have previously defined what the implicit subject is and at this juncture we continue to explain to you that it is of twelve types, this is because:

إما أن يدل على متكلم، وإما أن يدل على مخاطب، وإما أن يدل على غائب.

Sometimes it refers to the first person, sometimes to the second person and sometimes to the third person.

والذي يدل على متكلم، يتنوع إلى نوعين: لأنه إما أن يكون المتكلم واحداً، وإما أن يكون أكثر من واحد.

The subject that refers to the first person is categorised into two: sometimes it is singular and sometimes it is plural.

والذي يدل على مخاطب أو غائب يتنوع كل منهما إلى خمسة أنواع، لأنه إما أن يدل

على مفرد مذكر، وإما أن يدل على مفردة مؤنثة، وإما أن يدل على مثنى مطلقاً، وإما أن يدل على جمع مذكر، وإما أن يدل على جمع مؤنث، فيكون المجموع اثني عشر .

The subject that refers to the second person or third person is categorised into five in both cases: sometimes it indicates to the singular masculine, sometimes it indicates to the singular feminine, sometimes it indicates to the dual, sometimes it indicates to the masculine plural, and sometimes it indicates to the feminine plural. These all add up to twelve types.

فمثال ضمير المتكلم الواحد، مذكراً كان أو مؤنثاً (ضربتُ) ، و(حفظتُ)، و(اجتهدتُ) .

Examples of the pronoun in the first person singular—both masculine and feminine—are: "I hit", "I memorised" and "I strove".

ومثال ضمير المتكلم المتعدد أو الواحد الذي يعظم نفسه وينزلها منزلة الجماعة (ضربنا)، و(حفظنا) ، و(اجتهدنا).

Examples of the pronoun in the first person when referring to more than one, or when referring to one's own self in an overtly respectful manner that takes the style of the plural are: "we hit", "we memorised" and "we strove".

ومثال ضمير المخاطب الواحد المذكر (ضربتَ) ، و(حفظتَ) ، و(اجتهدتَ) .

Examples of the pronoun in the second person masculine singular are: "you hit", "you memorised" and, "you strove."

ومثال ضمير المخاطبة الواحدة المؤنثة (ضربتِ) ، و(حفظتِ) ، و(اجتهدتِ) .

Examples of the pronoun in the second person feminine singular are: "you hit", "you memorised" and, "you strove."

ومثال ضمير المخاطبين الاثنين مذكرين أو مؤنثتين (ضربتما) ، و(حفظتما) ، و(اجتهدتما) .

Examples of the pronoun in the second person dual—both masculine and feminine—are: “you two hit”, “you two memorised”, and “you two strove.”

ومثال ضمير المخاطبين من جمع الذكور (ضربتم) ، و(حفظتم) ، و(اجتهدتم) .

Examples of the pronoun in the second person masculine plural are: “you hit”, “you memorised” and, “you strove”.

ومثال ضمير المخاطبات من جمع المؤنثات (ضربتن) ، و(حفظتن) ، و(اجتهدتن) .

Examples of the pronoun in the second person feminine plural are: “you hit”, “you memorised” and, “you strove”.

ومثال ضمير الواحد المذكر الغائب (ضرب) في قولك: (محمد ضرب أخاه) و(حفظ) في قولك (إبراهيم حفظ درسه) و(اجتهدَ) في قولك: (خالد اجتهد في عمله)

Examples of the pronoun in the third person masculine singular are: “he hit” in the statement, “Muḥammad hit his brother”, “he memorised” in the statement, “Ibrāhīm memorised his lesson”, and “he strove” in the statement, “Khālid strove in his work.”

ومثال ضمير الواحدة المؤنَّثة الغائبة : (ضربت) في قولك : (هند ضربت أُختَها) ، و : (حفظتْ) في قولك : (سعادُ حَفِظَتْ دَرْسَها) ، و : (اجتَهَدَت) في قولك (زينب اجتهدتْ في عملها).

Examples of the pronoun in the third person feminine singular are: “she hit” in the statement, “Hind hit her sister”, “she memorised” in the statement, “Su‘ād memorised her lesson” and “she strove” in, “Zaynab strove in her work”.

ومثال ضمير الاثنين الغائبين مذكرين كانا أو مؤنثين (ضربا) في قولك: (المحمدان

ضربا بكراً) أو قولك: (الهندان ضربتا عامراً) و(حفظا) في قولك: (المحمدان حفظا درسهما) أو قولك: (الهندان حفظتا درسهما) و(اجتهدا) من نحو قولك: (البكران اجتهدا) أو قولك (الزينبان اجتهدتا) و(قاما) في نحو قولك: (المحمدان قاما بواجبهما) أو قولك (الهندان قامتا بواجبهما).

Examples of the pronoun in the third person masculine and feminine dual are: "those two hit" as in the statement, "the two Muḥammads hit Bakr" or "the two Hinds hit ʿĀmir, "those two memorised" as in the statement, "the two Muḥammads memorised their lessons" or "the two Hinds memorised their lessons", "those two strove" as in the statement, "the two Bakrs strove" or "the two Zaynabs strove", and "those two stood" as in the statement, "the two Muḥammads stood by their obligations" or "the two Hinds stood by their obligations."

ومثال ضمير الغائبين من جمع الذكور (ضربوا) من نحو قولك: (الرجال ضربوا أعداءهم) و(حفظوا) من نحو قولك: (التلاميذ حفظوا دروسهم) و(اجتهدوا) من نحو قولك: (التلاميذ اجتهدوا) .

Examples of the pronoun in the third person masculine plural are: "they hit" as in the statement, "the men hit their foes", "they memorised" as in the statement, "the students memorised their lessons", and "they strove" as in the statement, "the students strove".

ومثال ضمير الغائبات من جمع الإناث (ضربن) من نحو قولك: (الفتيات ضربن عدواتهن) وكذا (حفظن) من نحو قولك (النساء حفظن أماناتهن) وكذا (اجنهدن) من نحو قولك: (البنات اجتهدن) .

Examples of the pronoun in the third person feminine plural are: "they hit" as in the statement, "the girls hit their foes", "they maintain" as in the statement, "the women maintain their pacts", and "they strove" as in the statement, "the daughters strove".

وكل هذه الأنواع الأثني عشر السابقة يسمى الضمير فيها (الضمير المتصل) وتعريفه أنه هو: الذي لا يبتدأ به الكلام ولا يقع بعد (إلا) في حالة الاختيار.

In each of these twelve types that we have just mentioned the pronoun is referred to as "the attached pronoun". Its definition is: It is the one which does not commence speech and does not come after the word "*illā*" (except) in the case of displaying preference (i.e. "except for such and such").[137]

ومثلها يأتي في نوع آخر من الضمير يسمى (الضمير المنفصل) وهو: الذي يبتدأ به ويقع بعد (إلا) في حالة الاختيار، تقول (ما ضرب إلا أنا) و(ما ضرب إلا نحن) و(ما ضرب إلا أنت) ، و(ما ضرب إلا أنتِ) ، و(ما ضرب إلا أنتما) ، و(ما ضرب إلا أنتم) ، و(ما ضرب إلا أنتن) ، و(ما ضرب إلا هو)، و(ما ضرب إلا هي)، و(ما ضرب إلا هما) ، و(ما ضرب إلا هم)، و(ما ضرب إلا هن) وعلى هذا يجري القياس. وسيأتي بيان أنواع الضمير المنفصل بأوسع من هذه الإشارة في باب المبتدأ والخبر .

Examples of them coming in the different form of pronouns that we refer to as "the detached pronoun"—and its definition is that it is the one which can commence and it is placed after the word "except for" in the case of displaying preference—are: "Non hit except for me", "non hit except for us", "non hit except for you", "non hit except for you", "none hit except for you two", "none hit except for you", "none hit except for you", "none hit except for him", "none hit except for her", "none hit except for them two", "non hit except for them" and, "non hit except for them", and the pattern continues accordingly. And we will discuss the types of the detached pronoun in deeper detail than this in the Chapter of the Nominal Subject and Its Predicate.

تمرينات

Exercises

137 Ibn ʿAqīl said (1/89), "The attached pronoun is that which does not commence speech, such as the letter *kāf* in the statement (أكرمك). It does not follow the word *illā* in the case of displaying preference, so it is not right to say, (ما أكرمت إلا ك)."

١ ـ اجعل كل اسم من الأسماء الآتية فاعلاً في جملتين، بشرط أن يكون الفعل ماضياً في إحداهما، ومضارعاً في الأخرى :

One. Utilise each of the following nouns as the subject in two sentences with the condition that the verb is *māḍī* in the first sentence and *muḍāriʿ* in the other:

أبوك، صديقك، التجار، المخلصون، ابني، الأستاذ، الشجرة، الربيع، الحصان .

٢ ـ هات مع كل فعل من الأفعال الآتية اسمين، واجعل كل واحدا منهما فاعلاً له في جملة مناسبة:

Two. Bring two nouns with each of the following verbs, and give examples of each of them as a subject for the verb in an appropriate sentence:

حضر، اشترى، يربح، ينجو، نجح، أدى، أثمرت، أقبل، صهل .

٣ ـ أجب عن كل سؤال من الأسئلة الآتية بجملة مفيدة مشتملة على فعل وفاعل:

Three. Answer each of the following questions with a benefit deriving sentence that incorporates a verb and its subject.

(أ) متى تسافر؟

(ب) أين يذهب صاحبك ؟

(ج) هل حضر أخوك ؟

(د) كيف وجدتَ الكتاب ؟

(ه) ماذا تصنع ؟

(و) متى ألقاك ؟

(ز) أيان تقضي فصل الصيف ؟

(ح) ما الذي تدرسه ؟

٤ ـ كوِّن من الكلمات الآتية جملاً تشتمل كل واحدة منها على فعل وفاعل .

Three. Form sentences from the following words. Incorporate within each one a verb and a subject.

نجح، فاز، ربح، فاض، أينع، المجتهد، المخلص، الزهر، النيل، التاجر.

تدريب على الإعراب

Exercises on Grammatical Analysis

أعرب الجمل الآتية:

Provide a grammatical analysis of the following sentences:

حضر محمد، سافر المرتضى، سيزورنا القاضي، أقبل أخي .

Muḥammad was present. Al-Murtaḍā travelled. We will be visited by the judge. My brother came.

الجواب

Answer

١ ـ حضر محمد : (حضر) : فعل ماض مبني على الفتح لا محل له من الإعراب، (محمد) : فاعل مرفوع، وعلامة رفعه الضمة الظاهرة في آخره .

One. "Muḥammad was present": "Was present" is a *māḍī* verb that is un-inflectable upon a *fatḥah* with no grammatical state. "Muḥammad" is a *marfūʿ* subject, and the sign of it being in the state of *rafʿ* is the explicit *ḍammah* at its ending.

٢ ـ سافر المرتضى : (سافر) : فعل ماض مبني على الفتح لا محل له من الإعراب، (المرتضى) : فاعل مرفوع وعلامة رفعه ضمة مقدرة على الألف منع من ظهورها التعذر.

Two. "Al-Murtaḍā travelled": "Travelled" is a *māḍī* verb that is un-inflectable upon a *fatḥah* with no grammatical state. "Al-Murtaḍā" is a *marfūʿ* subject, and the sign of it being in the state of *rafʿ* is the implicit *ḍammah* upon its *alif*, prevented from being displayed due to impracticability.

٣ - سيزورنا القاضي : (سيزورنا) : السين: حرف دال على التنفيس، يزور: فعل مضارع مرفوع لتجرده من الناصب والجازم، وعلامة رفعه الضمة الظاهرة، و(نا) : مفعول به مبني على السكون في محل نصب، و(القاضي) فاعل مرفوع، وعلامة رفعه ضمة مقدرة على الياء منع من ظهورها الثقل .

Three. "We will be visited by the judge": The letter *sīn* is a particle that indicates *tanfīs* (the process that alters the *muḍāriʿ* verb from the present tense to the future tense). "He visits" is a *muḍāriʿ* verb which is *marfūʿ* due to the absence of a *nāṣib* or *jāzim* and the sign of it being in the state of *rafʿ* is the explicit *ḍammah*. "We" is the object, un-inflectable upon a *sukūn* in the state of *naṣb*. "The judge" is a *marfūʿ* subject and the sign of it being in the state of *rafʿ* is the implicit *ḍammah* on the letter *yā*, prevented from being displayed due to heaviness.

٤ - أقبل أخي : (أقبل) : فعل ماض مبني على الفتح لا محل له من الإعراب، و(أخ) : فاعل مرفوع، وعلامة رفعه ضمة مقدرة على آخره منع من ظهورها اشتغال المحل بحركة المناسبة، و(أخ) مضاف و(ياء المتكلم) ضمير مضاف إليه مبني على السكون في محل جر .

Four. "My brother came": "Came" is a *māḍī* verb that is un-inflectable upon a *fatḥah* with no grammatical state. "Brother" is a *marfūʿ* subject and the sign of it being in the state of *rafʿ* is the implicit *ḍammah* at its end, prevented from being displayed due to the position being occupied by the appropriate diacritic. "Brother" is the *muḍāf* (possessed part of a possessive compound) and the letter *yā* of the first person (my) is the *muḍāf ilayh* (possessor), it is a pronoun that is un-inflectable upon a *sukūn* in the state of *jarr*.

أسئلة

Questions

ما هو الفاعل لغة واصطلاحاً؟

What is the subject, both linguistically and technically?

مثل للفاعل الصريح بمثالين، والفاعل المؤول بالصريح بمثالين أيضا.

Provide two examples of the explicit subject and likewise do so for the subject which is a paraphrase of an explicit noun.

مثل للفاعل المرفوع باسم فعل بمثالين، وللفاعل المرفوع باسم فاعل بمثالين أيضا.

Provide two examples of the *marfūʿ* subject made from a verbal noun and also provide two examples of the *marfūʿ* subject made from a noun on the *fāʿil* word structure.

إلى كم قسم ينقسم الفاعل؟ ما هو الظاهر؟ ما هو المضمر؟ إلى كم قسم ينقسم المضمر؟

Into how many types is the subject categorised into? What is the apparent? What is the inferred? Into how many categories is the inferred divided into?

على كم نوع يتنوع الضمير المتصل؟ مثل لكل نوع من أنواع الضمير المتصل بمثلين. ما هو الضمير المتصل ؟

How many types of the attached pronoun are there? Provide two examples of each type of the attached pronoun. Define the attached pronoun.

ما هو الضمير المنفصل؟ مثل للضمير المنفصل الواقع فاعلاً باثني عشر مثالاً منوعة، وبين ما يدل الضمير عليه في كل منها .

What is the detached pronoun? Provide twelve examples from the different types of detached pronouns that serve as the subject, and explain what the pronoun indicates to in each of your examples.

ـ أعرب الجمل الآتية: كتب محمود درسه ... اشترى علي كتاباً ... ﴿**يا قومنآ أجيبوا داعي الله**﴾ ... ﴿**من عمل صالحاً فلنفسه**﴾ .

Provide a grammatical analysis of the following sentences: "Maḥmūd wrote his lesson", "'Alī brought a book", {**O our people, respond to the caller of Allah**}[138] and {**Whoever does a good deed—it is for himself.**}[139]

138 Al-Aḥqāf: 31
139 Al-Jāthiyah: 15

النائب عن الفاعل

The Deputy of the Subject

قال: (باب المفعول الذي لم يسم فاعله) وهو: الاسم، المرفوع، الذي لم يذكر معه فاعله .

He said: Chapter of the Object Where the Subject is not Named.[140] It is a noun, *marfūʿ*, and its subject is not mentioned.

وأقول: قد يكون الكلام مؤلفاً من فعل وفاعل ومفعول به، نحو (قطع محمود الغصن) ونحو (حفظ خليل الدرس)، ونحو (يقطع إبراهيم الغصن)، و(يحفظ علي الدرس) .

I say: Sometimes speech may comprise of a verb, its subject and its object. Examples are: "Mahmūd cut the branch", "Khalīl memorised the lesson", Ibrāhīm is cutting the branch" and "ʿAlī memorises the lesson."

وقد يحذف المتكلم الفاعل من هذا الكلام ويكتفي بذكر الفعل والمفعول، وحينئذ يجب عليه أن يغير صورة الفعل، ويغير صورة المفعول أيضاً، أما تغير صورة الفعل فسيأتي الكلام عليه.

And sometimes the speaker may omit the subject in this speech, instead sufficing with mentioning the verb and its object. In this circumstance it is mandatory for the speaker to alter the form of the verb and the form of the object as well. As for the alteration to the form of the verb, we will explain this shortly.

وأما تغيير صورة المفعول فإنه بعد أن كان منصوباً يصيره مرفوعاً، ويعطيه أحكام الفاعل:

140 Perhaps it would have been better for Ibn Ājurūm (may Allah have mercy upon) to express this here with the deputy of the subject (النائب عن الفاعل). See *Shudhūr al-Dhahab* (p. 159) and *Ḥāshiyat al-Ḥāmidī* (p. 82).

من وجوب تأخيره عن الفعل، وتأنيث فعله له إن كان مؤنثاً، وغير ذلك، ويسمى حينئذ (نائب الفاعل) أو (المفعول الذي لم يسم فاعله) .

As for the alteration of the form of the object, it changes from being *manṣūb* to becoming *marfūʿ* and it takes the rulings of the subject i.e. it is mandatory for it to be preceded by the verb, and for its verb to be feminine if it itself is feminine etc. We call this the deputy of the subject or the object where the subject is not named.

تغيير الفعل بعد حذف الفاعل

The Alteration of the Verb After the Removal of Its Subject

قال: فإن كان الفعل ماضياً ضُم أوله، وكسر الحرف الذي قبل آخره وإن كان مضارعاً ضم أوله وفتح ما قبل آخره .

He said: If it is a *māḍī* verb, it is given a *ḍammah* on the first letter and a *kasrah* on the letter that comes before the final one. If it is *muḍāriʿ*, it is given a *ḍammah* on the first letter and a *fatḥah* on the letter that comes before the final one.

أقول: ذكر المصنف في هذه العبارات التغييرات التي تحدث في الفعل عند حذف فاعله وإسناده إلى المفعول، وذلك أنه إذا كان ماضياً ضم أوله وكسر الحرف الذي قبل آخره، فتقول: (قُطِعَ الغُصْنُ) و(حُفِظَ الدَّرْسُ).

I say: The author has mentioned in the above statement the alteration of the verb that takes place when the subject is removed and the verb is connected to the object (where the subject is not mentioned). And the alteration is that the *māḍī* is given a *ḍammah* on the beginning letter and a *kasrah* upon the letter that comes before its final one. So one says, "The branch was cut" and, "The lesson was memorised".

وإن كان الفعل مضارعاً ضم أوله وفتح الحرف الذي قبل آخره، فتقول (يُقْطَعُ الغُصْنُ)، و(يُحْفَظُ الدَّرْسُ) .

And if it is a *muḍāri'* verb then the first letter is given a *ḍammah* and a *fatḥah* is placed upon the letter that comes before the final one. Examples are, "The branch is being cut" and, "The lesson is being memorised."

أقسام نائب الفاعل

Categories of the Deputy of the Subject

قال: وهو على قسمين: ظاهر، ومضمر، فالظاهر نحو قولك (ضُرِب زيدٌ)، و(يُضْرَبُ زيدٌ)، و(أُكْرِمَ عمرٌو)، و(يُكْرَمُ عمرٌو).

والمضمر اثنا عشر، نحو قولك (ضُرِبْتُ)، و(ضُرِبْنا)، و(ضُرِبْتَ)، و(ضُرِبْتِ)، و(ضُرِبْتُما)، و(ضُرِبْتم)، و(ضُرِبْتُنَّ)، و(ضُرِبَ)، و(ضُرِبَتْ)، و(ضُرِبا)، و(ضُرِبوا)، و(ضُرِبْنَ).

He said: It is of two types: the explicit and the inferred. Examples of the explicit type are: "Zayd was hit", "Zayd is hit", "'Amr was honoured" and "'Amr is honoured". The inferred consists of twelve, examples are: "I was hit", "We were hit", "You were hit", "You (fem.) were hit", "You two were hit", "You (pl.) were hit", "You (pl. fem.) were hit", "He was hit", "She was hit", "Them two were hit", "They were hit" and, "They (fem.) were hit".

أقول: ينقسم نائب الفاعل - كما انقسم الفاعل - إلى ظاهر ومضمر، والمضمر إلى متصل ومنفصل .

I say: The deputy of the subject is categorised—as the subject was categorised—into two: the explicit and the inferred, and the inferred is further sub-categorised into the attached and the detached.

وأنواع كل قسم من الضمير اثنا عشر: اثنان للمتكلم، وخمسة للمخاطب، وخمسة للغائب، وقد ذكرنا تفصيل ذلك كله في باب الفاعل، فلا حاجة بنا إلى تكراره هنا .

And the types of each category of the pronouns are twelve: Two for the first person, five for the second person and five for the third person. We have discussed this in detail in the "Chapter of the Subject" and there is no need in us repeating it here.

تدريب على الإعراب

Exercises on Grammatical Analysis

أعرب الجملتين الآتيتين: يُحتَرَمُ العالم، أُهِينَ الجَاهِلُ .

Provide a grammatical analysis of the following two sentences: "The scholar is honoured" and, "The ignorant was disdained".

الجواب

Answer

١ ـ يُحترم: فعل مضارع مبني للمجهول، مرفوع لتجرده من الناصب والجازم، وعلامة رفعه الضمة الظاهرة، العالم: نائب فاعل، مرفوع وعلامة رفعه الضمة الظاهرة .

One. "Is honoured": It is a *muḍāriʿ* verb that is un-inflectable due to being in the passive voice. It is *marfūʿ* due to the absence of a *nāṣib* or a *jāzim*, and the sign of it being in the state of *rafʿ* is the explicit *ḍammah*. "The scholar": It is the deputy of the subject. It is *marfūʿ* and the sign of it being so is the explicit *ḍammah*.

٢ ـ أُهِينَ: فعل ماض مبني للمجهول، مبني على الفتح لا محل له من الإعراب .
الجاهل: نائب فاعل، مرفوع وعلامة رفعه الضمة الظاهرة .

Two. "Is disdained": It is a *māḍī* verb that is un-inflectable due to being in the passive voice. It is un-inflectable upon a *fatḥah* and has no grammatical state. "The ignorant": It is the deputy of the subject. It is *marfūʿ* and the sign of it being so is the explicit *ḍammah*.

تمرينات

Exercises

١ ـ كل جملة من الجمل الآتية مؤلفة من فعل وفاعل ومفعول، فاحذف الفاعل واجعل المفعول نائباً عنه، واضبط الفعل بالشكل الكامل.

One. Each of the following sentences comprises of a verb, subject and object. Remove the subject and make the object its deputy. Express the full diacritics of the verbs.

قطع محمود زهرة، اشترى أخي كتاباً، قرأ إبراهيم درسه، يعطي أبي الفقراء، يكرم الأستاذ المجتهد، يتعلم ابني الرماية، يستغفر التائب ربنا .

٢ ـ اجعل كل اسم من الأسماء الآتية نائباً عن الفاعل في جملة مفيدة:

Two. Utilise each of the following nouns as the deputy of the subject in beneficial sentences.

الطبيب، النمر، النهر، الفأر، الحصان، الكتاب، القلم.

٣ ـ اِبنِ كل فعل من الأفعال الآتية للمجهول، واضبطه بالشكل، وضم إليه نائب فاعل يتم به معه الكلام.

Three. Alter each of the following verbs into the passive voice and express the appropriate diacritics. Combine with the verb a deputy of the subject which will complete speech alongside it.

يكرم، يقطع، يعبر، يأكل، يركب، يقرأ، يبري .

٤- عين الفاعل ونائبه، والفعل المبني للمعلوم والمبني للمجهول، من بين الكلمات التي في العبارات الآتية:

Four. Identify in the speech within the following paragraph: the subject and its deputy, the un-inflectable verb in the active voice and the passive voice:

لا خاب مَن استخار، ولا ندم مَن استشار، إذا عز أخوك فهنْ، مَن لم يحذر العواقب لم يجد له صاحباً، كان جعفر بن يحيى يقول: الخراج عمود المُلك، وما استُعزِزَ بمثل العدل، ولا استنزر بمثل الظلم . كلم الناس عبد الرحمن بن عوف أن يكلم عمر بن الخطاب في أن يلين لهم، فإنه قد أخافهم حتى أخاف الأبكار في خدورهِنَّ، فقال عمر: إني لا أجد لهم إلا ذلك، إنهم لو يعلمون ما لهم عندي، أخذوا ثوبي عن عاتقي، لا يُلامُ مَن احتاط لنفسه، من يوق شُح نفسه يسلم .

أسئلة

Questions

ما هو نائب الفاعل؟ هل تعرف له اسماً آخر؟

What is the deputy of the subject? Do you know another name for it?

ما الذي تعمله في الفعل عند إسناده للنائب عن فاعل؟

What is done to the verb when it is connected to a deputy subject instead of the subject?

ما الذي تفعله في المفعول إذا أقمته مقام الفاعل ؟

What is done to the object of the verb when it is placed in the position of the subject?

مثل بثلاثة أمثلة لنائب الفاعل الظاهر.

Provide three examples of the explicit deputy of the subject.

المبتدأ والخبر

The Nominal Subject and Predicate

قال: (باب المبتدأ والخبر) المبتدأ: هو الاسم المرفوع العاري عن العوامل اللفظية، والخبر: هو الاسم المرفوع المسند إليه، نحو قولك (زيد قائم)، و(الزيدان قائمان)، و(الزيدون قائمون) .

He said: The nominal subject and predicate. The nominal subject: It is a *marfūʿ* noun which is bare of any expressed governors of grammatical change. The predicate: It is a *marfūʿ* noun that refers back to the nominal subject. Examples are, "Zayd is standing", "The two Zayds are standing" and, "The Zayds are standing."

وأقول: المبتدأ عبارة عما اجتمع فيه ثلاثة أمور؛

I say: The nominal subject is a word that incorporates three characteristics:

الأول: أن يكون اسماً، فخرج عن ذلك الفعل والحرف، والثاني: أن يكون مرفوعاً، فخرج بذلك المنصوب والمجرور بحرف جر أصلي، والثالث: أن يكون عارياً عن العوامل اللفظية.

First: It is a noun. This removes the verb and the particle from its definition. Second: It is *marfūʿ*. This removes the *manṣūb* and the *majrūr* due to an original particle of *jarr*. Third: It is bare of any expressed governors of grammatical change.[141]

---

141 The grammatical governors are split into two: (i) the expressed governors of grammatical change (and they are many e.g. *kāna* and its sisters, *inna* and its sisters etc.) and, (ii) the implicit governors, and the most common of them are the commencement (الابتداء)—which makes the nominal subject *marfūʿ*, and the absence of a *nāṣib* and a *jāzim*—which makes the *muḍāriʿ* verb *marfūʿ*.

ومعنى هذا أن يكون خالياً من العوامل اللفظية مثل الفعل ومثل (كان) وأخواتها، فإن الاسم الواقع بعد الفعل يكون فاعلا، أو نائبا عن الفاعل.. على ما سبق، والاسم الواقع بعد (كان) أو إحدى أخواتها يسمى (اسم (كان)) ولا يسمى (مبتدأ) .

The meaning of this is that it is clear of any expressed governors of grammatical change such as the verb, and *kāna* or its sisters. So the noun present after the verb is its subject or the deputy of the subject, as we have spoken about previously. And the noun present after *kāna* or one of its sisters is termed as "the noun of *kāna*", and it is not termed as the subject.

ومثال المستوفي هذه الشروط الثلاثة (محمد) من قولك: (محمد حاضر) فإنه اسم مرفوع لم يتقدمه عامل لفظي .

The example of a word possessing all three of these characteristics is "Muḥammad" in the sentence, "Muḥammad is present." It is a *marfū'* noun that is not preceded by an expressed governor of grammatical change.

والخبر: هو الاسم المرفوع الذي يسند إلى المبتدأ ويحمل عليه، فيتم به معه الكلام، ومثاله (حاضر) من قولك: (محمد حاضر).

As for the predicate, it is a *marfū'* noun that refers back to the nominal subject[142] and combines with the nominal subject to complete speech. An example of it is "present" in the statement, "Muḥammad is present."

وحكم كل من المبتدأ والخبر الرفع كما رأيت، وهذا الرفع إما أن يكون بضمة ظاهرة، نحو (الله ربنا)، و(محمد نبينا) وإما أن يكون مرفوعاً بضمة مقدرة للتعذر نحو (موسى مصطفى من الله) ونحو (ليلى فضلى النساء)، وإما أن يكون بضمة مقدرة منع

142 There is somewhat of a deficiency in this definition due to the use of the word "noun" (الاسم) excluding the sentence and the quasi sentence (شبه الجملة)—though they both can be utilised as the predicate. A more encompassing definition is that which was stated by Ibn Hishām in *Sharḥ al-Qaṭr* (p. 161), "It is a supporting [statement] that, when coupled with the nominal subject, speech is completed properly." (هو المسند الذي تتم به مع المبتدأ فائدة).

من ظهورها الثقل نحو (القاضي هو الآتي) وإما أن يكون مرفوعاً بحرف من الحروف التي تنوب عن الضمة، نحو (المجتهدان فائزان).

The ruling of the nominal subject and the predicate is that they are in the state of *raf*ʿ, as you have seen. And the state of *raf*ʿ is sometimes displayed by way of an explicit *ḍammah*, as in, "Allah is our lord" and "Muḥammad is our prophet". Sometimes it is *marfū*ʿ with a *ḍammah* implicit due to impracticability, as in, "Mūsā was chosen by Allah" and, "Laylā is the best of women." Sometimes it is *marfū*ʿ with a *ḍammah* implicit due to heaviness, as in, "The judge is the one coming." Sometimes it is *marfū*ʿ with a letter from the letters that serve as deputies for the *ḍammah*, as in, "The two hard workers are successful."

ولابد في المبتدأ والخبر من أن يتطابقا في الإفراد، نحو (محمد قائم) والتثنية نحو (المحمدان قائمان) والجمع نحو (المحمدون قائمون)، وفي التذكير كهذه الأمثلة، وفي التأنيث نحو (هند قائمة)، و(الهندان قائمتان)، و(الهندات قائمات) .

It is essential for the nominal subject and predicate to correspond in singularity e.g. "Muḥammad is standing", in duality e.g. "The two Muḥammads are standing," and in plurality e.g. "The Muḥammads are standing." Likewise they both have to correspond in their gender e.g. "Hind is standing", "The two Hinds are standing", and, "The Hinds are standing."

المبتدأ قسمان ظاهر ومضمر

The Nominal Subject is of Two Types, the Apparent and the Inferred

قال: والمبتدأ قسمان: ظاهر ومضمر؛

فالظاهر ما تقدم ذكره، والمضمر اثنا عشر، وهي: (أنا)، و(نحن)، و(أنتَ)، و(أنتِ)، و(أنتما)، و(أنتم)، و(أنتن)، و(هو)، و(هي)، و(هما)،

و(هم)، و(هن)، نحو قولك: (أنا قائم)، و(نحن قائمون) وما أشبه ذلك .

He said: The nominal subject is of two types: the apparent and the inferred. We have already mentioned the apparent. The inferred is of twelve types: "I", "we", "you", "you" (fem.), "you two", "you (pl.)", "you (pl. fem.)", "he", "she", "they two", "they", "they (fem.)", such as in the sentences, "I am standing" and "We are standing" and that which resembles this.

وأقول: ينقسم المبتدأ إلى قسمين: الأول الظاهر، والثاني: المضمر، وقد سبق في باب الفاعل تعريف كل من الظاهر والمضمر .

I say: The nominal subject is categorised into two: the apparent and the inferred, and we have detailed both types in the Chapter of the Subject.

فمثال المبتدأ الظاهر (محمد رسول الله)، و(عائشة أم المؤمنين) .

Examples of the apparent nominal subject can be seen in the sentences: "Muḥammad is the Messenger of Allah" and, "'Āishah is the Mother of the Believers."

والمبتدأ المضمر اثنا عشر لفظاً :

The inferred nominal subject consists of twelve words:

الأول: (أنا) للمتكلم الواحد، نحو (أنا عبد الله) .

One. "I", for the first person singular. An example is, "I am ʿAbdullāh."

الثاني: (نحن) للمتكلم المتعدد أو الواحد المعظم نفسه، نحو (نحن قائمون).

Two. "We", for the first person plural or the singular when glorifying one's self. An example is, "We are standing."

الثالث: (أنتَ) للمخاطب المفرد المذكر، نحو (أنت فاهم).

Three. "You", for the masculine second person singular. An example is, "You are understanding."

الرابع: (أنتِ) للمخاطبة المفردة المؤنثة، نحو (أنت مطيعة).

Four. "You", for the feminine second person singular. An example is, "You are obedient.

الخامس: (أنتما) للمخاطبين مذكرين كانا أو مؤنثين، نحو (أنتما قائمان)، و(أنتما قائمتان).

Five. "You two" for the second person dual form, both masculine and feminine. Examples are, "You two [men] are standing" and, "You two [women] are standing."

السادس: (أنتم) لجمع الذكور المخاطبين، نحو (أنتم قائمون) .

Six. "You" for the second person masculine plural. An example is, "You are standing."

السابع: (أنتن) لجمع الإناث المخاطبات، نحو (أنتن قائمات).

Seven. "You" for the second person feminine plural. An example is, "You are standing."

الثامن: (هو) للمفرد الغائب المذكر، نحو (هو حاضر) .

Eight. "He" for the third person masculine singular. An example is, "He is present."

التاسع: (هي) للمفردة الغائبة المؤنثة ، نحو (هي مسافرة).

Nine. "She" for the third person feminine singular. An example is, "She is a traveller."

العاشر: (هما) للمثنى الغائب مطلقاً، مذكراً كان أو مؤنثاً نحو (هما قائمان)، و(

هما قائمتان) .

Ten. "They two" for the third person dual form, both masculine and feminine. Examples are, "They (two males) are standing" and, "They (two females) are standing."

الحادي عشر: (هم) لجمع الذكور الغائبين، نحو (هم قائمون).

Eleven. "They" for the third person masculine plural. An example is, "Those whom are standing."

الثاني عشر: (هن) لجمع الإناث الغائبات، نحو (هن قائمات) .

Twelve. "They", for the third person feminine plural. An example is, "Those [females] whom are standing."

وإذا كان المبتدأ ضميراً فإنه لا يكون إلا بارزاً منفصلاً، كما رأيت .

If the nominal subject is a pronoun, then it will not appear except as a clear detached pronoun, as you have seen.

أقسام الخبر

Categories of the Predicate

قال: والخبر قسمان: مفرد وغير مفرد فالمفرد نحو (زيد قائم) وغير المفرد أربعة أشياء: الجار والمجرور، والظرف، والفعل مع فاعله، والمبتدأ مع خبره، نحو قولك: (زيد في الدار) ، و(زيد عندك) ، و(زيد قام أبوه) ، و(زيد جاريته ذاهبة) .

He said: The predicate is of two categories: the singular and the non-singular. An example of the singular is, "Zayd is standing." The non-singular consists of four things: (i) a particle of *jarr* and its object, (ii) the adverbial expression, (iii) a verb with its subject and (iv) a nominal subject with its predicate. Examples are, "Zayd is in the house", "Zayd is with you", "Zayd's father is standing" and, "Zayd's girl is going."

وأقول: ينقسم الخبر إلى قسمين: الأول خبر مفرد، والثاني خبر غير مفرد.

I say: The predicate is categorised into two: the singular predicate and the non-singular predicate.

والمراد بالمفرد هنا: ما ليس جملة ولا شبيهاً بالجملة، نحو (قائم) من قولك (محمد قائم).

The meaning of singular here is that which is not a sentence or akin to a sentence. An example is "standing" in the statement, "Muḥammad is standing."

وغير المفرد نوعان: جملة، وشبه جملة، والجملة نوعان: جملة اسمية، وجملة فعلية .

The non-singular is of two types: the sentence and that which is akin to a sentence. And the sentence is of two types: the nominal sentence and the verbal sentence.

فالجملة الاسمية هي ما تألف من مبتدأ وخبر نحو (أبوه كريم) من قولك (محمد أبوه كريم).

The nominal sentence is that which is comprised of a nominal subject and its predicate. An example is, "His father is generous" in the statement, "Muḥammad, his father is generous."

والجملة الفعلية: ما تألفت من فعل وفاعل أو نائبه، نحو (سافر أبوه) من قولك (محمد سافر أبوه) ونحو (يضرب غلامه) من قولك (خالد يضرب غلامه).

The verbal sentence is that which is comprised of a verb and a subject or its deputy. Examples are, "His father travelled" in the statement, "Muḥammad's father travelled", and, "His servant boy is being hit" in the statement, "Khālid's servant boy is being hit".

فإن كان الخبر جملة فلابد له من رابط يربطه بالمبتدأ إما ضمير يعود إلى المبتدأ كما سمعتَ وإما اسم إشارة نحو (محمد هذا رجل كريم).

If the predicate is a sentence, then it is essential that there is a conjoining tool that conjoins it to the nominal subject. It can be a pronoun that returns to the nominal subject—as you have heard—and it can be a demonstrative pronoun such as, "This Muḥammad is a generous man."

وشبه الجملة نوعان أيضاً، الأول: الجار والمجرور، نحو (في المسجد) من قولك (علي في المسجد) . والثاني: الظرف، نحو (فوق الغصن) من قولك (الطائر فوق الغصن) .

If the predicate is akin to a sentence, it is of two types also. The first of them is the particle of *jarr* and its genitive word e.g. "in the *masjid*" in the statement, "'Alī is in the *masjid*." The second of them is the adverbial phrase e.g. "above the branch" in the statement, "The bird is above the branch.

ومن ذلك تعلم أن الخبر على التفصيل خمسة أنواع: مفرد، وجملة فعلية، وجملة اسمية، وجار مع مجرور، وظرف .

Based on the above, you should understand that in detail the predicate consists of five types: (i) the singular, (ii) the verbal sentence, (iii) the nominal sentence, (iv) the particle of *jarr* with its genitive word and (v) the adverbial phrase.

تدريب على الإعراب

Exercises on Grammatical Analysis

أعرب الجمل الآتية:

Provide a grammatical analysis of the following sentences:

محمد قائم، محمد حضر أبوه، محمد أبوه مسافر، محمد في الدار، محمد عندك .

"Muḥammad is standing." "Muḥammad's father was present." "Muḥammad's father is a traveller." "Muḥammad is in the abode." "Muḥammad is with you."

الجواب

Answers

١ ـ محمد قائم : (محمد): مبتدأ مرفوع بالابتداء، وعلامة رفعه ضمة ظاهرة في آخره، (قائم): خبر المبتدأ مرفوع بالمبتدأ، وعلامة رفعه ضمة ظاهرة في آخره .

One. "Muḥammad is standing": "Muḥammad" is the nominal subject, *marfūʿ* due to it initiating [the sentence.] The sign of it being in the state of *rafʿ* is the *ḍammah* that is explicit at its end. "Standing" is the predicate of the nominal subject and it is made *marfūʿ* by the nominal subject. The sign of it being in the state of *rafʿ* is the *ḍammah* that is explicit at its end.

٢ ـ محمد حضر أبوه : (محمد): مبتدأ، (حضر): فعل ماض مبني على الفتح لا محل له من الإعراب . (أبو): فاعل، (حضر) مرفوع بالواو نيابة عن الضمة لأنه من

الأسماء الخمسة، و(أبو) مضاف و(الهاء) مضاف إليه، مبني على الضم في محل خفض، والجملة من الفعل والفاعل في محل رفع خبر المبتدأ، والرابط بين الخبر والمبتدأ هو الضمير الواقع مضافاً إليه في قولك (أبوه).

Two. "Muḥammad's father was present": "Muḥammad" is the nominal subject. "Was present" is a *māḍī* verb un-inflectable upon a *fatḥah* without a grammatical state and "father" is the subject. "Was present" is *marfūʿ* with the letter *wāw* serving as a representative for the *ḍammah*, due to it being from the five nouns. "Father" is the possessed in a possessive compound and the attached pronoun "his" is the possessor, un-inflectable upon a *ḍammah* in the state of *khafḍ* (*majrūr*). And the verbal sentence (*ḥaḍara abūhu*) consisting of the verb and its subject is in the state of *rafʿ* as the predicate of the nominal subject. The connector between the predicate and the nominal subject is the attached pronoun serving as the possessor in the statement "his father."

٣ ـ محمد أبوه مسافر : (محمد): مبتدأ أول مرفوع بالضمة الظاهرة، و(أبو): مبتدأ ثان مرفوع بالواو نيابة عن الضمة لأنه من الأسماء الخمسة، و(أبو) مضاف، و(الهاء) مضاف إليه . (مسافر): خبر المبتدأ الثاني وجملة المبتدأ الثاني وخبره في محل رفع خبر المبتدأ الأول، والرابط بين هذه الجملة والمبتدأ الأول الضمير الذي في قولك (أبواه) .

Three. "Muḥammad's father is a traveller": "Muḥammad" is the first nominal subject, *marfūʿ* with an explicit *ḍammah*. "Father" is the second nominal subject, *marfūʿ* with the letter *wāw* serving as a representative for the *ḍammah* due to it being from the five nouns. "Father" is also the possessed in a possessive compound and the attached pronoun "his" is the possessor. "Traveller" is the predicate of the second nominal subject. The sentence consisting of the second nominal subject and its predicate is in the state of *rafʿ* as the predicate of the first nominal subject. The connector between this sentence and the first nominal subject is the attached pronoun serving as the possessor in the statement "his father."

٤ ـ محمد في الدار : (محمد): مبتدأ، (في الدار): جار ومجرور متعلق بمحذوف خبر المبتدأ.

Four. "Muḥammad is in the abode": "Muḥammad" is the nominal subject. "In the abode" is a preposition and its object, attached to the deleted predicate of the nominal subject.

٥ ـ محمد عندك : (محمد): مبتدأ، (عند): ظرف مكان متعلق بمحذوف خبر المبتدأ، و(عند): مضاف، و(الكاف) ضمير مضاف إليه مبني على الفتح في محل خفض.

Five. "Muḥammad is with you": "Muḥammad" is the nominal subject. "With" is an adverb of place, attached to the deleted predicate of the nominal subject. "With" is the possessed and the attached pronoun "you" is the possessor, un-inflectable upon a *fatḥah* in the state of *khafḍ*.

تمرينات

Exercises

١ ـ بين المبتدأ والخبر، ونوع كل واحد منهما، من بين الكلمات الواقعات في الجمل الآتية، وإذا كان الخبر جملة فبين الرابط بينها وبين مبتدئها ؟

One. Identify the nominal subject and its predicate, and the type of each one from the words found in the following sentences. And if there are sentences serving as predicates, then identify the connector between them and the nominal subject.

المجتهد يفوز بغايته، السائقان يشتدان في السير، النخلة تؤتي أكلها كل عام مرة، المؤمنات يُسبحن الله، كتابك نظيف، هذا القلم من خشب، الصوف يؤخذ من الغنم، والوبر من الجمال، الأحذية تصنع من جلد الماعز وغيره، القدر على النار، النيل يسقي أرض مصر، أنت أعرف بما ينفعك، أبوك الذي ينفق عليك، أمك أحق الناس ببرك،

العصفور يغرد فوق الشجرة، البرق يعقب المطر، المسكين مَن حرم نفسه وهو واجد، صديقي أبوه عنده، والدي عنده حصان .

٢ ـ استعمل كل اسم من الأسماء الآتية مبتدأ في جملتين مفيدتين، بحيث يكون خبره في واحدة منهما مفرداً وفي الثانية جملة:

Two. Utilise each of the following nouns as the nominal subject in two beneficial sentences, in the first of them its predicate should be singular and in the second of them it should be a sentence:

التلميذان، محمد، الثمرة، البطيخ، القلم، الكتاب، المعهد، النيل، عائشة، الفتيات.

٣ ـ أخبر عن كل اسم من السماء الآتية بشبه جملة:

Three. Make a predicate for the following nouns via a quasi sentence.

العصفور، الجوخ، الإسكندرية، القاهرة، الكتاب، الكرسي، نهر النيل.

٤ ـ ضع لكل جار ومجرور مما يأتي مبتدأً مناسباً يتم به معه الكلام:

Four. Place with each of the following preposition and *majrūr* word compounds an appropriate nominal subject that provides a completion to the speech:

في القفص، عند جبل المقطم، من الخشب، على شاطئ البحر، من الصوف، في القِمَطر، في الجهة الغربية من القاهرة.

٥ ـ كون ثلاث جمل في وصف الجَمَل تشتمل كل واحدة منها على مبتدأ وخبر.

Five. Make three sentences describing a camel using the formula of a nominal subject and predicate.

أسئلة

Questions

ما هو المبتدأ؟ ما هو الخبر؟ إلى كم قسم ينقسم المبتدأ ؟

What is the nominal subject? What is the predicate? Into how many categories is the nominal subject split into?

مثل للمبتدأ الظاهر، مثل للمبتدأ المضمر.

Provide an example of the explicit nominal subject. Provide an example of the implicit nominal subject.

إلى كم قسم ينقسم المضمر الذي يقع مبتدأ؟ إلى كم قسم ينقسم الخبر الجملة؟ إلى كم قسم ينقسم الخبر شبه الجملة؟ ما الذي يربط الخبر الجملة بالمبتدأ ؟ في أي شيء تجب مطابقة الخبر للمبتدأ، مثل لكل نوع من أنواع الخبر بمثالين .

Into how many types is the implicit nominal subject categorised into? Into how many types is the predicate sentence categorised into? Into how many types is the predicate akin to a sentence categorised into? What are the connectors that connect the predicate sentence with its nominal subject? What are the characteristics of the predicate that must conform with the nominal subject. Provide two examples of each type of the predicate.

نواسخ المبتدأ والخبر

The Abrogators of the Nominal Subject and Its Predicate

قال: (باب العوامل الداخلة على المبتدأ والخبر) وهي ثلاثة أشياء: (كان) وأخواتها، و(إن) وأخواتها، و(ظننت) وأخواتها .

He said: Chapter: The Governors that Impact the Nominal Subject and Its Predicate. They consist of three: (i) *kāna* and its sisters, (ii) *inna* and its sisters and (iii) *ẓanantu* and its sisters.

وأقول: قد عرفت أن المبتدأ والخبر مرفوعان، واعلم أنه قد يدخل عليهما أحد العوامل اللفظية فيغير إعرابهما، وهذه العوامل التي تدخل عليهما فتغير إعرابهما - بعد تتبع كلام العرب الموثوق به - على ثلاثة أقسام :

I say: I have explained that the nominal subject and its predicate are both *marfu'*, and at this juncture the reader should take note that sometimes certain expressed governors that change their grammatical state take affect upon them. These governors that enter upon them and alter their grammatical state—based upon what has become customarily accepted within the speech of the Arabs—are of three types:

القسم الأول: يرفع المبتدأ وينصب الخبر، وذلك ((كان) وأخواتها)، وهذا القسم كله أفعال، نحو (كان الجو صافياً) .

The first type makes the nominal subject *marfū'* and its predicate *manṣūb*. It is *kāna* and its sisters, and each of these is a verb e.g. "The weather was clear."

القسم الثاني: ينصب المبتدأ ويرفع الخبر، عكس الأول، وذلك ((إن) وأخواتها) وهذا القسم كله أحرف، نحو ﴿إِنَّ اللَّهَ عَزِيزٌ حَكِيمٌ﴾

The second type makes the nominal subject *manṣūb* and its predicate *marfu'*, and this is the opposite of the first one. It is *inna* and its sisters, and each of these is a particle e.g. **{Indeed, Allah is Exalted in Might and Wise.}**[143]

القسم الثالث: ينصب المبتدأ والخبر جميعاً، وذلك ((ظننت) وأخواتها)، وهذا القسم كله أفعال، نحو (ظننت الصديق أخاً) .

The third type makes the nominal subject and its predicate both *manṣūb*. It is *ẓanantu* and its sisters, and each of these is a verb e.g. "I thought the friend was a brother."

وتسمى هذه العوامل (النواسخ) لأنها نسخت حكم المبتدأ والخبر، أي: غيرته وجددت لهما حكماً آخر غير حكمهما الأول.

These governing agents are referred to as abrogators due to them abrogating i.e. changing the grammatical ruling of the nominal subject and its predicate. They refashion the ruling of the nominal subject and its predicate into rulings that contrast with the original one.

143 Al-Anfāl: 10

كان وأخواتها

Kāna and Its Sisters

قال: فأما ((كان) وأخواتها)، فإنها ترفع الاسم، وتنصب الخبر، وهي: (كان)، و(أمسى)، و(أصبح)، و(أضحى)، و(ظل)، و(بات)، و(صار)، و(ليس)، و(ما زال)، و(ما انفك)، و(ما فتِئ)، و(ما برح)، و(ما دام)، وما تصرف منها نحو: ((كان)، و(يكون)، و(كن)، و(أصبح)، و(يصبح)، و(أصبح))، تقول: (كان زيد قائماً) ، و(ليس عمرو شاخصاً) وما أشبه ذلك .

He said: As for *kāna* and its sisters, they make their noun *marfūʿ* and their predicate *manṣūb*. They are, *"kāna"*, *"amsā"*, *"aṣbaḥa"*, *"aḍḥā"*, *"ẓalla"*, *"bāta"*, *"ṣāra"*, *"laysa"*, *"mā zāla"*, *"mā anfakka"*, *"mā fatiʾ"*, *"mā bariḥa"*, *"mā dāma"*, and the conjugations of them e.g. *"kāna, yakūnu and kun"*, *"aṣbaḥa, yuṣbiḥu and aṣbiḥ."* It is said, "Zayd was standing" and "ʿAmr has not arrived yet " and that which is similar to this.

وأقول: القسم الأول من نواسخ المبتدأ والخبر (كان) وأخواتها، أي نظائرها في العمل .

I say: The first type of the abrogators of the nominal subject and its predicate is *kāna* and its sisters, meaning its counterparts in action.

وهذا القسم يدخل على المبتدأ فيزيل رفعه الأول ويحدث له رفعاً جديداً، ويسمى المبتدأ (اسمه) ، ويدخل على الخبر فينصبه، ويسمى (خبره) .

This type enters upon the nominal subject and lifts the original state of *rafʿ*, creating for it a new state of *rafʿ* and the name of the nominal subject is changed to "its (*kāna's*) noun". It enters upon the predicate and alters it to the state of *naṣb*, and its name is changed to "its predicate".

وهذا القسم ثلاثة عشر فعلاً :

This category consists of thirteen verbs:

الأول: (كان) وهو يفيد اتصاف الاسم بالخبر في الماضي، إما مع الانقطاع، نحو (كان محمد مجتهداً) وإما مع الاستمرار، نحو ﴿وَكَانَ رَبُّكَ قَدِيراً﴾ .

One. *Kāna*, and it indicates that the description of the noun with its predicate occurred in the past tense. Sometimes it indicates discontinuance e.g. "Muḥammad was a hard worker", and sometimes it indicates continuance[144] e.g. **{And ever is your Lord competent.}**[145]

والثاني: (أمسى) وهو يفيد اتصاف الاسم بالخبر في المساء، نحو (أمسى الجو بارداً).

Two. *Amsā*, and it indicates that the description of the noun with its predicate occurred during the evening e.g. "The weather became cold in the evening."

والثالث: (أصبح) وهو يفيد اتصاف الاسم بالخبر في الصباح، نحو (أصبح الجو مكفهِراً).

Third. "*Aṣbaḥa*", and it indicates that the description of the noun with its predicate occurred during the morning e.g. "The weather became overcast during the morning."

والرابع: (أضحى) وهو يفيد اتصاف الاسم بالخبر في الضحا، نحو (أضحى الطالب نشيطاً)

144 Benefit: The word *kāna* can refer to something which continues (present tense) or something which has been cut off (i.e. past tense). It indicates continuance when it is used in relation to the prerogatives of Allah. Al-Kafrāwī said (p. 95), "This is because a verb—when used in relation to Allah—loses a connection to time, and thus it is continuous." However, if *kāna* is used to describe the creation, this could refer to both present and past tenses.

145 Al-Furqān: 54

Fourth. "*Aḍḥā*", and it indicates that the description of the noun with its predicate occurred during the time of *ḍuḥā* e.g. "The student became active during the time of *ḍuḥā*."

والخامس: (ظل) وهو يفيد اتصاف الاسم بالخبر في جميع النهار، نحو ﴿ظَلَّ وَجْهُهُ مُسْوَدًّا﴾ .

Five. "*Ẓalla*", and it indicates that the description of the noun with its predicate occurred during the daytime e.g. **{His face becomes dark.}**[146]

والسادس: (بات) وهو يفيد اتصاف الاسم بالخبر في وقت البيات، نحو (بات محمد مسروراً) .

Six. "*Bāta*", and it indicates that the description of the noun with its predicate occurred during the time of resting e.g. "Muḥammad went to sleep happy."

والسابع: (صار) وهو يفيد تحول الاسم من حالته إلى الحالة التي يدل عليها الخبر، نحو (صار الطين إبريقاً).

Seven. "*Ṣāra*", and it indicates a change to the noun from its state to the state that is indicated by its predicate e.g. "The clay became a jug".

والثامن: (ليس) وهو يفيد نفي الخبر عن الاسم في وقت الحال، نحو (ليس محمد فاهماً).

Eight. "*Laysa*", and it indicates the negation of the predicate for the noun in the present tense[147] e.g. "Muḥammad is not comprehending."

والتاسع والعاشر والحادي عشر والثاني عشر: (ما زال)، و(ما انفك)، و(ما فتئ)،

146 Al-Naḥl: 58

147 However it can sometimes be understood in the future tense. Likewise it can mean continuance such as in the *āyah*: ﴿وأن الله ليس بظلام للعبيد﴾ {**... Because Allah is not ever unjust to [His] servants.**} (Āli ʿImrān: 182).

و(ما برح)، وهذه الأربعة تدل على ملازمة الخبر للاسم حسبما يقتضيه الحالُ، نحو (ما زال إبراهيم منكراً)، ونحو (ما برح علي صديقاً مخلصاً).

Nine, ten, eleven and twelve. "*Mā zāla*", "*mā anfakka*", "*mā fati*" and "*mā bariḥa*", each of these four indicate the existence of the predicate with the noun according to the requirement of the situation e.g. "Ibrāhīm remained censuring" and, "'Alī remained as a sincere friend."

والثالث عشر: (ما دام) وهو يفيد ملازمة الخبر للاسم أيضاً نحو (لا أعذل خالداً ما دمت حياً) .

Thirteen. "*Mā dāma*", and it likewise indicates the existence of the predicate with the noun e.g. "I will not blame Khālid for as long as I live."

وتنقسم هذه الأفعال - من جهة العمل - إلى ثلاثة أقسام:

These verbs are categorised into three—from the aspect of their function:

القسم الأول: ما يعمل هذا العمل - وهو رفع الاسم ونصب الخبر - بشرط تقدم (ما) المصدرية الظرفية عليه وهو فعل واحد وهو (دام) .

The first category: That which performs this function—which is making its noun *marfū'* and its predicate *manṣūb*—with the condition that it is preceded by the letter *mā al-masḍarīyyah* (gerundivial) *al-ẓarfiyyah* (adverbial). This consists of one verb, which is "*dāma*".

القسم الثاني: ما يعمل هذا العمل بشرط أن يتقدم عليه نفي، أو استفهام، أو نهي، وهو أربعة أفعال، وهي: (زال)، و(انفك)، و(فتئ)، و(برح).

The second category: That which performs this function with the condition that it is preceded by a negation, an interrogative particle, or a prohibition. This category consists of four verbs: (i) "*zāla*", (ii) "*anfakka*", (iii) "*fati'*" and (iv) "*bariḥa*".

القسم الثالث: ما يعمل هذا العمل بغير شرط، وهو ثمانية أفعال، وهي الباقي.

The third category: That which performs this function without any condition. This category consists of eight verbs, and they are those which remain.

وتنقسم هذه الفعال من جهة التصرف إلى ثلاثة أقسام :

And these verbs are categorised into three types from the aspect of their conjugation:

القسم الأول: ما يتصرف في الفعلية تصرفاً كاملاً، بمعنى أنه يأتي منه الماضي والمضارع والأمر، وهو سبعة أفعال، وهي: (كان) ، و(أمسى)، و(أصبح)، و(أضحى)، و(ظل)، و(بات)، و(صار).

The first category: That which comes in all of the different verbal forms, i.e. that which allows *māḍī*, *muḍāriʿ* and *ʾamr* forms to derive from it. This category consists of seven verbs: (i) *"kāna"*, (ii) *"amsā"*, (iii) *"asbaḥ"*, (iv) *"aḍḥā"*, (v) *"ẓalla"*, (vi) *"bāta"*, and (vii) *"ṣāra"*.

القسم الثاني: ما يتصرف تصرفاً ناقصاً، بمعنى أنه يأتي منه الماضي والمضارع ليس غير، وهو أربعة أفعال، وهي: (فتئ)، و(انفك)، و(برح)، و(زال).

The second category: That which is incomplete in the verbal forms it comes in, i.e. that which only allows the *māḍī* and *muḍāriʿ* forms to derive from it. This category consists of four verbs: (i) *"fatiʾ"*, (ii) *"anfaka"*, (iii) *"bariḥa"*, and (iv) *"zāla"*.

القسم الثالث: ما لا يتصرف أصلاً، وهو فعلان: أحدهما (ليس) اتفاقاً والثاني (دام) على الأصح .

The third category: That which does not come in different verbal forms entirely. This category consists of two verbs: (i) *"laysa"*—upon which there is agreement—, and (ii) *"dāma"* according to the strongest opinion.

وغير الماضي من هذه الأفعال يعمل عمل الماضي، نحو قوله تعالى: ﴿وَلَا يَزَالُونَ مُخْتَلِفِينَ﴾، ﴿لَن نَّبْرَحَ عَلَيْهِ عَاكِفِينَ﴾، ﴿تَاللَّهِ تَفْتَأُ تَذْكُرُ يُوسُفَ﴾.

When these verbs come in a form besides the *māḍī*, they still provide the function of the *māḍī*. Examples are in the statements of the Most High: {**They will not cease to differ**},[148] {**We will never cease being devoted**},[149] and, {**By Allah, you will not cease remembering Yūsuf**}.[150] [151]

148 Hūd: 118

149 Ṭaha: 91

150 Yūsuf: 85

151 In this *āyah* from Sūrah Yūsuf it may be asked why there is no visible particle of negation or a quasi negation (شبهه) preceding "تفتأ" (which is conjugated from *fati'* i.e. فتىء). The answer to this is that the negation can sometimes be explicit and sometimes implicit. In this particular *āyah* the negation is implicit i.e. "لا تفتأ". Ibn ʿAqīl said (1/263), "The negation is not omitted except after an oath—as in this noble *āyah*. It is a rarity for it to be omitted without an oath." If it is asked why the particle of negation was not mentioned, the answer was given by al-Imām al-Shawkānī in *Fatḥ al-Qadīr* (3/48), "The particle of negation was omitted due to the absence of any doubt regarding this matter."

إنّ وأخواتها

Inna and Its Sisters

قال: وأما ((إنَّ) وأخواتها) فإنها تنصب الاسم وترفع الخبر، وهي: (إنَّ)، و(أنَّ)، و(لكنَّ)، و(كأنَّ)، و(ليت)، و(لعلَّ)، تقول: (إنَّ زيداً قائمٌ)، و(ليت عمراً شاخصٌ)، وما أشبه ذلك، ومعنى (إنَّ) و(أنَّ) التوكيد، و(لكنَّ) للاستدراك، و(كأنَّ) للتشبيه، و(ليت) للتمني، و(لعل) للترجي والتوقع .

He said: As for *inna* and its sisters, they cause their nouns to become *manṣūb* and their predicates to become *marfūʿ*. They consist of "*inna*", "*anna*", "*lakinna*", "*ka'anna*", "*layta*" and "*laʿalla*". This can be seen in the statements, "Indeed Zayd is standing", "Would that ʿAmr come over" and similar statements. The meaning of "*inna*" and "*anna*" denotes emphasis, *lakinna* serves as a disjunctive clause, "*ka'anna*" denotes likeness, "*layta*" denotes wishing [something that is unlikely to be attained], and "*laʿalla*" denotes hope and expectation.

وأقول: القسم الثاني من نواسخ المبتدأ والخبر ((إنَّ) وأخواتها)، أي: نظائرها في العمل، وهي تدخل على المبتدأ والخبر، فتنصب المبتدأ ويسمى اسمها، وترفع الخبر بمعنى أنها تجدد له رفعاً غير الذي كان له قبل دخولها، ويسمى خبرها، وهذه الأدوات كلها حروف، وهي ستة:

I say: The second type from the abrogators of the nominal subject and its predicate is *inna* and its sisters, i.e. its counterparts in action. These governors take effect upon the nominal subject and its predicate by making the nominal subject *manṣūb* and causing it to be termed as its noun, and making its predicate *marfūʿ* i.e. it refashions it into a state of *rafʿ* different to the one present before it entered upon it, and causing it to be termed as its predicate. All of these apparatus are particles, and they consist of six:

الأول: (إنَّ) بكسر الهمزة . والثاني: (أنَّ) بفتح الهمزة.

One. "*Inna*", which has a *kasrah* upon the letter *hamzah*. Two. "*Anna*", which has a *fatḥah* upon the letter *hamzah*.

وهما يدلان على التوكيد، ومعناه تقوية نسبة الخبر للمبتدأ، نحو (إن أباك حاضر)، ونحو (علمت أن أباك مسافر).

Both of these indicate an element of emphasis. The meaning of emphasis is that the relationship of the predicate to its nominal subject is intensified. Examples are, "Indeed your father is present" and, "I know that your father is a traveller."

والثالث: (لكنَّ) ومعناه الاستدراك، وهو تعقيب الكلام بنفي ما يتوهم ثبوته أو إثبات ما يتوهم نفيه، نحو (محمد شجاع لكن صديقه جبان).

Three. "*Lakinna*", which serves as a disjunctive clause.[152] The meaning of this is that it provides a commentary on speech by negating that which is assumed to be certain or making certain that which is assumed to be negated. An example of this is, "Muḥammad is brave however his friend is cowardly."

والرابع: (كأنَّ) وهو يدل على تشبيه المبتدأ بالخبر، نحو: (كأنَّ الجارية بدر) .

Four. "*Ka'anna*", it indicates towards a similarity between the nominal subject and its predicate e.g. "It is as if the young girl is like a full moon."

والخامس: (ليت) ومعناه التمني، وهو: طلب المستحيل أو ما فيه عسر، نحو: (ليت الشبابَ عائدٌ) ونحو (ليت البليدَ ينجحُ).

Five. "*Layta*", it denotes a wish i.e. the seeking of something impossible or where attainment of it is has an element of difficulty. Examples are, "If only youth would return", and, "If only the foolish would succeed."

152 *Lakinna* serves as a disjunctive clause when it is preceded by speech. See *al-Kawākib* (1/252).

والسادس: (لعل) وهو يدل على الترجي أو التوقع، ومعنى الترجي: طلب الأمر المحبوب، ولا يكون إلا في الممكن نحو: (لعل اللهَ يرحمُني)، ومعنى التوقع: انتظار وقوع الأمر المكروه في ذاته، نحو (لعل العدوَ قريبٌ منا) .

Six. "*La'alla*", it denotes hope and expectation. The meaning of hope is the attainment of something dear and [for something to fall under this definition] its attainment must be possible. An example is, "That Allah forgives me." The meaning of expectation here is the anticipation of the occurrence of something within which there is dislike. An example is, "It seems the enemy is close to us."

ظنّ وأخواتها

Ẓanna and Its Sisters

قال: وأما ((ظننت) وأخواتها) فإنها تنصب المبتدأ والخبر على انهما مفعولان لها، وهي: (ظننت)، و(حسبت)، و(خِلتُ)، و(زعمتُ) ، و(رأيتُ) ، و(علمتُ) ، و(وجدتُ) ، و(اتَّخذتُ) ، و(جعلتُ) ، و(سمعتُ) ، تقولُ: (ظننتُ زيداً قائماً) ، و(رأيتُ عمراً شاخصاً) ، وما أشبه ذلك.

He said: As for *ẓanantu* and its sisters,[153] they make the nominal subject and its predicate both *manṣūb* and they both become the objects for them. They are "*ẓannatu*", "*ḥasibtu*", "*khiltu*", "*zaʿamtu*", "*raʾaytu*", "*ʿalimtu*", "*wajadtu*", "*ittakadhtu*", "*jaʿaltu*" and "*samiʿtu*". It is said, "I thought Zayd was standing", "I saw ʿAmr coming", and such similar statements.

وأقول: القسم الثالث من نواسخ المبتدأ والخبر، (ظننت) وأخواتها أي نظائرها في العمل، وهي تدخل على المبتدأ والخبر فتنصبهما جميعاً، ويقال للمبتدأ (مفعول أول) وللخبر (مفعول ثان) ، وهذا القسم عشرة أفعال:

I say: The third type from the abrogators of the nominal subject and its predicate is *ẓanantu* and its sisters, i.e. its counterparts in action. They enter upon the nominal subject and its predicate and make both of them *manṣūb*. The name of the nominal subject is changed to the "first object" and the name of the predicate is changed to the "second object." This type consists of ten verbs:

---

153 If it is asked why *ẓanna* and its sisters are mentioned here when they could have been mentioned in the chapter of *manṣūb* words, the answer was given by al-Kafrāwī (p. 103), "This type—i.e. *ẓanna* and its sisters—was mentioned under the *marfūʿ* words as a form of digression in order to complete the abrogators. If not for this it would have been better to mention them under the *manṣūb* words."

والأول: (ظننت) نحو (ظننت محمداً صديقاً).

One. "*Ẓanantu*" e.g. "I thought Muḥammad to be a friend."

والثاني: (حسبت) نحو (حسبتُ المال نافعاً).

Two. "*Ḥasibtu*" e.g. "I considered the wealth to be beneficial."

والثالث: (خِلت) نحو (خلت الحديقة مثمرة).

Three. "*Khiltu*" e.g. "I supposed that the garden was fruitful."

والرابع: (زعمت) نحو (زعمت بكراً جريئاً).

Four. "*Zaʿamtu*" e.g. "I contended that Bakr was valiant."

والخامس: (رأيت) نحو (رأيت إبراهيم مفلحاً).

Five. "I viewed" e.g. "I viewed Ibrāhīm as being successful."

والسادس: (علمت) نحو (علمت الصدق منجياً).

Six. "I knew" e.g. "I knew that honesty was a saviour."

والسابع: (وجدت) نحو (وجدت الصلاح باب الخير).

Seven. "I found" e.g. "I found righteousness to be a door to goodness."

والثامن: (اتخذت) نحو (اتخذت محمداً صديقاً).

Eight. "I took" e.g. "I took Muḥammad to be a friend."

والتاسع: (جعلت) نحو (جعلت الذهب خاتماً).

Nine. "I made" e.g. "I made the gold into a ring."

والعاشر: (سمعت) نحو (سمعت خليلاً يقرأ).

Ten. "I heard" e.g. "I heard Khalīl reading."

هذه الأفعال العشرة تنقسم إلى أربعة أقسام:

These ten verbs are categorised into four categories:

القسم الأول: يفيد ترجيح وقوع الخبر، وهو أربعة أفعال ، وهي : (ظننت) ، و(حسبت) ، و(خلت) ، و(زعمت) .

The first category denotes the preponderance of the occurrence of the predicate. It consists of four verbs: "*ẓanantu*", "*ḥasibtu*", "*khiltu*" and "*za'amtu*".

والقسم الثاني: يفيد اليقين وتحقيق وقوع الخبر، وهو ثلاثة أفعال، وهي : (رأيت) ، و(علمت) ، و(وجدت).

The second category denotes certainty and affirmation of the occurrence of the predicate. It consists of three verbs: "*ra'aytu*", "'*alimtu*" and "*wajadtu*".

والقسم الثالث: يفيد التصيير والانتقال، وهو فعلان، وهما: (اتخذت)، و(جعلت) .

The third category denotes changing or transferring. It consists of two verbs, and they are: "*ittakhadhtu*" and "*ja'altu*".

والقسم الرابع: يفيد النسبة في السمع، وهو فعل واحد، وهو (سمعت) .

The fourth category denotes a connection to hearing. It consists of one verb: "*sami'tu*".

تمرينات

Exercises

١ ـ أدخل (كان) أو إحدى أخواتها على كل جملة من الجمل الآتية ثم اضبط آخر

كل كلمة بالشكل.

One. Enter "*kāna*" or one of its sisters upon each of the following sentences, and then express the diacritics of the ending of each word.

الجو صحو، الحارس مستيقظ، الهواء طلق، الحديقة مثمرة، البستاني منتبه، القراءة مفيدة، الصدق نافع، الزكاة واجبة، الشمس حارة، البرد قارس .

❖❖❖

٢ ـ أدخل (إنَّ) أو إحدى أخواتها على كل جملة من الجمل الآتية، ثم اضبط بالشكل آخر كل كلمة:

Two. Enter "*inna*" or one of its sisters upon each of the following sentences, and then express the diacritics of the ending of each word.

أبي حاضر، كتابك جديد، مِحبَرتُكَ قذرة، قلمُكَ مكسور، يدك نظيفة، الكتاب خير رفيق، الأدب حميد، البطيخ يظهر في الصيف، البرتقال من فواكه الشتاء، القطن سبب ثروة مصر، النيل عذب الماء، مصر تُربَتُها صالحة للزراعة.

❖❖❖

٣ ـ أدخل (ظنَّ) أو إحدى أخواتها على كل جملة من الجمل الآتية ثم اضبط بالشكل آخر كل كلمة:

Three. Enter "*ẓanna*" or one of its sisters upon each of the following sentences, and then express the diacritics of the ending of each word.

محمد صديقك، أبوك أحب الناس إليك، أمك أرأف الناس بك، الحقل ناضر، البستان مثمر، الصيف قائظ، الأصدقاء أعوانك عند الشدة، الصمت زين، الثياب البيضاء لُبوس الصيف، عثرة اللسان أشد من عثرة الرجل.

٤- ضع في المكان الخالي من كل مثال من الأمثلة الآتية كلمة مناسبة، واضبطها بالشكل:

Four. Place in the below empty spaces an appropriate word, and express the diacritics.

(أ) إنَّ الحارس ...

(ب) صارت الزكاة ...

(ج) أضحتِ الشمس ...

(د) رأيتُ الأصدقاء ...

(ه) إنَّ عثرة اللسان ...

(و) علمتُ أن الكتاب ...

(ز) محمد صديقك لكن أخاه ...

(ح) حسبتُ أباك ...

(ط) حسن المنطق من دلائل النجاح لكن الصمت ...

(ي) كأن الحقل ...

(ك) رأيتُ عمك ...

(ل) اعتقد أن القطن ...

(م) أمسى الهواء ...

(ن) سمعت أخاك ...

(س) ما فتئ إبراهيم ...

(ع) لأصحبُك ما دمت ...

(ف) ظل الجو ...

٥- ضع أداة من الأدوات الناسخة تناسب المقام في كل مكان خال من الأمثلة الآتية :

Five. Place the appropriate tool of abrogation in each of the below empty spaces:

(أ) ... الكتابَ خيرُ سميرٍ.

(ب) ... الجوَّ ملبدٌ بالغيوم.

(ج) ... الصدقُ منجياً.

(د) ... أخاكَ صديقاً لي.

(ه) ... أخوكَ زميلي في المدرسة.

(و) ... الحارسُ مستيقظاً.

(ز) ... المعلمُ مرشداً.

(ح) ... الجنَّة تحت أقدام أمك.

(ط) ... البنتَ مدرسَة.

(ي) ... الكتابُ سميري.

(ك) ... الصدقاءُ عونكَ في الشدةِ.

٦- ضع في المكان الخالي من كل مثال من الأمثلة الأتية اسماً واضبطه بالشكل الكامل:

Six. Place within each of the empty places below a noun, and express its full diacritics.

(أ) كان ... جباراً.

(ج) رأيت ... مكفهراً.

(ه) صار ... خبزاً .

(د) علمت أن العدل ...

(و) ليس ... عاراً.

(ز) أمسى ... فرحاً.

(ب) يبيت ... كئيباً.

(ح) إنَّ ... ناضرةٌ.

(ط) ليت ... طالعٌ.

(ي) كأن ... معلمٌ.

(ك) ما زال ... صديقي.

(ل) إن ... واجبة.

٧ - كون ثلاث جمل في وصف الكتاب، كل واحدة مشتملة على مبتدأ وخبر، ثم أدخل على كل جملة منها (كان) واضبط كلماتها بالشكل .

Seven. Make three sentences describing a book, each of which should contain a nominal subject and its predicate. Then enter into each sentence "*kāna*" and express the diacritics of the words.

٨ ـ كون ثلاث جمل في وصف المطر، كل واحدة تشتمل على مبتدأ وخبر، ثم أدخل على كل جملة منها (إنَّ) واضبط كلماتها بالشكل .

Eight. Make three sentences describing the rain, each of which should contain a nominal subject and its predicate. Then enter into each sentence "*inna*" and express the diacritics of the words.

٩ ـ كون ثلاث جمل في وصف النهر، كل واحدة منها تشتمل على مبتدأ وخبر، ثم أدخل على كل جملة منها (رأيت) واضبط كلماتها بالشكل .

Nine. Make three sentences describing a river, each of which should contain a nominal subject and its predicate. Then enter into each sentence "*ra'aytu*" and express the diacritics of the words.

تدريب على الإعراب

Exercises on Grammatical Analysis

أعرب الجمل الآتية: ﴿إِنَّ إِبْرَاهِيمَ كَانَ أُمَّةً﴾، كأنَّ القمر مصباح، حسبتُ المال نافعاً، ما زال الكتاب رفيقي .

Provide a grammatical analysis of the following sentences: **{Indeed, Ibrāhīm was an Ummah}**,[154] "It is as if the moon is a lamp", "I considered the wealth to be beneficial", and, "The book continues to be my friend."

الجواب

Answers

١ ـ (إنَّ): حرف توكيد ونصب، ينصب الاسم ويرفع الخبر، و(إبراهيم): اسم (إنَّ) منصوب به، وعلامة نصبه الفتحة الظاهرة، (كان): فعل ماض ناقص، يرفع الاسم وينصب الخبر، واسمه ضمير مستتر فيه جوازاً تقديره هو؛ يعود على (إبراهيم)، (أمة): خبر (كان) منصوب به، وعلامة نصبه الفتحة الظاهرة، والجملة من ((كان) واسمه

154 Al-Naḥl: 120

وخبره) في محل رفع خبر (إنَّ) .

One. "*Inna*" (indeed) is a particle of emphasis and *naṣb*, it makes its noun *manṣūb* and its predicate *marfūʿ*. "Ibrāhīm" is the noun of *inna* and is *manṣūb* due to this, the sign of it being so is the explicit *fatḥah*. "*Kāna*" (was) is a deficient *māḍī* verb, it makes its noun *marfūʿ* and its predicate *manṣūb*. Its noun is a hidden pronoun which can be assessed as "*huwa*" (he), referring to Ibrāhīm. "Ummah" is the predicate of *kāna* and *manṣūb* due to this, and the sign of it being so is the explicit *fatḥah*. The sentence which consists of the word *kāna*, its noun and predicate is in the state of *rafʿ* due to being the predicate of *inna*.

٢- (كأنَّ) : حرف تشبيه ونصب، ينصب الاسم ويرفع الخبر، و(القمر) : اسم (كأنَّ) منصوب به وعلامة نصبه الفتحة الظاهرة، و(مصباح): خبر (كأنَّ) مرفوع به، وعلامة رفعه الضمة الظاهرة.

Two. "*Ka'anna*" (it is as if) is a particle of similitude and *naṣb*, it makes its noun *manṣūb* and its predicate *marfūʿ*. "The moon" is the noun of *ka'anna* and *manṣūb* due to this, and the sign of it being so is the explicit *fatḥah*. "Lamp" is the predicate of *ka'anna* and *marfūʿ* due to this, and the sign of it being so is the explicit *ḍammah*.

٣ - (حسبت): فعل ماض مبني على فتح مقدر على آخره منع من ظهوره اشتغال المحل بالسكون العارض لدفع كراهة توالي أربع متحركات فيما هو كالكلمة الواحدة، و(التاء) ضمير المتكلم فاعل (حسب)، مبني على الضم في محل رفع، و(المال): مفعول أول لـ(حسب) منصوب به، وعلامة نصبه الفتحة الظاهرة، و(نافعاً): مفعول ثان لـ(حسب) منصوب به، وعلامة نصبه الفتحة الظاهرة.

Three. "*Ḥasibtu*" (I considered) is a *māḍī* verb un-inflectable upon an estimated *fatḥah* at its end, prevented from being displayed due to its place being assumed by a *sukūn* to prevent the disliked meeting of four diacritics in what appears as one word. The letter *tā* (I) is a first person pronoun and the subject of "*ḥasiba*", un-inflectable upon a *ḍammah* in the state of *rafʿ*. "Wealth" is the first object of "*ḥasiba*" and it is *manṣūb* due to this, and the sign of it being so is the explicit *fatḥah*. "Beneficial" is the second object of "*ḥasiba*" and it is *manṣūb* due to this, the sign of it being so is the explicit *fatḥah*.

٤- (ما): حرف نفي مبني على السكون، لا محل له من الإعراب، و(زال) : فعل ماض ناقص يرفع الاسم وينصب الخبر، و(الكتاب): اسم (زال) مرفوع به، وعلامة رفعه ضمة ظاهرة في آخره، و(رفيق): خبر (زال) منصوب به، وعلامة نصبه فتحة مقدرة على آخره منع من ظهورها اشتغال المحل بحركة المناسبة لياء المتكلم، و(رفيق) مضاف و(ياء المتكلم) مضاف إليه مبني على السكون في محل خفض .

Four. "*Mā*" (not) is a particle of negation, un-inflectable upon a *sukūn* without a grammatical state. "*Zāla*" (disappear) is a deficient *māḍī* verb, and it makes its noun *marfūʿ* and its predicate *manṣūb*. "The book" is the noun of *zāla* and is *marfūʿ* due to this, the sign of it being so is the explicit *ḍammah* at its end. "Companion" is the predicate of *zāla* and *manṣūb* due to this. The sign of it being *manṣūb* is the estimated *fatḥah* upon its ending, prevented from being displayed due to its place being occupied by the appropriate diacritic due to the letter *yā* of the first person. "Companion" is the *muḍāf* in a possessive compound while the *yā* of the first person (my) is the *muḍāf ilayh*, un-inflectable upon a *sukūn* in the state of *khafḍ*.

أسئلة على أقسام النواسخ

Questions Regarding the Categories of the Abrogators

إلى كم قسم تنقسم النواسخ؟

Into how many categories are the abrogators split into?

ما الذي تعمله (كان) وأخواتها؟

What action do *kāna* and its sisters perform?

إلى كم قسم تنقسم أخوات (كان) من جهة العمل؟

Into how many types are the sisters of *kāna* categorised into in terms of their action.

وإلى كم قسم تنقسم من جهة التصرف؟

Into how many types are they categorised into in terms of their verbal forms?

ما الذي تعمله (إنَّ) وأخواتها؟

What action do *inna* and its sisters perform?

ما الذي تدل عليه (كأنَّ)، و(ليت)؟

What is indicated by *ka'anna* and *layta*.

ما معنى الاستدراك؟ ما معنى الترجي؟ ما معنى التوقع؟

What is the meaning of *al-istidrāk*? What is the meaning *al-tarjī*? What is the meaning of *al-tawaqqu'*?

ما الذي تعمله (ظننت) وأخواتها؟

What action do *ẓanantu* and its sisters perform?

إلى كم قسم تنقسم أخوات (ظننت)؟

Into how many types are the sisters of *ẓanantu* categorised into?

هات ثلاث جمل مكونة من مبتدأ وخبر بحيث تكون الأولى من مبتدأ ظاهر، وخبر جملة فعلية، والثانية من مبتدأٍ ضمير لجماعة الذكور وخبر مفرد، والثالثة من مبتدأٍ ظاهر وجملة اسمية، ثم أدخل على كل واحدة من هذه الجمل (كان) و(لعل) و(زعمت) .

Bring three sentences that consist of a nominal subject and its predicate. In the first of them the nominal subject should be explicit and its predicate should be a verbal sentence. In the second of them the nominal subject should be a masculine plural pronoun and its predicate should be singular. In the third of them there should be an explicit nominal subject and a nominal sentence. Then enter upon each of these sentences *kāna*, *laʿalla* and *ẓanantu*.

أعرب الأمثلة الآتية: ﴿وَاتَّخَذَ اللهُ إِبْرَاهِيمَ خَلِيلاً﴾، ﴿يَا لَيْتَنِي مِتُّ قَبْلَ هَذَا﴾، ﴿لَعَلِّي أَبْلُغُ الْأَسْبَابَ﴾.

Provide a grammatical analysis of the following *āyāt*: **{And Allah took Abraham as an intimate friend}**,[155] **{O, I wish I had died before this}**,[156] and, **{That I might reach the ways.}**[157]

155 Al-Nisā: 125
156 Maryam: 23
157 Ghāfir: 36

النعت

The Adjective

قال: (باب النعت) النعت: تابع للمنعوت في رفعه ونصبه وخفضه، وتعريفه وتنكيره؛ قام زيدٌ العاقلُ، ورأيتُ زيداً العاقل، ومررت بزيد العاقل.

He said: Chapter of the Adjective: The adjective follows the described in its *raf*ʿ, *naṣb* and *khafḍ* while also following the described in its definiteness or indefiniteness as in the following examples: "Zayd the intelligent stood", "I saw Zayd the intelligent" and, "I passed by Zayd the intelligent."

وأقول: النعت في اللغة هو الوصف، وفي اصطلاح النحويين هو: التابع المشتق أو المؤوَّلُ بالمشتق، الموضِّح لمتبوعه في المعارف، المخصِّصُ له في النكرات.

I say: *Al-naʿt* (the adjective) in the linguistic sense refers to the descriptive word. According to the nomenclature of the grammarians it refers to the grammatically following derived noun or clause which indicates the derived noun, which clarifies the definite noun that it follows or specifies the indefinite noun that it follows.

والنعتُ ينقسمُ إلى قسمين: الأولُ: النعتُ الحقيقي، والثاني: النعت السببي.

The adjective is categorised into two: (i) the actual adjective and (ii) the causal adjective.

أما النعتُ الحقيقي فهو: ما رفع ضميراً مستتراً يعود إلى المنعوت، نحو (جاء محمدٌ العاقلُ)، فالعاقل: نعتٌ لـ(محمد)، وهو رافع لضمير مستتر تقديره هو يعود إلى (محمد).

As for the actual adjective, it is that which makes the hidden pronoun that refers to the described into the state of *rafʿ*. An example is, "Muḥammad the intelligent arrived." "The intelligent" is an adjective for "Muḥammad", and it makes *marfūʿ* the hidden pronoun which is implied as "*huwa*" (he) and which refers to Muḥammad.

وأما النعت السببي فهو: ما رفع اسماً ظاهراً متصلاً بضمير يعود إلى المنعوت نحو (جاء محمدٌ الفاضلُ أبوه) فالفاضلُ: نعت لـ(محمد)، و(أبوه): فاعل لـ(الفاضل)، مرفوع بالواو نيابة من الضمة لأنه من الأسماء الخمسة، وهو مضاف إلى الهاء التي هي ضمير عائد إلى محمد.

As for the causative adjective, it is that which makes *marfūʿ* the explicit noun that is connected to the pronoun which refers back to the described. An example is seen in the statement, "Muḥammad—whose father is virtuous—arrived." "The virtuous" is the adjective of Muḥammad. "His father" is the subject of "the virtuous", and it is *marfūʿ* with the letter *wāw* serving in place of the *ḍammah* due to it being from the five nouns. It is possessed by the pronoun *hā* to which it is attached to, and which refers back to Muḥammad.

وحكم النعت أنه يتبع منعوته في إعرابه، وفي تعريفه أو تنكيره، سواءٌ أكان حقيقياً أم سببياً.

The ruling of the adjective: It follows the described in its grammatical state and in its definiteness or indefiniteness, and this is the case regardless if it is an actual adjective or a causal one.

ومعنى هذا أنه إن كان المنعوت مرفوعاً كان النعت مرفوعاً، نحو: (حضر محمدٌ الفاضلُ) أو (حضر محمدٌ الفاضلُ أبوه)، وإن كان المنعوت منصوباً كان النعت منصوباً نحو: (رأيتُ محمداً الفاضلَ) أو (رأيتُ محمداً الفاضلَ أبوه)، وإن كان المنعوت مخفوضاً كان النعت مخفوضاً نحو: (نظرتُ إلى محمدٍ الفاضلِ) أو (نظرتُ إلى محمدٍ الفاضلِ أبوه)، وإن كان المنعوت معرفة كان النعت معرفة، كما في جميع الأمثلة السابقة، وإن

كان المنعوت نكرة كان النعتُ نكرة، نحو (رأيتُ رجلاً عاقلاً) أو (رأيتُ رجلاً عاقلاً أبوهُ).

The meaning of this is that if the described is *marfū‘* then its adjective will be *marfū‘*. Examples are, "The virtuous Muḥammad was present" and, "Muḥammad—whose father is virtuous—arrived." And if the described is *makhfūḍ* then its adjective will be *makhfūḍ*. Examples are, "I saw the virtuous Muḥammad" and, "I looked at Muḥammad—whose father is virtuous." And if the described is definite then its adjective will be definite, as in all of the aforementioned examples. And if the described is indefinite then its adjective will be indefinite. Examples are, "I saw an intelligent man" and, "I saw an intelligent man whose father is intelligent".

ثم إذا كان النعت حقيقياً زاد على ذلك أنه يتبع منعوته في تذكيره أو تأنيثه، وفي إفراده أو تثنيته أو جمعه.

Furthermore, in the case of the actual adjective, additional rulings are that it follows the described in gender and in number.

ومعنى ذلك أنه إن كان المنعوت مذكراً كان النعتُ مذكراً، نحو: (رأيتُ محمداً العاقلَ) وإن كان المنعوتُ مؤنثاً كان النعتُ مؤنثاً نحو: (رأيتُ فاطمةَ المهذبةَ) وإن كان المنعوت مفرداً كان النعتُ مفرداً كما رأيتَ في هذين المثالين، وإن كان المنعوت مثنى كان النعت مثنى، نحو: (رأيت المحمدين العاقلين) وإن كان المنعوت جمعاً كان النعتُ جمعاً نحو: (رأيتُ الرجال العقلاءَ).

The meaning of this is that if the described word is masculine then its adjective will be masculine. An example is, "I saw the intelligent Muḥammad." And if the described word is feminine then its adjective will be feminine. An example is, "I saw the courteous Fāṭimah." And if the described word is singular then its adjective will be singular, as in the two previous examples. And if the described word is dual then its adjective will be dual. An example is, "I saw the two intelligent Muḥammads." And if the described word is plural then its adjective will be plural. An example is, "I saw the intelligent men."

أما النعتُ السببي فإنه يكون مفرداً دائماً ولو كان منعوته مثنى أو مجموعاً تقول: (رأيتُ الوَلدينِ العاقلِ أبوهما) وتقول: (رأيتُ الأولاد العاقل أبوهم) .

As for the causative adjective, it remains in the singular always—regardless if the described is dual or plural. Examples are, "I saw the two boys whose father is intelligent," and, "I saw the boys whose father is intelligent".

ويتبع النعت السببي ما بعده في التذكير أو التأنيث، تقول: (رأيتُ البنات العاقل أبوهنَّ)، وتقول: (رأيتُ الأولاد العاقلة أُمُّهم).

And the causative adjective follows that which comes after it in gender. Examples are, "I saw the girls whose father is intelligent" and, "I saw the boys whose mother is intelligent".

فتلخص من هذا الإيضاح أنَّ النعت الحقيقي يتبع منعوته في أربعة من عشرة. واحد من الإفراد والتثنية والجمع، وواحد من الرفع والنصب والخفض، وواحد من التذكير والتأنيث، وواحد من التعريف والتنكير.

This explanation can be summarised as follows: The actual adjective follows the described in four traits from ten: one consists of the singular, dual and plural, one consists of the states of *rafʿ*, *naṣb* and *khafḍ*, one consists of the masculine and feminine, and one consists of definiteness and indefiniteness.

والنعت السببي يتبع منعوته في اثنين من خمسة: واحد من الرفع والنصب والخفض، وواحد من التعريف والتنكير، ويتبع مرفوعه الذي بعده في واحد من اثنين وهما التذكير والتأنيث، ولا يتبع شيئاً في الإفراد والتثنية والجمع، بل يكون مفرداً دائماً وأبداً، والله أعلم.

The causative adjective follows the described in two traits from five: one consists of the states of *rafʿ*, *naṣb* and *khafḍ*, and one consists of definiteness and indefiniteness. And it follows the *marfūʿ* word after it in one of two things, and they are the masculine and feminine genders. However it does not follow anything in number, rather it stays in the singular always. And Allah knows best.

المعرفة وأقسامها

The Definite and Its Types

قال: والمعرفة خمسة أشياء: الاسم المضمر نحو: (أنا) و(أنت)، والاسم العَلم نحو: (زيدٌ) و(مكةُ)، والاسم المبهمُ نحو: (هذا) و(هذه) و(هؤلاء) والاسم الذي فيه الألف واللام نحو: (الرجلُ) و(الغلامُ)، وما أضيف إلى واحدٍ من هذه الأربعة.

He said: The definite consists of five things: (i) the implicit noun e.g. "me" and "you", (ii) the proper nouns e.g. "Zayd" and "Makkah", (iii) the ambiguous nouns e.g. "this", "this (fem.)" and "these", (iv) the noun preceded by the letters *alif* and *lām* (i.e. the definite article) e.g. "the men", "the servant", (v) nouns which are compounded to any of these four.

وأقولُ: اعلم أنَّ الاسم ينقسم إلى قسمين الأول: النكرة وستأتي، والثاني: المعرفة وهي: اللفظ الذي يدل على معَيَّنٍ، وأقسامها خمسة:

I say: Know that the noun is categorised into two: (i) the indefinite—regarding which we will speak about later, (ii) the definite, and this refers to the word that indicates towards something particular. It consists of five categories:

القسم الأول: المضمر أو الضمير، وهو ما دل على متكلم، نحو: (أنا)، أو مخاطب نحو: (أنت)، أو غائب نحو: (هو)، ومن هنا تعلم أنَّ الضمير ثلاثة أنواع.

The first category: The implicit, i.e. the pronoun. It is that which indicates towards the first person i.e. "I", the second person i.e. "you" or the third person i.e. "him". From here it can be identified that there are three types of pronouns:

النوع الأول: ما وضع للدلالة على المتكلم وهو كلمتان، وهما: (أنا) للمتكلم وحده،

و(نحن) للمتكلم المعظِّم نَفسَهُ أو معه غيره.

The first type: That which is utilised to indicate towards the first person, and it comprises of two words: "I" for the singular first person, "we" for the first person when glorifying one's self or when there is another (one or more) accompanying the speaker.

والنوع الثاني: ما وضع للدلالة على المخاطب وهو خمسة ألفاظ، وهي: (أنتَ) بفتح التاء للمخاطب المذكر المفرد، و(أنتِ) بكسر التاء للمخاطبة المؤنثة المفردة و(أنتما) للمخاطب المثنى مذكراً كان أو مؤنثاً و(أنتُم) لجمع الذكور المخاطبين، و(أنتُنَّ) لجمع الإناث المخاطبات.

The second type: That which is utilised to indicate towards the second person, and it comprises of five words: "You" which has a *fatḥah* on the letter *tā* in the Arabic and which refers to the singular second person masculine, "you" which has a *kasrah* on its *tā* and which refers to the singular second person feminine, "you two" for the dual form second person from both genders, "you" for the plural second person masculine, "you" for the plural second person feminine.

والنوع الثالث: ما وضع للدلالة على الغائب، وهو خمسة ألفاظ أيضاً، وهي: (هو) للغائب المذكر المفرد، و(هِيَ) للغائبة المؤنثة المفردة، و(هُمَا) للمثنى الغائبُ مطلقاً، مذكراً كان أو مؤنثاً، و(هُم) لجمع الذكور الغائبين، و(هُنَّ) لجمع الإناث الغائبات.

The third type: That which is utilised to indicate towards the third person, and it likewise comprises of five words: "Him" for the singular third person masculine, "her" for the singular third person feminine, "those two" for the dual third person in both genders, "they" for the plural third person masculine and "they" for the plural third person feminine.

وتقدم هذا البيانُ في (بحث الفاعل)؛ وفي (بحث المبتدأ والخبر).

And we have preceded in explanation regarding these in the section regarding the subject [of the verb] and the nominal subject and its predicate.

القسم الثاني من المعرفة: العَلمُ، وهو ما يدل على معين بدون احتياج إلى قرينة تكلم أو خطاب أو غيرهما، وهو نوعان: مذكر نحو (محمد)، و(إبراهيم)، و(جبل)، ومؤنث نحو (فاطمة)، و(زينب) و(مكة).

The second category from the definite nouns: The proper noun, and it is that which indicates towards a specific thing without needing a sign towards the first person, second person, or other than these two. It has two sub-categories: (i) the masculine e.g. "Muḥammad", "Ibrāhīm" and "Jabal", (ii) the feminine e.g. "Fāṭimah", "Zaynab" and "Makkah."

القسم الثالث: الاسم المبهم، وهو نوعان: اسمُ الإشارة، والاسمُ الموصول.

The third category: The ambiguous noun, and it is of two types: the demonstrative pronoun and the relative pronoun.

أما اسم الإشارة: فهو: ما وضع ليدل على معين بواسطة إشارة حسية؛ أو معنوية، وله ألفاظ معينة، وهي: (هذا) للمذكر المفرد، و(هذه) للمفردة المؤنثة، و(هذين) أو (هذين) للمثنى المذكر، و(هاتَانِ) أو (هاتينِ) للمثنى المؤنث، و(هؤلاء) للجمع مطلقاً.

As for the demonstrative pronoun, it is that which is utilised to indicate towards a specific thing through the means of a tangible signal (e.g. this is a pen/هذا قلم) or an intangible one (e.g. this is a view (or opinion)/هذا رأي). It consists of a number of specific words: "This" referring to the singular masculine, "this" for the singular feminine", "these two" (utilised by one of the two variations *hādhān* or *hādhayn*) for the dual masculine, "these two" (utilised by one of the two variations *hātān* or *hātayn*) for the dual feminine, and "them" for the plural of both genders.

وأما الاسم الموصول فهو: ما يدل على معين بواسطة جملة أو شبهها تذكر بعده البتة

وتسمى (صِلة)، وتكون مشتملة على ضمير يطابق الموصول ويسمى (عائداً)، وله ألفاظ معينة أيضاً، وهي: (الذي) للمفرد المذكر، و(التي) للمفردة المؤنثة، و(اللذان) أو (اللذين) للمثنى المذكر، و(اللتان) أو (اللتَينِ) للمثنى المؤنث، و(الَّذين) لجمع الذكور، و(اللَّائي) أو (الأتي) لجمع الإناث.

As for the relative pronoun, it is that which is utilised to indicate towards a specific thing through the means of a sentence or the quasi sentence, and it (i.e. the sentence or quasi sentence) must always be mentioned after it as it is termed as a *ṣilah* (i.e. a subordinate clause connected to the sentence which preceded it).[158] A *ṣilah* will include a pronoun which conforms to the relative pronoun hence it is termed as being a "returner". It has specific words, and they are: "The one that" for the singular masculine", "the one that" for the singular feminine, "the two that" (utilised by one of the two variations *alladhān* or *alladhayn*) for the dual masculine, "the two that" (utilised by one of the two variations *allatān* or *allatayn*) for the dual feminine, "they that" for the plural masculine and "they that" for the plural feminine.

القسم الرابع: المحلى بالألف واللام، وهو: كل اسم اقترنت به (أل) فأفادته التعريف ، نحو (الرجل)، و(الكتاب)، و(الغلام)، و(الجارية) .

The fourth category: That which is adorned by the letters *alif* and *lām* i.e. every word connected to "*al-*" [at its start], and this makes the word definite. Examples are, "the man", "the book", "the boy" and "the girl".

والقسم الخامس: الاسم الذي أضيف إلى واحد من الأربعة المتقدمة فاكتسب التعريف من المضاف إليه نحو: (غلامك)، و(غلام محمد)، و(غلام هذا الرجل)، و(غلام الذي زارنا أمس)، و(غلام الأستاذ).

The fifth category: The noun that is compounded to one of these four aforementioned categories and it attains definitiveness due to being possessed by it. Examples are, "Your boy", "Muḥammad's boy", "This man's boy," "The boy,

158 Meaning, the relative pronoun must have a *ṣilah* attached to it in order for it to make sense.

the one who visited us yesterday", and, "The teacher's boy."

وأعرف هذه المعارف بعد لفظ الجلالة: الضميرُ، ثم العلمُ، ثم اسم الإشارة، ثم الاسمُ الموصول، ثم المحلى بـ(أل)، ثم المضاف إليها.

The level of definitiveness of these words—after the name of Allah—is as follows: the pronoun, the proper noun, the demonstrative pronoun, the relative pronoun, that which is adorned by "*al-*" and that which is possessed by any of these four.

والمضاف في رتبة المضاف إليه، إلا المضاف إلى الضمير فإنه في رتبة العلم، والله أعلم.

The *muḍāf's* definitiveness is classified in accordance to that of the *muḍāf ilayh*. However the exception to this rule is that which is a *muḍāf* to a pronoun, as it is classified as a proper noun. And Allah knows best.

النكرةُ

The Indefinite

قال: والنكرةُ: كلُ اسم شائعٍ في جنسه لا يختصُّ به واحدٌ دون آخر، وتقريبُهُ: كل ما صَلَحَ دخولُ الألِفِ واللامِ عليه، نحوُ (الرجُلِ) و(الفَرَسِ).

He said: The indefinite consists of every noun which is general in its genus and is not easily distinguished from other nouns of the same type. One might approximate that the indefinite includes all of the words that can accept the definite article *"al-"*, such as "the man" and "the horse."

وأقول: النكرة: هي كل اسم وضع لا ليخصَّ واحداً بعينه من بين أفراد جنسه، بل ليصلح إطلاقُهُ على كل واحدٍ على سبيل البدل، نحو (رجل) و(امرأة)؛ فإن الأول يصح إطلاقه على كل ذكر بالغ من بني آدم، والثاني يصح إطلاقه على كل أنثى بالغة من بني آدم.

I say: The indefinite is every noun that is not utilised to refer to an individual thing from its type. Rather it is utilised to refer to each individual from its type in a general manner where each individual from the type is interchangeable.[159] Examples are "a man" and "a woman". The first of them is appropriate to be utilised as a general reference to every mature man from the Children of Ādam. The second of them is appropriate to be utilised as a general reference to every mature woman from the Children of Ādam.

وعلامة النكرة أن تصلح لأن تدخُلَ عليها (أل) وتؤثر فيها التعريف نحو (رجل) فإنه يصح دخول (أل) عليه، ويؤثر فيه التعريف؛ فتقول: (الرجل) وكذلك (غلام) ، و(

159 Al-Ahdal said in *al-Kawākib* (1/103), "I.e. It is correct to be used interchangeably for each type and not for each type all at once."

جارية)، و(صبي)، و(معلم) فإنك تقول: (الغلام)، و(الجارية)، و(الصبي)، و(الفتاة)، و(المعلم).

The sign of the indefinite is that it can be adapted by the entry of "*al-*" upon it,[160] which would cause it to become definite. An example is the word "a man". It is valid to enter "*al-*" upon it, and it causes it to become definite so one would now say, "the man." Likewise is the case for words such as: "a boy", "a girl", "a child", and "a teacher." They would become, "the boy", "the girl", "the child" and, "the teacher."

تمرينات

Exercises

١ - ضع كل اسم من الأسماء الأتية في ثلاث جمل مفيدة، بحيث يكون مرفوعاً في واحدة، ومنصوباً في الثانية، ومخفوضاً في الثالثة، وانعت ذلك الاسم في كل جملة بنعت حقيقي مناسب:

One. Place each of the following nouns into three beneficial sentences, in the first of them the noun should be *marfū'*, in the second of them it should be *manṣūb* and in the third of them it should be *makhfūḍ*. Give each of these nouns in the sentences an appropriate actual adjective:

الرجلان. محمد. العصفور. الأستاذ. فتاة. زهرة. المسلمون. أبوك.

٢ - ضع نعتاً مناسباً في كل مكان من الأمكنة الخالية في الأمثلة الآتية، واضبطه

160 Al-Ahdal said in *al-Kawākib* (1/104-105), "This definition omits nouns which do not accept *alif* and *lām* e.g. Zayd, 'Amr and Bakr. Also omitted from it are the nouns which accept *alif* and *lām* but which do not become definite through this, such as al-Faḍl, al-Ḥārith, al-Ḥasan etc. Furthermore, omitting *alif* and *lām* in these cases does not make them indefinite nouns. [Therefore, the inclusion of *alif* and *lām* in proper nouns is not included in the definition and in making something definite.]"

بالشكل:

Two. Place an appropriate adjective in each empty place found in the below examples, and express their diacritics.

(أ) الطالب ... يُحِبُّهُ أُستاذه.

(ب) الفتاة ... تُرضي والديها.

(ج) النيل ... يخصب الأرض.

(د) أنا أحب الكتب ... .

(ه) وطني مصرُ ... .

(و) الطلاب ... يخدمون بلادهم.

(ز) الحدائق ... للتنزه.

(ح) لقيت رجلاً ... فتصدقت عليه.

(ط) سكنت في بيت ... .

(ي) ما أحسَنَ الغرَف ... .

(ك) عند أخي عصاً ... .

(ل) أهديتُ إلى أخي كتاباً ... .

(م) الثيابَ ... لَبُوس الصيف.

٣ ـ ضع منعوتاً مناسباً في كل مكان من الأماكن الآتية، واضبطه بالشكل:

Three. Place an appropriate described word in each empty place found below, and express their diacritics.

(أ) ... المجتهد يحبه أستاذه.

(ب) ... العالمون يخدمون أمتهم.

(ج) أنا أحب ... النافعة .

(د) ... الأمين ينجح نجاحاً باهراً.

(ه) ... الشديدة تقتلع الأشجار.

(و) قطفت ... ناضرة.

(ز) رأيت ... بائسة فتصدقت عليها.

(ح) ... القارس لا يحتمله الجسم.

(ط) ... المجتهدون خدموا الشريعة الإسلامية.

(ي) أفدت من آثار... المتقدمين.

(ل) ... العزيزة وطني.

٤ ـ أوجِد منعوتاً مناسباً لكل من النعوت الآتية، ثم استعمل النعت والمنعوت جميعاً في جملة مفيدة، واضبط آخرهما بالشكل:

Four. Identify an appropriate described word for each of the following adjectives. Then utilise the adjective and the described word together in a beneficial sentence, and express the vowelling at their ends.

الضخم، المؤدبات، الشاهقة، العذبة، الناضرة، العقلاء، البعيدة، الكريم، الأمين، العاقلات، المهذبين، شاسع، واسعة.

تدريب على الإعراب

Exercises on Grammatical Analysis

أعرب الجمل الآتية:

Provide a grammatical analysis of the following sentences:

(الكتاب جليس ممتع)، (الطالب المجتهد يحبه أستاذه)، (الفتيات المهذبات يخدمن بلادهنّ)، (شربت من الماء العذب).

"The book is a delightful companion", "The hard working student is loved by his teacher", "The polite girls serve their country", and, "I drank from the fresh water."

الجواب

Answers

١ ـ (الكتاب) : مبتدأ مرفوع بالابتداء، وعلامة رفعه الضمة الظاهرة في آخره. (جليس) : خبر المبتدأ، مرفوع بالمبتدأ وعلامة رفعه الضمة الظاهرة في آخره. (ممتع) : نعت

لـ(جليس) ، و(نعت) المرفوع مرفوع، وعلامة رفعه الضمة الظاهرة في آخره

One. “The book” is a *marfū‘* nominal subject due to it commencing the sentence, and the sign of it being *marfū‘* is the explicit *ḍammah* at its end. “Companion” is the predicate of the nominal subject, *marfū‘* due to its nominal subject, and the sign of it being *marfū‘* is the explicit *ḍammah* at its end. “Delightful” is the adjective of “companion” and the adjective of a *marfū‘* word is also *marfū‘*, the sign of it being *marfū‘* is the explicit *ḍammah* at its end.

٢ - (الطالب) : مبتدأ مرفوع بالابتداء، وعلامة رفعه الضمة الظاهرة في آخره. و(المجتهد) : نعت (للطالب)، ونعت المرفوع مرفوع، وعلامة رفعه الضمة الظاهرة في آخره. و(يحب) : فعل مضارع مرفوع لتجرده من الناصب والجازم، وعلامة رفعه الضمة الظاهرة في آخره، والهاء: ضمير الغائب مفعول به، مبني على الضم في محل نصب. و(أستاذ): فاعل (يحب) مرفوع، وعلامة رفعه الضمة الظاهرة في آخره، و(أستاذ) مضاف و(الهاء) ضمير الغائب مضاف إليه، مبني على الضم في محل خفض، والجملة من الفعل وفاعله في محل رفع خبر المبتدأ الذي هو (الطالب)، والرابط بين هو الضمير المنصوب في (يحبه).

Two. “The student” is a *marfū‘* nominal subject due to it commencing the sentence, and the sign of it being *marfū‘* is the explicit *ḍammah* at its end. “The hard working” is the adjective of “the student” and the adjective of a *marfū‘* word is also *marfū‘*, the sign of it being so is the explicit *ḍammah* at its end. “He loves” (i.e. “is loved” in the above sentence) is a *marfū‘ muḍāri‘* verb due to the absence of a *nāṣib* or *jāzim*, and the sign of it being so is the explicit *ḍammah* at its end. The letter *hā* (him) is a third person pronoun serving as an object, un-inflectable upon a *ḍammah* in the state of *naṣb*. “Teacher” is the subject of the verb “he loves”, it is *marfū‘* and the sign of it being so is the explicit *ḍammah* at its end. “Teacher” is the possessed in the possessive compound and the third person pronoun *hā* (his) is the possessor, un-inflectable upon a *ḍammah* in the state of *khafḍ*. And the sentence consisting of the verb and its subject is in the state of *raf‘* due to being the predicate of the nominal subject i.e. “the students”. The connector is the *manṣūb* pronoun in “he loves him".

٣ - (الفتيات) : مبتدأ مرفوع بالابتداء، وعلامة رفعه الضمة الظاهرة . و(المهذبات) : نعت لـ(الفتيات)، ونعت المرفوع مرفوع، وعلامة رفعه الضمة الظاهرة. و(يخدم) : فعل مضارع مبني على السكون لاتصاله بنون النسوة، ونون النسوة فاعل، مبني على الفتح في محل رفع. و(بلاد) : مفعول به لـ(يخدم) منصوب، وعلامة نصبه الفتحة الظاهرة، و(بلاد) مضاف و(هن) ضمير جماعة الإناث الغائبات مضاف إليه، مبني على الفتح في محل خفض، والجملة من الفعل والفاعل في محل رفع خبر المبتدأ الذي هو (الفتيات)، والرابط هو: نون النسوة في (يخدمن).

Three. "Girls" is the nominal subject, *marfūʿ* due to it commencing the sentence. The sign of it being so is the explicit *ḍammah*. "The polite" is the adjective of "girls" and the adjective of a *marfūʿ* word is likewise *marfūʿ* and the sign of it being so is the explicit *ḍammah*. "Serve" is a *muḍāriʿ* verb un-inflectable upon a *sukūn* due to it being connected to the letter *nūn* of feminine plurality. The *nūn* of feminine plurality is the subject, un-inflectable upon a *fatḥah* in the state of *rafʿ*. "Country" is the object of "serve" and *manṣūb*, the sign of it being so is the explicit *fatḥah*. "Country" is the possessed, and "their" (*hunna*) is a pronoun denoting the plural third person feminine and it is the possessor, un-inflectable upon a *fatḥah* in the state of *khafḍ*. The sentence consisting of the verb and its subject is in the state of *rafʿ* due to it being the predicate of the nominal subject i.e. "the girls." The connector is the *nūn* of feminine plurality in the word "serve".

٤ - (شرب) : فعل ماض و(التاء) ضمير المتكلم فاعل، مبني على الضم في محل رفع. و(من) : حرف جر، مبني على السكون لا محل له من الإعراب. و(الماء) : مجرور بـ(من)، وعلامة جره الكسرة الظاهرة، والجار والمجرور متعلق بـ(شرب). و(العذب): نعت لـ(الماء)، ونعت المجرور مجرور، وعلامة جره الكسرة الظاهرة في آخره.

Four. "Drank" is a *māḍi* verb and the letter *tā* (I) is the first person pronoun serving as the subject, un-inflectable upon a *ḍammah* in the state of *rafʿ*. "From" is a particle of *jarr*, un-inflectable upon a *sukūn* without a grammatical state. "Water" is *majrūr* due to the particle "from" and the sign of it being so is the explicit *kasrah*. The *jārr* and *majrūr* compound is connected to the verb drink. "Fresh" is the adjective of "water" and the adjective of a *majrūr* word is also *majrūr*, the sign of it being so is the explicit *fatḥah* at its end.

أسئلة على ما تقدم

Questions Regarding What Has Preceded

ما هو النعت؟ إلى كم قسم ينقسم النعت؟

What is an adjective? Into how many categories is it categorised into?

ما هو النعت الحقيقي؟ ما هو النعت السببي؟

What is the actual adjective? What is the causal adjective?

ما هي الأشياء التي يتبع فيها النعت الحقيقي منعوته؟

What are the things that the actual adjective follows the described word in?

ما هي الأشياء التي يتبع فيها النعت السببي منعوته؟

What are the things that the causal adjective follows the described word in?

ما الذي يتبعه النعت السببي في التذكير والتأنيث؟

In what manner does gender affect the actual adjective ?

ما هي المعرفة؟ ما هو الضمير؟ ما هو العلم؟ ما هو اسم الإشارة ؟ ما هو الاسم الموصول؟

What is the definite? What is the pronoun? What is the proper noun? What is the demonstrative pronoun? What is the relative pronoun?

مثل لكل من الضمير، والعلم، واسم الإشارة، والاسم الموصول ... بثلاثة أمثلة في جمل مفيدة.

Provide three examples each for the pronoun, proper noun, demonstrative pronoun and relative pronoun in beneficial sentences.

حروف العطف

The Particles of Conjunction

قال: (باب العطف)، وحروف العطف عشرة، وهي: (الواو)، و(الفاء)، و(ثمَّ)، و(أو)، و(أم)، و(إمَّا)، و(بل)، و(لا)، و(لكن)، و(حتى) في بعض المواضع.

He said: Chapter of the Conjunction: The particles of conjunction are ten[161]: the letter *wāw*, the letter *fā*, *thumma*, *aw*, *am*, *immā*, *bal*, *lā*, *lakin* and *ḥatā* in some instances.

وأقول: للعطف معنيان: أحدهما لغوي والآخر اصطلاحي.

I say: The conjunction has two meanings, the first of them is the linguistic meaning and the second of them is according to the nomenclature of the grammarians.

أما معناه لغة فهو: الميل، تقول: (عطف فلان على فلان)، تريد أنه مال إليه وأشفق عليه. وأما العطف في الاصطلاح فهو قسمان: الأول: عطف البيان، والثاني: عطف النسق.

As for its linguistic meaning, it means inclination e.g. "So-and-so inclined towards so-and-so." The intention behind this statement is that the person inclines towards the other and has compassion for him. As for its meaning according to the nomenclature of the grammarians, it consists of two types: (i) the conjunct of proclamation and (ii) the conjunct of correlating.

---

161 Al-Imām Ibn al-Qayyim said in *al-Badāʾī* (4/201), "The correct view is that the particles of conjunction are nine, not ten." This is because he did not consider *immā* to be from them. This will be explained below in the appropriate place.

فأما عطف البيان فهو (التابع الجامد الموضَّح لمتبوعه في المعارف المخصص له في النكرات) فمثال عطف البيان في المعارف : (جاءني محمد أبوك) فـ(أبوك): عطف بيان على (محمد)، وكلاهما معرفة، والثاني في المثال موضِّح للأول، ومثاله في النكرات قوله تعالى: ﴿مِنْ مَاءٍ صَدِيدٍ﴾ [إبراهيم : ٦١] فـ(صديد) عطف بيان على (ماء)، وكلاهما نكرة، والثاني في المثال مخصِّص للأول.

As for the conjunct of proclamation, its definition is, "The *jāmid* (i.e. non-derivative) follower which serves as a clarifier[162] for what preceded it in the case of a definite, and as a specifier of it in the case of the indefinite." An example of the conjunct of proclamation after a definite noun is, "Muḥammad, your father, came." "Your father" is the conjunct of proclamation for "Muḥammad" and both of them are definite. It is mentioned to clarify what comes before it. An example of it after an indefinite noun is, **{Of water, purulent [water.]}**[163] We can see that "purulent" here is a conjunct of proclamation for "water" and both of them are indefinite. The second of them (i.e. "purulent") is utilised to specify the first.

وأما عطف النسق فهو (التابع الذي يتوسط بينه وبين متبوعه أحدُ الحروف العشرة) وهذه الحروف هي:

As for the conjunct of correlation, its definition is, "The grammatical follower that has between it and the followed word one of ten particles." These particles are as follows:

١ ـ الواو، وهي لمطلق الجمع؛ فيُعطف بها المتقارنان، نحو: (جاء محمدٌ وعليٌ) إذا كان مجيئهما معاً، ويعطف بها السابق على المتأخر، نحو: (جاء عليٌ ومحمود) إذا كان مجيءِ محمودٍ سابقاً على مجيءِ عليٍّ، ويعطف بها المتأخر على السابق، نحو: (

162 Al-Ḥāmidī said (P. 109), 'It is called a clarifier because the latter part of the statement is connected to the former, this is in order to add clarification or specification.' See *Sharh al-Fakihi* (2/170).

163 Ibrāhīm: 16

جاء عليٌ ومحمد) إذا كان مجيءُ محمد متأخراً عن مجيءِ عليٍّ.

One. The letter *wāw*, it is for general combining, and so it is utilised to attach together the associated e.g. "Muḥammad and 'Alī came" if they arrived together. It can be used to attach the preceding to the latter e.g. "'Alī and Maḥmūd came" if the arrival of Maḥmūd preceded the arrival of 'Alī. It can also be used to attach the latter to the preceding e.g. "'Alī and Muḥammad came" if the arrival of Muḥammad was after the arrival of 'Alī.

٢ ـ الفاءُ، وهي للترتيب والتعقيب، ومعنى الترتيب: أن الثاني بعد الأول، ومعنى التعقيب: أنه عقيبهُ بلا مُهلة، نحو: (قدِمَ الفرسان فالمشاةُ) إذا كان مجيء الفرسان سابقا ؛ ولم يكن بين قدوم الفريقين مهلة.

Two. The letter *fā* (then/subsequently), it expresses *al-tartīb* and *al-ta'qīb* i.e. immediate (*al-ta'qīb*) succession (*al-tartīb*). An example is, "The cavalry arrived and then the ground forces," when the arrival of the cavalry is first but there is not a gap in-between the two groups.

٣ ـ (ثمَّ)، وهي للترتيب مع التراخي، ومعنى الترتيب قد سبق، ومعنى التراخي: أن بين الأول والثاني مُهلة، نحو: (أرسل الله موسى ثمَّ عيسى ثمَّ محمداً عليهم الصلاة والسلام).

Three. *Thumma* (then), and it is used to express *al-tartīb* with *al-tarākhī*. We have just explained the meaning of *al-tartīb*. The meaning of *al-tarākhī* is that there is a gap between the first thing and the second. An example of this is in the statement, "Allah sent Mūsā, then 'Īsā, then Muḥammad (peace and blessings be upon them)."

٤ ـ (أوْ)، وهو للتأخير أو الإباحة، والفرق بينهما أن التخيير لا يجوز معه الجمع. والإباحة يجوز معها الجمع؛ فمثال التخيير (تزوَّج هنداً أو أختها)، ومثال الإباحة (ادرس الفقه أو النحو) فإن لديك من الشرع دليلاً على أنه لا يجوز الجمع بين (هند وأختها) بالزواج، ولا تشكَّ في أنه يجوز الجمع بين الفقه والنحو بالدراسة.

Four. *Aw* (or), it is utilised for two things, selection and allowance. The difference between the two is that the word *al-ta'khīr* (selection) here does not allow the different things to be combined, whereas the word *ibāḥah* (allowance) does allow this. An example of selection is in the statement, "Marry Hind or her sister." An example of allowance is in the statement, "Study *fiqh* or grammar." So in these two cases you have proof from Islamic legislation that it is not permissible to combine between Hind and her sister in marriage, whereas you have no doubt that it is permissible for you to combine between *fiqh* and grammar lessons.

٥ - (أمْ)، وهي لطلب التعيين بعد همزة الاستفهام نحو: (أدرست الفقه أم النحو؟).

Five. *Am* (or), it is used to seek a specific [answer] after one has utilised the letter *hamza* of interrogation. An example is, "Did you study *fiqh* or grammar?"

٦ - (إمَّا)، بشرط أن تسبق بمثلها، وهي مثل (أو) في المعنيين، نحو قوله تعالى: ﴿فَشُدُّوا الْوَثَاقَ فَإِمَّا مَنًّا بَعْدُ وَإِمَّا فِدَاءً﴾ [محمد : ٤]، ونحو: (تزوج إمَّا هنداً وإمَّا أُختها).

Six. *Immā* (or/either),[164] if it meets the condition of being preceded by its like, then it is the equivalent of the particle *aw* in its two meanings. It can be seen in the *āyah*: {**Then secure their bonds, and either [confer] favour afterwards or ransom [them]**}[165] and the statement, "Marry either Hind or her sister."

٧ - (بل)، وهي للإضراب، ومعناهُ جعلُ ما قبلها في حكم المسكوت عنه، نحو: (ما جاء محمدٌ بل بَكرٌ)، ويشترط للعطف بها شرطان؛ الأول: أن يكون المعطوف بها مفرداً لا جملة، والثاني: ألا يسبقها استفهام.

164 Shaykh Ibn al-'Uthaymīn said (pp. 321-322), "It is a matter of difference amongst the scholars of grammar regarding whether "*immā*" is a particle of conjunction or not… The correct view is that it is not a conjunction, rather it is a *ḥarf tafṣīl* (particle of explanation)."

165 Muḥammad: 4

Seven. *Bal* (rather), it is used for *iḍrāb* and the meaning of this is to overturn what preceded it with the meaning of negation. An example is, "Muḥammad did not come, rather Bakr." There are two conditions for this to be used as a particle of conjunction: (i) that the word following it is a single word and not a sentence, (ii) it is not preceded by a question.

٨ - (لا)، وهي تنفي عما بعدها نفسَ الحكم الذي ثبت لما قبلها نحو: (جاء بكرٌ لا خالدٌ).

Eight. *Lā* (not), it is utilised to negate for the following word the matter which was established for the preceding word. An example is, "Bakr came, not Khālid."

٩ - (لكن)، وهي تدلُ على تقرير حكم ما قبلها وإثبات ضده لما بعدها، نحو: (لا أحبُّ الكسالى لكنِ المجتهدين). ويشترط للعطف بها ثلاثة شروط: أن يسبقها نفي أو نهي، وأن يكون المعطوف بها مفرداً، وألا تسبقها الواو.

Nine. *Lakin* (however), it indicates towards affirmation of the matter that came before it and affirmation of the opposite for that which comes after it. An example is, "I do not like the lazy, however I like the industrious." There are three conditions for it to be utilised as a particle of conjunction: (i) it is preceded by a negation or a prohibition, (ii) there must be a single word after it,[166] and (iii) it is not preceded by the letter *wāw*.

١٠- (حتَّى)، وهي للتدريج والغاية، والتدريج: هو الدلالة على انقضاء الحكم شيئاً فشيئاً، نحو: (يَموتُ الناسُ حتَّى الأنبياءُ).

166 Ibn Hishām said in *al-Mughnī* (1/292), "If it is followed by speech then it is a particle of commencement and only gives the meaning of rectification (الاستدراك), it is not a particle of conjunction. In this case it is permissible to use the letter *wāw* with it, e.g.

﴿وَمَا ظَلَمْنَاهُمْ وَلَٰكِن كَانُوا هُمُ الظَّالِمِينَ﴾

{**And we did not wrong them, but it was they who were the wrongdoers**} (al-Zukhruf: 76)."

Al-Ahdal said (2/556), "If a sentence arises after it then it is a particle of commencement and rectification and not a particle of conjunction."

Ten. *Ḥattā* (until), it is utilised for *al-tadrīj* and providing a terminal point. *Al-tadrīj* is an indication of the completion of a matter gradually, little by little. An example is the statement, "The people die, even the Prophets."

وتأتي (حتَّى) ابتدائية غير عاطفة، إذا كان ما بعدها جملة، نحو: (جاء أصحابُنا حتى خالد حاضر) وتأتي جارة نحو قوله تعالى: ﴿حَتَّى مَطْلَعِ الْفَجْرِ﴾ ولهذا قال المؤلف: (و(حتَّى) في بعض المواضع).

Ḥatta is also utilised as an initiator instead of as a particle of conjunction, and this is the case when a sentence follows it. An example is, "Our companions came. Even Khālid was present." It will also come as a governing agent of *jarr*, an example being in the statement, "Until the rise of dawn." This is why the author said, "And *ḥatā* (until) in some instances."

حكم حروف العطف

The Ruling of the Particles of Conjunction

قال: فإن عطفت على مرفوع رفعت، أو على منصوب نُصبت، أو على مخفوض خفضت، أو على مجزوم جزمت، تقُولُ: (قام زيد وعمرٌو) ، و(رأيتُ زيداً وعمراً) ، و(مررتُ بزيدٍ وعمرٍو) ، و(زيدٌ لم يقُم ولم يقعُدْ).

He said: So if a word is conjoined with another which is *marfūʿ* then the conjoined word is also *marfūʿ*, and if a word is conjoined with another which is *manṣūb* then the conjoined word is also *manṣūb*, and if a word is conjoined with another which is *makhfūḍ* then the conjoined word is also *makhfūḍ*, and if a word is conjoined with another which is in the state of *jazm* then the conjoined word is also *majzūm*. Examples of this can be found in the following statements: "Zayd and ʿAmr stood", "I saw Zayd and ʿAmr", "I passed by Zayd and ʿAmr" and, "Zayd did not stand and did not sit."[167]

وأقول: هذه الأحرف العشرة تجعل ما بعدها تابعاً لما قبلها في حكمه الإعرابي، فإن كان المتبوع مرفوعاً كان التابع مرفوعاً، نحو: (قابلني محمد وخالدٌ) فـ(خالد): معطوف

---

167 Benefit:

(i) Al-Ḥāmidī said in *Ḥāshiyat ʿalā al-Kafrāwī* (p. 86), "If the conjoined words are repeated then each of them is conjoined to the first if the conjunction is not one that provides ordering e.g. *al-wāw* and *aw*. If this is not the case then each is conjoined to the one before it."

(ii) Al-Imām ibn al-Qayyim said in *al-Badāʾi* (3/52)—in regards to the names and attributes of Allah, "If there is a place where a number of attributes of Allah are mentioned together without regards to combining them or singling them out, it is better to leave out the particle of conjunction. On the other hand, if there is an intention to combine between the attributes or give attention to their differences then it is better to utilise a particle of conjunction." He said (3/53), "And whenever the difference is clear then using the particle of conjunction is better."

على (محمد)، والمعطوف على المرفوع مرفوع، وعلامة رفعه الضمة الظاهرة، وإن كان المتبوع منصوباً كان التابع منصوباً، نحو: (قابلت محمداً وخالداً) فـ(خالداً) معطوف على (محمد)، والمعطوف على المنصوب منصوب، وعلامة نصبه الفتحة الظاهرة، وإن كان المتبوع مخفوضاً كان التابع مخفوضاً مثله، نحو: (مررت بمحمدٍ وخالد) فـ(خالد) معطوف على (محمد)، والمعطوف على المخفوض مخفوض، وعلامة خفضه الكسرة الظاهرة، وإن كان المتبوع مجزوماً كان التابع مجزوماً أيضاً، نحو: (لمْ يَحْضُر خالد أو يُرسِل رسُولاً) فـ(يرسل): معطوف على (يحضر)، والمعطوف على المجزوم مجزوم، وعلامة جزمه السكون.

I say: These ten particles cause that which follows them to follow that which precedes them in terms of grammatical ruling. If the followed word is *marfūʿ* then the follower will be *marfūʿ* e.g. "Muḥammad and Khālid met me." In this example, "Khālid" is conjoined to "Muḥammad" and that which is conjoined to a *marfūʿ* word is also *marfūʿ*, and the sign of it being so is the explicit *ḍammah*. If the followed word is *manṣūb* then the follower will be *manṣūb* e.g. "I met Muḥammad and Khālid." "Khālid" is conjoined to "Muḥammad" and that which is conjoined to a *manṣūb* word is also *manṣūb*, and the sign of it being so is the explicit *fatḥah*. If the followed word is *makhfūḍ* then the follower will be *makhfūḍ* likewise e.g. "I passed by Muḥammad and Khālid. "Khālid is conjoined to "Muḥammad" and that which is conjoined to a *makhfūḍ* word is also *makhfūḍ*, and the sign of it being so is the explicit *kasrah*. If the followed word is *majzūm* then its follower will be *majzūm* likewise e.g. "Khālid did not attend or send a messenger." "Send" is conjoined to "attend" and that which is conjoined to a *majzūm* word is also *majzūm*, and the sign of it being so is the *sukūn*.

ومن هذه الأمثلة تعرف أن الاسم يعطف على الاسم، وأن الفعل يُعْطفُ على الفعل.

From these examples one can perceive that nouns are conjoined to nouns and verbs are conjoined to verbs.

تمرينات

Exercises

١- ضع معطوفاً مناسباً بعد حروف العطف المذكورة في الأمثلة الآتية:

One. Place an appropriate conjoined word after the particles of conjunction that are present in the following examples:

(أ) ما اشتريت كتاباً بل ....   (ب) ما أكلت تفاحاً لكن ....

(ج) بنى أخي بيتاً و ....   (و) خرج من بالمعهد حتى ....

(د) حضر الطلاب فـ ....   (ح) ما زرت أخي لكن ....

(ه) سافرت يوم الخميس و ....   (ز) صاحِبِ الأخيار لا ....

٢ ـ ضع معطوفاً مناسباً في الأماكن الخالية من الأمثلة الآتية:

Two. Place an appropriate conjoined word in the empty spaces that are present in the following examples:

(أ) كل من الفاكهة .... لا الفجَّ.   (ه) نظم .... وأدواتِك.

(ب) بقي عندنا أبوك .... أو بعض يوم.   (و) رحلتُ إلى .... فالإسكندرية.

(ج) ما قرأت الكتاب .... بل بعضه.   (ز) يعجبني .... لا قولُهُ.

(د) ما رأيت .... بل وكيله.   (ح) أيهما تفضل .... أم الشتاء.

٣ ـ اجعل كل كلمة من الكلمات الآتية في جملتين، بحيث تكون في إحداهما معطوفاً وفي الثانية معطوفاً عليه:

Three. Utilise each of the following words in two sentences, in the first of them it should be the conjoined and in the second of them it should be the word conjoined upon.

العلماءُ، العِنبُ، القَصر، القاهرةُ، يسافر، يأكل، المجتهدون، الأتقياء، أحمد، عمر، أبو بكر، اقرأ، كَتَبَ.

تدريب على الإعراب

Exercises on Grammatical Analysis

أعرب الجمل الآتية:

Provide a grammatical analysis of the following sentences:

ما رأيت محمداً لكن وكيله، زارنا أخوك وصديقه، أخي يأكل ويشرب كثيراً.

"I did not see Muḥammad however [I saw] his representative", "We were visited by your brother and his friend" and, "My brother eats and drinks a lot."

الجواب

Answer

١ـ (ما): حرف نفي، مبني على السكون لا محل له من الإعراب. (رأى) من (رأيت): فعل ماض مبني على فتح مقدر على آخره منع من ظهوره اشتغال المحل بالسكون. و(التاءُ) ضمير المتكلم فاعل، مبني على الضم في محل رفع. (محمداً) : مفعول به منصوب، وعلامة نصبه الفتحة الظاهرة. (لكن) : حرف عطف. (وكيل) : معطوف على (محمد) ، والمعطوف على المنصوب منصوب، وعلامة نصبه الفتحة الظاهرة، و(وكيل) مضاف و(الهاء) ضمير الغائب مضاف إليه، مبني على الضم في محل جر.

One. "*Mā*" (did not) is a particle of negation that is un-inflectable upon a *sukūn* without a grammatical state. "See" is a *māḍī* verb un-inflectable upon an implicit *fatḥah* at its end, prevented from being displayed due to its position being occupied by a *sukūn*. The letter *tā* at the end of the verb is a first person pronoun and the subject, un-inflectable upon a *ḍammah* in the state of *rafʿ*. "Muḥammad" is a *manṣūb* object and the sign of it being *manṣūb* is the explicit *fatḥah*. "*Lākin*" is a particle of conjunction. "Representative" is conjoined to "Muḥammad" and that which is conjoined to a *manṣūb* word is also *manṣūb*, the sign of it being so is the explicit *fatḥah*. "Representative" is also the *muḍāf* while the attached pronoun "*hā*" (his) is the third person pronoun and the *muḍāf ilayhi* in this compound, un-inflectable upon a *ḍammah* in the state of *jarr*.

٢ - (زار) : فعل ماض مبني على الفتح لا محل له من الإعراب، و(نا) : مفعول به مبني على السكون في محل نصب. (أخو) : فاعل مرفوع وعلامة رفعه الواو نيابة عن الضمة لأنه من الأسماء الخمسة، و(أخو) مضاف و(الكاف) ضمير المخاطب مضاف إليه مبني على الفتح في محل خفض، و(الواو) حرف عطف، (صديق) معطوف على (أخو)، والمعطوف على المرفوع مرفوع، وعلامة رفعه الضمة الظاهرة. و(صديق): مضاف و(الهاءُ) ضمير الغائب مضاف إليه، مبني على الضم في محل خفض.

Two. "Visited" is a *māḍī* verb un-inflectable upon a *fatḥah* without a grammatical state. The attached pronoun "*nā*" (us) is the object, un-inflectable upon a *sukūn* in the state of *naṣb*. "Brother" is a *marfūʿ* subject, and the sign of it being *marfūʿ* is the letter *wāw* serving as a representative for the *ḍammah* due to it being from the five nouns. "Brother" is also the *muḍāf* while the letter *kāf* is a pronoun of the second person and the *muḍāf ilayhi* in this compound, un-inflectable upon a *fatḥah* in the state of *khafḍ*. The letter *wāw* is a particle of conjunction. "Friend" is conjoined to "brother", and that which is conjoined to a *marfūʿ* word is also *marfūʿ* and the sign of it being so is the explicit *ḍammah*. "Friend" is also the *muḍāf* and the letter *hā* (his) is the third person pronoun and the *muḍāf ilayhi* in this compound, un-inflectable upon a *ḍammah* in the state of *khafḍ*.

٣ - (أخ) من (أخي) : مبتدأ مرفوع بالابتداء وعلامة رفعه ضمة مقدرة على آخره منع من ظهورها اشتغال المحل بحركة المناسبة، و(أخ) مضاف و(ياءُ المتكلم) مضاف إليه، مبني على السكون في محل خفض. (يأكل): فعل مضارع مرفوع لتجرده من الناصب والجازم، وعلامة رفعه الضمة الظاهرة، والفاعل ضمير مستتر فيه جوازاً تقديره هو يعود على (أخي)، والجملة من الفعل والفاعل في محل رفع خبر المبتدأ، والرابط بين جملة الخبر والمبتدأ هو الضمير المستتر في (يأكل) و(الواو) حرف عطف. (يشرب): فعل مضارع معطوف على (يأكل)، والمعطوف على المرفوع مرفوع، وعلامة رفعه الضمة الظاهرة. (كثيراً): نائب مفعول مطلق منصوب وعلامة نصبه الفتحة الظاهرة.

Three. The word "brother" from "my brother" is the nominal subject and *marfūʿ* due to it being the commencement, and the sign of it being so is the implicit *ḍammah* upon its end, prevented from being displayed due to its place being occupied by the appropriate diacritic. "Brother" is also the *muḍāf* and the letter *yā* of the first person is the *muḍāf ilayhi* in this compound, un-inflectable upon a *sukūn* in the state of *khafḍ*. "He eats" is a *muḍāriʿ* verb which is *marfūʿ* due to the absence of a *nāṣib* or a *jāzim*, and the sign of it being *marfūʿ* is the explicit *ḍammah*. The subject is the hidden pronoun which is allowed to be implicit as "*huwa*" (he), which refers back to "my brother." The sentence from the verb and the subject is in the state of *rafʿ* and the predicate of the nominal subject. The connection between the predicate sentence and the nominal subject is the hidden pronoun in "he eats". The letter *wāw* (and) is a particle of conjunction. "He drinks" is a *muḍāriʿ* verb conjoined to "he eats", and the word which is conjoined to a *marfūʿ* word is also *marfūʿ*, the sign of it being so is the explicit *ḍammah*. "A lot" is the *nāʾib mafʿūl muṭlaq* (representative absolute object) and the sign of it being *manṣūb* is the explicit *fatḥah*.

أسئلة

Questions

ما هو العطف؟

What is a conjunct?

إلى كم قسم ينقسم العطف؟

Into how many types has the conjunct been categorised into?

ما هو عطف البيان؟

What is the conjunct of proclamation?

مثِّل لعطف البيان بمثالين.

Provide two examples of the explanatory conjunct.

ما هو عطف النسق؟

What is the correlative conjunct?

ما معنى (الواو)؟

What is the meaning of the letter *wāw*?

ما معنى (أم)؟

What is the meaning of the particle "*am*"?

ما معنى (إمَّا)؟

What is the meaning of the particle "*immā*"?

ما الذي يشترط للعطف بـ(بَل)؟

What are the conditions for "*bal*" to be utilised as a particle of conjunction?

ما الذي يشترط للعطف بـ(لكن)؟

What are the conditions for "*lakin*" to be utilised as a particle of conjunction?

فيم يشترك المعطوف والمعطوف عليه؟

What does the conjoined word share with the word with which it has been conjoined to?

أعرب الأمثلة الآتية، وبين المعطوف والمعطوف عليه، وأداة العطف ﴿وَجَاوَزْنَا بِبَنِي إِسْرَآئِيلَ الْبَحْرَ فَأَتْبَعَهُمْ فِرْعَوْنُ وَجُنُودُهُ﴾، ﴿فَئَاتِ ذَا الْقُرْبَى حَقَّهُ وَالْمِسْكِينَ وَابْنَ السَّبِيلِ﴾، ﴿سَبَّحَ لِلَّهِ مَا فِي السَّمَوَاتِ وَالأَرْضِ وَهُوَ العَزِيزُ الحَكِيمُ﴾، ﴿وَإِنَّ مِنْ أَهْلِ الكِتَابِ لَمَن يُؤْمِنُ بِاللهِ وَمَآ أُنزِلَ إِلَيْكُمْ وَمَآ أُنزِلَ إِلَيْهِمْ﴾، ﴿وَلَسَوْفَ يُعْطِيكَ رَبُّكَ فَتَرْضَى ﴿٥﴾ أَلَمْ يَجِدْكَ يَتِيماً فَئَاوَى ﴿٦﴾ وَوَجَدَكَ ضَالًّا فَهَدَى ﴿٧﴾ وَوَجَدَكَ عَآئِلاً فَأَغْنَى﴾، ﴿خُذُوهُ فَغُلُّوهُ ﴿٣٠﴾ ثُمَّ الجَحِيمَ صَلُّوهُ ﴿٣١﴾ ثُمَّ فِي سِلْسِلَةٍ ذَرْعُهَا سَبْعُونَ ذِرَاعاً فَاسْلُكُوهُ﴾.

Provide a grammatical analysis of the following examples, and identify the conjoined words and those which they are conjoined to, and the particles of conjunction: **{And We took the Children of Israel across the sea, and Pharaoh and his soldiers pursued them}**,[168] **{So give the relative his right, as well as the needy and the traveller}**,[169] **{Whatever is in the heavens and earth exalts Allah, and He is the Exalted in Might, the Wise}**,[170] **{And indeed, among the People of the Scripture are those who believe in Allah and what was revealed to you and what was revealed to them}**,[171] **{And your Lord is going to give you, and you will be satisfied. Did He not find you an orphan and give [you] refuge? And He found you lost and guided [you], and He found you poor and made [you] self-sufficient.}**[172] **{[Allah will say], "Seize him and shackle him. Then into Hellfire drive him. Then into a chain whose length is seventy cubits insert him."}**[173]

168 Yūnus: 90

169 Al-Rūm: 38

170 Al-Ḥadīd: 1

171 Āli 'Imrān: 199

172 Al-Ḍuḥā: 5-8

173 Al-Ḥāqqah: 30-32

التوكيد، وأنواعه، وحكمه

The Emphasis, Its Types and Its Rulings

قال: (باب التوكيد)، التوكيد: (تابعٌ للمُؤكدِّ في رفعه ونصبه وخفضِه وتعريفه).

He said: Chapter of the Emphasis. The emphasis follows the emphasised object in its *raf*ʿ, *naṣb*, *khafḍ* and its definitiveness.[174]

أقول: التأكيد - ويقال التوكيد - معناه في اللغة: التقوية، تقول: (أكَّدتُ الشيء) وتقول: (وكَّدتُهُ) أيضاً: إذا قويته.

I say: Emphasis (which can also be pronounced in Arabic with the letter *hamza* instead of the letter *wāw*)[175] means—in the linguistic sense—to strengthen e.g. "I asserted something", and "I asserted it" when one reinforces a statement.

وهو في اصطلاح النحويين نوعان، الأول: التوكيد اللفظي، والثاني: التوكيد المعنوي.

And according to the nomenclature of the grammarians it has two types: (i) verbal emphasis and (ii) emphasis through meaning.

أما التوكيد اللفظي: فيكون بتكرير اللفظ وإعادته بعينه أو بمرادفه، سواء أكان اسماً نحو: (جاء محمدٌ محمدٌ) أم كان فعلاً نحو (جاء جاء محمد) أم كان حرفاً نحو (نَعَمْ

174 Al-Kafrāwī said (p. 114), "The emphasis follows the emphasised object in definiteness but not in indefiniteness. This is because the words of emphasis are definite and so they do not follow the indefinite. For this reason, he did not say 'and its indefiniteness, that would be the opposite view of the Kufis'." See *al-Kawākib* (p. 571).

175 Al-Ahdal said in *al-Kawākib* (2/558), "*Tawkīd* is more eloquent and it is the word used in the Qur'ān: ﴿وَلَا تَنقُضُوا الْأَيْمَانَ بَعْدَ تَوْكِيدِهَا﴾ **{And do not break oaths after their confirmation}** (al-Naḥl: 91)." See *al-Taṣrīḥ* (2/12).

نَعَمْ جاء محمد) أم كان مرادفا نحو (جاء حضر أبو بكر).

As for verbal emphasis: It is achieved by repeating the wording, either by repeating the same word or through the use of a synonym. This form of emphasis can be utilised for the noun e.g. "Muḥammad, Muḥammad came", the verb e.g. "Muḥammad came, came", or a particle e.g. "Yes, yes Muḥammad came." An example of the utilisation of a synonym is, "Muḥammad came, he was present."

وأما التوكيد المعنوي فهو: (التابع الذي يرفع احتمال السهو أو التوسع في المتبوع)، وتوضيح هذا أنك لو قلت: (جاء الأميرُ) احتمل أنك سهوت أو توسعت في الكلام، وأن غرضك مَجِيءُ رسولِ الأمير، فإذا قلت: (جاء الأميرُ نفسُهُ) أو قلت: (جاء الأميرُ عينُهُ) ارتفع الاحتمالُ وتقرر عند السامع أنك لم تُرِد إلا مجيءَ الأمير نفسه.

As for emphasis through meaning: It is, "A follower that removes the possibility that one is speaking forgetfully or that he spoke regarding something with a wider scope [than he intended.]" This can be understood by pondering over the statement, "The leader came." It could be assumed that the speaker in this case is speaking forgetfully or that he intended something with a wider scope i.e. that the leader's messenger was in fact whom was truly meant. Whereas if it is said, "The leader, himself, came" then the possibility of these kinds of assumptions are removed and it is established to the listener that the speaker is referring to nothing besides the coming of the leader.

وحكمُ هذا التابع أنه يوافق متبوعه في إعرابه، على معنى أنه إن كان المتبوع مرفوعاً كان التابع مرفوعاً أيضاً، نحو: (حضر خالدٌ نفسُهُ) وإن كان المتبوع منصوباً كان التابع منصوباً مثله، نحو: (حفظتُ القرآنَ كُلَّهُ) وإن كان المتبوع مخفوضاً كان التابع مخفوضاً كذلك، نحو: (تدبرتُ في الكتاب كُلِّه) ويتبعه أيضاً في تعريفه، كما ترى في هذه الأمثلة كلها.

The ruling regarding this particular follower is that it matches the followed word in its inflection, i.e.: If the followed word is *marfūʿ* then its follower will be *marfūʿ* e.g. "Khālid was present himself." If the followed word is *manṣūb* then its follower will be *manṣūb* e.g. "I memorised the Qur'ān in its entirety." If the followed word is *makhfūḍ* then its follower will be *makhfūḍ* e.g. "I reflected within this book in its entirety." It also matches the followed word in definitiveness, as the reader can see in the aforementioned examples.

ألفاظ التوكيد المعنوي

The Words Utilised to Derive the Emphasis Through Meaning

قال: ويكون بألفاظ معلومة، وهي: (النفسُ)، و(العين)، و(كلٌّ)، و(أجمعُ)، و(توابعُ (أجمعُ))، وهي: (أكتعُ)، و(أبتعُ)، و(أبصعُ)، تقولُ: (قام زيدٌ نفسهُ)، و(رأيتُ القومَ كُلَّهم)، و(مررت بالقوم أجمعينَ).

He said: It occurs with certain known words and they are: "*al-nafsu*" (self), "*al-ʿaynu*" (self), "*kullun*" (all), "*ajmaʿu*" (all) and its followers: "*aktaʿu*", "*abtaʿu*" and "*abṣaʿu*". Thus one says, "Zayd—himself—stood", "I saw the people, all of them", and, "I passed by the people, all of them."

وأقول: للتوكيد المعنوي ألفاظ معينة عَرَفها النُحاةُ من تتبُّع كلام العرب ومن هذه الألفاظ: (النفسُ) و(العينُ)، ويجب أن يضاف كل واحدٍ من هذين إلى ضمير عائدٍ على المؤَكَدِ - بفتح الكاف -، فإن كان المؤكد مفرداً كان الضمير مفرداً، ولفظ التوكيد مفرداً أيضاً، تقول: (جاء عليٌ نفسُهُ)، و(حضر بكرٌ عينُهُ)، وإن كان المؤكد جمعاً كان الضمير ضمير الجمع، ولفظُ التوكيد مجموعاً أيضاً، تقول: (جاء الرجالُ أنفُسُهُم)، و(حضر الكتَّابُ أعينهم)، وإن كان المؤكد مثنى؛ فالأفصح أن يكون الضمير مثنى، ولفظ التوكيد مجموعاً، تقول: (حضر الرجلان أنفُسُهما) و(جاء الكاتبان أعينهما).

I say: The emphasis through meaning has specific words used for it that have been identified by the grammarians through following the speech of the Arabs. From these words are "*al-nafsu*" and "*al-ʿaynu*". It is mandatory that each of these two words are possessed by a pronoun that refers to the word that is being emphasised. If the word being emphasised is singular, then its pronoun and the emphasis will be singular also. Examples are, "'Alī himself came" and, "Bakr himself was present". If the word being emphasised is a plural, then its pronoun and the emphasis will be plural also. Examples are, "The men themselves came", and, "The scribes themselves were present". If the word being emphasised is a dual form then it is more eloquent for one to use a dual pronoun whilst utilising a plural word for the emphasis. Examples of this are, "The two men themselves were present" (i.e. the word *anfusu* is in the plural and it is attached to a dual form pronoun), and, "The two scribes themselves came."

ومن ألفاظ التوكيد: (كلُّ)، ومثلُهُ (جميعٌ) ويشترط فيهما إضافة كل منهما إلى ضمير مطابق للمؤكد، نحو: (جاء الجيشُ كلهُ) و(حضر الرجالُ جميعُهُم).

From the words of emphasis are "*kullu*" and "*jāmī'*" and they likewise have to be attached to a pronoun which corresponds to the word being emphasised. Examples are, "The army came, all of it", and, "The men were present, all of them."

ومن الألفاظ (أجمعُ) ولا يؤكد بهذا اللفظ غالباً إلا بعد (كلٍّ) ومن الغالب قوله تعالى: ﴿فَسَجَدَ الْمَلَائِكَةُ كُلُّهُمْ أَجْمَعُونَ﴾ ومن غير الغالب قول الراجز: (إذن ظَلِلْتُ الدَّهرَ أبكي أجمعَا)، وربما احتيج إلى زيادة التقوية، فجيء بعد (أجمع) بألفاظ أخرى، وهي: (أكتَعُ) و(أبتعُ) و(أبصعُ) وهذه الألفاظ لا يؤكَّدُ بها استقلالاً، نحو: (جاء القومُ أجمعون، أكتعون، أبتعون، أبصعون) والله أعلم.

From the words of emphasis is "*ajma'u*", and emphasis is not normally denoted through the use of this except after *kullu*, and an example of this emphasis is in the statement of Allah: **{So the angels prostrated themselves, all of them.}**[176] An example of the utilisation of this word in the less frequent manner is the statement of the poet:

176 Ṣad: 73

As a result I spent my time crying, all of it.

Sometimes more emphasis may be needed, in which case "*ajmaʿu*" will be followed by another word, and this word can be any of "*aktaʿu*", "*abtaʿu*" and "*abṣaʿu*". These words do not provide emphasis independently. An example is, "The people came, all of them [...] (emphasised)." And Allah knows best.

تدريب على الإعراب

Exercises on Grammatical Analysis

أعرب الجمل الآتية:

Provide a grammatical analysis for the following sentences:

(قرأت الكتاب كلَّهُ)، (زارنا الوزيرُ نفسُهُ)، (سلمت على أخيك عينه)، (جاء رجال الجيش أجمعون).

"I read the book, all of it." "The minister himself visited us." "I greeted your brother himself." "The men of the army came, all of them."

١- (قرأ): فعل ماض، مبني على فتح مقدر على آخره منع من ظهوره اشتغال المحل بالسكون العارض لدفع كراهة توال أربع متحركات فيما هو كالكلمة الواحدة، و(التاء) ضمير المتكلم فاعل، مبني على الضم في محل رفع، و(الكتاب) مفعول به منصوب، وعلامة نصبه الفتحة الظاهرة، و(كل): توكيد لـ(الكتاب)، وتوكيد المنصوب منصوب، وعلامة نصبه الفتحة الظاهرة، و(كل) مضاف و(الهاء) ضمير الغائب مضاف إليه، مبني على الضم في محل خفض.

One. "Read" is a *māḍī* verb, un-inflectable upon an implicit *fatḥah* at its end, prevented from being displayed due to its position being occupied by a *sukūn* which prevents the disliked following of four diacritics in what appears to be one word. The letter *tā* is the first person pronoun and the subject, un-inflectable upon a *ḍammah* in the state of *rafʿ*. "The book is the *manṣūb* object, and the sign of it being *manṣūb* is the explicit *fatḥah*. "All of it" (*kulla*) is an emphasis of "the book", and the emphasis of a *manṣūb* word is also *manṣūb*. The sign of it being *manṣūb* is the explicit *fatḥah*. It is also the possessed in a possessive compound and the letter *hā* (which refers to the book) is a third person pronoun and the possessor in this compound, un-inflectable upon a *ḍammah* in the state of *khafḍ*.

٢ - (زار): فعل ماض مبني على الفتح لا محل له من الإعراب، و(نا) مفعول به مبني على السكون في محل نصب، و(الوزير): فاعل (زار) مرفوع، وعلامة رفعه الضمة الظاهرة في آخره، و(نفس) : توكيد لـ(الوزير)، وتوكيد المرفوع مرفوع، وعلامة رفعه الضمة الظاهرة، و(نفس) مضاف و(الهاء) ضمير الغائب مضاف إليه، مبني على الضم في محل خفض.

Two. "Visited" is a *māḍi* verb, un-inflectable upon a *fatḥah* without a grammatical state. "Us" is the object, un-inflectable upon a *sukūn* in the state of *naṣb*. "The minister" is the subject of "visited" and it is *marfūʿ*, the sign of it being so is the explicit *ḍammah* at its end. "Himself" is an emphasis of "the minister", and the emphasis of a *marfūʿ* word is itself *marfūʿ*, the sign of it being so is the explicit *ḍammah*. "Himself" is also the possessed in a possessive compound and the letter *hā* (which refers to the minister) is a third person pronoun and the possessor, un-inflectable upon a *ḍammah* in the state of *khafḍ*.

٣- (سلمت): فعل وفاعل، (على): حرف خفض مبني على السكون لا محل له من الإعراب، (أخي): مخفوض بـ(على)، وعلامة خفضه الياء نيابة عن الكسرة لأنه من الأسماء الخمسة، و(أخي) مضاف و(الكاف) ضمير المخاطب مضاف إليه، مبني على الفتح في محل خفض، (عين): توكيد (لأخي)، وتوكيد المخفوض مخفوض، وعلامة خفضه الكسرة الظاهرة، و(عين) مضاف و(الهاء) ضمير الغائب مضاف إليه، مبني على الكسر في محل خفض.

Three. "I greeted" consists of the verb and its subject. "*ʿAlā*" is a particle of *khafḍ* that is un-inflectable upon a *sukūn* without a grammatical state.

"Brother" is made *makhfūḍ* by "*ʿalā*" and the sign of it being so is the letter *yā* serving in place of the *kasrah* due to it being from the five nouns. "Brother" is also the possessed in a possessive compound and the letter *kāf* is a second person pronoun and the possessor, un-inflectable upon a *fatḥah* in the state of *khafḍ*. "Himself" is an emphasis of the word "brother" and the emphasis of a *makhfūḍ* word is itself *makhfūḍ*, and the sign of it being so is the explicit *kasrah*. "Himself" is also the possessed in a possessive compound and the letter *hā* (which refers to the brother) is a third person pronoun and the possessor, un-inflectable upon a *kasrah* in the state of *khafḍ*.

٤- (جاء) : فعل ماض مبني على الفتح لا محل له من الإعراب، (رجال): فاعل مرفوع وعلامة رفعه الضمة الظاهرة في آخره، و(رجال) مضاف، و(الجيش): مضاف إليه مخفوض، وعلامة خفضه الكسرة الظاهرة، و(كل): توكيد لـ(رجال)، وتوكيد المرفوع مرفوع، وعلامة رفعه الضمة الظاهرة، و(كل) مضاف، و(هم): ضمير جماعة الغائبين مضاف إليه، مبني على السكون في محل خفض، (أجمعون): توكيد ثان مرفوع، وعلامة رفعه الواو نيابة عن الضمة لأنه جمع مذكر سالم.

Four. "Came" is a *māḍi* verb un-inflectable upon a *fatḥah* without a grammatical state. "The men" is the subject and *marfūʿ*, the sign of it being so is the explicit *ḍammah* at its end. It is also the possessed in a possessive compound and "the army" is the possessor and *makhfūḍ*, the sign of it being so is the explicit *kasrah*. "All" is an emphasis of "men" and the emphasis of a *marfūʿ* word is also *marfūʿ*, the sign of it being so is the explicit *ḍammah*. "All" is also the possessed in a possessive compound and "*hum*" (which refers to the men) is a third person plural pronoun and the possessor, un-inflectable upon a *sukūn* in the state of *khafḍ*. "*Ajmaʿūn*" is the second emphasis and *marfūʿ*, the sign of it being so is the letter *wāw* serving as a representative of the *ḍammah* due to it being a sound masculine plural.

أسئلة

Questions

ما هو التوكيد؟ إلى كم قسم ينقسم التوكيد؟

What is *tawkīd*? Into how many categories has it been split into?

مثل بثلاثة أمثلة مختلفة للتوكيد اللفظي.

Provide three different examples of the verbal emphasis.

ما هي الألفاظ التي تستعمل في التوكيد المعنوي؟

What are the words that are utilised to provide emphasis through meaning?

ما الذي يشترط للتوكيد بالنفس والعين؟

What are the conditions for the words *al-nafs* and *al-ʿayn* to bring forth emphasis?

ما الذي يشترط للتوكيد بـ(كل)، و(جميع)؟

What are the conditions for the words *kullu* and *jāmīʿu* to bring forth emphasis?

هل يستعمل (أجمعون) في التوكيد غير مسبوق بـ(كل)؟

Can *ajmaʿūn* be utilised as an emphasis if it is not preceded by *kullu*?

أعرب الأمثلة الآتية:

Provide a grammatical analysis of the following examples:

أيُّ إنسانٍ تُرضى سجاياهُ كُلّها؟ الطلاب جميعُهم فائزون، رأيتُ علياً نفسه، زرت الشيخين أنفُسَهُما.

Which person has their characteristics loved, all of them? The students, all of them, were successful. I saw ʿAlī himself. I visited the two scholars themselves.

البدل وحكمه

The Substitute and Its Rulings

قال: إذا أُبدل اسمٌ من اسمٍ أو فعلٌ من فعلٍ تَبِعه في جميع إعرابِهِ.

He said: If a noun is substituted for another noun or a verb for another verb, then the substitute follows the original word's grammatical state.

وأقول: البدل معناه في اللغة: العِوَضَ، تقول: (استبدلتُ كذا بكذا)، و(أبدلتُ كذا من كذا)؛ أي: استعضتهُ منه.

I say: Linguistically, the Arabic word *al-badl* refers to exchanging. It is said, "I sought to exchange this with this" and, "I exchanged this from this", meaning, I substituted something with it.

وهو في اصطلاح النحويين (التابع المقصود بالحكم بلا واسطة).

The meaning according to the nomenclature of the grammarians is, "The follower (i.e. the exchanged) that takes the same ruling without there being an intermediary."[177]

وحكمه: أنه يتبع المبدل منه في إعرابه، على معنى أنه إن كان المبدل منه مرفوعاً كان البدلُ مرفوعاً، نحو: (حضر إبراهيمُ أبوكَ) وإن كان المبدل منه منصوباً كان البدل منصوباً، نحو: (قابلت إبراهيمَ أخاك) وإن كان المبدل منه مخفوضاً كان البدلُ

177 Ibn Hishām said in *Sharḥ al-Qaṭr* (p. 439), "The statement 'the follower' includes all followers and 'takes the same ruling' excludes the adjective, the emphasis and the conjunct of proclamation, for they are compliments to the followed word which is intended by the ruling. 'That it comes without an intermediary' meaning, it comes without a conjunction e.g. 'Zayd and 'Amr came', though it is a follower and is intended by the ruling, it comes with the particle of conjunction as an intermediary." See *Shudhūr al-Dhahab* (pp. 439-440), *al-Kawākib* (2/573) and *Ḥāshiyat al-Kafrāwī* (pp. 115-116).

مخفوضاً، نحو: (أعجبتني أخلاق محمدٍ خالِكَ) وإن كان المبدل منه مجزوماً كان البدل مجزوماً، نحو: (من يشكر ربَّهُ يسجد له يَفُزْ).

Its ruling is that it follows the word it substitutes in its grammatical state. The meaning of this is that if the word it substitutes is *marfūʿ* then the substitute will also be *marfūʿ* e.g. "Ibrāhīm, [i.e.] your father, was present." And if the word it substitutes is *manṣūb* then the substitute will be *manṣūb* e.g. "I met Ibrāhīm, [i.e.] your brother." And if the word it substitutes is *makhfūḍ* then the substitute will be *makhfūḍ* e.g. "The manners of Muḥammad, [i.e.] your uncle, amazed me." And if the word it substitutes is *majzūm* then the substitute will be *majzūm* e.g. "Whoever thanks his Lord [and] prostrates to him will be victorious."[178]

أنواع البدل

Types of the Substitute

قال: وهو على أربعةِ أقسام: بدلُ الشيءِ من الشيءِ، وبدلُ البعضِ من الكل، وبدل الاشتمالِ، وبدل الغلطِ، نحو قولك: (قام زيدٌ أخوكَ)، و(أكلتُ الرغيفَ ثُلُثَه)، و(نفعني زيدٌ علمُهُ)، و(ورأيتُ زيداً الفرسَ)، أردت أن تقول (الفرَسَ) فَغَلِطت فأبدلت (زيداً) منه.

He said: Substitution is categorised into four: (i) Substitution of something for another, (ii) the substitution of a part for the whole, (iii) the theoretical substitution (iv) the substitution of error. Some examples of these types of substitution include, "Zayd, [i.e.] your brother, stood", "I ate the loaf, a third of it", "I was benefited by Zayd, [i.e.] his knowledge", and, "I saw Zayd, the horse" where one intended to say "the horse" but made a mistake and so substituted "Zayd" with it.

178 This is a conditional sentence. The verb "thanks" is in the state of *jazm* in this sentence due to it being the verb of the condition. The word "who" (*man*) is the noun of the condition.

وأقول: البدلُ على أربعة أنواع:

I say: There are four types of substitution:

النوع الأول: بدل الكل من الكل، ويسمى البدل المطابق، وضابطه: أن يكون البدل عينَ المبدل منه، نحو: (زارني محمدٌ عمُكَ).

The first type: Substituting the complete with the complete, and it is known as the substitution of the concordant. The governing principle for this is that the substitute refers to the same thing as the word substituted e.g. "I was visited by Muḥammad, [i.e.] your uncle."

النوع الثاني: بدل البعض من الكل، وضابطه: أن يكون البدل جزءاً من المبدل منه، سواءٌ أكان أقلَّ من الباقي أم مساوياً له أم أكثر منه، نحو: (حفظت القرآنَ ثُلُثَه) أو (نصفه) أو (ثلثَيهِ) ويجب في هذا النوع أن يضاف إلى ضمير عائدٍ إلى المبدل منه، كما رأيت.

The second type: The substitution of a part for the whole. The governing principle for this is that the substitute is a part from the thing substituted, regardless if it is small compared to the remainder, equal or bigger. Examples are, "I memorised the Qur'ān, a third of it", and this portion could be "half of it" or "two thirds of it." It is mandatory in this type that the substitute is compounded with a pronoun that refers back to the word substituted, as the reader should have noticed.

النوع الثالث: بدلُ الاشتمال، وضابطه: أن يكون بين البدل والمبدل منه ارتباط بغير الكلية والجزئية، ويجب فيه إضافة البدل إلى ضمير عائد إلى المبدل منه أيضاً، نحو: (أعجبتني الجاريةُ حديثُهَا) و(نَفَعني الأستاذ حُسنُ أخلاقِهِ).

The third type: The theoretical substitution. The governing principle for this is that there is a relationship between the substitute and the thing substituted that is not absolute nor partial.[179] It is mandatory for the substitute to be compounded to a pronoun that refers back to the word substituted, as was also the case above. Examples are, "I was surprised by the girl, her speech" and, "I attained benefit from the teacher, his good manners."

النوع الرابع: بدل الغلطِ، وهذا النوع على ثلاثة أضرب:

The fourth type: The substitution of error. This type is of three kinds:

١ - بدل البداءِ، وضابطه: أن تقصد شيئاً فتقوله، ثم يظهر لك أن غيره أفضلُ منه فتعدل إليه، وذلك كما لو قلت: (هذه الجارية بدرٌ) ثم قلت بعد ذلك: (شمسٌ).

One. The substitution of the commencement. The governing principle for this is that one intends something and states it, then it becomes apparent to the speaker that something else is more appropriate to be utilised and so he alters towards it. This can be seen if one says, "This girl is a full moon" and then says after this, "... a sun."

٢ - بدل النسيان، وضابطه: أن تبني كلامك في الأول على ظنٍّ، ثم تعلم خطأهُ فتعدل عنه، كما لو رأيت شبحاً من بعيد فظننته إنساناً فقلت: (رأيتُ إنساناً) ثم قرب منك فوجَدْتَه فرساً فقلت: (فرساً).

Two. The substitution of "inattention". The governing principle for this is that one speaks at first based upon an assumption, then he realises he is mistaken and alters away from this course. An example of this is if one sees an obscure figure from afar and assumes it to be a human, so he says, "I see a human". But then as the figure draws closer the speaker realises that it is a horse, and so he says "... a horse."

٣ - بدل الغلط، وضابطه: أن تريد كلاماً فيسبق لسانُك إلى غيره وبعد النطق تعدل إلى ما أردتَ أوّلاً، نحو: (رأيت محمداً الفرسَ).

---

179 Ibn 'Aqīl said (3/249), "The theoretical substitution provides a meaning for the followed word."

Three. The substitution of an error. The governing principle for this is that one intends to say something but a slip of the tongue causes the utterance of something else, and so the speaker alters towards what he intended to state originally. An example is, "I saw Muḥammad … the horse."

تمرينات

Exercises

١ - ميز أنواع البدل الواردة في الجمل الآتية:

One. Identify the types of substitutes found in the following examples:

سرتني أخلاقُ خالك محمدٍ، رأيتَ السفينةَ شِراعَهَا، بَشَّرتني أختي فاطمة بمجيءِ أبي، أعجبتني الحديقة أزهارُها، هالني الأسدُ زَئِيرُهُ، شربت ماءً عسلاً، ذهبتُ إلى البيتِ المسجد، ركبت القطار الفرس.

٢ - ضع في كل مكان من الأمكنة الخالية بدلاً مناسباً، واضبطه بالشكل:

Two. Fill in the gaps below with an appropriate substitute, and express its diacritics.

(أ) أكرمتُ إخوَتَكَ .... وكبيرهم. (ج) احترم جميع أهلك .... ونساءهم.

(ب) جاءَ الحُجَّاجُ .... ومُشاتُهم. (د) اجتمعت كملة الأمة .... وشِيبُهَا.

٣ - ضع في كل مكان من الأمكنة الخالية بدلاً مطابقاً مناسباً واضبطه بالشكل:

Three. Fill in the gaps below with an appropriate concordant substitute, and express its diacritics.

(أ) كان أمير المؤمنين .... مثالاً للعدل. (ج) يسر الحَاكِمُ .... أن ترقى أُمَّتُهُ.

(ب) اشتهر خليفة النبي .... برقة القلب. (د) سافر أخي .... إلى الإسكندرية.

٤ ـ ضع في كل مكان من الأمكنة الخالية بدل اشتمالٍ مناسباً، واضبطه بالشكل:

Four. Fill in the gaps below with an appropriate theoretical substitute, and express its diacritics.

(أ) راقتني حديقة دارك .... .

(ب) أعجبني الأستاذ .... .

(ج) وثِقتُ بصديقك .... .

(د) فرحت بهذا الطالب .... .

(ه) أحببت محمداً .... .

(و) رضيت خالداً .... .

٥ ـ ضع في كل مكان من الأمكنة الخالية مبدلاً منه مناسباً، واضبطه بالشكل، ثم بين نوع البدل:

Five. Fill in the gaps below with an appropriate substituted word, and express its diacritics. Then identify what type the substitute falls under.

(أ) نفعني .... علمه.

(ب) اشتريت .... نصفها.

(ج) زارني .... محمد.

(د) إن .... أباك تكرِمُهُ تُفلِح.

(ه) شاقتني .... أزهارها .

(و) رحلت رحلة طويلة ركبت فيها .... سيارة.

أسئلة

Questions

ما هو البدلُ؟

What is *al-badl*?

فيم يتبع البدل المبدل منه؟

What does the substitute follow the substituted word in?

إلى كم قسم ينقسم البدل؟

Into how many categories is the substitute split into?

ما الذي يشترط في بدل البعض وبدل الاشتمال؟

What are the conditions for the substitution of a part and the theoretical substitution?

ما ضابط بدل الكل؟ ما أقسامه؟ وما ضابط كل قسم؟

What is the governing principle for the complete substitution? What are its categories? What is the governing principle for each category?

ما هو بدل الغلط؟ وما أقسامه؟ وما ضابط كل قسم؟

What is the substitution of an error? What are its categories? What is the governing principle for each category?

أعرب الأمثلة الآتية: رسول الله محمد خاتم النبيين، عَجَزَ العربُ عن الإتيانِ بالقرآنِ عشرِ آياتٍ منه، أعجبتني السماء نُجُومُهَا.

Provide a grammatical analysis of the following examples: "The Messenger of Allah, Muḥammad ﷺ is the seal of the Prophets", "The Arabs were not able to bring forth [the similitude] of the Qur'ān, ten *āyāt* from it" and "I was amazed by the sky, its stars".

عدد المنصوبات، وأمثلتها

The Number of *Manṣūb* Words and Examples of Them

قال: منصوبات خمسة عشر، وهيَ: المفعولُ بِهِ، والمصدرُ، وظرفُ الزمانِ، وظرفُ المكانِ، والحال، والتمييزُ، والمُستثنى، واسم (لا)، والمُنادى، والمفعول من أجله، والمفعولُ معهُ، وخبرُ ((كان) وأخواتِها)، واسم ((إن) واخواتها)، والتابعُ للمنصوب، وهو أربعة أشياء: النَّعتُ، والعطفُ، والتوكيدُ، والبدلُ .

He said: The nouns in the state of *naṣb* are fifteen: The object, the infinitive, the adverb of time, the adverb of place, the state, the distinction, the exception, the noun negated by *lā*, the vocative (i.e. that which is called), the object of reason, the object of accompaniment, the predicate of *kāna* and its sisters, the noun of *inna* and its sisters, and the followers of a *manṣūb* word, which are four: the adjective, the conjunction, the emphasis and the substitute.

أقول: ينصبُ الاسمُ إذا وقع في موقع من خمسة عشر موقعاً.

I say: The noun is *manṣūb* if it falls under one of fifteen things.

وسنتكلم على كل واحد من هذه المواقع في باب يخصه، على النحو الذي سلكناه في أبواب المرفوعات، ونضرب لها ههنا الأمثلة بقصد البيان والإيضاح:

We will delve into all of these in a dedicated section for each, similar to the method we used in the Chapter of *Marfūʿ* Words. At the current juncture we will just give examples of each so as to display and clarify them:

١ ـ أن يقع مفعولاً به، نحو (نوحاً) من قوله تعالى: ﴿إنا أرسلنا نوحاً﴾.

One. If it is an object e.g. "Nūḥ" in the statement of the Most High: **{Verily we**

sent Nūḥ.}

٢ ـ أن يقع مصدراً، نحو (جذلاً) من قولك: (جَذِلَ محمدٌ جذلاً).

Two. If it is an infinitive e.g. the word "rejoicing" in "Muḥammad rejoiced a rejoicing."

٣ ـ أن يكون ظرف مكان أو ظرف زمان؛ فالأول نحو (أمام الأستاذ) من قولك: (جلست أمام الأستاذ) والثاني نحو (يوم الخميس) من قولك: (حضر أبي يوم الخميس).

Three. If it is an adverb of place or an adverb of time. An example of the former is "in front of the teacher" in the statement, "I sat in front of the teacher." An example of the latter is "Thursday" in the statement, "My father was present on Thursday.

٤ ـ أن يقع حالاً، نحو (ضَاحِكاً) من قوله تعالى: ﴿فَتَبَسَّمَ ضَاحِكًا﴾.

Four. If it is a *ḥāl* (a state) e.g. "laughing" in the statement of the Most High: **{So he smiled, laughing.}**

٥ ـ أن يقع تمييزاً، نحو (عَرَقا) من قولك: (تصبب زيدٌ عرقاً).

Five. If it is a distinction e.g. "sweat" in the statement, "Zayd poured sweat."

٦ ـ أن يقع مستثنى، نحو (محمداً) من قولك: (حضر القوم إلا محمداً).

Six. If it is an exception e.g. "Muḥammad" in the statement, "The people were present except Muḥammad."

٧ ـ أن يقع اسماً لـ((لا) النافية)، نحو (طالب علم) من قولك: (لا طالب علم مذموم).

Seven. If it is the noun of the *lā* of negation e.g. "student of knowledge" in the statement, "The student of knowledge is not disparaged."

٨ - أن يقع منادى، نحو (رسول الله) من قولك: (يا رسول الله).

Eight. If it is a vocative e.g. "Messenger of Allah" in the statement, "O Messenger of Allah."

٩ - أن يقع مفعولاً لأجله، نحو (تأديباً) من قولك: (عنَّف الأستاذ التلميذ تأديباً).

Nine. If it is an object of reason e.g. "to induce discipline" in the statement, "The teacher scolded the student in order to induce discipline."

١٠ - أن يقع مفعولاً معه، نحو (المصباح) من قولك: (ذاكرت والمصباح).

Ten. If it is an object of accompaniment e.g. "the lamp" in the statement, "I studied and the lamp."

١١ - أن يقع خبراً لـ(كان) أو إحدى أخواتها أو اسماً لـ(إن) أو إحدى أخواتها؛ فالأول نحو (صديقاً) من قولك: (كان إبراهيم صديقاً لعلي)، والثاني نحو (محمداً) من قولك (ليت محمداً يزورنا).

Eleven. If it is the predicate of *kāna* or one of its sisters, or the noun of *inna* or one of its sisters. An example of the former is "a friend" in the statement, "Ibrāhīm was a friend to 'Alī." An example of the latter is "Muḥammad" in the statement, "If only Muḥammad visited us."

١٢ - أن يقع نعتاً لمنصوب، نحو (الفاضل) من قولك: (صاحبت محمداً الفاضل).

Twelve. If it is an adjective of a *manṣūb* word e.g. "the honourable" in the statement, "I accompanied Muḥammad the honourable."

١٣ - أن يقع معطوفاً على منصوب، نحو (بكراً) من قولك: (ضرب خالد عمراً وبكراً).

Thirteen. If it is conjoined to a *manṣūb* word e.g. "Bakr" in the statement, "Khālid hit 'Amr and Bakr."

١٤ - أن يقع توكيداً لمنصوب، نحو (كُلَّهُ) من قولك: (حفظت القرآن كله).

Fourteen. If it is an emphasis of a *manṣūb* word e.g. "all of it" in the statement, "I memorised the Qur'ān, all of it."

١٥ ـ أن يقع بدلاً من منصوب، نحو (نصفه) من قوله تعالى: ﴿قُمِ اللَّيْلَ إِلَّا قَلِيلاً ﴿٢﴾ نِصْفَهُ أَوِ انْقُصْ مِنْهُ قَلِيلاً﴾.

Fifteen. If it is a substitute for a *manṣūb* word e.g. "half of it" in the statement of the Most High: {**Arise [to pray] the night, except for a little, half of it—or subtract from it a little.**}[180]

180 Al-Muzzamil: 2-3

المفعول به

The Object

قال: (باب المفعول به) وهو: الاسم، المنصوب، الذي يقع عليه الفعل، نحو قولك: (ضربتُ زيداً) و(ركبت الفرسَ).

He said: Chapter of the Object. It is a *manṣūb* noun upon which the action takes place. Examples are: "I hit Zayd" and, "I rode the horse."[181]

وأقول: المفعول به يطلق عند النحويين على ما استجمع ثلاثةَ أمور:

I say: According to the grammarians, the object is that which encompasses three things:

الأول: أن يكون اسماً؛ فلا يكون المفعول به فعلاً ولا حرفاً.

First. That it is a noun. The object can never be a verb or a particle.

والثاني: أن يكون منصوباً؛ فلا يكون المفعول به مرفوعاً ولا مجروراً.

Second. That it is *manṣūb*. The object can never be *marfūʿ* or *majrūr*.

والثالث: أن يكون فعل الفاعل قد وقع عليه، والمراد بوقوعه عليه تَعَلُّقه به، سواء أكان ذلك من جهة الثبوت، نحو (فهمت الدرسَ) أم كان على جهة النفي، نحو (لم أفهم الدرس).

---

181 Al-Kafrāwī said (p. 125), "He provided these two examples to indicate that there is no difference in the object being rational (عاقل) e.g. 'Zayd' or non-rational (غير عاقل) e.g. 'the horse'." Al-Ahdal said in *al-Kawākib* (p. 327), "The sign of the object is that it is valid to talk about it through an i*sm mafʿūl* constructed with the letters of its verb. So in the examples of the text it would be said, "زيد مضروب" and "الفرس مركوب"."

Third. That the verb is carried out by the subject, meaning the subject is connected to the verb, regardless if the intention is to affirm the occurrence e.g. "I comprehended the lesson" or if it is to negate it e.g. "I did not comprehend the lesson."

أنواع المفعول به

The Types of the Object

قال: وهو قسمان: ظاهر، ومضمر؛ فالظاهر ما تقدم ذكره، والمضمر قسمان: متصل، ومنفصل، فالمتصل اثنا عشر، وهي: ضَرَبني، وضربنا، وضربكَ، وضربكِ، وضربكما، وضربكم، وضربكنَّ، وضربهُ، وضَرَبها، وضربهما، وضربهم، وضربهنَّ. والمنفصل اثنا عشر، وهي: إيَّاي، وإيانا، وإياكَ، وإياكِ، وإياكما، وإياكم، وإياكنَّ، وإياهُ، وإياها، وإياهما، وإياهم، وإياهن.

He said: It is divided into two categories: the explicit and the implicit. We have already explained the explicit. The implicit is of two types: the attached and the detached. The attached consists of twelve: He hit me, he hit us, he hit you, he hit you (fem.), he hit you two, he hit you (pl.), he hit you (pl. fem.), he hit him, he hit her, he hit them two, he hit them and he hit them (fem.). The detached also consists of twelve: me, us, you, you (fem.), you two, you (pl.), you (pl. fem.), him, her, them two, them and them (fem.).

وأقول: ينقسم المفعول به إلى قسمين: الأول الظاهر، والثاني: المضمر.

I say: The object is categorised into two: (i) the explicit and (ii) the implicit.

وقد عرفت أن الظاهر ما يدل على معناه بدون احتياج إلى قرينة تكلم أو خطاب أو غيبة، وأن المضمر ما لا يدل على معناه إلا بقرينة من هذه القرائن الثلاث؛ فمثال الظاهر (ضرب محمد بكراً) و(يضرب خالد عمراً) و(قطف إسماعيلُ زهرةً) و(يقطف

إسماعيلُ زهرة) .

We have already discussed that the explicit is that which indicates a meaning without requiring a sign of it being first person, second person or third person. The implicit is that which does not indicate towards a meaning except with additional information of it being one of these three. Examples of the explicit are, "Muḥammad hit <u>Bakr</u>", "Khālid hits <u>ʿAmr</u>", "Ismāʿīl plucked <u>a flower</u>" and, "Ismāʿīl plucks <u>a flower</u>."

وينقسم المضمر المنصوب إلى قسمين: الأول المتصل؛ والثاني المنفصل.

The *manṣūb* implicit is categorised into two: (i) the attached and (ii) the detached.

أما المتصل فهو: ما لا يُبتدأُ به الكلام ولا يصح وقوعه بعد (إلا) في الاختيار، وأما المنفصل فهو: ما يُبتدأُ به الكلام ويصح وقوعه بعد (إلا) في الاختيار.

As for the attached, it is that which does not commence a sentence and it does not appear after "*illā*" (except) is used for selection. As for the detached, it is that which can commence a sentence and it can appear after "*illā*" is used for selection.

وللمتصل اثنا عشر لفظاً:

The attached consists of twelve words:

الأول: الياءُ، وهي للمتكلم الواحد، ويجب أن يُفصلَ بينها وبين الفعل بنونٍ تسمى نون الوقاية، نحو (أطاعني محمدٌ)، و(يطيعني بكرٌ) و(أطِعني يا بكرُ).

One. The letter *yā*, and it denotes the first person singular. It is mandatory to separate it from the verb by utilising the letter *nūn*, which in this case is termed as the letter *nūn* of protection. Examples are, "Muḥammad obeyed me", "Bakr obeys me" and "Obey me O Bakr."

والثاني: (نا) وهو للمتكلم المعظم نفسه أو معه غيره، نحو (أطاعنا أبناؤنا).

Two. "*Nā*", and it denotes the first person when glorifying one's self or when accompanied by other than oneself e.g. "Our sons obeyed us."

والثالث: الكاف المفتوحة وهي للمخاطب المفرد المذكر، نحو (أطاعكَ ابنُك).

Three. The letter *kāf* with a *fatḥah* (i.e. "*ka*"), and it denotes the second person singular masculine e.g. "Your sons obeyed you."

والرابع: الكاف المكسورة وهي للمخاطبة المفردة المؤنثة، نحو (أطاعكِ ابنكِ).

Four. The letter *kāf* with a *kasrah* (i.e. "*ki*"), and it denotes the second person singular feminine e.g. "Your son obeyed you."

والخامس: الكاف المتصل بها الميم والألف، وهي للمثنى المخاطب مطلقاً نحو (أطاعَكُما).

Five. The letter *kāf* which is attached to the letters *mīm* and *alif* (i.e. "*kuma*"), and it denotes the dual form second person in both genders e.g. "He obeyed them both."

والسادس: الكاف المتصل بها الميم وحدها، وهي لجماعة الذكور المخاطبين، نحو (أطاعكم)

Six. The letter *kāf* which is attached to the letter *mīm* (i.e. "*kum*"), and it denotes the second person masculine plural e.g. "He obeyed you."

والسابع: الكاف المتصل بها النون المشددة، وهي لجماعة الإناث المخاطبات نحو (أطاعكنَّ)

Seven. The letter *kāf* which is attached to the letter *nūn* which has a *shaddah* (i.e. "*kunna*"), and it denotes the second person feminine plural e.g. "He obeyed you."

والثامن: الهاء المضمومة، وهي للغائب المفرد المذكر، نحو (أطاعَهُ).

Eight. The letter *hā* with a *ḍammah* (i.e. "*hu*"), and it denotes the third person masculine singular e.g. "He obeyed him."

والتاسع: الهاءُ المتصل بها الألف، وهي للغائبة المفردة المؤنثة نحو (أطاعها).

Nine. The letter *hā* which is connected to the letter *alif* (i.e. "*hā*"), and it denotes the third person feminine singular e.g. "He obeyed her."

والعاشر: الهاءُ المتصل بها الميم والألف، وهي للمثنى الغائب مطلقاً نحو (أطاعهما).

Ten. The letter *hā* which is connected to the letters *mīm* and *alif*, and it denotes the third person dual form in both genders e.g. "He obeyed them two."

والحادي عشر: الهاءُ المتصل بها الميم وحدها، وهي لجماعة الذكور الغائبين نحو (أطاعهم).

Eleven. The letter *hā* which is connected to the letter *mīm*, and it denotes the third person masculine plural e.g. "He obeyed them."

والثاني عشر: الهاءُ المتصل بها النون المشددة، وهي لجماعة الإناث الغائبات، نحو (أطاعهن).

Twelve. The letter *hā* which is connected to the letter *nūn* with a *shaddah*, and it denotes the third person feminine plural e.g. "He obeyed them."

وللمنفصل: اثنا عشر لفظاً أيضا، وهي: (إيَّا) مُردَفَةً بالياء للمتكلم وحده، أو (نا) للمعظم نفسهُ، أو مع غيره، أو بالكاف مفتوحة للمخاطب المفرد المذكر، أو بالكاف مكسورة للمخاطبة المفردة المؤنثة، ولا تخفى عليك معرفة الباقي.

The detached also consists of twelve words: "*iyyā*" which is used as a synonym of the *yā* of the singular first person, or [*iyyā* attached with] "*nā*" (us) when magnifying one's self or in a plural form, or with the letter *kāf* with a *fatḥah* that denotes the second person masculine singular, or with the letter *kāf* with a *kasrah* that denotes the second person feminine singular, and the remainder should be evident to the reader.

والصحيح أن الضمير هو (إيَّا) وأن ما بعده لواحق تدلُ على التكلم، أو الخطاب أو الغيبة، تقول: (إيَّايَ أطاعَ التلاميذ) و(ما أطاع التلاميذ إلا إيَّايَ) ومنه قوله تعالى: ﴿إِيَّاكَ نَعْبُدُ وَإِيَّاكَ نَسْتَعِينُ﴾ وقوله سبحانه: ﴿أَمَرَ أَلَّا تَعْبُدُوا إِلَّا إِيَّاهُ﴾.

According to the correct opinion, "*iyyā*" is the pronoun and that which comes after it is a suffix that indicates towards the first person, second person or the third person. Examples are the statements, "The students obeyed me" and, "The students did not obey except me." There are also the statements of the Most High: **{It is you we worship and to you we seek aid}** and, **{He has commanded that you worship not except Him.}**

تمرينات

Exercises

١ - ضع ضميراً منفصلاً مناسباً في كل مكان من الأمكنة الخالية ليكون مفعولاً به، ثم بين معناه بعد أن تضبطه بالشكل:

One. Fill the gaps with a detached pronoun so that it becomes the object. Then identify the meaning after you have expressed its diacritics.

(أ) أيها الطلبة .... ينتظر المستقبل.

(ب) يا أَيَّتُهَا الفتيات .... ترتقب البلاد.

(ج) أيها المتقي .... يرجو المصلحون.

(د) أيتها الفتاة .... ينتظر أبوك.

(ه) أيها المؤمنون .... يثيب الله.

(و) إنَّ محمداً قد تأخر و .... انتظرت طويلاً.

(ز) هؤلاء الفتيات .... يرجو المصلحون.

(ح) يا محمد ما انتظرتُ إلا ....

٢ - ضع كل اسم من الأسماء الآتية في جملة مفيدة بحيث يكون مفعولاً به:

Two. Place each of the following nouns into a beneficial sentence where they are utilised as an object.

الكتاب، الشجر، القلم، الجبل، الفرس، حذاء، النافذة، البيت.

٣ ـ حول الضمائر الآتية إلى ضمائر متصله، ثم اجعل كل واحد منها مفعولاً به في جملة مفيدة:

Three. Convert each of the following pronouns into attached pronouns, then utilise each of them as an object in beneficial sentences.

إياهما، إياكم، إياي، إياكنَّ، إياه، إياكما، إيانا.

٤ ـ هات لكل فعل من الأفعال الآتية فاعلاً ومفعولاً به مناسبين:

Four. Provide for each of the following verbs an appropriate subject and an object.

قرأ، برى، تسلَّق، ركب، اشترى، سكن، فتح، قتل، صعد.

٥ ـ كون ست جمل، واجعل في كل جملة اسمين من الأسماء الآتية بحيث يكون أحد الاسمين فاعلاً والآخر مفعولاً به:

Five. Formulate six sentences, and place in each of them two nouns from the following, where one of them is the subject and the other is an object.

محمد، الكتاب، علي، الشجرة، إبراهيم، الحبل، خليل، الماء، أحمد، الرسالة، بكر، المسألة.

٦ ـ هات سبع جمل مفيدة بحيث تكون كل جملة مؤلفة من فعل وفاعل ومفعول به، ويكون المفعول به ضميراً منفصلاً، بشرط ألا تذكر الضمير الواحد مرتين.

Six. Provide seven beneficial sentences where each of them consists of a verb, subject and an object. Do not mention the same pronoun twice.

٧ ـ هات سبع جمل مفيدة بحيث تكون كل جملة مؤلفة من فعل وفاعل ومفعول به، ويكون المفعول به ضميراً متصلاً، بشرط أن يكون الضمير في كل واحدة مخالفاً لأخواته.

Seven. Provide seven beneficial sentences where each of them consists of a verb, subject and an object. The object should be an attached pronoun. The pronoun should be different in each one.

أسئلة

Questions

ما هو المفعول به؟ إلى كم قسم ينقسم المفعول به؟

What is an object? How many categories is it split into?

ما هو الظاهر؟ مثل بثلاثة أمثلة للمفعول به الظاهر.

What is the apparent object? Provide three examples of it.

ما هو المضمر؟ إلى كم قسم ينقسم المضمر؟

What is the implicit object? How many categories is it split into?

ما هو المضمر المتصل؟ كم لفظاً للمضمر المتصل الذي يقع مفعولاً به؟

What is the attached implicit object? How many words are utilised for it?

ما هو المضمر المنفصل؟ كم لفظا للمضمر المنفصل الذي يقع مفعولا به؟

What is the detached implicit object? How many words are utilised for it?

ما الذي يجب أن يُفصَل به، بين الفعل وياء المتكلم؟

What is the mandatory separation between the letter *yā* of the first person singular and the verb?

مثّل بثلاثة أمثلة للمضمر المتصل الواقع مفعولاً به، وبثلاثة أمثلة أخرىٰ للمضمر المنفصل الواقع مفعولاً به.

Provide three examples of the attached implicit object, and three examples of the detached implicit object.

أعرب الأمثلة الآتية: ﴿فَلَا تَخْشَوْهُمْ وَاخْشَوْنِ﴾ [المائدة:٣]، ﴿وَاعْبُدُوا اللهَ وَلَا تُشْرِكُوا بِهِ شَيْئًا﴾، ﴿ذَلِكَ الْكِتَابُ لَا رَيْبَ فِيهِ هُدًى لِلْمُتَّقِينَ ٢ الَّذِينَ يُؤْمِنُونَ بِالْغَيْبِ وَيُقِيمُونَ الصَّلَاةَ وَمِمَّا رَزَقْنَاهُمْ يُنْفِقُونَ﴾ [البقرة:٣]

Provide a grammatical analysis of the following examples, {So do not fear them, fear me},[182] {Worship Allah and associate nothing with Him},[183] and, {This is the Book about which there is no doubt, a guidance for those conscious of Allah, who believe in the unseen, establish prayer, and spend out of what We have provided for them.}[184]

يخزُونَ مِن ظُلمِ أهلِ الظُلمِ مغفِرَةً   ومن إساءةِ أهلِ السوءِ إحساناً.

In abasement, they meet the oppression of those who oppress with forgiveness,

And the harm of those who cause harm with beneficence.

---

182 Al-Māʾidah: 3
183 Al-Nisā: 36
184 Al-Baqarah: 2-3

المصدر

The Infinitive

قال: (باب المصدر) المصدر هو: الاسم، المنصوب، الذي يجيءُ ثالثاً في تصريف الفعل، نحو: (ضرب يضرب ضرباً).

He said: The infinitive is the *manṣūb* noun that comes third when conjugating a verb e.g. "*ḍaraba, yaḍribu, ḍarban*."

أقول: قد عرَّف المؤلف المصدر بأنه (الذي يجيءُ ثالثاً في تصريف الفعل) ومعنى ذلك أنه لو قال لك قائل: (صرِّف (ضَرَبَ) ... مثلاً)، فإنك تذكر الماضي أولاً، ثمَّ تجيء بالمضارع، ثم بالمصدر، فتقول: (ضرب يضرب ضربا).

I say: The author has identified the infinitive as that which, "Comes third when conjugating a verb." The meaning of this is that if one was asked to conjugate a verb such as *ḍaraba* (he hit), he would mention the *māḍī* form first, then the *muḍāriʿ* and then the *maṣdar*. Thus he would say, "*Ḍaraba, yaḍribu, ḍarban*."

وليس الغرض ههنا معرفة المصدر لذاته، وإنما الغرض معرفة المفعول المطلق، وهو يكون مصدراً، وهو عبارة عن (مَا ليسَ خبراً ممَّا دلَّ على تأكيد عامله، أو نَوعِهِ، أو عَدَدِهِ).

The purpose at this juncture is not to understand the infinitive in of itself, rather the purpose is to understand the absolute object. It comes as an infinitive and it is defined as, "That which is not a predicate, from that which indicates an emphasis regarding its governor (i.e. the action), its type or its number.

فقولنا: (ليس خبراً) مخرجٌ لما كان خبراً من المصادر، نحو قولك: (فهمُك فهمٌ

دقيق).

Our statement, "not a predicate" removes from our definition the infinitive that serves as the predicate e.g. the statement, "Your understanding is a precise understanding."

وقولنا: (مما دل .... إلخ) يفيد أن المفعول المطلق ثلاثة أنواع:

Our statement, "From that which indicates [...]" derives for us the understanding that the absolute object is of three types:

الأول: المؤكِّدُ لعامله، نحو (حفظتُ الدرسَ حفظاً)، و نحو (فرحتُ بقدومك جذلاً).

First. Giving emphasis to its governor e.g. "I memorised the lesson, a memorisation (i.e. emphasising the fact)", and, "I was happy with your arrival, [with] elation."

والثاني: المبين لنوعِ العامل، نحو (أحببت أستاذي حب الولد أباه)، ونحو (وقفتُ للأستاذِ وقوف المؤدَّبِ).

Second. Clarifying the type of its governor e.g. "I loved my teacher in the manner a child loves his father," and, "I stood for my teacher, the standing of good manners."

والثالث: المبين للعدد، نحو (ضربتُ الكسولَ ضربتينِ)، ونحو (ضربتُهُ ثلاث ضرباتٍ).

Third. Clarifying the number [of the action] e.g. "I hit the idle person twice" and, "I hit him thrice."

أنواع المفعول المطلق

Types of the Absolute Object

قال: وهو قسمان: لفظيٌّ، ومعنويٌّ، فإن وافق لفظُهُ لفظَ فعله فهو لفظي، نحو (قَتَلتُهُ ... قتلاً)، وإن وافق معنى فعله دون لفظه فهو معنوي، نحو (جلستُ قُعوداً)، و(قمتُ وقوفاً)، وما أشبه ذلك.

He said: And the infinitive can be divided into two groups: the verbal,[185] and the abstract. So if the letter composition of the infinitive agrees with the verb which is extracted from it then it is the verbal type, and the infinitive is written like, "I fought him a (hard) fight." If it agrees with the verb in terms of meaning but not in letter composition then it is the abstract type e.g. "I sat a sitting", "I stood a standing" and other similar statements.

وأقولُ: ينقسم المصدر الذي ينصب على أنه مفعول مطلق إلى قسمين:

I say: The infinitive that is *manṣūb* due to it being the absolute object is of two types:

القسمُ الأول: ما يوافق الفعل الناصب له في لفظه، بأن يكون مشتملاً على حروفه، وفي معناه أيضاً بأن يكون المعنى المراد من الفعل هو المعنى المراد من المصدر، وذلك نحو (قعدت قعوداً)، (ضربته ضرباً) و(ذهبتُ ذهاباً) وما أشبه ذلك.

The first type: That which is in accordance verbally (i.e. in pronunciation) to its verb—which serves as a *nāṣib* for it—whereby it concords in both structure of composition and in terms of meaning i.e. the intended meaning of the verb is the same as the intended meaning of the infinitive. Examples are, "I sat, a sitting", "I hit him, a hitting", "I go, a going" and other similar statements.

والقسم الثاني: ما يوافق الفعل الناصب له في معناه، ولا يوافقه في حروفه، بأن تكون حروف المصدر غير حروف الفعل، وذلك نحو (جلستُ قُعوداً) فإن معنى (جلس) هو معنى القعود، وليست حروف الكلمتين واحدة، ومثل ذلك (فرحت جذلاً) و(

185 Al-Ḥāmidī said (p. 124), "He preceded with this because it is more numerous."

ضربته لَكْماً) و(أهنته احتقاراً) و(قمت وقوفاً) وما أشبه ذلك، والله سبحانه وتعالى أعلى وأعلم.

The second type: That which is in accordance in meaning to its verb—which serves as a *nāṣib* for it—and not in its composition, as the letters of the infinitive differ from those of the verb. In this case the infinitive's composition of letters will be different to that of the verb. An example of this is, "I sat, sitting." In this case, the Arabic word *jalasa* (he sat) is in concordance with the meaning of *al-quʿūd*, however they vary in the composition of their letters. Other examples are, "I rejoiced, a jubilation", "I struck him, a punch", "I demeaned him, a belittling", "I stood up, a standing" and other similar statements. And Allah (the Most Glorified and Most High) is the Most High and Knowledgeable.

تمرينات

Exercises

١ ـ اجعل كل فعل من الأفعال الآتية في جملتين مفيدتين، وهات لكل فعل بمصدره منصوباً على أنه مفعول مطلق: مؤكد لعامله مرة، ومبين لنوعه مرة أخرى:

One. Utilise each of the following words in two beneficial sentences, and bring for each of the verbs an infinitive that is *manṣūb* due to being an absolute object, emphasising the governor in one instance and a clarification of its type in the other instance:

حفظ، شرب، لعب، استغفر، باع، سار.

٢ ـ اجعل كل اسم من الأسماء الآتية مفعولاً مطلقاً في جملة مفيدة:

Two. Utilise each of the following nouns as an absolute object in a beneficial sentence:

حفظاً، لعباً هادئاً، بيع المضطر، سيراً سريعاً، سهراً طويلاً، غضبة الأسد، وثبة النمر،

اختصاراً.

٣ ـ ضع مفعولاً مطلقاً مناسباً في كل مكان من الأماكن الخالية الآتية:

Three. Fill in the gaps with an appropriate absolute object within each empty space below:

(أ) يخاف علي ....

(ب) ظهر البدر ....

(ج) يثور البركان ....

(د) اترك الهذر ....

(ه) تَجَنّبِ المزاح ....

(و) غَلَتِ المِرجلُ ....

(ز) فاض النيلُ ....

(ح) صرخ الطفلُ ....

أسئلة

Questions

ما هو المصدر؟

What is the infinitive noun?

ما هو المفعول المطلق؟

What is the absolute object?

إلى كم قسم ينقسم المفعول المطلق من جهة ما يراد منه؟

Into how many categories has the absolute object been categorised into in relation to its intended meaning?

إلى كم قسم ينقسم المفعول المطلق من حيث موافقته لعامله وعدمها.

Into how many categories has the absolute object been categorised in terms of its agreement with the governor or the lack of agreement?

مثل بثلاثة أمثلة للمفعول المطلق المؤكد لعامله.

Provide three examples of the absolute object that serves as an emphasis for its governor.

مثل بثلاثة أمثلة للمفعول المطلق المبين لنوع العامل.

Provide three examples of the absolute object that serves as a clarification of the type of its governor.

مثل بثلاثة أمثلة للمفعول المطلق المبين للعدد.

Provide three examples of the absolute object that serves as a clarification of the number.

مثل بثلاثة أمثلة لمفعول مطلق منصوب بعامل من لفظه، وبثلاثة أمثلة لمفعول مطلق منصوب بعامل من معناه.

Provide three examples of the absolute object which is made *manṣūb* by its verbal governor and likewise for the absolute object made *manṣub* due to a governor of its meaning.

ظرف الزمان، وظرف المكان

The Adverb of Time and the Adverb of Place

قال: (باب ظرف الزمان، و ظرف المكان) ظرف الزمان هو: اسم الزمان المنصوب بتقدير (في) نحو (اليوم)، و(الليلة)، و(غدوة)، و(بكرة)، و(سحرا)، و(غدا)، و(عتمةً)، و(صباحاً)، و(مساءً)، و(أبداً)، و(أمداً)، و(حيناً) وما أشبه ذلك.

He said: Chapter: The Adverb of Time and the Adverb of Place.[186] The adverb of time is a noun denoting time which is *manṣūb* and has an implicit meaning of "in"[187] or "during" as in the following examples: "the day", "tonight/nighttime", "early morning", "early daytime", "late night", "tomorrow", "early night", "morning", "post meridiem[188]", "always[189]", "long-term", "moment" and anything resembling these.

وأقول: الظرف معناه في اللغة: الوعاء، والمراد به في عُرف النحاة المفعول فيه، وهو نوعان: الأول: ظرف الزمان، والثاني: ظرف المكان.

I say: The meaning of *al-ẓarf* linguistically is a container. And according to

---

186 Al-Ḥāmidī said (p. 125), "These two were mentioned together by the author (i.e. Ibn Ājurūm) in one chapter due to their similarities and closeness in ruling. He individually defined them in their appropriate places so that similar terminologies are not a matter of confusion for beginner learners."

187 Al-Ahdal said in *al-Kawākib* (2/352), "Their intention of mentioning "*fī*" being inferred is its meaning and not its utterance, for this may not be valid to be inferred before the adverb, e.g. in the examples (سرتَ قبله) and (صليت معه)." Al-Kafrāwī said (p. 127), "If he said 'with the meaning of in' (على معنى في), it would have been better than (بتقدير في). This is because there are adverbs of place for which "*fī*" cannot be inferred with, such as (عند)."

188 The common use for this word is either "late afternoon" or "early evening".

189 This adverb and the one following it can be used to mean "always" but can also mean the antonym, "never".

the convention of the grammarians it refers to the *maf'ūl fīhi* (a locative adverb)[190]. It consists of two types: (i) the adverb of time and (ii) the adverb of place.

أما ظرف الزمان: فهو عبارة عن الاسم الذي يدل على الزمان المنصوب باللفظ الدال على المعنى الواقع ذلك المعنى فيه، بملاحظة معنى (في) الدالة على الظرفية، وذلك مثل قولك: (صمت يوم الاثنين) فإنَّ (يوم الاثنين) ظرف زمان مفعول فيه، وهو منصوب بقولك: (صمت) وهذا العامل دال على معنى وهو الصيام، والكلام على ملاحظة معنى (في) أي: أن الصيام حدث في اليوم المذكور؛ بخلاف قولك: (يخاف الكسول يوم الامتحان) فإن معنى ذلك أنه يخاف نفس يوم الامتحان وليس معناه أنَّه يخاف شيئا واقعا في هذا اليوم.

As for the adverb of time, it refers to the *manṣūb* noun that indicates time through the use of a word denoting the occurrence of an event within it, bearing the meaning of "in" which expresses an adverb of time in which the action took place in. An example is the statement, "I fasted Monday." In this sentence "Monday" is an adverb of time and a *maf'ūl fīhi*, and it is *manṣūb* due to the words "I fasted". This governor (i.e. I fasted) infers the meaning of fasting, and the rest of the sentence serves the purpose of noting the meaning of "in" i.e. that the fasting took place during that specific day. This is in contrast to the statement, "The idle person fears the day of examination." In this example the meaning is that the person fears the day itself, and not something that takes place within it.

واعلم أنَّ الزمان ينقسم إلى قسمين: الأول المختص، والثاني المبهم.

Know that the adverb of time is categorised into two: (i) the specified and (ii) the unspecified.

أما المختص فهو (ما دال على مقدار معين محدود من الزمان).

As for the specified, it is a definitive measure and time bounded.

190 A locative adverb denotes where or when an action was performed.

وأما المبهم فهو (ما دال على مقدار غير معين ولا محدود).

As for the unspecified, it is an indefinite measure and it is not time bounded.

ومثال المختص: الشهر، والسنة، واليوم، والعام، والأسبوع.

Examples of the specified are: "the month", "the year", "the day", "the year" and "the week".

ومثال المبهم: اللحظة، والوقت، والزمان، والحين.

Examples of the unspecified are: "the instant", "the time period", "the time" and "the moment".

وكل واحد من هذين النوعين يجوز أنتصابه على أنه مفعول فيه.

It is permissible for both of these kinds of words to become *manṣūb* as the *maf'ūl fīhi*.

وقد ذكر المؤلف من الألفاظ الدالة على الزمان اثني عشر لفظا:

The author has mentioned above twelve words that can refer to time periods:

الأول: (اليوم) وهو من طلوع الفجر إلى غروب الشمس، تقول: (صمت اليوم) أو (صمت يوم الخميس) أو (صمت يوما طويلا).

(i) "The day", it is the time period between the rise of dawn until sunset.[191] Examples are, "I fasted today", "I fasted on Thursday" and, "I fasted a long day."

والثاني: (الليلة) وهى من غروب الشمس إلى طلوع الفجر تقول: (اعتكفت الليلة البارحة) أو (اعتكفت ليلة) أو (اعتكفت ليلة الجمعة).

191 Al-Kafrāwī said (p. 125), "I.e. the real dawn, as there are two dawns—which is derived from the established *marfū' ḥadīth* from the Prophet ﷺ. The false dawn does not rise past the night, in contrast to the true dawn. The day was also defined as being from the rise of the sun until it sets."

(ii) "Tonight/nighttime", it is the time period between sunset until the rise of dawn. Examples are, "I performed *iʿtikāf* last night", "I performed *iʿtikāf* during a night" and, "I performed *iʿtikāf* on Friday night"

الثالث: (غدوة) وهى الوقت ما بين صلاة الصبح وطلوع الشمس، تقول: (زارني صديقي غدوة الأحد) أو (زارني غدوة).

(iii) "Early morning", it is the time period between the *fajr* prayer and sunrise. Examples are, "My friend visited early Sunday morning" and, "He visited me early in the morning."

والرابع: (بكرة) وهى أول النهار، تقول: (أزورك بكرةَ السبت)، و(أزورك بكرة).

(iv) "Early daytime", it refers to the early morning time period. Examples are, "I will visit you early on Saturday" and, "I will visit you early in the day."

والخامس: (سحراً) وهو آخر الليل قبيل الفجر، تقول: (ذاكرت درسي سحراً).

(v) "Late night", it refers to the late night period before the dawn. An example is, "I studied my lesson late at night."

والسادس: (غداً) وهو اسم لليوم الذي بعد يومك الذي أنت فيه، تقول: (إذا جِئتني غداً أكرمتُك).

(vi) "Tomorrow", it [evidently] refers to the day after the present one. An example is, "If you come to me tomorrow I will serve you."

والسابع: (عَتمة) وهي اسم لثلث الليل الأول، تقول: (سأزورك عتمة).

(vii) "Early night", it is the name given to the first third of the night. An example is, "I will visit you early in the night."

والثامن: (صباحاً) وهو اسم الوقت الذي يبتدئ من أول نصف الليل الثاني إلى الزوال، تقول: (سافر أخي صباحاً).

(viii) "Morning", it is the time period between the commencement of the second half of the night until *al-zawāl* i.e. when the sun reaches its zenith.[192] An example is, "My brother travelled in the morning."

والتاسع: (مساءً) وهو اسم للوقت الذي يبتدئ من الزوال إلى نصف الليل، تقول: (وصل القِطارُ بنا مساءً).

(ix) "Post meridiem", it is the time period which commences at the sun's zenith and ends at midnight. An example is, "The train arrived to us during the p.m."

والعاشر: (أبداً)، والحادي عشر: (أمداً): وكل منهما اسم للزمان المستقبل الذي لا غاية لانتهائه، تقول: (لا أصحب الأشرار أبداً) و(لا أقترفُ الشرَّ أمداً).

(x) "Always" and (xi) "long-term", both of these are nouns referring to the future with no point of ending. Examples are, "I will never (antonym of always) befriend evildoers" and, "I will never (antonym of always) commit evil."

والثاني عشر: (حيناً) وهو اسمٌ لزمان مبهمٍ غير معلوم الابتداء ولا الانتهاء، تقول: (صاحبتُ عليّاً حيناً من الدهر).

(xii) "Moment", it is a noun that refers to an ambiguous time-frame of which the commencement and conclusion are unknown. An example is, "I accompanied ʿAlī for a moment of time."

ويلحق بذلك ما أشبهه من كل اسم دال على الزمان: سواء أكان مختصاً مثل: (ضحوة)، و(ضحا) أم كان مبهماً مثل (وقت)، و(ساعة)، و(لحظة)، و(زمان)، و(بُرهة)؛ فإن هذه وما ماثلها يجوز نصب كل واحد منها على أنه مفعول فيه.

Any other word that indicates a time can also fall under this group, regardless if it is specified e.g. the time after sunrise known as *ḍuḥā*, or unspecified e.g.

192 Al-Ahdal said in *al-Kawākib* (2/353), "It can refer to the first part of the day from the true dawn until *al-zawāl*."

"time", "hour", "instant", "time" or "a short time". Each of these words and their likeness are allowed to be made *manṣūb* and utilised as the *maf'ūl fīhi*.

ظرف المكان

The Adverb of Place

قال: وظرف المكان هو: اسم المكان المنصوب بتقدير (في)، نحو: (أمامَ)، و(خلف)، و(قُدَّامَ)، وَ(وَراءَ)، و(فوق)، و(تحت)، و(عندَ)، و(إزاءَ)، و(حِذاءَ)، و(تلقاءَ) و(ثَمَّ)، و(هُنا)، وما أشبه ذلك.

He said: The adverb of time is a noun denoting time which is *manṣūb* and has an implicit meaning of "in," for example: "in front", "rear of", "before", "behind", "above"[193], "under", "with/by", "opposite to", "close to", "facing towards/opposite to", "there", "here" and that which is similar to these.

وأقول: قد عرفت فيما سبق ظرف الزمان، وأنه ينقسم إلى قسمين: مختص، ومبهم، وعرفت أن كل واحد منهما يجوز نصبه على أنه مفعول فيه.

I say: We have previously defined the adverb of time and that it is categorised into two: (i) the specified and (ii) the unspecified. Likewise, I have previously explained that each word that denotes an adverb of place becomes *manṣūb* as the *maf'ūl fīhi*.

واعلم هنا أن ظرف المكان عبارة عن: الاسم، الدال على المكان، المنصوب باللفظ الدال على المعنى الواقِع فيه بملاحظة معنى (في) الدالة على الظرفية.

And the reader should note here that the adverb of place refers to the *manṣūb* noun that indicates place through the use of a word denoting the occurrence of an event within it, inferring the meaning of "in" that expresses the locative case.

---

193 فوق can refer to different adverbial locations, such as "on", "above", "over" etc.

وهو أيضاً ينقسم إلى قسمين: مختصٌ، ومبهم؛ أما المختصُ فهو: (ما له صورةٌ وحدودٌ محصورة) مثل: الدار، والمسجد، والحديقة، والبستان؛ وأما المبهم فهو: (ما ليس له صورة ولا حدود محصورة) مثل: (وراء)، و(أَمام).

It is also categorised into two, the specified and the unspecified. As for the specified, its definition is, "It is that which has a form and defined boundaries." Examples are, "the residence", "the *masjid*", "the garden", "the orchard". As for the unspecified, it is that which does not meet the aforementioned definition. Examples are, "behind" and "in front".

ولا يجوز أن ينصب على أنه مفعول فيه من هذين القسمين إلا الثاني، وهو المُبهَم؛ أمَّا الأول - وهو المختص - فيجب جرُّهُ بحرف جر يدل على المراد، نحو: (اعتكفتُ في المسجد) و(زُرتُ علياً في داره).

It is important to note that it is only permissible to make the second category (i.e. the unspecified) *manṣūb* as the *maf'ūl fīhi*. As for the first category (i.e. the specified), it is mandatory to make it *majrūr* by using the particle of *jarr* that is suited to the intended meaning e.g. "I performed *i'tikāf* in the *masjid*" and, "I visited 'Alī in his abode."

وقد ذكر المؤلف من الألفاظ الدالة على المكان ثلاثةَ عشر لفظاً:

The author has mentioned above thirteen words from the words that indicate place:

الأول: (أَمام) نحو: (جلستُ أمامَ الأستاذِ مؤدَّباً).

One. "In front", e.g. "I sat in front of the teacher politely."

الثاني: (خلفَ) نحو: (سار المشاة خلف الركبانِ).

Two. "Rear of", e.g. "The walkers marched to the rear of the riders."

الثالث: (قُدَّامَ) نحو: (مشى الشرطيُّ قُدَّامَ الأمير).

Three. “Before”, e.g. “The police officer walked before the leader.”

الرابع: (وَرَاءَ) نحو: (وقفَ المصلون بعضهم وراءَ بعض).

Four. “Behind”, e.g. “Those in prayer stood, some of them behind others.”

الخامس: (فوق) نحو: (جلستُ فوق الكرسيِّ).

Five. “Above”, e.g. “I sat on the chair.”

السادس: (تحتَ) نحو: (وقف القطُّ تحت المائدة).

Six. “Under”, e.g. “The cat stood under the table.”

السابع: (عِندَ) نحو: (لِمحمَّدٍ منزلةٌ عندَ الأستاذِ).

Seven. “With/by”, e.g. “Muhammad has a high standing with his teacher.”

الثامنُ: (معَ) نحو: (سار مع سليمان أخوه).

Eight. “With”, e.g. “He travelled with Sulaymān, his brother.”

التاسع: (إزاءَ) نحو: (لنا دارٌ إزاءَ النيل).

Nine. “Opposite to”, e.g. “We have an abode opposite to the Nile.”

العاشر: (حِذاء) نحو: (جلس أخي حِذاءَ أخيك).

Ten. “Close to”, e.g. “My brother sat close to your brother.”

الحادي عشر: (تِلقاءَ) نحو: (جلس أخي تِلقاءَ دارِ أخيك).

Eleven. “Facing towards/opposite to”, e.g. “My brother sat opposite your brother’s house.”

الثاني عشر: (ثَمَّ) نحو قول الله تعالى: ﴿وَأَزْلَفْنَا ثَمَّ الْآخَرِينَ﴾.

Twelve. "There", as in the statement of Allah: **{And then we brought near there the others.}**[194]

الثالث عشر: (هُنا) نحو قولك: (جلس محمدٌ هُنا لحظة).

Thirteen. "Here", as in the statement, "Muḥammad sat here for a moment."

ومثلُ هذه الألفاظ كلُّ ما دل على مكانٍ مبهم، نحو: يمينٍ، وشمالٍ.

[Furthermore,] the case is similar for all words besides these that indicate towards [something occurring within] an obscure location e.g. "right" and "left".

أسئلة وتمرينات

Questions and Exercises

١ - ما هو الظرف؟

One. What is the adverb?

إلى كم قسم ينقسم الظرف؟

Into how many categories is the adverb split into?

ما هو ظرف الزمان؟

What is the adverb of time?

إلى كم قسم ينقسم ظرف الزمان؟

Into how many categories is the adverb of time split into?

مَثِّل بثلاثة أمثلة في جمل مفيدة لظرف الزمان المختص، وبثلاثة أمثلة أخرى لظرف الزمان المبهم.

194 Al-Shuʿarā: 26

Provide three examples of the specified adverb of time in beneficial sentences, and do likewise for the unspecified adverb of time.

هل ينصب على أنه مفعول فيه كل ظرف زمان؟

Do all of the adverbs of time become *manṣūb* due to being the *maf'ūl fīhi*?

٢ ـ اجعل كل واحد من اللفاظ الآتية مفعولاً فيه في جملة مفيدة، وبيِّن معناه:

Two. Utilise each of the following words as the *maf'ūl fīhi* in beneficial sentences, and explain the meaning of each of them.

عتمة، صباحاً، زماناً، لحظة، ضحوةً، غداً.

٣ ـ ما هو ظرف المكان؟

Three. What is the adverb of place?

ما هو ظرف المكان المبهم؟

What is the unspecified adverb of place?

ما هو ظرف المكان المختص؟

What is the specified adverb of place?

مَثِّل بثلاثة أمثلة لكلٍ من ظرف المكان المبهم، وظرف المكان المختص.

Provide three examples for both the unspecified adverb of place and the specified adverb of place.

وهل ينصب على أنه مفعول فيه كل ظرفِ مكان؟

Do all of the adverbs of place become *manṣūb* due to being the *maf'ūl fīhi*?

٤ ـ اذكر سبع جمل تصفُ فيها عملك يوم الجمعة، بشرط أن تشتمل كل جملة على مفعول فيه.

Four. Provide seven sentences describing therein your actions on Fridays. A condition is that each sentence must include a *maf'ūl fīhi*.

الحال

The Circumstantial Adverb

قال: (باب الحال) الحال هو: الاسمُ المنصوبُ، المفسِّرُ لما انبهم من الهيئات، نحو قولك: (جاء زيدٌ راكباً) و(ركبتُ الفرسَ مسرجاً) و(لقيتُ عَبدَ الله راكباً) وما أشبه ذلك.

He said: "Chapter of the Circumstantial Adverb". The Circumstantial adverb is a *manṣūb* noun which gives explanation to ambiguities in regards to circumstances like the following, "Zayd came riding", "I rode the horse, saddled", "I met 'Abdullāh riding" and other similar statements.

وأقول: الحال في اللغة: ما عليه الإنسان من خير أو شر (وهو في اصطلاح النحاة عبارة عن: الاسم الفَضْلَة، المنصوب، المفسِّرُ لما انبهم من الهيئات.

I say: The linguistic meaning of the word *al-ḥāl* is the state of a person in terms of good or evil. According to the nomenclature of the grammarians it refers to: the *al-fadlah*[195] (the supplementary) noun which is *manṣūb*, which gives explanation to ambiguities in regards to circumstances.

وقولنا: (الاسم) يشمل الصريح مثل (ضاحكاً). في قولك: (جاء محمدٌ ضاحكاً) ويشمل المؤول بالصريح مثل (يضحَكُ) في قولك: (جاء محمدٌ يضحكُ) فإنه في تأويل قولك: (ضاحكاً) .

Our statement "the noun" includes (i) the explicit noun e.g. "laughing" in the

---

195 In English, this is known as an adverb clause which modifies the word by telling us how or how much. Ibn Hishām said in *al-Qaṭr* (p. 329), "It is that which is utilised after the completion of a sentence, not that the added piece of information is a clause in and of itself. "

statement, "Muḥammad came laughing." (ii) The paraphrase of the explicit noun e.g. "he laughs" in the statement, "Muḥammad came laughing" as this verb can be interpreted as "laughing".

وقولنا: (الفَضْلَة) معناه أنه ليس جزءًا من الكلام؛ فخرج به الخبرُ.

Our statement "*al-fadlah*" means that the adverb alone is not a part of speech (according to the conditions which constitute speech), thus the predicate is omitted from the definition by this stipulation.

وقولنا: (المنصوب) خرج به المرفوع والمجرور.

Our statement "*manṣūb*" excludes from the definition the *marfū'* and *majrūr* words.

وإنما ينصب الحال بالفعل أوشبه الفعل: كاسم الفاعل، والمصدر، والظرف، واسم الإشارة.

The circumstantial adverb is made *manṣūb* by the verb or that which is similar to the verb, e.g. the noun on the *fā'il* word composition, the infinitive, the adverb and the demonstrative pronoun.

وقولنا: (المفسِّرُ لما انبهم من الهيئات) معناه أن الحال يُفَسِّر ما خفي واستتر من صفات ذَوِي العَقلِ أو غيرهم .

Our statement "which gives explanation to ambiguities in regards to circumstances" means that the circumstantial adverb explains that which is hidden or concealed regarding the traits of intelligent beings or other than them.

ثم إنه قد يكون بياناً لصفة الفاعل، نحو: (جاء عبد الله راكباً) أو بياناً لصفة المفعول به، نحو: (ركبتُ الفرسَ مُسرجاً)، وقد يكون محتملاً للأمرين جميعاً، نحو: (لقيتُ عبدَ اللهِ راكباً).

It can clarify the traits of the subject e.g. "'Abdullāh came riding", the traits of the object e.g. "I rode the horse, saddled", and sometimes it can be applicable to both of them e.g. "I met ʿAbdullāh riding."

وكما يجيء الحال من الفاعل والمفعول به فإنه يجيء من الخبر، نحو: (أنت صديقي مخلصاً)، وقد يجيء من المجرور بحرف الجر، نحو: (مَرَرتُ بِهندٍ راكبةً) وقد يجيءُ من المجرور بالإضافة، نحو قوله تعالى: ﴿أَنِ اتَّبِعْ مِلَّةَ إِبْرَاهِيمَ حَنِيفاً﴾ فـ(حنيفاً): حال من (إبراهيم)، و(إبراهيم) مجرور بالفتحة نيابة عن الكسرة، وهو مجرور بإضافة (ملة) إليه.

As the circumstantial adverb can arise in explanation of the subject and the object, it can also arise from the predicate e.g. "You are my friend, sincere", that which is made *majrūr* due to a particle of *jarr* e.g. "I passed by Hind [who was] riding", and that which is *majrūr* due to the possessive compound e.g. the statement of the Most High: **{That you follow the religion of Ibrāhīm, Ḥanīfa (Islamic monotheism).}**[196] So in this example, the word "*ḥanīfan*" is the circumstantial adverb of "Ibrāhīm". "Ibrāhīm" is *majrūr* with a *fatḥah* serving in place of the *kasrah*, and it is *majrūr* due to the word "religion" being compounded with it.[197]

شروط الحال وشروط صاحبها

The Conditions of the Circumstantial Adverb and the Conditions of the Word that Accompanies It

قال: ولا يكون إلا نكرة، ولا يكون إلا بعد تمام الكلام، ولا يكون صاحبها إلا معرفة.

He said: The circumstantial adverb does not exist except in the indefinite

196 Al-Naḥl: 123

197 The author of the commentary did not mention the circumstantial adverb that arises from the nominal subject due to the difference amongst the grammarians regarding this. See *Ḥāshiyat al-Ḥāmidī* (p. 130).

state[198] and does not occur except after completed speech. The companion of the situational cannot be anything besides the definite.[199]

وأقول: يجب في الحال أن يكون نكرة، ولا يجوز أن يكون معرفة، وإذا جاء تركيب فيه الحال معرفة في الظاهر، فإنه يجب تأويل هذه المعرفة بنكرة مثل قولهم: (جاء الأميرُ وحدَهُ)، فإنَّ (وحده) حال من (الأمير)، وهو معرفة بالإضافة إلى الضمير، ولكنه في تأويل نكرة هي قولك: (منفرداً) فكأنك قلت: (جاء الأمير منفرداً)، ومثل ذلك قولهم: (أرسَلَهَا العِرَاك)، أي: مُعتَرِكَةً، و(جَاءُوا الأوَّل فالأوَّل) أي مُتَرَتِّبِينَ.

I say: It is mandatory for the circumstantial adverb to be indefinite, and it is not allowed for it to be definite. If it comes as part of a composite within which it (i.e. the circumstantial adverb) appears to be definite, then it is mandatory to re-interpret this definite word with an indefinite meaning. An example of this is the statement, "The leader came by himself." Here the word "himself" is the circumstance for "the leader", and it is definite due to being compounded to the pronoun "*hu*" (him). However it is reinterpreted into an indefinite word with the same meaning, which in this case is the word "*munfaridan*" (alone) i.e. it is as if it is being said, "The leader came alone." Other examples of this are, *"It sent it to drink in the crowded place"* (a line from a famous poem) which is reinterpreted as "entering the crowd". Also, "They came one by one", which is reinterpreted as "in sequential order".

والأصل في الحال أنَّ يجيء بعد استيفاء الكلام، ومعنى (استيفاء الكلام): أنَّ يأخذ الفعل فاعله والمبتدأُ خبره.

198 Al-Ḥāmidī said (p. 130), "This is because its purpose is to clarify the circumstance, and this is attained by being in the indefinite. Thus there is no need to make it definite as it is considered to be an addition."

199 Al-Kafrāwī said (p. 130), "I.e. the root principle of the circumstantial is that it is indefinite to quell any false assumption that it is an adjective—if the word accompanying it is *manṣūb* or its grammatical state is unclear." Al-Ḥāmidī explained his statement with examples, "His statement 'If the word accompanying it is *manṣūb*' e.g. in 'رأيت زيداً الراكب' it would be falsely assumed that the word الراكب is an adjective. His statement, 'Or its grammatical state is unclear' e.g. in 'جاء زيد الفتى' the same false assumption would arise."

The root principle for the circumstantial adverb is that it comes after the completion of speech. The meaning of this is that the verb has its subject and the nominal subject has its predicate.

وربما وجب تقديم الحال على جميع أجزاء الكلام، كما إذا كان الحال اسم استفهام، نحو: (كيفَ قَدِمَ علي) فـ(كيف): اسم استفهام مبني على الفتح في محل نصب حال من (علي)، ولا يجوز تأخير اسم الاستفهام.

At times it is mandatory to precede with the circumstantial before all of the components of speech, as is the case when the circumstantial is an interrogative noun. An example is, "How did ʿAlī come? In this sentence "how" is an interrogative noun un-inflectable upon a *fatḥah* in the state of *naṣb* as the situational of ʿAlī, and it is not allowed to defer the interrogative noun [from the beginning of the sentence].

ويشترط في صاحب الحال أنَّ يكون معرفة، فلا يجوز أن يكون نكرة بغير مُسَوِّغ.

The condition for the word that accompanies the circumstantial is that it must be definite and it is not permissible for it to be indefinite except if something makes this justifiable.

ومما يُسَوِّغ مجيء الحال من النكرة أن تتقدم الحال عليها، كقول الشاعر:

From the matters that justify that which accompanies the circumstantial to become indefinite is when it is preceded by the situational, as in the statement of the poet:

لِمَيَّة مُوحِشا طلَل   يَلُوحُ كأنه خِلل

Mayyah has desolate ruins,

Brandished akin to the sword sheath's engravings.

فـ(موحشاً): حال من (طلل)، و(طللٌ) نكرة، وسوغ مجيء الحال منه تقدُّمها عليه.

So here, "desolate" is the circumstance of "ruins" and "desolate" is indefinite.

This is justified by the circumstantial preceding it.

ومما يسوِّغ مجيء الحال من النكرة أن تُخَصَّصَ هذه النكرة بإضافةٍ أو وصفٍ. فمثال الأول قوله تعالى: ﴿فِي أَرْبَعَةِ أَيَّامٍ سَوَآءً﴾ فـ(سواء): حال من (أربعة) وهو نكرة، وساغ مجيء الحال منها لكونها مضافة، ومثال الثاني قول الشاعر:

From that which permits the coming of a circumstantial to an indefinite is when the indefinite is specified by being part of a compound or by an adjective. An example of the former is the statement of the Most High: **{In four days equal.}**[200] Here, "equal" is the circumstantial of "four", which is indefinite. However it is justified to bring a circumstantial for it, due to it being the possessed in a possessive compound. An example of the latter is the statement of the poet:

نَجَّيْتَ يَا ربِّ نُوحاً واستجبت لهُ   في فُلُكٍ مَاخِرٍ في اليمِّ مشحوناً.

You saved—O my Lord—Nūḥ and responded to him,

In an <u>ark</u> plowing through the sea [while] <u>carrying a load</u>.

تمرينات

Exercises

١ - ضع في كل مكان من الأمكنة الخالية الآتية حالاً مناسباً:

One. Complete the sentence with an appropriate circumstantial adverb:

(أ) يعود الطالب المجتهد إلى بلده ...   (ه) لا تنم في الليل ...

(ب) لا تأكلِ الطعام ...   (و) رَجَعَ أخي من ديوانه ...

(ج) لا تَسِر في الطريق ...   (ز) لا تمشِ في الأرض ...

(د) البس ثوبك ...   (ح) رأيت خالداً ...

200 Fuṣṣilat: 10

٢ ـ اجعل كل اسم من الأسماء الآتية حالاً مبيناً لهيئة الفاعل في جملة مفيدة:

Two. Use each of the following nouns as a circumstantial adverb, clarifying the condition of the subject to make complete sentences:

مسروراً، مختالاً، عريانَ، مُتْعباً، حارًّا، حافياً، مجتهداً.

٣ ـ اجعل كل اسم من الأسماء الآتية حالاً مبيناً لهيئة المفعول به في جملة مفيدة:

Three. Use the following nouns as circumstantial adverbs clarifying the condition of the object to make complete sentences:

مَكتُوفاً، كئيباً، سريعاً، صافياً، نظيفاً، جديداً، ضاحكاً، لامعاً، ناضراً، مستبشرات.

٤ ـ صف الفرسَ بأربع جمل، بشرط أن تجيء في كل جملة بحال.

Four. Describe a horse with four sentences, using a circumstantial adverb in each sentence.

تدريب على الإعراب

Exercises on Grammatical Analysis

أعرب الجملتين الآتيتين: لقيتني هند باكية، لبست الثوب جديداً.

Provide a grammatical analysis of the following sentences: "Hind, while crying, met me." And, "I wore a new robe."

الجواب

Answers

١ - (لقي): فعل ماض مبني على الفتح لا محل له من الإعراب، و(التاء) علامة التأنيث، والنون للوقاية، و(الياء) ضمير المتكلم مفعول به، مبني على السكون في محل نصب. و(هند): فاعل (لقي) مرفوع، وعلامة رفعه الضمة الظاهرة. و(باكية) حال مبين لهيئة الفاعل منصوب بالفتحة الظاهرة.

One. "Met" is a *māḍī* verb un-inflectable upon a *fatḥah* without a grammatical state. The letter *tā* is the sign of femininity and the letter *nūn* is for preservation. The letter *yā* is the pronoun of first person and the object, un-inflectable upon a *sukūn* in the state of *naṣb*. "Hind" is the subject of "met" and *marfūʿ*, the sign of it being so is the explicit *ḍammah*. "Crying" is the situational, clarifying the condition of the subject, and it is *manṣūb* with an explicit *fatḥah*.

٢ - (لبس) : فعل ماض مبني على فتح مقدر على آخره منع من ظهوره اشتغال المحل بالسكون المأتي به لدفع كراهة توالي أربع متحركات فيما هو كالكلمة الواحدة، و(التاء) ضمير المتكلم فاعل مبني على الضم في محل رفع. و(الثوب): مفعول به منصوب، وعلامة نصبه الفتحة الظاهرة، (جديداً): حال مبين لهيئة المفعول به منصوب، وعلامة نصبه الفتحة الظاهرة.

Two. "Wore" is a *māḍī* verb un-inflectable upon a *fatḥah* which is implicit at its end, prevented from being displayed due to its position being occupied by a *sukūn* which comes to prevent the disliked succession of four *mutaḥarik* (vowelised) letters in that which appears as one word. The letter *tā* is the first person pronoun, and it is the subject, un-inflectable upon a *ḍammah* in the state of *rafʿ*. "Robe" is the object and *manṣūb*, the sign of it being so is the explicit *fatḥah*. "New" is the situational, clarifying the condition of the object, and it is *manṣūb* with an explicit *fatḥah*.

أسئلة

Questions

ما هو الحال لغة واصطلاحاً؟

What is the meaning of the word *al-ḥāl* linguistically and according to the nomenclature of the grammarians?

ما الذي تأتي الحال منه؟

What can the circumstantial adverb arise from?

هل تأتي الحال من المضاف إليه؟

Can the circumstantial adverb arise from the possessed word in a possessive compound?

ما الذي يشترط في الحال، وما الذي يشترط في صاحب الحال؟

What are the conditions imposed upon the circumstantial adverb, and what are those imposed upon the word that accompanies the circumstantial adverb?

ما الذي يُسَوِّغ مجيء الحال من النكرة؟

What justifies the circumstantial adverb to arise from an indefinite word?

مَثِّل للحال بثلاثة أمثلة، وطبق على كل واحد منها شروط الحال كلها، واعربها.

Provide three examples of a circumstantial adverb, apply the rules of the circumstantial adverb to each example and provide the grammatical analysis.

التمييز

The Disambiguation

قال: (باب التمييز) التمييز هو: الاسم المنصوبُ، المفَسِّر لما انبهم من الذوات، نحو قولك: (تصَبَّبَ زيدٌ عرقاً) و(تَفَقَّأَ بكرٌ شحماً) و(طابَ محمدٌ نفساً) و(اشتريتُ عشرين [كتاباً]) و(ملكتُ تسعين نعجة) و(زيدٌ أكرمَ منكَ أباً) و(أجملُ منكَ وجهاً).

He said: The Chapter of the Disambiguation. The disambiguation[201] is a *manṣūb* noun which gives description to an ambiguous object, as in the following statements: "Zayd poured out sweat", "Bakr expanded with fat", "Muḥammad made pleasant in his self", "I purchased twenty [books]", "I possessed ninety ewes", "Zayd is nobler than you in terms of fatherhood" and, "More handsome than you facially."

وأقول: للتمييز في اللغة معنيان؛ الأول: التفسير مطلقاً، تقول: (ميّزتُ كذا)؛ أي فسّرتَهُ. والثاني: فصلُ بعضِ الأمور عن بعض تقول: (ميَّزتُ القوم)، أي فصلتُ بعضَهم عن بعض.

I say: The word *al-tamyīz* has two linguistic meanings: (i) Explanation in the general sense e.g. "I made it distinct (i.e. I explained it)." (ii) To separate part of something from another e.g. "I made the people distinct (i.e. I separated some of them from others)."[202]

---

201 In English grammar, a disambiguation refers to the process of clarifying a word with multiple meanings due to its given context.

202 Al-Ḥāmidī said (p. 133), "Linguistically it means separating one thing from something else e.g. *āyah* fifty nine in Sūrah Yasīn : ﴿وَامْتَازُوا الْيَوْمَ أَيُّهَا الْمُجْرِمُونَ﴾ **{But stand apart today, you criminals}**".

والتمييز في اصطلاح النحاة عبارة عن: الاسم الصريح، المنصوب، المُفَسِر لما انبهم من الذوات أو النَّسب.

The definition of the word *al-tamyīz* according to the nomenclature of the grammarians is: an explicit noun, *manṣūb*, which gives clarification to an ambiguity in an entity or its relationship [to the context].

فقولنا: (الاسم) معناه أن التمييز لا يكون فعلاً ولا حرفاً.

Our statement "a noun" means that the disambiguation is neither a verb nor a particle.

وقولنا: (الصريح) لإخراج الاسم المؤول، فإن التمييز لا يكون جملة ولا ظرفاً، بخلاف الحال.

Our statement "explicit" excludes the paraphrase of a noun as the disambiguation is neither a sentence nor an adverb—in contrast to the circumstantial adverb.

وقولنا: (المفسر لما انبهم من الذوات أو النسب) يشير إلى أنَّ التمييز على نوعين، الأول: تمييز الذات، والثاني: تمييز النسبة.

Our statement "which gives clarification to an ambiguity in an entity or its relationship [to the context]" indicates that the disambiguation consists of two types: (i) clarifying the entity and (ii) clarifying the relationship of the word within its context.

أما تمييز الذات - ويسمى أيضاً (تمييز المفرد) - فهو: ما رفع إبهام اسم مذكور قَبلَهُ مُجملِ الحقيقة. ويكون بعد العدد، نحو قوله تعالى: ﴿إِنِّي رَأَيْتُ أَحَدَ عَشَرَ كَوْكَباً﴾، ﴿إِنَّ عِدَّةَ الشُّهُورِ عِنْدَ اللهِ اثْنَا عَشَرَ شَهراً﴾ أو بعد المقادير، من الموزونات، نحو (اشتريتُ رطلا زيتاً) أو المَكيلاتِ، نحو (اشتريتُ إردَبَّاً قمحاً) أو المساحات، نحو (اشتريتُ فداناً أرضاً).

As for the disambiguation of an entity (which is also termed as the disambiguation of the singular), it is that which clarifies the ambiguity of a noun which comes before it. It can arise after a number e.g. the statement of the Most High: {**Indeed I have seen [in a dream] eleven stars**}[203] and: {**Indeed, the number of months with Allah is twelve months.**}[204] It can arise after a measurement: (a) a measurement of weight e.g. "I purchased a *raṭl*[205] of oil", (b) a dry measure e.g. "I purchased an *irdab*[206] of wheat", or (c) a measure of area e.g. "I purchased an acre of land."

وأما تمييز النسبة - ويسمى أيضاً (تمييز الجملة) - فهو: ما رفع إبهام نسبة في جملة سابقة عليه، وهو ضربان؛ الأول: مُحوَّل، والثاني: غير محول.

As for the disambiguation of the relationship (which is also termed as the disambiguation of a sentence), it is that which clarifies the ambiguity in relationship of the sentence which precedes it, and it consists of two categories: (i) the transformed and (ii) the non-transformed.

فأما المحول فهو على ثلاثة أنواع:

As for the transformed, it consists of three types:

النوع الأول: المحول عن الفاعل، وذلك نحو (تَفَقَّأ زيدٌ شحماً) الأصل فيه (تفقأ شحمُ زيد) فحذف المضاف - وهو شحم - وأقيم المضاف إليه - وهو زيدٌ - مُقامَهُ، فارتفع ارتفاعه، ثم أتي بالمضاف المحذوف فانتصب على التمييز.

The first type: Transformed from the subject e.g. "Zayd expanded with fat." The original composition of this sentence was, "The fat of Zayd expanded." So the possessed in the possessive compound—i.e. "fat"—was omitted and its possessor "Zayd" took its place and its state of *raf*ʿ, then the possessed (i.e. fat) was brought and made *manṣūb* due to it becoming the disambiguation.

203 Yūsuf: 4

204 Al-Tawbah: 36

205 A *raṭl* is a measurement used at the time of early Islam and it weighs approximately 400g.

206 A measurement used at the time of early Islam which weighs approximately 85g.

والنوع الثاني: المحول عن المفعول وذلك نحو قوله تعالى: ﴿وَفَجَّرْنَا الْأَرْضَ عُيُونًا﴾ أصله (وفجرنا عيون الأرض) ففُعل فيه مثلُ ما سبق.

The second type: Transformed from the object, as in the statement of the Most High: **{And caused the earth to burst with springs.}**[207] The original construction of this *āyah* would be, "And we caused to burst the springs of the earth," and this is similar to what occurred in the previous type (i.e. in this case the word "springs" is the object and it is replaced by the word "earth").

النوع الثالث: المحوَّلُ عن المبتدأ، وذلك نحو قوله تعالى: ﴿أَنَا أَكْثَرُ مِنْكَ مَالًا﴾ وأصله (مالي أكثرَ من مالِكَ) فحذف المضاف، وهو (مال) وأُقيمَ المضاف إليه - وهو الضمير الذي هو ياء المتكلم - مقامه فارتفع ارتفاعاً وانفصل؛ لأن ياء المتكلم ضميرٌ متصل كما عرفت، وهو لا يبتدأ به، ثم جيء بالمضاف المحذوف فَجُعلَ تمييزاً، فصار كما ترى.

The third type: Transformed from the nominal subject, as in the statement of the Most High: **{I am greater than you in wealth.}**[208] The original construction of this *āyah* would be, "My wealth is greater than your wealth." So the possessed in the possessive compound i.e. "wealth" was removed and its possessor—i.e. the letter *yā* which is utilised as the first person pronoun ("my", which correlates to "I" in the *āyah*)—took its place and its state of *rafʿ*, and it subsequently became a detached pronoun. The reason for it becoming detached has previously been explained, i.e. the letter *yā* of the first person is an attached pronoun and they do not commence sentences. Then the possessed word which was removed is brought back as the disambiguation and the sentence becomes as you see it above.

وأما غير المحول فنحو (امتلأ الإناءُ ماءً).

As for the non-transformed, an example is the statement, "The container was filled with water."

---

207 Al-Qamar: 12

208 Al-Kahf: 34

شروط التمييز

The Conditions of the Disambiguation

قال: ولا يكون إلا نكرة، ولا يكون إلا بعد تمام الكلام.

He said: It does not arise except in the indefinite state, and it does not arise except after completed speech.

وأقول: يشترط في التمييز أن يكون نكرة، فلا يجوز أن يكون معرفة، وأما قول الشاعر:

I say: It is a condition upon the disambiguation that it be indefinite, so it is not permissible for it to arise in the definite. As for the statement of the poet:

رَأيتُكَ لمَّا أن عَرَفتَ وُجُوهَنا صَدَدْتَ وطِبتَ النَّفسَ يَا قيسُ عن عمرِو

I found you when you recognised our faces,

That you turned away and gave in the self O Qays the betrayer of ʿAmr.

فإن قوله (النفس) تمييز، وليست (أل) هذه ((أل) المُعَرِّفة) حتى يلزم منه مجيء التمييز معرفة، بل هي زائدة لا تفيد ما دخلت تعريفاً؛ فهو نكرة، وهو موافق لما ذكرنا من الشرط.

The word "the self" here is a disambiguation, and the "*al-*" here is not considered to be the "*al-*" of definiteness or it would necessitate that a disambiguation can be definite. Rather it is an addition that is not a sign of the word being definite.[209] So the word here is indefinite and it satisfies the conditions that we have laid forth.

ولا يجوز في التمييز أن يتقدم على عامله، بل لا يجيء إلا بعد تمام الكلام، أي: بعد

209 This is the view of the Baṣrī grammarians and their view is more famous. As for the Kūfī grammarians, they permit it being definite and they use this couplet as a proof. See *Sharḥ Ibn ʿAqīl* (1/182-183).

استيفاء الفعل فاعله، والمبتدأ خبره.

And it is not permissible for the disambiguation to precede its governor. Rather it does not come except after the completion of the speech i.e. after the verb's attainment of its subject and the nominal subject's attainment of its predicate.

تمرينات

Exercises

١ - بيّن أنواع التمييز تفصيلاً في الجمل الآتية:

One. Identify and provide details of the types of disambiguation found in each of the following sentences:

شربتُ كوباً ماءً، اشتريتُ قِنطاراً عسلاً، ملكت عشرة مثاقيل ذهباً، زَرَعتُ فَدَّاناً قُطناً، رأيتُ أحد عشر فارساً، ركب القطارَ خمسونَ مسافراً، محمد أكملُ من خالد خلقاً وأشرفُ نفساً وأطهر ذَيلاً، امتلأ إبراهيم كبراً.

٢ - ضع في كل مكان من الأمكنة الخالية من الأمثلة الآتية تمييزاً مناسباً:

Two. Fill in the gaps with an appropriate disambiguation:

(أ) الذهب أغلى ... من الفضة.

(ب) الحديد أقوى ... من الرصاص.

(ج) العلماء أصدق الناس ...

(د) طالب العلم أكرم ... من الجهال.

(ه) الزرافة أطول الحيوانات ...

(و) الشمس أكبر ... من الأرض.

(ز) أكلت خمسة عشرَ ...

(ح) شربت قدحاً ...

٣ ـ اجعل كل اسم من الأسماء الآتية تمييزاً في جملة مفيدة:

Three. Use each of the following nouns as a disambiguation to form a complete sentence.

شعيراً، قصباً، خُلُقاً، أدباً، شربا، ضَحكاً، بأساً، بَسَالة .

٤ ـ هات ثلاث جمل يكون في كل جملة منها تمييز مسبوق باسم عدد، بشرط أن يكون اسم العدد مرفوعاً في واحدة ومنصوباً في الثانية ومخفوضاً في الثالثة.

Four. Make three sentences where included therein is a disambiguation preceded by a number, with the condition that the number should be *marfūʿ* in the first example, *manṣūb* in the second and *makhfūḍ* in the third example.

تدريب على الإعراب

Exercises on Grammatical Analysis

أعرب الجملتين الآتيتين:

Provide a grammatical analysis of the following two sentences:

محمد أكرم من خالد نفساً، عندي عشرون ذراعاً حريراً.

Muḥammad is a more honourable person than Khālid. I have twenty cubits of silk.

الجواب

Answer

١ ـ (محمد): مبتدأ مرفوع بالابتداء، وعلامة رفعه الضمة الظاهرة. (أكرم): خبر المبتدأ مرفوع بالمبتدأ، وعلامة رفعه الضمة الظاهرة. (من خالد): جار ومجرور متعلق بـ(أكرم) . (نفساً) : تمييز نسبة محول عن المبتدأ منصوب وعلامة نصبه الفتحة الظاهرة.

One. "Muḥammad" is the nominal subject, *marfū'* due to it being the initiation, the sign of it being *marfū'* is the explicit *ḍammah*. "More honourable" is the predicate of the nominal subject and it is made *marfū'* by the nominal subject, the sign of it being so is the explicit *ḍammah*. "From Khālid" is a *jārr* and *majrūr* compound that connects to "more honourable". "Spiritually" is the disambiguation of a sentence transformed from the nominal subject and it is *manṣūb*, the sign of which is the explicit *fatḥah*.

٢ - (عند) : ظرف مكان متعلق بمحذوف خبر مقدم، و(عند) مضاف وياء المتكلم مضاف إليه، مبني على السكون في محل خفض. (عشرون) : مبتدأ مؤخر مرفوع بالابتداء، وعلامة رفعة الواو نيابة عن الضمة؛ لأنه ملحق بجمع المذكر السالم. (ذراعاً) : تمييز لـ(عشرين) ، منصوب بالفتحة الظاهرة. (حريراً) : تمييز لـ(ذراع) ، منصوب بالفتحة الظاهرة.

Two. "With" is an adverb of place which is connected to a predicate that has been omitted. "With" is also the possessed in a possessive compound and the letter *yā* of the first person is the possessor, un-inflectable upon a *sukūn* in the state of *khafḍ*. "Twenty" is the delayed nominal subject and *marfū'* due to it being the commencement, the sign of it being so is the letter *wāw* serving in place of the *ḍammah* due to being connected to a sound masculine plural. "Cubits" is the disambiguation of "twenty" and it is *manṣūb* with an explicit *fatḥah*. "Silk" is the disambiguation of "cubits" and it is *manṣūb* with an explicit *fatḥah*.

أسئلة

Questions

ما هو التمييز لغة واصطلاحاً؟

What is the meaning of *al-tamyīz* linguistically and according to the nomenclature of the grammarians?

إلى كم قسم ينقسم التمييز؟

Into how many categories has the disambiguation been categorised into?

ما هو تمييز الذات؟

What is the disambiguation of an entity?

ما هو تمييز النسبة؟

What is the disambiguation of relationship?

بماذا يسمى (تمييز الذات)؟

What is the other name given to the disambiguation of an essence?

بماذا يسمى (تمييز النسبة)؟

What is the other name given to the disambiguation of relationship?

ما الذي يقع قبل تمييز الذات؟

What comes before the disambiguation of an entity?

مَثِّل لتمييز الذات بثلاثة أمثلة مختلفة وأعرب كل واحد منها؟

Provide three varying examples of the disambiguation of an entity and provide a grammatical analysis of each one.

إلى كم قسم ينقسم تمييز النسبة المحوَّل؟

How many types of the transformed disambiguation are there?

مَثِّل للتمييز المحول عن الفاعل وعن المفعول وعن المبتدأ.

Provide examples of the transformed from a subject, object and from a nominal subject.

مَثِّل لتمييز النسبة غير المحول.

Provide an example of the non-transformed disambiguation.

ما هي شروط التمييز؟

What are the conditions of the disambiguation?

ما معنى أنَّ التمييز لا يجيء إلا بعد تمام الكلام؟

What is the meaning of the disambiguation not coming except after the completion of speech?

الاستثناء

The Exception

قال: (باب الاستثناء) وحروف الاستثناء ثمانية، وهي: (إلَّا)، و(غير)، وَ(سِوَى)، وَ(سُوى)، وَ(سوَاءٌ)، وَ(خلا)، و(عدا)، وَ(حاشا).

He said: Chapter of the Exception: The particles of exception are eight: *illā*, *ghayru*, *siwa*, *suwan*, *sawā'*, *khalā*, *'adā* and *ḥāshā*.

وأقول: الاستثناء معناه في اللغة مطلق الإخراج، وهو في اصطلاح النحاة عبارة عن الإخراج بـ(إلا) أو إحدى أخواتها لشيء لولا ذلك الإخراج لكان داخلاً فيما قبل الأداة. ومثالُه قولك: (نجح التلاميذُ إلا عامراً) فقد أخرجت بقولك (إلا عامراً) أحد التلاميذ، وهو (عامر)، ولولا ذلك الإخراج لكان (عامر) داخلاً في جملة التلاميذ الناجحين.

I say: The linguistic meaning of the word *al-istithnā* (the exception) is absolute removal. And the meaning according to the nomenclature of the grammarians refers to the removal of something using "*illā*" or one of its sisters, where that thing would be part of what came before the tool of exception [if it was not present.] An example of this is the statement, "The students passed except for *'Āmir*." In this statement the removal is "except for *'Āmir*" i.e. one of the students. If not for the [tool of exception causing this] exception, "*'Āmir*" would be considered part of the phrase "the students passed."

واعلم أنَّ أدوات الاستثناء كثيرة، وقد ذكر منها المؤلف ثمان أدوات، والذي ذكره منها على ثلاثة أنواع:

Know that the tools of exception are abundant, and the author has mentioned eight from them. The ones which he has mentioned can be split into three types:

النوع الأول: ما يكون حرفاً دائماً وهو (إلّا).

The first type: That which is always a particle, and this is "*illā*".

النوع الثاني: ما يكون اسماً دائماً، وهو أربعة، وهي: (سِوى) بالقصر وكسر السين، و(سُوَى) بالقصر وضم السين، و(سَواءُ) بالمد وفتح السين، و(غير).

The second type: That which is always a noun, and it consists of four: (i) "*siwa*", (ii) "*suwa*", (iii) "*sawā*" and (iv) "*ghayru*".

النوع الثالث: ما يكون حرفاً تارة ويكون فعلاً تارة أخرى، وهي ثلاثُ أدواتٍ وهي: (خلا)، و(عدا)، و(حاشا).

The third type: That which is considered to be a particle at times and as a verb at other times, and it consists of three instruments: (i) "*khalā*", (ii) "'*adā*", and (iii) "*ḥāshā*".

حكم المستثنى بـ(إلا)

The Ruling of the Exception with "*Illā*"

قال: فالمستثنى بـ(إلّا) يُنصبُ إذا كان الكلام تامّاً موجباً، نحو (قام القومُ إلا زيداً) و(خرج الناسُ إلا عمراً) وإن كان الكلام منفياً تاماً جاز فيه البدلُ والنصبُ على الاستثناء، نحو: (ما قام القومُ إلا زيدٌ) و(إلا زيداً) ، وإن كان الكلام ناقصا كان على حسب العوامل، نحو: (ما قام إلا زيد)، و(ما ضربتُ إلا زيداً) و(ما مررتُ إلا بزيدٍ).

He said: The word made into an exception with *illā* is made *manṣūb* if the speech which has preceded it is complete and affirmative e.g. "The people stood except for Zayd" and "The people left except for 'Amr." If the speech is complete and negative then [making the exception a grammatical follower

as a] substitution *(al-badl)* here is permissible as well as making it *manṣūb* as an exception e.g. "The people did not stand except Zayd." If the speech is deficient then [the exception's] grammatical classification depends upon the presence of other grammatical agents like those found in the following examples, "None stood except for Zayd", "I did not hit except Zayd", and "I did not pass except by Zayd."

وأقول: اعلم أنَّ للاسم الواقع بعد (إلّا) ثلاثةَ أحوالٍ؛

I say: Know that there are three states for the noun present after "*illā*":

الحالة الأولى: وجوب النصب على الاستثناء.

The first state: It is mandatory that the exception be *manṣūb*.

الحالة الثانية: جواز إتباعه لما قبل (إلّا) على أنه بدل منه مع جواز نصبه على الاستثناء.

The second state: It is permissible for the exception to follow grammatically what comes before "*illā*" as a substitution (*al-badl*) for it, and it is also permissible for it to be *manṣūb* as an exception.

الحالة الثالثة: وجوب إجرائه على حسب ما يقتضيه العامل المذكورُ قبل (إلّا).

The third state: It is mandatory that the exception follows upon that which is dictated by its governor which is mentioned before "*illā*".

وبيان ذلك أنَّ الكلام الذي قبل (إلّا) إما أن يكون تامّاً موجباً، وإما أن يكون تاماً منفياً، وإما أن يكون ناقصاً ولا يكون حينئذٍ إلا منفياً.

The reason behind this is that the speech before "*illā*" is sometimes: (i) complete and affirmative, (ii) complete and negative, and (iii) incomplete, and this will always be negative.

ومعنى كون الكلام السابق تاماً: أن يُذكر فيه المستثنى منه، ومعنى كونه ناقصاً: ألا يذكر فيه المستثنى منه، ومعنى كونه موجباً: ألا يسبقه نفي أو شبهه، وشِبهُ النفي: النهي،

والاستفهام، ومعنى كونه منفياً: أنَّ يسبقه أحد هذه الأشياء.

The meaning of the preceding speech being "complete" is that it mentions what is being made an exception from. The meaning of it being "incomplete" is that it does not mention what is being made an exception from. The meaning of it being "affirmative" is that it is not preceded by a negation or that which is similar to the negation i.e. the prohibition and the interrogative. The meaning of it being "negative" is that it is preceded by one of the aforementioned things.

فإن كان الكلام السابق (تاماً موجباً) وجب نصب الاسم الواقع بعد (إلّا) على الاستثناء نحو قولك: (قامَ القومُ إلّا زيداً) وقولك: (خرج الناس إلّا عمراً) فـ(زيداً) و(عمراً): مستثنيان من كلام تام لذكر المستثنى منه، وهو (القوم) في الأول و(الناس) في الثاني، والكلام مع ذلك مُوجبٌ لعدم تقدم نفي أو شبهه؛ فوجب نصبهما، وهذه هي الحالة الأولى.

So if the preceding speech is complete and affirmative, it is mandatory to make the noun following "*illā*" *manṣūb* due to it being an exception. Examples are, "The people stood except for Zayd" and, "The people left except for ʿAmr." So "Zayd" and "ʿAmr" are both exceptions to complete speech where the thing made exception to is mentioned. In the former example this thing is "the people (*al-qawm*)" and in the latter example this thing is "the people (*al-nās*). The speech is also affirmative due to the absence of a negation or that which is similar to it. Hence it is obligatory to make these two words *manṣūb*, and this is the first of the aforementioned states.

وإن كان الكلام السابق (تاماً منفياً) جاز فيه الاتباعُ على البدلية أو النصب على الاستثناء، نحو قولك: (ما قام القوم إلا زيدٌ) فـ(زيدٌ): مستثنى من كلام تام لذكر المستثنى منه، وهو القوم، والكلام مع ذلك منفي لتقدم ((ما) النافية)؛ فيجوز فيه الإتباع؛ فتقولُ (إلّا زيدٌ) بالرفع؛ لأن المستثنى منه مرفوع، وبدل المرفوع مرفوع، ويجوز فيه على قلةٍ النصبُ على الاستثناء؛ فتقول: (إلا زيداً) وهذه هي الحالة الثانية.

If the preceding speech is complete and negative then two options are allowed for the grammatical status of the noun following "*illā*": (i) it can grammatically follow as a substitute or (ii) it can be *manṣūb* as an exception. An example of the former is, "The people did not stand except Zayd." In this example Zayd is an exception to complete speech where the thing being made exception to (i.e. "the people") is mentioned. The speech is also negative as it is preceded by the particle of negation "*mā*". So it is permissible for it to (i) grammatically follow or (ii) become *manṣūb* due to being an exception. For the first option it would be said "*illā Zaydun*" in the state of *rafʿ* as the word being made exception to is *marfūʿ* and the substitute of the *marfūʿ* is also *marfūʿ*. And the second option—though permissible—is less frequently utilised. In this option it would have been said instead, "*illā Zaydan*." This is the second of the aforementioned states.

وإن كان الكلام السابق (ناقصاً، ولا يكون إلا منفياً)، كان المستثنى على حسب ما قبل (إلّا) من العوامل؛ فإن كان العامل يقتضي الرفع على الفاعلية رفعته عليها، نحو (ما حضر إلا عليٌّ)، وإن كان العامل يقتضي النصب على المفعولية، نصبته عليها، نحو (ما رأيتُ إلا علياً) وإن كان العامل يقتضي الجر بحرف من حروف الجر جررته به نحو (ما مررتُ إلا بزيدٍ) وهذه هي الحالة الثالثة.

If the preceding speech is "incomplete and this will always be negative", then the grammatical state of the exception will be based upon the influence of its governor that precedes "*illā*". If this governor dictates that a subject be *marfūʿ* then the exception will be *marfūʿ* e.g. "None were present except ʿAlī." If the governor dictates that an object be *manṣūb* then the exception will become *manṣūb* e.g. "I did not see except ʿAlī. If the governor dictates the state of *jarr* through the particles of *jarr* then the exception becomes *majrūr* e.g. "I did not pass except by Zayd." And this is the third of the aforementioned states.

المستثنى بـ(غير) وأخواتها

The Exception with "*Ghayru*" and Its Sisters

قال: والمستثنى بـ(سِوى)، وَ(سُوى)، وَ(سَوَاءٍ)، وَ(غَيرٍ) مجرورٌ لا غيرُ.

He said: The word made into an exception with *"siwā"*, *"suwan"*, *"sawā'i"* and *"ghayrin"* is *majrūr* and nothing else.

وأقول: الاسم الواقع بعد أداة من هذه الأدوات الأربعة يجب جرهُ بإضافة الأداة إليه، أما الأداةُ نفسُها فإنها تأخذ حكم الاسم الواقع بعد (إلا) على التفصيل الذي سبق: فإن كان الكلام تاماً موجباً نصبتها وجوباً على الاستثناء، نحو (قام القومُ غيرَ زيدٍ)، وإن كان الكلام تاماً منفياً أتبعتها لما قبلها أو نصبتها، نحو (ما يزورَني أحدٌ غيرُ الأخيارِ)، أو (غيرَ الأخيارِ)، وإن كان الكلام ناقصاً منفياً أجريتها على حسب العوامل، نحو (لا تتصل بغيرِ الأخيارِ).

I say: It is mandatory that the noun that is present after one of these four apparatus of exception is in the state of *jarr* due to these apparatus being compounded to it. As for these apparatus themselves, they take the ruling of the word that follows "*illā*" that we detailed above. So if the speech is complete and affirmative then it is mandatory to be *manṣūb* as the exception e.g. "The people stood except for Zayd." If the speech is complete and negative then it can either grammatically follow that which preceded it or become *manṣūb* e.g. "No one visits me except for (*ghayru*) the best" or "Except for (*ghayra*) the best." If the speech is incomplete and negative then it falls according to its governor e.g. "Do not connect yourself except to the best."

المستثنى بـ(عدا) وأخواته

The Exception with *ʿAdā* and Its Sisters

قال: والمستثنى بـ(خلا)، و(عدا)، و(حاشا)، يجوزُ نصبُهُ وجرُهُ، نحو (قام القومُ خلا زيداً)، و(زيدٍ) و(عدا عمراً) و(عمرٍو)، و(حاشا بكراً) و(بكرٍ).

He said: The word used as an exception with *khalā*, *ʿadā* and *ḥāshā* is allowed to be *manṣūb* or *majrūr* e.g. "The people stood except for Zaydan/Zaydin", "... except for ʿAmran/ʿAmrin", and, "... except for Bakran/Bakrin."

وأقول: الاسم الواقع بعد أداة من هذه الأدوات الثلاثة يجوز لك أن تنصبه، ويجوز لك أن تجره، والسر في ذلك أنَّ هذه الأدوات تستعمل أفعالاً تارة، وتستعمل حروفاً تارة أخرى على ما سبق، فإن قدّرتَهُنَّ أفعالاً نصبتَ ما بعدها على أنّه مفعول به، والفاعل ضمير مستتر وجوباً، وإن قدّرتَهنَّ حروفاً خفضت ما بعدها على أنّه مجرور بها.

I say: The noun present after one of these apparatus of exception is permissible to be either: (i) *manṣūb* or (ii) *majrūr*. The reason behind this is that these apparatus are sometimes utilised as verbs and sometimes utilised as particles, and we have discussed this earlier. If they are utilised as verbs, then that which follows them is made *manṣūb* due to them being regarded as objects, and the subject appears as a hidden pronoun compulsorily. If they are utilised as particles, then that which follows them is made *makhfūḍ* due to them being dictated so by them.

ومحلُّ هذا التردد فيما إذا لم تتقدم عليهنَّ ((ما) المصدرية)؛ فإن تقدمت على واحدة منهن (ما) هذه، وجب نصب ما بعدها، وسببُ ذلك أنَّ ((ما) المصدرية) لا تدخلُ إلا على الأفعال؛ فهنَّ أفعالٌ ألبتة إن سبقتهنَّ ، فنحو (قام القومُ خلا زيد) يجوز فيه نصب (زيد) وخفضه، ونحو (قام القوم ما خلا زيداً) لا يجوز فيه إلا نصب (زيد)

والله سبحانه وتعالى أعلى وأعلم.

This option is present in these apparatus of exception that are not preceded by the *mā* of the infinitive. This is because if this *mā* precedes them, it is obligatory to make that which comes after them *manṣūb* [without any option]. The reason behind this is that the *mā* of the infinitive does not enter onto anything except the verb, and so they are taken as verbs absolutely if they are preceded as such. An example of the case where there are two possibilities is, "The people stood except Zayd." In this example it is permissible to make the word "Zayd" (i) *manṣūb* or (ii) *khafḍ*. An example of the other aforementioned scenario is, "The people stood except for Zayd." Here it is not permissible except to make the word "Zayd" *manṣūb* and Allah the Most High knows best.

أسئلة

Questions

ما هو الاستثناء لغة واصطلاحاً؟

What is the linguistic meaning of the word "*al-istithnā*" and its meaning according to the nomenclature of the grammarians?

ما هي أدوات الاستثناء؟

What are the apparatus of exception?

إلى كم قسم تنقسم أدوات الاستثناء؟

Into how many categories are the apparatus of exception split into?

كم حالة للاسم الواقع بعد (إلّا)؟

How many states are allowed for the noun that arises after "*illā*"?

متى يجب نصب الاسم الواقع بعد (إلا) ؟

When is it mandatory to make the noun present after "*illā*" *manṣūb*?

متى يجوز نصب الاسم الواقع بعد (إلا) وإتباعه لما قبلها؟

When is it allowed to either make the noun present after "*illā*" *manṣūb* or a grammatical follower of what preceded it?

ما معنى كون الكلام تاماً؟

What is the meaning of speech being complete?

ما معنى كون الكلام منفياً؟

What is the meaning of speech being negative?

ما حكم الاسم الواقع بعد (سوى) ؟

What is the ruling of the noun present after "*siwa*"?

كيف تعرب (سواء) ؟

What is the grammatical structure that comes in the context of "*sawā*"?

ما حكم الاسم الواقع بعد (خلا) ؟

What is the ruling of the noun present after "*khalā*"?

شروط إعمال (لا) عمل (إنّ)

The Conditions for Using "*Lā*" with the Function of *Innā*

قال: باب (لا)، اعلم أنَّ (لا) تنصبُ النكرات بغير تنوين إذا باشرتِ النكرة ولم تتكرر (لا) نحو (لا رجلَ في الدار).

He said: The Chapter of "*Lā*": Know that "*lā*" places indefinite nouns into the state of *naṣb* without the *tanwīn* if it is immediately followed by an indefinite noun and the "*lā*" is not repeated, as in the following sentence, "There is no man in the house."

وأقول: اعلم أنَّ ((لا) النافية للجنس) تعمل عمل (إن) فتنصب الاسم لفظاً أو محلاً وترفع الخبر.

I say: Know that the "*lā*" of negation of an entire type serves the function of "*inna*" and so its noun is made *manṣūb* verbally or in state and its predicate is made *marfū'*.

وهي لا تعمل هذا العمل وجوباً إلا بأربعةِ شروط:

It is not mandatory for it to be given this function except if it meets four conditions:

الأول: أن يكون اسمها نكرة.

First. Its noun is indefinite.[210]

الثاني: أن يكون اسمها متصلاً بها: أي غير مفصول منها ولو بالخبر.

---

210 Al-Ahdal said (1/283), "The purpose of the noun being indefinite is to indicate through the wording a general negation."

Second. Its noun is connected to it i.e. there is no separation between them, even if this separation is the predicate.

والثالث: أن يكون خبرها نكرة أيضاً.

Third. Its predicate must also be indefinite.[211]

والرابع: ألّا تتكرر (لا) .

Fourth. The word "*lā*" is not repeated.

ثم اعلم أنَّ اسم (لا) على ثلاثة أنواع، الأولُ المفرد، والثاني المضاف إلى نكرة، والثالث الشبيه بالمضاف.

It should also be known that the noun of "*lā*" is of three types: (i) the singular, (ii) the *muḍāf* (possessed) of an indefinite and (iii) that which is similar to a *muḍāf*.

أما المفرد في هذا الباب، وفي باب المنادى، فهو: ما ليس مضافاً ولا شبيهاً بالمضاف، فيدخل فيه المثنى، وجمعُ التكسير، وجمع المذكر السالم، وجمع المؤنث السالم.

As for the singular in relation to this—and in relation to the vocative—it is that which is not a *muḍāf* and not similar to a *muḍāf*. So the dual form, broken plural, sound masculine plural and sound feminine plural will also fall under this type.

وحكمه أنه يُبنى على ما ينصبُ به: فإذا كان نصبه بالفتحة بني على الفتح، نحو (لا رجلَ في الدار)، وإن كان نصبه بالياء - وذلك المثنى وجمع المذكر السالم - بني على الياء نحو (لا رجُلَينِ في الدار) وإن كان نصبه بالكسرة نيابة عن الفتحة - وذلك جمع المؤنث السالم - بني على الكسر، نحو (لا صالحاتٍ اليومَ) .

211 Al-Ahdal said (1/283), "The purpose of the predicate being indefinite is so a definite predicate is not given to an indefinite noun."

Its grammatical ruling is that it is formed upon whatever it becomes *manṣūb* with. If it is made *manṣūb* with a *fatḥah* then it is formed upon a *fatḥah* e.g. "There is no man (*rajula*) in the house." If it is made *manṣūb* with the letter *yā*—and this is the case for the dual form and the sound masculine plural—it is formed upon a *yā* e.g. "There is not two men (*rajulayn*) in the house." If it is made *manṣūb* with a *kasrah* serving in place of the *fatḥah*—and this is the case for the sound feminine plural—it is formed upon a *kasrah* e.g. "There is not good women (*ṣāliḥātin*) today."

وأما المضاف فينصب بالفتحة الظاهرة أو بما ناب عنها، نحو (لا طالبَ علمٍ ممقوتٌ)

As for the *muḍāf*, it becomes *manṣūb* with an explicit *fatḥah* or that which serves in its place e.g. "There is not a student of knowledge who is abhorred."

وأما الشبيه بالمضاف ؛ وهو ما اتصل به شيءٌ من تمام معناه، فمثلُ المضاف في الحكم: أي ينصب بالفتحة، نحو (لا مستقيماً حاله بين الناس).

As for that which resembles the *muḍāf*, it is that which is connected to something that completes its meaning. It is akin in its grammatical ruling to the *muḍāf* i.e. it becomes *manṣūb* with the *fatḥah*. An example is "There is no upright person amongst the people."

قال: فإن لم تُباشِرها وجبَ الرفعُ ووجبَ تكرارُ (لا) نحو (لا في الدار رجلٌ ولا امرأةٌ) فإن تكررت جاز إعمالُها وإلغاؤُها، فإن شئت قلت: (لا رجُلَ في الدارِ ولا امرأةَ)؛ فإن شئت قلت: (لا رجلٌ في الدار ولا امرأةٌ).

He said: And if it is not immediately followed by an indefinite noun then the state of *rafʿ* becomes obligatory as does the repetition of *"lā"* as in the following example: "There is not a man in the house nor a woman." If the *"lā"* is repeated then it is permissible for it to have its effect and it is also permissible for the effect to be cancelled. So it can be said, "There is not a man *(rajula)* in the house and not a woman *(imra'ata)*" or, "There is not a man *(rajulun)* in the house and not a woman *(imra'ata)*."

وأقول: قد عرفت أنَّ شروط وجوب عمل (لا) عملَ (إنَّ) أربعة، وهذا الكلام في بيان الحال إذا اختل شرط من الشروط الأربعة السابقة.

I say: I have previously explained that the conditions that mandate the effect of "*lā*" being the same as the effect of "*inna*" are four. What we are discussing now is the situation where one of the aforementioned four conditions are not met.

وبيان ذلك أنه إذا وقع بعد (لا) معرفة وجب إلغاءُ (لا) وتكرارها، نحو (لا محمدٌ زارني ولا بكرٌ) وإذا فصل بين (لا) واسمها فاصلٌ ما، وجب كذلك إلغاؤها وتكرارها نحو ﴿لا فِيهَا غَوْلٌ وَلا هُمْ عَنْهَا يُنْزَفُونَ﴾ فـ(غولٌ) : مبتدأ مؤخر، و(فيها): متعلق بمحذوف خبر مقدم، و(لا) نافية مهملة.

To illustrate this: If a definite word arises after "*lā*" then it is mandatory to cancel the effect of "*lā*" and to repeat it, e.g. "Neither did Muḥammad visit me nor Bakr." If there is anything separating "*lā*" and its noun then it is mandatory to cancel its effect and repeat it e.g. {**No bad effect is there in it, nor from it will they be intoxicated.**}[212] Here "*ghawlun*" (bad effect) is the delayed nominal subject and "*fīhā*" (in it) is connected to an omitted preceding predicate. "*Lā*" here is of absolute negation but with its effect cancelled.

وإذا تكررت (لا) لم يجب إعمالها، بل يجوز إعمالها إذا استوفت بقية الشروط، ويجوز إهمالها؛ فتقول على الإعمال (لا رجلَ في الدار ولا امرأةَ)، بفتح (رجل) و(امرأة) وتقول على الإهمال: (لا رجلٌ في الدار ولا امرأةٌ) برفع رجل وامرأة.

If "*lā*" is repeated then it is not mandatory to give it its effect, rather it is permissible to (i) give it its effect, if the other conditions are met, or (ii) neglect the effect. So an example of when the effect is *utilised* is, "There is no man and no woman in the house" with a *fatḥah* on the words "*rajula*" and "*imra'ata*". An example of when the effect is neglected is, "There is no man and no woman in the house" with the words "*rajulun*" and "*imra'atun*" in the state of *rafʿ*.

---

212 Al-Ṣāffāt: 47

أسئلة

Questions

ما الذي تعمله (لا) النافية للجنس؟

What grammatical effect is performed by the "*lā*" of negation of an entire type?

ما شروط وجوب عمل (لا) النافية للجنس؟

What are the conditions that make the grammatical effect of the "*lā*" of negation of an entire type mandatory?

إلى كم قسم ينقسم اسم (لا) ؟

Into how many categories is the noun of "*lā*" split into?

ما حكم اسم (لا) المفرد ؟

What is the grammatical ruling of the singular noun of "*lā*"?

ما هو المفرد في باب (لا) والمنادى ؟

What constitutes the singular in relation to "*lā*" and the vocative?

ما حكم اسم (لا) إذا كان مضافاً أو شبيهاً به ؟

What is the grammatical ruling of the noun of "*lā*" if it is a *muḍāf* or similar to a *muḍāf*?

ما الحكم إذا تكررت (لا) النافية ؟

What is the grammatical ruling if there is a repetition of the "*lā*" of negation?

ما الحكم إذا وقع بعد (لا) النافية معرفة ؟

What is the grammatical ruling if there is a definite noun after the "*lā*" of negation?

ما الحكم إذا فصل بين (لا) واسمها فاصل ؟

What is the grammatical ruling if there is a separation between the "*lā*" and its noun?

المنادى

The Vocative

قال: (باب المنادى) المنادى خمسة أنواع: المفردُ العلم، والنكرة المقصودة، والنكرةُ غير المقصودةُ، والمضافُ، والشبيه بالمضافِ.

He said: Chapter of the Vocative: The vocative is of five types: (i) the singular proper noun, (ii) the intended indefinite noun, (iii) the unintended indefinite noun, (iv) the *muḍāf*, and (v) that which resembles the *muḍāf*.

وأقول: المنادى في اللغة هو: المطلوب إقباله مطلقاً، وفي اصطلاح النحاة هو: المطلوب إقباله بـ(يا) أو إحدى أخواتها.

I say: The linguistic meaning of the word "*munādā*" refers to the seeking of someone's approach in an absolute sense.[213] Its meaning according to the nomenclature of the grammarians refers to the seeking of someone's approach through the use of the word "*yā*" ("O [so and so]") or one of its sisters.

وأخواتُ (يا) هي الهمزة نحو (أزيدُ أقبل) و(أي) نحو (أي إبراهيمُ تَفهم) و(أيا) نحو:

The sisters of "*yā*" are: (i) The letter *hamzah* e.g. "O Zayd, approach." (ii) "*Ay*" e.g. "O Ibrāhīm, understand." (iii) "*Ayā*", as in the Arabic couplet:

أَيَا شَجَرَ الخابُورِ مَا لَكَ مُورقاً　　كأنك لم تجزع على ابنِ طريف

O trees of al-Khābur, what is this foliage?

---

213 I.e. where one's response is sought without answering the seeker verbally, e.g. "*yā Allah*". See *Ḥāshiyat Yasīn ʿalā al-Fākihi* (2/72) and *Ḥāshiyat al-Sajāʿī* (pp. 77-78).

It is as if you do not mourn Ibn Turayf.[214]

و(هيا) نحو (هيا محمد تعالَ).

And (iv) "*hayā*" e.g. "O Muḥammad, come."

ثم المنادى على خمسة أنواع:

Furthermore, the vocative is of five types:

١ ـ المفردُ العلمُ، وقد مضى في باب (لا) تعريف المفرد، ومثاله (يا محمد) و(يا فاطمة) و(يا محمدان) و(يا فاطمتان) و(يا محمدون) و(يا فاطمات).

One. The singular proper noun. We have previously discussed the definition of the singular in the Chapter of "*Lā*". Examples are: "O Muḥammad", "O Fāṭimah", "O two Muḥammads", "O two Fāṭimahs", "O Muḥammads" and "O Fāṭimahs."

٢ ـ النكرة المقصودة؛ وهي: التي يقصد بها واحدٌ معينٌ ممَّا يصحُ إطلاق لفظها عليه، نحو (يا ظالمُ) تريد واحداً بعينه.

Two. The intended indefinite noun. This refers to when an individual is specified with a wording that is suitable to refer to a wide group e.g. saying "O oppressor" whilst intending a specific oppressor.

٣ ـ النكرة غير المقصودة؛ وهي: التي يقصد بها واحدٌ غير معين، نحو قول الواعظ: (يا غافلاً تنبَّه)، فإنَّه لا يريد واحداً معيناً، بل يريد كل من يطلق عليه لفظ (غافل).

Three. The unintended indefinite noun. This refers to when an unspecified

214 This was stated by the sister of al-Walīd ibn Turayf, mourning his death. This couplet is present in al-Dhahabī's *Siyar A'lām al-Nubalā* (8/232), but the couplet was not narrated with the same wording mentioned here, rather it states (فيا شجر الخابور). Based on this wording, the evidence cited by the author (i.e. al-Shaykh Muḥī al-Dīn) is not provided by it, unless there is another route with his wording, in which case there is no harm.

individual from a wide group is intended e.g. the preacher saying, "O negligent, pay heed" whilst not intending a specific individual, rather intending everyone who could be considered to be negligent.

٤ ـ المضاف، نحو (يا طالبَ العلمِ اجتهد).

Four. The *muḍāf* e.g. "O student of knowledge, strive."

٥ ـ الشبيه بالمضاف، وهو ما اتصل به شيء من تمام معناه، سواءٌ أكان المتصل به مرفوعاً به، نحو (يا حميداً فعْلهُ) أم كان منصوباً به نحو (يا حافظاً درسَهُ) أم كان مجروراً بحرف جر يتعلق به نحو (يا محباً للخير).

Five. That which resembles the *muḍāf*. This refers to that which is connected to something to complete its meaning, regardless if the word connected to it is *marfūʿ* e.g. "O one with praiseworthy actions", *manṣūb* e.g. "O memoriser of his lesson", or *majrūr* due to being connected to a particle of *jarr* e.g. "O lover of the good."

❁❁❁

قال: فأمَّا المفرد العلَم، والنكرة المقصودة فيبنيان على الضم من غير تنوين، نحو (يا زيدُ) و(يا رجلُ) والثلاثة الباقية منصوبة لا غير.

He said: As for the singular proper noun and the intended indefinite noun then they are both linguistically constructed upon the *ḍammah* without the presence of *tanwīn* e.g. "O Zayd" and "O man". And the three remaining types remain *manṣūb* and do not change.

وأقول: إذا كان المنادى علما مفرداً أو نكرة مقصودة فإنَّه يُبنى على ما يرفع به؛

I say: If the vocative is a singular proper noun or an intended indefinite noun, then it is constructed upon that which it becomes *marfūʿ* with.

فإن كان يُرفع بالضمة فإنه يبنى على الضم، نحو (يا محمدُ) و(يا فاطمةُ) و(يا رجلُ

) و(يا فاطماتُ) .

If it becomes *marfū'* with a *ḍammah*, then it is constructed upon a *ḍammah* e.g. "O Muḥammad", "O Fāṭimah", "O man", "O Fāṭimas".

وإن كان يرفع بالألف نيابةً عن الضمة - وذلك المثنى - فإنَّه يبنى على الألف، نحو (يا محمدان) و(يا فاطمتان)

If it becomes *marfū'* with the letter *alif* serving in place of the *ḍammah*—and this is the case for the dual form—then it is constructed upon an *alif* e.g. "O two Muḥammads" and "O two Fāṭimahs".

وإن كان يُرفع بالواو نيابة عن الضمة - وذلك جمع المذكر السالم - فإنَّه يبنى على الواو نحو (يا محمدون).

If it becomes *marfū'* with the letter *wāw* serving in place of the *ḍammah*—and this is the case for the sound masculine plural—then it is constructed upon a *wāw* e.g. "O Muḥammads".

وإن كان المنادى نكرة غير مقصودة أو مضافاً أو شبيهاً بالمضاف فإنَّه ينصب بالفتحة أو ما ناب عنها نحو (يا جاهلاً تعلّم) و(يا كسولاً أقبل على ما ينفعك) ونحو (يا راغبَ المجدِ اعمل له) و(يا محبَّ الرِّفعةِ ثابر على السعي) ونحو (يا راغباً في السُّؤدُدِ لا تَضجر من العمل) و(يا حريصاً على الخير استقم).

And if the vocative is an unintended indefinite noun, a *muḍāf* or that which resembles the *muḍāf* then it becomes *manṣūb* with a *fatḥah* or that which serves in place of the *fatḥah*. Examples are: "O ignorant, learn", "O lazy one, dedicate yourself to that which will benefit you", "O aspirer of glory, endeavour for it", "O lover of prestige, persevere [in its] pursuit", "O aspirer of honour, do not abscond from working hard" and, "O covetous of goodness, be upright."[215]

215 If it is asked why the vocative is *manṣūb*, the answer is that the noun of the vocative is at its origin an object (مفعول به). Thus if one said, "O 'Abdullāh" (يا عبدالله), its original

أسئلة

Questions

ما هو المنادى لغة واصطلاحاً ؟

What is the meaning of the word "*al-munāḍā*" linguistically and according to the nomenclature of the grammarians?

ما هي أدوات النداء ؟ مَثِل لكل أداة بمثال.

What are the apparatus of the vocative? Provide an example for each one.

إلى كم قسم ينقسم المنادى ؟

How many types has the vocative been categorised into?

ما هو المفرد العَلم؟ ومَثِّل له بمثالين مختلفين.

What is the singular proper noun? Provide two different examples of it.

ما هي النكرة المقصودة مع التمثيل؟

What is the intended indefinite noun? Provide an example of it.

ما هو الشبيه بالمضاف؟

What is meant by "that which resembles the *muḍāf*"?

إلى كم نوع يتنوع الشبيه بالمضاف مع التمثيل لكل نوع .

How many types are there of the resemblance of the *muḍāf*? Provide an example of each type.

ما حكم المنادى المفرد العلم؟

wording is "I call ʿAbdullāh" (أدعو عبدالله).

What is the grammatical ruling of the singular proper noun vocative?

ما حكم المنادى المضاف؟

What is the grammatical ruling of the *muḍāf* vocative?

مثّل لكل نوع من أنواع المنادى الخمسة بمثالين، وأعرب واحداً منهما.

Exemplify each type of the vocative with five examples. Provide a grammatical analysis of one of them.

المفعول له

The Causative Object

قال: (باب المفعول من أجله) وهو: الاسم المنصوبُ، الذي يَذكرُ بياناً لسبب وقوع الفعل، نحو قولك: (قام زيد إجلالاً لعمرو) و(قصدتك ابتغاء معروفك).

He said: Chapter of the Causative Object: The causative object is the noun in the state of *naṣb*[216] which is mentioned in order to explain the reason why a verb occurred, as in the following examples: "Zayd stood out of reverence for 'Amr" and, "I have sought you out desiring your favour."

وأقول: المفعول من أجله - ويقال (المفعول لأجله)، و(المفعول له) - هو في اصطلاح النحاة: عبارة عن (الاسم، المنصوب، الذي يذكر بياناً لسبب وقوع الفعل).

I say: The causative object—which is referred to with the names "*al-maf'ūl min ajlihi*", "*al-maf'ūl li ajlihi*" and "*al-maf'ūl lahu*", according to the nomenclature of the grammarians refers to a *manṣūb* noun which is mentioned to detail the reason behind the occurrence of a verb.

وقولنا: (الاسم) يشمل الصريح والمؤول به.

Our statement "a noun" includes the explicit noun and its paraphrase.

ولا بد في الاسم الذي يقع مفعولاً له من أن يجتمع فيه خمسة أمور:

It is essential for the noun that serves as a causative object to possess five matters:

---

216 Al-Azharī said in *al-Taṣrīḥ* (1/337), "There is a difference of opinion regarding the *nāṣib* of the causative object. The majority of the Baṣrī grammarians said that it is made *manṣūb* by the verb due to the implicit *lām* of reasoning. This was differed upon by al-Zajāj and the Kūfī grammarians..." See *Ḥāshiyat al-Sibān* (2/122).

الأول: أن يكون مصدراً.

First: It must be an infinitive.

والثاني: أن يكون قَلبيّاً، ومعنى كونه قَلبيّاً ألا يكون دالاً على عمل من أعمال الجوارح كاليد واللسان مثل (قراءة) و(ضرب).

Second: It must be *qalbiyyan* (occur by heart), meaning that it does not refer to the actions of the limbs such as the hand or the tongue e.g. "reading" and "he hit".

والثالث: أن يكون علة لما قبله.

Third: It must be a reason for that which precedes it.

والرابع: أن يكون متحداً مع عامله في الوقت.

Fourth: It must be united with its governor in time.

والخامس: أن يتحد مع عامله في الفاعل.

Fifth: It must also be united with its governor in terms of their subject.

ومثال الاسم المستجمع لهذه الشروط (تأديباً) من قولك: (ضربتُ ابني تأديباً) فإنَّه مصدر، وهو قلبي؛ لأنَّه ليس من أعمال الجوارح، وهو علة للضرب، وهو متحد مع (ضربت) في الزمان، وفي الفاعل أيضاً.

An example of a noun that encompasses these conditions is the word "discipline" in the statement, "I hit my son for discipline." It is an infinitive, it is *qalbiyyun* due to it not being an action of the limbs, it is the reason for the hitting and it is united with the word "I hit" in terms of time and in terms of the subject also.

وكل اسم استوفى هذه الشروط يجوز فيه أمران: النصب، والجر بحرف من حروف الجر

الدالة على التعليل كاللام.

Every noun that meets these conditions is permissible to be made: (i) *manṣūb* or (ii) *majrūr* due to a particle of *jarr* that indicates reason [for the action], like the letter *lām*.

واعلم أنَّ للاسم الذي يقع مفعولاً لأجله ثلاث حالاتٍ:

Furthermore, know that the noun that is utilised as a causative object has three situations:

الأولى: أنَّ يكون مقترناً بـ(أل) .

One. It is connected to "*al-*".

الثانية: أنَّ يكون مضافاً.

Two. It is a *muḍāf*.

الثالثة: أن يكون مجرداً من (أل) ومن الإضافة.

Third. It is free from "*al-*" and from the possessive construction.

وفي جميع هذه الأحوال يجوز فيه النصب والجر بحرف الجر، إلا أنَّه قد يترجح أحد الوجهين، وقد يستويان في الجواز.

In all of these situations it is permissible for the causative object to be *manṣūb* and *majrūr* due to a particle of *jarr*, however either one of the situations may be most correct (under certain conditions)—or both may be equal in permissibility.

فإن كان مقترناً بـ(أل) فالأكثر فيه أن يجرَّ بحرف جر دال على التعليل، نحو: (ضربت ابني للتأديب) ويقلُّ نصبُه.

If it is connected to "*al-*" then it is more commonly *majrūr* due to a particle of *jarr* that indicates cause e.g. "I hit my son for discipline." It is rarely in the state of *naṣb*.

وإن كان مضافاً جاز جوازاً متساوياً أن يجر بالحرف وأن ينصب، نحو: (زرتك محبة أدبِكَ) أو (زرتك لمحبَّةِ أدبِكَ).

If it is *muḍāf* then it is equally permissible for it to be *majrūr* due to a particle or *manṣūb*. Examples are, "I visited you out of love (*maḥabbata*) for your manners" and, "I visited you out of love (*li muḥabbati*) for your manners."

وإن كان مجرداً من (أل) ومن الإضافة فالأكثر فيه أن ينصب، نحو: (قمتُ إجلالاً للأستاذ) ويقلُّ جره بالحرف ، والله أعلم.

If it is free of "*al-*" and not a *muḍāf* then it is more commonly *manṣūb* e.g. "I stood due to reverence for the teacher."[217] It is rarely *majrūr* due to a particle.[218] And Allah knows best.

أسئلة

Questions

ما هو المفعول لأجله؟

217 It says in *Mirqāt al-Mafātīḥ Sharḥ Mishkāt al-Maṣābīḥ* (8/511), "There is a stern punishment [of one being asked to take his seat in the fire] for those who have pride and take pleasure in having those who are present stand as they enter. However, if they stand for them whilst they have not sought it, standing either to gain reward or to show humility when greeting, then there is no harm in this."

218 There are other conditions. Khālid al-Azharī said in *al-Taṣrīḥ* (1/335) that Abu al-Baqā said in *Sharḥ al-Lamaʿ* of Ibn Jinni that the *mafʿūl lahu* has conditions, and from them: 1) It must be an answer to *"lima"*, i.e. the interrogative *mā*. 2) It is valid to serve as a predicate for the governing verb e.g. "I visited you out of desire to serve you" or the nominal subject e.g. "the desire is the one who made me visit you" 3) It is correct to have inferred the meaning of the *lām* [of reason] 4) The governor is not verbally correspondent to it, thus it is not correct for you to say that the word "*ziyarah*" (visit) in, "*zurtuk ziyarah*" (I visited you a visit) is a causative object because the infinitive is of the same verb, and something is not considered as its cause if it is existent by itself. [End quote.]

What is the *maf'ūl li ajlihi*?

ما الذي يشترط في الاسم الذي يقع مفعولاً لأجله؟

What are the conditions for a noun to be utilised as a causative object?

كم حالة للاسم الواقع مفعولاً له؟

How many situations are there of the noun utilised as a causative object?

ما حكم المفعول له المقترن بـ(أل) والمضاف؟

What is the grammatical ruling of the causative object that is connected to "*al-*" or the one which is a *muḍāf*?

مَثِّل بثلاثة أمثلة للمفعول لأجله بشرط أن يكون الأول مقترناً بـ(أل) والثاني مضافاً والثالث مجرداً من (أل) والإضافة، وأعرب كل واحد منها، وبين في كل مثال ما يجوز فيه من الوجوه مع بيان الأرجح إن كان.

Provide three examples of the causative object with the condition that the first is connected to "*al-*", the second is a *muḍāf* and the third is free of "*al-*" and not a *muḍāf*. Provide a grammatical analysis of each, and explain for each example what is the permissible alternative, and explain the reason for its preference —if any.

المفعول معه

The Object of Accompaniment

قال: (باب المفعول معه) وهو: الاسمُ المنصوب الذي يُذكر لبيان من فُعِلَ مَعَهُ الفعل، نحو قولك: (جاء الأميرُ والجيشَ) و(استوى الماءُ والخشبةَ).

He said: Chapter of the Object of Accompaniment: It is a *manṣūb* noun which is mentioned in order to explain who or what participated in the enactment of the action, as in the following examples: "The leader came with the army" and, "The water became level with the wood."

وأقول: المفعول معه عند النحاة هو: الاسم، الفضلة، المنصوب بالفعل أو ما فيه معنى الفعل وحروفه، الدّالُّ على الذات التي وقع الفعل بمصاحبتها، المسبوق بواو تفيد المعيةَ نصاً.

I say: The object of accompaniment according to the grammarians is: a noun, surplus (i.e. not an essential component of the speech), *manṣūb* due to a verb or that which has the meaning and linguistic structure of a verb, it indicates towards an entity that accompanied at the occurrence of the action and it is preceded by the letter *wāw* that textually indicates accompaniment.

فقولنا: (الاسم) يشمل المفرد والمثنى والجمع، والمذكر والمؤنث والمراد به: الاسم الصريح دون المؤول، وخرج عنه الفعل والحرف والجملة.

Our statement "a noun" encompasses the singular, dual form and the plural—masculine and feminine. Here it refers to the explicit noun and not to the paraphrase of an explicit noun. Likewise the verb, particle and sentence are removed from the definition.

وقولنا: (الفضلة) معناه أنّه ليس ركناً في الكلام؛ فليس فاعلاً، ولا مبتدأً ولا خبراً، وخرج

به العمدة، نحو (اشترك زيدٌ وعمروٌ).

Our statement "surplus" means that it is not an essential part of the speech, so it cannot be the subject, nominal subject or the predicate. Thus this clause excludes the main component [of a sentence.][219] An example is, "Zayd and 'Amr shared."

وقولنا: (المنصوب بالفعل أو ما فيه معنى الفعل وحروفه) يدل على أنَّ العامل في المفعول معه على ضربين:

Our statement "*manṣūb* due to a verb or that which has the meaning and linguistic structure of a verb"[220] indicates that the grammatical governor for the object of accompaniment is of two types:

الأول: الفعل، نحو (حضر الأمير والجيشَ).

First: The verb e.g. "The leader was present with the army."

الثاني: الاسم الدال على معنى الفعل المشتمل على حروفه، كاسم الفاعل في نحو (الأمير حاضرٌ والجيش).

Second: A noun that indicates towards the meaning of a verb and encompasses its letters. An example is the noun on the *fā'il* pattern in the statement, "The leader is present (*ḥāḍir*, which is on the *fā'il* word pattern with the root words *ḥ-ḍ-r*) with the army."

وقولنا: (المسبوق بواو هي نص في الدلالة على المعية) يخرج به الاسم المسبوق بواو ليست نصاً في الدلالة على المعية، نحو (حضر محمدٌ وخالدٌ).

---

219 Ibn Hishām said in *al-Qaṭr* (p. 323), "This is because the verb is not free from it. If it is said, 'Zayd shared,' it would not be considered to be correct as sharing cannot take place except between two."

220 This is the view of the majority of the Baṣrī grammarians and a group from the Kūfīs. Ibn Hishām considered this view to be preponderant. See *Awḍaḥ al-Masālik* (2/54), *al-Taṣrīḥ* by al-Azharī (1/343) and *Ḥāshiyat al-Khuḍarī* (1/200).

Our statement "it is preceded by the letter *wāw* that textually indicates accompaniment" excludes from the definition the noun that is preceded by the letter *wāw* that does not textually indicate this e.g. "Muḥammad and Walīd were present."[221]

واعلم أنَّ الاسم الواقع بعد الواو على نوعين:

Know that the noun arising after the letter *wāw* is of two types:

١ - ما يتعين نَصبُهُ على أنَّه مفعول معه.

One. That which is required to be *manṣūb* due to being the object of accompaniment.

٢ - ما يجوز نَصبُهُ على ذلك واتباعُه لما قبله في إعرابه معطوفاً عليه.

Two. That which is allowed to be (i) *manṣūb* due to being the object of accompaniment and (ii) a grammatical follower of what preceded it due to being conjoined to it.

أما النوع الأول فمحله إذا لم يصحَّ تشريك ما بعد الواو لما قبلها في الحكم، نحو (أنا سائرٌ والجبلَ) ونحو (ذاكرتُ والمصباحَ) فإنَّ الجبل لا يصح تشريكه للمتكلم في السير، وكذلك المصباح لا يصح تشريكه للمتكلم في المذاكرة، وقد مَثَّل المؤلف لهذا النوع بقوله: (استوى الماءُ والخشبةَ).

As for the first type, it is the case when it is not appropriate for that which comes after the letter *wāw* to share the ruling of what preceded it e.g. "I am walking alongside the mountain" and, "I studied with the lamp" Evidently it is not tangible for the word "the mountain" to share in the "walking" of the one speaking the sentence. Likewise is the case for the lamp in relation to the speaker's studying. The author provided an example of this type with his statement, "The water became level with the wood."

---

221 Ibn Hishām said in *al-Qaṭr* (p. 323), "[I.e.] when a conjunction is only intended."

وأما الثاني فمحله إذا صح تشريك ما بعد الواو لما قبلها في الحكم، نحو (حضر عليٌّ ومحمدٌ) فإنه يجوز نصب (محمد) على أنَّه مفعول معه، ويجوز رفعه على أنَّه معطوف على (علي)؛ لأن محمداً يجوز اشتراكه مع علي في الحضور، وقد مَثَّل المؤلف لهذا النوع بقوله: (جاء الأميرُ والجيشَ).

As for the second type, it is the case when it is correct for that which comes after the letter *wāw* to share the ruling of what preceded it e.g. "'Alī and Muḥammad were present." Here it is permissible to make "Muḥammad" *manṣūb* due to it being the accompanying object and it is also permissible to make it *marfū'* due to it being conjoined to "'Alī". This is because it is allowed for Muḥammad to share in the act of "presence" with 'Alī. The author exemplified this type in his statement, "The leader came with the army."

أسئلة

Questions

ما هو المفعول معه؟

What is the *maf'ūl ma'ahu*?

ما المراد بالاسم هنا؟

What is meant by the noun in the context of the *maf'ūl ma'ahu*?

ما المراد بالفضْلة؟

What is meant by "surplus" here?

ما الذي يعمل في المفعول معه؟

What governs the object of accompaniment?

إلى كم قسم ينقسم المفعول معه؟

Into how many categories is the object of accompaniment split into?

مثِّل للمفعول معه الذي يجب نصبه بمثالين.

Provide two examples of the object of accompaniment that is mandatory to be made *manṣūb*.

مثِّل للمفعول معه الذي يجوز نصبه واتباعه لما قبله بمثالين،

Provide two examples of the object of accompaniment that is allowed to be either *manṣūb* or a grammatical follower of what precedes it.

أعرب المثالين اللذين في كلام المؤلف، وبين في كل مثال منهما من أي نوع هو.

Provide a grammatical analysis of the two examples given by the author in the text of *al-Ājrūmiyyah*. Also clarify as to what type of object of accompaniment each example is.

❖❖❖

قال: وأما خبر ((كان) وأخواتِها) واسم ((إنَّ) وأخواتِها) فقد تقدم ذكرُهُما في المرفوعاتِ، وكذلك التوابعُ؛ فقد تقدَّمَتْ هُناكَ.

He said: As for the predicate of *kāna* and its sisters and the noun of *inna* and its sisters, we have discussed these previously under the *marfūʿ* nouns and likewise under the grammatical followers.

وأقول: من المنصوبات اسم (إنَّ) وأخواتها، وخبر (كان) وأخواتها، وتابعُ المنصوب، وقد تقدم بيان ذلك في أبوابه؛ فلا حاجة بنا إلى إعادة شيءٍ منه.

I say: From the *manṣūb* nouns is the noun of *inna* and its sisters, the predicate of *kāna* and its sisters and the grammatical follower of a *manṣūb* word. We have already spoken about these matters in the relevant chapters, and there is no need for us to repeat anything from them.

المخفوضات من الأسماء

The Nouns in the State of *Khafḍ*

قال: (باب المخفوضات من الأسماء)، المخفوضات ثلاثة أنواع، مخفوض بالحرف، ومخفوض بالإضافة، وتابعٌ للمخفوض.

He said: Chapter of the Nouns in the State of *Khafḍ*: The nouns in the state of *khafḍ* are of three types: (i) *makhfūḍ* due to a particle, (ii) *makhfūḍ* due to the possessive construction, and (iii) *makhfūḍ* due to being a grammatical follower of a *makhfūḍ* word.

وأقول: الاسم المخفوض على ثلاثة أنواع؛ وذلك لأن الخافض له :

I say: The *makhfūḍ* noun is of three types, and this is due to the governor of its *khafḍ*:

إما أن يكون حرفاً من حروف الخفض التي سبق بيانها في أوَّل الكتاب والتي سيذكرها المؤلف بعد ذلك، وذلك نحو (خالد) من قولك: (أشفقت على خالدٍ) فإنَّه مجرور بـ(على)، وهو حرف من حروف الخفض.

Sometimes the governor is a particle from the particles *khafḍ*, upon which we have spoken about earlier in the book, and which the author will mention below. An example of this is the word "Khālid" in the statement "I yearned for Khālid." It is *majrūr* due to the word "*ʿalā*" and it is a particle from the particles of *khafḍ*.

وإما أن يكون الخافض للاسم إضافة اسم قبله إليه، ومعنى الإضافة: نسبة الثاني للأول، وذلك نحو (محمد) من قولك: (جاء غلام محمدٍ) فإنَّه مخفوض بسبب إضافة (غلام) إليه.

Sometimes the governor of *khafḍ* for the noun is the possessive construction of a preceding noun to it—and the meaning of the possessive construction is the attribution of the second word to the first. An example is the word "Muḥammad" in the statement, "The son of Muḥammad came." Here it is *makhfūḍ* due to the compounding of the word "son" to it (i.e. to Muḥammad).

وإما أن يكون الخافض للاسم تبعِيَّته لاسم مخفوض: بأن يكون نعتاً له، نحو (الفاضل) من قولك: (أخذتُ العلم عن محمدٍ الفاضلِ) أو معطوفاً عليه، نحو (خالد) من قولك: (مررت بمحمدٍ وخالدٍ) أو غير هذين من التوابع التي سبق ذكرها.

Sometimes the governor of *khafḍ* for the noun is due to being a follower of a *makhfūḍ* noun (thus taking the same state as the followed noun). It could be an adjective e.g. "the virtuous" in the statement, "I took knowledge from Muḥammad the virtuous." It could be conjoined to a *makhfūḍ* noun e.g. "Khālid" in the statement, "I passed by Muḥammad and Khālid." Or it could be onc of the other aforementioned grammatical followers besides these.

قال: فأما المخفوض بالحرف فهو: ما يخفضُ بـ(مِن)، و(إلى)، و(عن)، و(على)، و(في)، و(ربَّ)، و(الباءِ)، و(الكافِ)، و(اللام)، وحُرُوفِ القسمِ، وهي: (الواوُ)، و(الباءُ)، و(التاءُ)، أو بـ(واوِ (رُبَّ))، وبـ(مُذْ)، و(مُنذُ).

He said: As for the word made *makhfūḍ* by a particle, it is that which is made *makhfūḍ* by: *min*, *ilā*, *ʿan*, *ʿalā*, *fī*, *rubba*, the letter *bā*, the letter *kāf*, the letter *lām*, the particles of oath i.e. the letters *wāw*, *bā* and *tā*, *wāw* of *rubba*, *mudh* and *mundhu*.

وأقول: النوع الأول من المخفوضات: المخفوض بحرف من حروف الخفض وحروف الخفض كثيرة.

I say: The first type of the *makhfūḍ* words is that which is made so by a particle of *khafḍ*. The particles of *khafḍ* are many:

منها (مِنْ) ومن معانيها الابتداءُ، وتجر الاسم الظاهر والمضمر، نحو قوله تعالى: ﴿وَمِنكَ وَمِن نُّوحٍ﴾ .

From them is "*min*", and from its meanings is starting or beginning. It makes both explicit and implicit nouns *majrūr* e.g. in the statement of the Most High: **{And from you and from Nuḥ.}**[222]

ومنها (إلى) ومن معانيها الانتهاء، وتجر الاسم الظاهر والمضمر أيضاً، نحو قوله تعالى: ﴿إِلَيْهِ يُرَدُّ عِلْمُ السَّاعَةِ﴾، وقوله ﴿إِلَى اللهِ مَرْجِعُكُمْ جَمِيعاً﴾.

From them is "*ilā*", and from its meanings is ending. It makes both explicit and implicit nouns *majrūr* e.g. in the two statements of the Most High: **{To him [alone] is attributed knowledge of the Hour}**[223] and **{To Allah is your return all together.}**[224]

ومنها (عن) ومن معانيها المجاوزة، وتجر الاسم الظاهر والضمير أيضاً، نحو قوله تعالى: ﴿لَقَدْ رَضِيَ اللهُ عَنِ الْمُؤْمِنِينَ﴾ وقوله: ﴿رَضِيَ اللهُ عَنْهُمْ وَرَضُوا عَنْهُ﴾.

From them is "*'an*", and from its meanings is exceeding something. It makes both explicit nouns and pronouns *majrūr* e.g. the two statements of the Most High: **{Certainly was Allah pleased with the believers}**[225] and, **{Allah being pleased with them and they with Him.}**[226]

ومنها (على) ومن معانيها الاستعلاء، وتجر الاسم الظاهر والمضمر أيضاً، نحو قوله تعالى: ﴿وَعَلَيْهَا وَعَلَى الْفُلْكِ تُحْمَلُونَ﴾.

From them is "*'alā*", and from its meanings is rising above. It makes both explicit and implicit nouns *majrūr* e.g. the statement of the Most High: **{And**

---

222 Al-Aḥzāb: 7
223 Al-Aḥzāb: 47
224 Al-Mā'idah: 48
225 Al-Fatḥ: 18
226 Al-Bayyinah: 8

upon them and on ships you are carried.}[227]

ومنها (في) ومن معانيها الظرفية، وتجر الاسم الظاهر والضمير أيضاً، نحو قوله تعالى: ﴿وَفِي السَّمَآءِ رِزْقُكُمْ﴾ وقوله: ﴿لا فِيهَا غَوْلٌ﴾.

From them is "*fī*", and from its meanings is to serve as an adverb. It makes both explicit nouns and pronouns *majrūr* e.g. the two statements of the Most High: **{And in the heaven is your provision}**[228] and, **{No bad effect is there in it.}**[229]

ومنها (رُبَّ) ومن معانيها التقليل، ولا تجر إلَّا الاسم الظاهر النكرة، نحو قولك: (رُبَّ رَجُلٍ كريمٍ لَقِيتُهُ).

From them is "*rubba*", and from its meanings is reduction. It only makes the explicit, indefinite noun *majrūr* e.g. in the statement, "Few a noble man have I met."

ومنها (الباء) ومن معانيها التعديةُ، وتجر الاسم الظاهر والضمير جميعاً، نحو قوله تعالى: ﴿فَإِمَّا نَذْهَبَنَّ بِكَ﴾ وقوله ﴿ذَهَبَ اللهُ بِنُورِهِمْ﴾.

From them is the letter *bā*, and from its uses is to make something transitive. It makes both explicit nouns and pronouns *majrūr* as in the two statements of the Most High: **{And whether [or not] We take you away}**[230] and **{Allah took away their light.}**[231]

ومنها (الكاف) ومن معانيها التشبيه، ولا تجر إلَّا الاسم الظاهر، نحو قوله تعالى: ﴿مَثَلُ نُورِهِ كَمِشْكَاةٍ﴾.

From them is the letter *kāf*, and from its meanings is similitude. It only makes

227 Al-Mu'minūn: 22
228 Al-Dhāriyāt: 22
229 Al-Ṣaffāt: 47
230 Al-Zukhruf: 41
231 Al-Baqarah: 17

explicit nouns *majrūr* as in the statement of the Most High: **{The example of His light is like a niche.}**[232]

ومنها (اللام) ومن معانيها الاستحقاق والمِلكُ، وتجر الاسم الظاهر والمضمر جميعاً، نحو قوله سبحانه وتعالى: ﴿سَبَّحَ لِلَّهِ مَا فِي السَّمَاوَاتِ وَالْأَرْضِ﴾، وقوله: ﴿لَهُ مُلْكُ السَّمَاوَاتِ وَالْأَرْضِ﴾.

From them is the letter *lām*, and from its meanings is entitlement and possession. It makes both the explicit noun and the implicit noun *majrūr*, as in the statements of the Most High: **{Whatever is in the heavens and earth exalts Allah}**[233] and, **{His is the dominion of the heavens and earth.}**[234]

ومنها حروف القسم الثلاثة - وهي: (الباء)، و(التاءُ)، و(الواو) - وقد تكلمنا عليها كلاماً مُستوفى في أول الكتاب؛ فلا حاجة بنا إلى إعادة شيء منه.

From them are the three particles of oath, which are: the letters *bā*, *tā* and *wāw*. We have already provided details regarding these at the start of the book so there is no need to repeat anything regarding them.

ومنها (واو (رُبَّ)) ومثالُها قول امرئ القيس:

From them is the *wāw* of *rubba* (i.e. it has the meaning of *rubba*). Its use can be seen in the following statement of Imru' al-Qays:

وليلٍ كَمَوجِ البحرِ أَرْخَى سُدُولهُ

Possibly the night is like the waves of the sea, its curtain let loose.[235]

232 Al-Nūr: 35

233 Al-Ḥadīd: 1

234 Al-Ḥadīd: 5

235 The poet, Imru' al-Qays, is a well-known Arab pre-Islamic versifier. The deeper meaning of this verse is to draw a parable between being at sea and the opportunity for terror and mishaps the night brings; all of which is a test of nerve and patience from the Lord that created man, his feelings and the environment one is placed in. See *Awḍah al-Masālik ila Alfiyyatu ibnu Mālik* (3/65).

وقوله أيضاً:

And also in his statement:

وَبَيْضَةِ خِدْرٍ لا يُرامُ خِباؤُها .

Perhaps the maiden [akin to an] egg [in beauty, virginity and seclusion from view] whose tent cannot be approached...

ومنها (مُذْ) و(منذُ) ويجرانِ الأزمانِ، وهما يدلان على معنى (من) إن كان ما بعدها ماضياً، نحو (ما رأيتُه مُذْ يومِ الخميسِ)، و(ما كلمتُهُ منذ شهرٍ)، ويكونانِ بمعنى (في) إن كان ما بعدهما حاضراً، نحو (لا أُكلِّمُهُ مُذْ يَومِنا)، و(لا ألقاهُ مُنْذُ يومِنا).

From them are "mudhu" and "mundhu", and they are both connected to time. They indicate the meaning of "min" (from or since) if that which follows them is in the past, as in the examples, "I have not seen him since Thursday" and, "I have not spoken to him for one month". They indicate the meaning of "fī" (in) if that which follows them is in the present, as in the examples, "I did not speak to him today" and, "I did not meet him today."

فإن وقع بعد (مذ) أو (منذ) فعلٌ، أو كانَ الاسم الذي بعدهما مرفوعاً فهما اسمان.

If that which follows "mudhu" and "mundhu" is a verb or a marfūʿ noun then they are both considered to be nouns [and not particles of jarr.][236]

قال: وأما ما يخفض بالإضافة، فنو قولك: (غلامُ زيدٍ) وهو على قسمين: ما يُقَدَّرُ باللامِ، وما يُقَدَّرُ بِ(مِن)؛ فالذي يقدر باللام نحو (غلامُ زيدٍ) والذي يقدرُ

---

[236] This statement needs some clarification, if *mudh* and *mundhu* are used before a verb then they take the form of being a noun, they are *manṣūb*, act as adverbs and come as the *muḍāf* to these verbal sentences. For example, "I have come *mudh* (since) the *muʾadhin* called the *adhan*". If a *marfūʿ* noun only comes after them then they are nominal subjects and the *marfūʿ* word after them is the predicate. See: *al-Mughnī* (1/335/336), *Sharḥ ibn ʿAqīl* (3/31) and *al-Kawākib* (2/420).

بـ(مِن)، نحو (ثوبُ خَزٍّ) و(بابُ ساجٍ) و(خاتَمُ حديد).

He said: And as for the noun which is placed into the state of *khafḍ* by way of the possessive construction then its example is like that of the following: "The boy of Zayd." It is divided into two groups: (i) that which implies the meaning of "*lām*" (i.e. for) and (ii) that which implies the meaning of "*min*" (i.e. from). An example of the former is, "The boy of Zayd" and examples of the latter are, "a garment made from silk", "a door made from teak" and, "a ring made from iron."

وأقول: القسم الثاني من المخفوضات: المخفوض بالإضافة، وهو على ثلاثة أنواع، ذكر المؤلف منها نوعين؛ الأول: ما تكون الإضافة فيه على معنى (مِن) والثاني: ما تكون الإضافة فيه على معنى (اللام)، والثالث: ما تكون الإضافة فيه على معنى (في).

I say: The second type from the *makhfūḍ* words is that which is *makhfūḍ* due to a possessive construction.[237] [238] It is of three types, though the author has

237 The grammarians have differed over the *jārr* (governor of the *majrūr/makhfūḍ* state) of the *muḍāf ilayh*, and this has brought forth three views. Some of them said that it is made *majrūr* by the removed particle of *jarr*, and this view is weak as it is weak to say that the *jārr* is removed but its function remains. Some of them said that it is *majrūr* due to the possessive construction—and this is famous amongst the scholars of inflection—however it is not correct based on what we will mention. Some of them said—and this is the correct view—that it is made *majrūr* by the *muḍāf*, and this is the view of Sībawayh and the majority of the grammarians. From their proofs is that, "The pronoun connects to the *muḍāf* and the pronoun connects to its grammatical governor" [The Arabic text of this quotation is:] (اتصال الضمير بالمضاف والضمير إنما يتصل بعامله)

And they said, "That it dictates the *muḍāf ilayhi* and demands from it like the grammatical agent demands upon the word it impacts upon—whilst also implying the meaning of the particle of *jarr*. It is not a valid objection, therefore, to claim that the nouns do not play a part in the effect." [The Arabic text of this quotation is:]

(لأنه يقتضي المضاف إليه ويطلبه كطلب العامل معموله مع تضمنه معنى الحرف الجار، فلا يرد أن الأسماء المحضة لا حظ لها في العمل).

See *Sharḥ ibn ʿAqīl* (3/43), *Ḥāshiyat al-Khuḍrī* (2/3), *al-Taṣrīḥ* of al-Azharī (2/24-25), *Ḥāshiyat al-Ṣabbān* (2/237), *al-Kawākib* (2/457) and *Ḥāshiyat al-Fākihī maʿa Yasīn* (2/132-133).

238 Al-Suyūṭī said in *al-Ashbāh wa al-Naẓā'ir* (2/110), "The word '*al-jarr*' is from the

only mentioned two types here. The first type is the possessive construction which implies the meaning of "*min*" (from). The second type is the possessive construction which implies the meaning of "*lām*" (for). The third type is the possessive construction which implies the meaning of "*fī*" (in).[239]

أما ما تكون الإضافة فيه على معنى (مِنْ) فضابِطُهُ: أن يكون المضاف جزءاً وبعضاً من المضاف إليه، نحو (جُبَّةُ صوفٍ) فإنَّ الجبة بعض الصوف وجزء منه، وكذلك أمثلة المؤلف.

As for the possessive construction which implies the meaning of "*min*", the governing rule for it is that the *muḍāf* is a part of the *muḍāf ilayhi*. An example is, "An outer garment of wool", wherein the outer garment is partly made of wool and is a portion from it. There were also similar examples given by the author above.

وأما ما تكون الإضافة فيه على معنى (في) فضابطهُ: أن يكون المضاف إليه ظرفاً للمضاف، نحو قوله تعالى: ﴿بَلْ مَكْرُ اللَّيْلِ﴾ فإنَّ الليل ظرفٌ للمكر ووقتٌ يَقعُ المكرُ فيه.

As for the possessive construction which implies the meaning of "*fī*", the governing rule for it is that the *muḍaf ilayhi* is an adverb for the *muḍaf*. An example is in the statement of the Most High: **{Rather, [your] conspiracy of night.}**[240] The word "night" here is an adverb for "conspiracy" and it is when the conspiracy takes place.

---

nomenclature of the Baṣrī grammarians, and '*al-khafḍ*' is from the nomenclature of the Kūfīs, and this was mentioned by al-Khabāz and others." Another benefit that was mentioned by al-Suyūṭī is that Ibn al-Dahān said in *al-Ghurah*, "'*Min*' is the strongest of the particles of *jarr*, and for this reason it has a more specific meaning and usage than '*inda*."

239 Benefit: Yasīn said in his *Ḥāshiyat 'ala 'l-Taṣrīḥ* (2/24), that al-Danūsharī said, "The *muḍāf* will always be a noun for its infliction with *tanwīn* or a *nūn* and because the main objective of *al-iḍāfah* is to make the *muḍāf* definite, whereas a verb cannot be definite. Likewise is the case for the *muḍāf ilayhi* as it is being ruled upon, and only nouns can be ruled upon."

240 Saba: 33

وأما ما تكون الإضافة فيه على معنى (اللام)؛ فكُلُّ ما لا يصلح فيه أحَدُ النوعين المذكورين، نحو (غلامُ زيدٍ) و(حصيرُ المسجدِ).

As for the possessive construction which implies the meaning of "*lām*", this type encompasses any case which doesn't comply with the two aforementioned types. Examples are, "The boy of Zayd" and "The mat of the *masjid*."

وقد ترك المؤلف الكلام على القسم الثالث من المخفوضات، وهو المخفوضُ بالتبعية، وعُذرُه في ذلك أنَّه قد سبق القول عليه في آخر أبواب المرفوعات مُفَصَّلا، والله سبحانه وتعالى أعلى وأعلم وأعزُّ وأكرم.

The author has omitted the mention of the third type of the *makhfūḍ* nouns, and this is that which is *makhfūḍ* due to being a grammatical follower. The justification for him doing so is that he mentioned in detail regarding the grammatical follower during the final chapters of *marfūʿ* words. Allah is the Highest and Most Knowledge, the Most Honoured and the Most Generous.

أسئلة

Questions

على كم نوع تتنوع المخفوضات؟

Into how many types have the *makhfūḍ* words been categorised into?

ما المعنى الذي تدل عليه الحروف: (من) ، (عن) ، (في) ، (رُبَّ) ، (الكاف)، (اللام) ؟ وما الذي يجُرُهُ كُلُّ واحد منها ؟

What meaning is indicated by the following particles and what is made *majrūr* by each of them: "*min*", "*ʿan*", "*fī*", "*rubba*", "*al-kāf*" and "*al-lām*"?

مَثِّل بمثالين من إنشائك لاسم مخفوض بكل واحد من الحروف: (على) ، (الباءُ)

، (إلى) ، ((واو) القسم) .

Provide two examples of your own design of a noun that is made *makhfūḍ* by each of the following particles: "*'alā*", "*al-bā*", "*ilā*" and "*wāw al-qasam*."

على كم نوع تأتي الإضافة ؟ مع التمثيل لكل نوع بمثالين.

How many types of possessive constructions are there? Provide two examples of each type.

ما ضابط الإضافة التي على معنى (من)؟ مع التمثيل.

What is the governing principle for the possessive construction that implies the meaning of "*min*"? Provide an example.

ما ضابط الإضافة التي على معنى (في) ؟ مع التمثيل

What is the governing principle in the possessive construction that implies the meaning of "*fī*"? Provide an example.

خاتمة الشارح

Conclusion of the Commentator

وقد كان الفراغ من كتابة هذا الشرح في ليلة القدر (ليلة الخميس ٢٧ من شهرِ رمضان سنة ١٣٥٣ من الهجرة) أعاد الله تعالى علينا من بركاته، آمين، والحمد لله ربِّ العالمين، وصلاته وسلامه على صفْوة الصفْوة من خلقه أجمعين، وعلى سادتنا آله وصحبه والتابعين، ولا عدوان إلا على الظالمين، والعاقبة للمتقين.

The completion of writing this commentary occurred during Laylat al-Qadr (Thursday night, 27th Ramaḍān 1353H [2nd January 1935]). I ask Allah to repeat it for us from His Blessings, *amīn*. All praises are to Allah the Lord of all creation, may peace and blessings be upon the elite of the elite from the entire creation, upon our master, his family, his companions and their followers. And there is no persecution except to the oppressors, and the final end is with the god-fearing.

[Translator: And I completed this translation during the early hours of 13th November 2017. May Allah accept this deed and bless it.]